# NATIONAL LEAGUE PLAYERS

D1444344

# NATIONAL LEAGUE PLAYERS

## By Barry Shapiro

LITTLE, BROWN AND COMPANY

Boston  Toronto  London

Produced by
Cloverdale Press, Inc.
96 Morton Street
New York, New York 10014

Copyright (c) 1990 by Cloverdale Press, Inc.

All Rights Reserved.

No part of this book may be reproduced in any form or by any electronic or mechanical means, including information storage and retrieval systems, without permission in writing from the publisher, except by a reviewer, who may quote brief passages in a review.

First Edition

Library of Congress Catalog Card Number: 89-63983

ISBN 0-316-08310-0

10  9  8  7  6  5  4  3  2  1

*Published simultaneously in Canada
by Little, Brown & Company (Canada) Limited*

RRD OH

PRINTED IN THE UNITED STATES OF AMERICA

This book is neither endorsed nor authorized by the National League or by the National League Baseball Association.

Statistics provided by Stats Inc.
7250 N. Cicero
Lincolnwood, IL 60646

# CONTENTS

Introduction . . . . . . . . . . . . . . . . . . . . . . . .ix

First Basemen. . . . . . . . . . . . . . . . . . . . . . .1

Second Basemen . . . . . . . . . . . . . . . . . .15

Third Basemen. . . . . . . . . . . . . . . . . . . .27

Shortstops. . . . . . . . . . . . . . . . . . . . . . . .39

Catchers . . . . . . . . . . . . . . . . . . . . . . . . .51

Outfielders . . . . . . . . . . . . . . . . . . . . . . .67

Pitchers. . . . . . . . . . . . . . . . . . . . . . . . .105

Contest Rules . . . . . . . . . . . . . . . . . . . .173

Official Entry Form . . . . . . . . . . . . . . . .175

# INTRODUCTION

# INTRODUCTION

Welcome to *Baseball Contest 1990: National League Players*, in which you test your managerial mettle against tens of thousands of fantasy baseball enthusiasts. Beyond the pride and the glory, the person who assembles the team that does best will be awarded $10,000 in cash!

Let's start with the ground rules. You are going to pick 24 players from this book to fill out your roster:

- Six outfielders

- Six infielders—one first baseman, one second baseman, one third baseman, one shortstop, and two additional players from any of the infield positions

- Two catchers

- Ten pitchers

You can pick six left fielders if you wish, but not three shortstops or three third basemen.

You can pick a player who has played more than one position, but in our game he qualifies only at the position at which he's listed. For example, Jose Oquendo, the man of a thousand gloves, is strictly a second baseman. The only eligible players are those listed in this book.

You must choose at least one player from at least 6 of the 12 National League teams.

You must follow all the other contest rules printed on page 173.

How will the contest umpires make their calls? There are eight basic statistical measurements, four for hitters and four for pitchers.

*First, the offensive categories:*

- *Batting average:* You earn one point for each .001 in every player's average. San Diego outfielder Tony Gwynn hit .336 last season. That would produce 336 points for his manager.

- *Home Runs:* Each player's home run total is multiplied by 10. Kevin Mitchell's 47 homers in 1989 would have been worth 470 points for anyone who put him on their roster.

- *Runs Batted In:* A player's RBI total is multiplied by three. Howard Johnson knocked in 101 runs last season, which would be worth 303 points.

- *Runs Scored:* Like RBIs, a multiple of three is assigned to a player's runs scored. Ryne Sandberg scored 104 runs in 1989, good for a total of 312 points in *Baseball Contest 1990*.

*Now, the pitching categories:*

• *Earned Run Average:* One point for each .01 below 6.00. Subtract your pitcher's ERA from that number, then divide by .01. Mike Scott's 1989 ERA was 3.10. That's a difference of 2.90 (6.00 − 3.10). Divided by .01, Scott's performance earns 290 points.

• *Wins:* Every pitcher's victory total is multiplied by 30. Orel Hershiser won 15 games last season, which would have been good for 450 points.

• *Losses:* There's jeopardy in a loss. The umpires will deduct 10 points for every defeat. Hershiser also *lost* 15 games in 1989. That would cost his manager 150 points.

• *Saves:* Ten points will be awarded for every save. John Franco saved 32 games for the Reds last season. In our game, that would be worth 320 points.

In assembling your team, you have a salary cap of 75 points. Every player in this book has been rated on a scale of 1 to 5, with 5 points being the highest. The rating is clearly displayed next to each player profile.

To arrive at this rating, each player's amateur, minor league, and major league performances were reviewed. Close attention was paid to their play over the past three seasons (for second-year players, this meant looking at their minor league numbers as well). The result is what professional scouts call a "projection evaluation"—a rating indicating the level at which the player can be expected to perform in 1990.

To simplify the ratings, consider a player rated 5 to be a superstar, one who will help you in most or all categories and dominate one or two; a 4 is an above-average player who will help you in two or three categories and stand out in one or two; a 3 is an average major league player, who will contribute in most categories, or will stand out in one or two; a 2 is a below-average major leaguer; and a 1 is a player of little impact.

Each player was rated relative to his position. Therefore, a 5-rated catcher is not necessarily as good as a 5-rated outfielder—but he is the best of the catching corps. Likewise, a 5-rated reliever is not necessarily a better pitcher than a 5-rated starter. A 5-rated starter won't get any saves, while a 5-rated reliever may not pick up many wins.

You might not agree with some of the ratings in this book. You might think a player rated 3 really warrants a 5. If that's the case, what are you waiting for? Add him to your team and spend the two points elsewhere! Or, if we've rated someone a 5 who you think is really a 2, it's your prerogative to stay away from this player. That's what baseball savvy is all about!

We've done our best to include as much of the off-season trading activity and free-agent signings as possible, but since general managers never seem to sleep and have a knack for doing things at the last minute, inevitably a few things may have changed since this book went to press.

What kind of players do you want for your team? Well, that's entirely your decision. If I were playing (the rules prevent me from doing so), I'd look for multitalented position players who contribute in many categories. You've noticed that stolen bases are not counted in this contest, but they are valuable nonetheless; a player who steals bases gets into scoring position. Since runs scored is a contest category, stolen bases are essentially built in to our game.

As for pitchers, you have to decide the best breakdown of starters and relievers. Some fantasy players like having a predominance of starters who will give them lots of wins and low-scoring innings. Others favor a staff loaded with relievers who'll provide saves while allowing few runs.

So grab a pencil and paper, go through the player evaluations, and start making notes. Then get your lineup card (entry form) ready for the season. Keep in mind, there are bonus points available for early entries.

If you've been hollering at your favorite team's general manager for not producing a winner every year, here's your opportunity to build your own championship franchise. It will be a great season. Enjoy! And good luck!

# FIRST BASEMEN

# FIRST BASEMEN

## Todd Benzinger

**Birth Date:** 2/11/63
**Bats:** Right and Left
**Throws:** Right
**1989 Club:**
Cincinnati Reds
**Contest Code #:** 101

**Rating: 2**

**B**oy, did the Reds have to pay for former manager Pete Rose's impatience with first baseman Nick Esasky! Having waited six seasons for Esasky to fulfill his potential, the Reds dealt Esasky, who'd long been in Rose's doghouse, and reliever Rob Murphy to the Red Sox in December 1988 for pitcher Jeff Sellers and first baseman Todd Benzinger. In Boston, Esasky belted 30 home runs and knocked in 108 runs, and Murphy saved 9 games and posted a 2.74 ERA. In Cincinnati, Sellers blew out his arm, was released, and has since undergone reconstructive surgery, while Benzinger basically reproduced his run-of-the-mill 1988 season.

Benzinger's chronic problem is his appetite for pitches outside the strike zone. In 1988, he walked only 22 times in 405 at-bats, and in 1989 accepted just 44 free passes in 628 at-bats. Last season, Benzinger also struck out 120 times. How can he ever become a good first baseman if he can't get to first base?

| Year | Team | G | AB | R | H | 2B | 3B | HR | RBI | BB | SB | AVG |
|------|------|-----|------|-----|-----|-----|-----|-----|-----|-----|-----|------|
| 1987 | Bos .... | 73 | 223 | 36 | 62 | 11 | 1 | 8 | 43 | 22 | 5 | .278 |
| 1988 | Bos .... | 120 | 405 | 47 | 103 | 28 | 1 | 13 | 70 | 22 | 2 | .254 |
| 1989 | Cin .... | 161 | 628 | 79 | 154 | 28 | 3 | 17 | 76 | 44 | 3 | .245 |
| | | 354 | 1256 | 162 | 319 | 67 | 5 | 38 | 189 | 88 | 10 | .254 |

## Sid Bream

**Birth Date:** 8/3/60
**Bats:** Left
**Throws:** Left
**1989 Club:**
Pittsburgh Pirates
**Contest Code #:** 102

**Rating: 3**

**S**id Bream had constantly been fighting off attempts to platoon him until 1988, when he took over the position on a full-time basis. However, last season Bream severely injured his right knee and played in only 19 games.

Bream is no Will Clark, but when healthy, his numbers are easy to predict. He'll bat between .260 and .270, hit around 15 home runs, drive in about 65 runs, and score between 50 and 70 runs.

The Pirates are so sure that Bream will be back strong that they plan to move Jeff King to third base and Bobby Bonilla to right field. If Bream falters, look for him to platoon once more, this time with King.

| Year | Team | G | AB | R | H | 2B | 3B | HR | RBI | BB | SB | AVG |
|------|------|-----|------|-----|-----|-----|-----|-----|-----|-----|-----|------|
| 1983 | LA ..... | 15 | 11 | 0 | 2 | 0 | 0 | 0 | 2 | 2 | 0 | .182 |
| 1984 | LA ..... | 27 | 49 | 2 | 9 | 3 | 0 | 0 | 6 | 6 | 1 | .184 |
| 1985 | LA ..... | 24 | 53 | 4 | 7 | 0 | 0 | 3 | 6 | 7 | 0 | .132 |
| 1985 | Pit .... | 26 | 95 | 14 | 27 | 7 | 0 | 3 | 15 | 11 | 0 | .284 |
| 1986 | Pit .... | 154 | 522 | 73 | 140 | 37 | 5 | 16 | 77 | 60 | 13 | .268 |
| 1987 | Pit .... | 149 | 516 | 64 | 142 | 25 | 3 | 13 | 65 | 49 | 9 | .275 |
| 1988 | Pit .... | 148 | 462 | 50 | 122 | 37 | 0 | 10 | 65 | 47 | 9 | .264 |
| 1989 | Pit ..... | 19 | 36 | 3 | 8 | 3 | 0 | 0 | 4 | 12 | 0 | .222 |
| | | 562 | 1744 | 210 | 457 | 112 | 8 | 45 | 240 | 194 | 32 | .262 |

# Jack Clark

Birth Date: 11/10/55
Bats: Right
Throws: Right
1989 Club:
San Diego Padres
Contest Code #: 103

### Rating: 4

**J**ack Clark, acquired from the Yankees during the 1988 winter meetings, struggled so much during the first half of the 1989 season—a .227 average, 9 home runs, and 40 RBI's—that at times he spoke of retirement. But the Padres knew that all Clark needed was, as the media called it, "Yankee Detox."

Sure enough, as the Padres' staff continued to show confidence in Clark, "The Ripper," a streaky hitter throughout his career, went on a 17-home run, 54-RBI tear in the second half.

A fast-ball hitter, Clark strikes out a lot, but, unlike Todd Benzinger, he knows when to say when. Last year, Clark walked a league-leading 132 times, the second time he's led the National League in walks over the past three seasons.

The best thing about Clark—for your purposes—is that he can drive in runs even when he's the lone power hitter in a team's lineup. He did that with the Cardinals in 1987 and during the second half of 1989 with the Padres.

| Year | Team | G | AB | R | H | 2B | 3B | HR | RBI | BB | SB | AVG |
|------|------|-----|------|-----|------|-----|----|-----|-----|------|----|------|
| 1975 | SF..... | 8 | 17 | 3 | 4 | 0 | 0 | 0 | 2 | 1 | 1 | .235 |
| 1976 | SF..... | 26 | 102 | 14 | 23 | 6 | 2 | 2 | 10 | 8 | 6 | .225 |
| 1977 | SF..... | 136 | 413 | 64 | 104 | 17 | 4 | 13 | 51 | 49 | 12 | .252 |
| 1978 | SF..... | 156 | 592 | 90 | 181 | 46 | 8 | 25 | 98 | 50 | 15 | .306 |
| 1979 | SF..... | 143 | 527 | 84 | 144 | 25 | 2 | 26 | 86 | 63 | 11 | .273 |
| 1980 | SF..... | 127 | 437 | 77 | 124 | 20 | 8 | 22 | 82 | 74 | 2 | .284 |
| 1981 | SF..... | 99 | 385 | 60 | 103 | 19 | 2 | 17 | 53 | 45 | 1 | .268 |
| 1982 | SF..... | 157 | 563 | 90 | 154 | 30 | 3 | 27 | 103 | 90 | 6 | .274 |
| 1983 | SF..... | 135 | 492 | 82 | 132 | 25 | 0 | 20 | 66 | 74 | 5 | .268 |
| 1984 | SF..... | 57 | 203 | 33 | 65 | 9 | 1 | 11 | 44 | 43 | 1 | .320 |
| 1985 | StL .... | 126 | 442 | 71 | 124 | 26 | 3 | 22 | 87 | 83 | 1 | .281 |
| 1986 | StL .... | 65 | 232 | 34 | 55 | 12 | 2 | 9 | 23 | 45 | 1 | .237 |
| 1987 | StL .... | 131 | 419 | 93 | 120 | 23 | 1 | 35 | 106 | 136 | 1 | .286 |
| 1988 | NYA.... | 150 | 496 | 81 | 120 | 14 | 0 | 27 | 93 | 113 | 3 | .242 |
| 1989 | SD..... | 142 | 455 | 76 | 110 | 19 | 1 | 26 | 94 | 132 | 6 | .242 |
| | | 1658 | 5775 | 952 | 1563 | 291 | 37 | 282 | 998 | 1006 | 72 | .271 |

# Will Clark

Birth Date: 3/13/64
Bats: Left
Throws: Left
1989 Club:
San Francisco Giants
Contest Code #: 104

### Rating: 5

**N**ear the end of the movie Bull Durham, veteran catcher Crash Davis tells young phenom Nuke La-loosh that the keys to success in The Show are "fear and arrogance." Will Clark's arrogance is apparent, from his strut to his glower. But beneath the popinjay exterior is a fear that drives Clark to be the best player in the game.

During each off season Clark works untold hours on his batting and his physical conditioning. Always a good hitter for average, he's now developed into a consistent power threat, as well as one of the league's finest hitters.

Last year Clark's name popped up among the leaders in most categories: tied for first in runs scored (104); second in batting average (.333) and hits (196); tied for third in triples (9); fourth in doubles (38).

Clark is the type of player who likes challenges, so this season expect him to resemble his sweet-swinging MVP performance in the 1989 League Championship Series and erase all memories of his miserable performance in the 1989 World Series.

| Year | Team | G | AB | R | H | 2B | 3B | HR | RBI | BB | SB | AVG |
|------|------|---|----|---|---|----|----|----|-----|----|----|-----|
| 1986 | SF . . . . . | 111 | 408 | 66 | 117 | 27 | 2 | 11 | 41 | 34 | 4 | .287 |
| 1987 | SF . . . . . | 150 | 529 | 89 | 163 | 29 | 5 | 35 | 91 | 49 | 5 | .308 |
| 1988 | SF . . . . . | 162 | 575 | 102 | 162 | 31 | 6 | 29 | 109 | 100 | 9 | .282 |
| 1989 | SF . . . . . | 159 | 588 | 104 | 196 | 38 | 9 | 23 | 111 | 74 | 8 | .333 |
| | | 582 | 2100 | 361 | 638 | 125 | 22 | 98 | 352 | 257 | 26 | .304 |

# Glenn Davis

**Birth Date: 3/28/61**
**Bats: Right**
**Throws: Right**
**1989 Club:**
**Houston Astros**
**Contest Code #: 105**

**Rating: 4**

Glenn Davis deserves to be recognized as one of the National League's finest home-run hitters. In the past four seasons he's averaged 31 home runs annually despite playing in a pitcher's park and being surrounded in the Astros' lineup by singles hitters.

Like many power hitters, Davis goes through hot and cold streaks. When he's slumping, he will chase curveballs out of the strike zone. When he's hot, Davis will hit just about any pitch to all parts of the ball park. His opposite field power makes him truly dangerous.

Two factors negatively influence Davis' rating: He has only driven in 100 RBI's once in his career, and he doesn't hit for high average. But if you want a guy who'll give you 30-plus home runs, Davis is the one.

| Year | Team | G | AB | R | H | 2B | 3B | HR | RBI | BB | SB | AVG |
|------|------|---|----|---|---|----|----|----|-----|----|----|-----|
| 1984 | Hou . . . . | 18 | 61 | 6 | 13 | 5 | 0 | 2 | 8 | 4 | 0 | .213 |
| 1985 | Hou . . . . | 100 | 350 | 51 | 95 | 11 | 0 | 20 | 64 | 27 | 0 | .271 |
| 1986 | Hou . . . . | 158 | 574 | 91 | 152 | 32 | 3 | 31 | 101 | 64 | 3 | .265 |
| 1987 | Hou . . . . | 151 | 578 | 70 | 145 | 35 | 2 | 27 | 93 | 47 | 4 | .251 |
| 1988 | Hou . . . . | 152 | 561 | 78 | 152 | 26 | 0 | 30 | 99 | 53 | 4 | .271 |
| 1989 | Hou . . . . | 158 | 581 | 87 | 156 | 26 | 1 | 34 | 89 | 69 | 4 | .269 |
| | | 737 | 2705 | 383 | 713 | 135 | 6 | 144 | 454 | 264 | 15 | .264 |

# Benny Distefano

**Birth Date: 1/23/62**
**Bats: Left**
**Throws: Left**
**1989 Club:**
**Pittsburgh Pirates**
**Contest Code #: 106**

**Rating: 1**

Benny Distefano gets the most out of his abilities. As a minor leaguer, he made the record books by leading the Pacific Coast League in 1987 and the American Association in 1988 in being hit by pitches. Last season, Distefano filled in behind the plate, earning a footnote as the National League's only left-handed-throwing catcher.

At the Triple A level, Distefano showed himself to be capable of hitting for power. In 1987 he hit 15 home runs and drove in 77 runs, and in 1988 popped 19 dingers and knocked in 63 runs. Given a full-time role, Distefano might put up some respectable numbers. But the Pirates see him strictly as bench material.

| Year | Team | G | AB | R | H | 2B | 3B | HR | RBI | BB | SB | AVG |
|------|------|---|----|---|---|----|----|----|-----|----|----|-----|
| 1984 | Pit . . . . . | 45 | 78 | 10 | 13 | 1 | 2 | 3 | 9 | 5 | 0 | .167 |
| 1986 | Pit . . . . . | 31 | 39 | 3 | 7 | 1 | 0 | 1 | 5 | 1 | 0 | .179 |
| 1988 | Pit . . . . . | 16 | 29 | 6 | 10 | 3 | 1 | 1 | 6 | 3 | 0 | .345 |
| 1989 | Pit . . . . . | 96 | 154 | 12 | 38 | 8 | 0 | 2 | 15 | 17 | 1 | .247 |
| | | 188 | 300 | 31 | 68 | 13 | 3 | 7 | 35 | 26 | 1 | .227 |

# Nick Esasky

**Birth Date:** 2/24/60
**Bats:** Right
**Throws:** Right
**1989 Club:** Boston Red Sox
**Contest Code #:** 124

**Rating: 4**

The Red Sox practically stole Nick Esasky (along with ace reliever Rob Murphy) from the Reds in December 1988. The 30-year-old bounced back from a pair of trips to the disabled list in 1988 to hit .277 with 30 homers and 108 RBI's for Boston in 1989. The Green Monster helped, of course, but the scouts always felt that Esasky had that type of talent. Still, Nick had never come close to those numbers in six seasons with Cincy, and the change of scenery obviously helped.

The only problem for Boston was Esasky's off-season free-agency. After his 1989 season, he could practically write his own contract—and he did, going home to Atlanta, where he should continue to flourish in the Fulton County launching pad. Scouts love Esasky's work habits and rate him high on the "aggressive" scale. He hits, hits with power, makes contact, and does a fine job at first base. If 1989 wasn't a fluke, Esasky will become one of the game's premier front-line players.

| Year | Team | G | AB | R | H | 2B | 3B | HR | RBI | BB | SB | AVG |
|------|------|----|------|-----|-----|-----|----|-----|-----|-----|----|------|
| 1983 | Cin .... | 85 | 302 | 41 | 80 | 10 | 5 | 12 | 46 | 27 | 6 | .265 |
| 1984 | Cin .... | 113 | 322 | 30 | 62 | 10 | 5 | 10 | 45 | 52 | 1 | .193 |
| 1985 | Cin .... | 125 | 413 | 61 | 108 | 21 | 0 | 21 | 66 | 41 | 3 | .262 |
| 1986 | Cin .... | 102 | 330 | 35 | 76 | 17 | 2 | 12 | 41 | 47 | 0 | .230 |
| 1987 | Cin .... | 100 | 346 | 48 | 94 | 19 | 2 | 22 | 59 | 29 | 0 | .272 |
| 1988 | Cin .... | 122 | 391 | 40 | 95 | 17 | 2 | 15 | 62 | 48 | 7 | .243 |
| 1989 | Bos .... | 154 | 564 | 79 | 156 | 26 | 5 | 30 | 108 | 66 | 1 | .277 |
| | | 801 | 2668 | 334 | 671 | 120 | 21 | 122 | 427 | 310 | 18 | .251 |

# Darrell Evans

**Birth Date:** 5/26/47
**Bats:** Left
**Throws:** Right
**1989 Club:** Atlanta Braves
**Contest Code #:** 107

**Rating: 1**

Braves general manager Bobby Cox seems to have an affinity for old, slow, once-proud ballplayers. From 1986 to 1988 he carried Ted Simmons as a catcher/first baseman/third baseman/pinch-hitter. Following the 1988 season, Simmons, then thirty-nine, hung up his uniform and joined the Cardinals' front office. So, in his quest for another experienced player for his bench, Cox signed Darrell Evans, who was two years older than Simmons.

Evans, the oldest player reviewed in this book, managed to hit 11 home runs, fifth-best on the Braves. In fact, 20 percent of his total hits were home runs. Unfortunately, Evans had 57 hits all year.

If I were Braves owner Ted Turner and I saw Evans back in the Braves' camp this spring, I'd wonder if there wasn't something seriously wrong with the player-development system.

| Year | Team | G | AB | R | H | 2B | 3B | HR | RBI | BB | SB | AVG |
|------|------|-----|-----|-----|-----|----|----|----|-----|-----|----|------|
| 1969 | Atl ..... | 12 | 26 | 3 | 6 | 0 | 0 | 0 | 1 | 1 | 0 | .231 |
| 1970 | Atl ..... | 12 | 44 | 4 | 14 | 1 | 1 | 0 | 9 | 7 | 0 | .318 |
| 1971 | Atl ..... | 89 | 260 | 42 | 63 | 11 | 1 | 12 | 38 | 39 | 2 | .242 |
| 1972 | Atl ..... | 125 | 418 | 67 | 106 | 12 | 0 | 19 | 71 | 90 | 4 | .254 |
| 1973 | Atl ..... | 161 | 595 | 114 | 167 | 25 | 8 | 41 | 104 | 124 | 6 | .281 |
| 1974 | Atl ..... | 160 | 571 | 99 | 137 | 21 | 3 | 25 | 79 | 126 | 4 | .240 |
| 1975 | Atl ..... | 156 | 567 | 82 | 138 | 22 | 2 | 22 | 73 | 105 | 12 | .243 |
| 1976 | Atl ..... | 44 | 139 | 11 | 24 | 0 | 0 | 1 | 10 | 30 | 3 | .173 |
| 1976 | SF ..... | 92 | 257 | 42 | 57 | 9 | 1 | 10 | 36 | 42 | 6 | .222 |
| 1977 | SF ..... | 144 | 461 | 64 | 117 | 18 | 3 | 17 | 72 | 69 | 9 | .254 |
| 1978 | SF ..... | 159 | 547 | 82 | 133 | 24 | 2 | 20 | 78 | 105 | 4 | .243 |
| 1979 | SF ..... | 160 | 562 | 68 | 142 | 23 | 2 | 17 | 70 | 91 | 6 | .253 |
| 1980 | SF ..... | 154 | 556 | 69 | 147 | 23 | 0 | 20 | 78 | 83 | 17 | .264 |
| 1981 | SF ..... | 102 | 357 | 51 | 92 | 13 | 4 | 12 | 48 | 54 | 2 | .258 |

| Year | Team | G | AB | R | H | 2B | 3B | HR | RBI | BB | SB | AVG |
|---|---|---|---|---|---|---|---|---|---|---|---|---|
| 1982 | SF | 141 | 465 | 64 | 119 | 20 | 4 | 16 | 61 | 77 | 5 | .256 |
| 1983 | SF | 142 | 523 | 94 | 145 | 29 | 3 | 30 | 82 | 84 | 6 | .277 |
| 1984 | Det | 131 | 401 | 60 | 93 | 11 | 1 | 16 | 63 | 77 | 2 | .232 |
| 1985 | Det | 151 | 505 | 81 | 125 | 17 | 0 | 40 | 94 | 85 | 0 | .248 |
| 1986 | Det | 151 | 507 | 78 | 122 | 15 | 0 | 29 | 85 | 91 | 3 | .241 |
| 1987 | Det | 150 | 499 | 90 | 128 | 20 | 0 | 34 | 99 | 100 | 6 | .257 |
| 1988 | Det | 144 | 437 | 48 | 91 | 9 | 0 | 22 | 64 | 84 | 1 | .208 |
| 1989 | Atl | 107 | 276 | 31 | 57 | 6 | 1 | 11 | 39 | 41 | 0 | .207 |
| | | 2687 | 8973 | 1344 | 2223 | 329 | 36 | 414 | 1354 | 1605 | 98 | .248 |

# Andres Galarraga

Birth Date: 6/18/61
Bats: Right
Throws: Right
1989 Club:
Montreal Expos
Contest Code #: 108

Rating: 4

Normally, I admire players who remain in the lineup despite injuries. It shows character, fortitude, and leadership. When I traded for Andres Galarraga during the middle of last season, I remembered how in 1987, when a wrist injury sapped him of his power, he rapped out 40 doubles. My kind of guy. But I could barely endure Galarraga's sub-par performance last year, which was caused in part by a knee injury sore enough to hamper his hitting but just sound enough to keep him from the disabled list.

A healthy Galarraga is among the National League's top players. He hits for average, has power to all fields, and steals a few bases. "The Big Cat" would be even better if he didn't strike out so often. In 1988, Galarraga, fourth in batting, led the league with 153 strikeouts. Last season, he batted 45 points less and struck out 158 times, once again the most in the league.

Injuries heal, but strikeouts can linger. If Galarraga would merely choke up for better bat control, the increase in contact would mean more hits and RBI's, and fewer K's.

| Year | Team | G | AB | R | H | 2B | 3B | HR | RBI | BB | SB | AVG |
|---|---|---|---|---|---|---|---|---|---|---|---|---|
| 1985 | Mon | 24 | 75 | 9 | 14 | 1 | 0 | 2 | 4 | 3 | 1 | .187 |
| 1986 | Mon | 105 | 321 | 39 | 87 | 13 | 0 | 10 | 42 | 30 | 6 | .271 |
| 1987 | Mon | 147 | 551 | 72 | 168 | 40 | 3 | 13 | 90 | 41 | 7 | .305 |
| 1988 | Mon | 157 | 609 | 99 | 184 | 42 | 8 | 29 | 92 | 39 | 13 | .302 |
| 1989 | Mon | 152 | 572 | 76 | 147 | 30 | 1 | 23 | 85 | 48 | 12 | .257 |
| | | 585 | 2128 | 295 | 600 | 126 | 12 | 77 | 313 | 161 | 39 | .282 |

# Mark Grace

Birth Date: 6/28/64
Bats: Left
Throws: Left
1989 Club:
Chicago Cubs
Contest Code #: 109

Rating: 5

Baseball scouts have long compared Mark Grace to Don Mattingly. Both can drive the ball to the opposite field. Both hit for high average. You'll recall that Mattingly didn't pull the ball when he first came to the major leagues, but after a year of work and maturation he grew into a consistent power threat. I believe Grace is ready to rise to that next level.

As a hitter, Grace, who just three seasons ago played in Double A, is equaled by few players. He turns the count to his advantage, always swinging at strikes and pressuring the pitcher into mistakes. He goes with the pitch. And he makes it all look easy.

As a run producer, last year Grace compiled a .493 slugging average. On the bases, Grace swiped 14, 11 more than he did in 1988. All indicators are pointing upward. This is the season when Grace challenges for the batting title and develops into a more consistent home-run hitter.

| Year | Team | G | AB | R | H | 2B | 3B | HR | RBI | BB | SB | AVG |
|------|------|---|-----|----|-----|----|----|----|-----|-----|----|------|
| 1988 | ChN.... | 134 | 486 | 65 | 144 | 23 | 4 | 7 | 57 | 60 | 3 | .296 |
| 1989 | ChN.... | 142 | 510 | 74 | 160 | 28 | 3 | 13 | 79 | 80 | 14 | .314 |
| | | 276 | 996 | 139 | 304 | 51 | 7 | 20 | 136 | 140 | 17 | .305 |

# Tommy Gregg

Birth Date: 7/29/63
Bats: Left
Throws: Left
1989 Club:
Atlanta Braves
Contest Code #: 110

Rating: 3

In his days as an outfielder, Tommy Gregg banged into more walls and hit more potholes than Richard Petty. He's had so many collisions that his Braves teammates have nicknamed him "Crash." When Gerald Perry was lost for the season, the Braves tried Gregg at first. Considering his track record, that's probably the safest place to put him.

Gregg was originally selected by the Indians in the June 1981 draft, but he opted to attend Wake Forest University instead. Three years later, the Indians drafted him again, but Gregg passed once more. In 1985, he was drafted by—and signed with—the Pirates. Gregg shined in the Pirates' system, batting .313 in 1985 and .371 in 1987. But injuries have stymied him since. Gregg's grade is a projection of his potential for 25 home runs, 75 RBI's and a .275 batting average.

| Year | Team | G | AB | R | H | 2B | 3B | HR | RBI | BB | SB | AVG |
|------|------|---|-----|----|----|----|----|----|-----|----|----|------|
| 1987 | Pit..... | 10 | 8 | 3 | 2 | 1 | 0 | 0 | 0 | 0 | 0 | .250 |
| 1988 | Pit..... | 14 | 15 | 4 | 3 | 1 | 0 | 1 | 3 | 1 | 0 | .200 |
| 1988 | Atl..... | 11 | 29 | 1 | 10 | 3 | 0 | 0 | 4 | 2 | 0 | .345 |
| 1989 | Atl..... | 102 | 276 | 24 | 67 | 8 | 0 | 6 | 23 | 18 | 3 | .243 |
| | | 137 | 328 | 32 | 82 | 13 | 0 | 7 | 30 | 21 | 3 | .250 |

# Pedro Guerrero

Birth Date: 6/29/56
Bats: Right
Throws: Right
1989 Club:
St. Louis Cardinals
Contest Code #: 111

Rating: 4

How did the Cardinals stay in the National League East race despite a slew of injuries to their pitching staff and a pop-gun offense that hit a league-low 73 home runs? Pedro Guerrero carried the team on his back all season long.

Guerrero got my vote for the 1989 National League MVP. Kevin Mitchell may have hit more home runs, but he had Will Clark in front of him and, during the second half, a power-hitting Matt Williams behind him. Guerrero had a slumping Tom Brunansky.

In 162 games last year, Guerrero tied for the league lead in doubles (42), was second in RBI's (117), and fifth in batting average (.311). In fact, 66 percent of his hits drove in runs. That's a clutch performer.

| Year | Team | G | AB | R | H | 2B | 3B | HR | RBI | BB | SB | AVG |
|------|------|---|-----|----|-----|----|----|----|-----|----|----|------|
| 1978 | LA .... | 5 | 8 | 3 | 5 | 0 | 1 | 0 | 1 | 0 | 0 | .625 |
| 1979 | LA .... | 25 | 62 | 7 | 15 | 2 | 0 | 2 | 9 | 1 | 2 | .242 |
| 1980 | LA .... | 75 | 183 | 27 | 59 | 9 | 1 | 7 | 31 | 12 | 2 | .322 |
| 1981 | LA .... | 98 | 347 | 46 | 104 | 17 | 2 | 12 | 48 | 34 | 5 | .300 |
| 1982 | LA .... | 150 | 575 | 87 | 175 | 27 | 5 | 32 | 100 | 65 | 22 | .304 |
| 1983 | LA .... | 160 | 584 | 87 | 174 | 28 | 6 | 32 | 103 | 72 | 23 | .298 |
| 1984 | LA .... | 144 | 535 | 85 | 162 | 29 | 4 | 16 | 72 | 49 | 9 | .303 |
| 1985 | LA .... | 137 | 487 | 99 | 156 | 22 | 2 | 33 | 87 | 83 | 12 | .320 |
| 1986 | LA .... | 31 | 61 | 7 | 15 | 3 | 0 | 5 | 10 | 2 | 0 | .246 |
| 1987 | LA .... | 152 | 545 | 89 | 184 | 25 | 2 | 27 | 89 | 74 | 9 | .338 |

| | | | | | | | | | | | |
|---|---|---|---|---|---|---|---|---|---|---|---|
| 1988 | LA..... | 59 | 215 | 24 | 64 | 7 | 1 | 5 | 35 | 25 | 2 | .298 |
| 1988 | StL .... | 44 | 149 | 16 | 40 | 7 | 1 | 5 | 30 | 21 | 2 | .268 |
| 1989 | StL .... | 162 | 570 | 60 | 177 | 42 | 1 | 17 | 117 | 79 | 2 | .311 |
| | | 1242 | 4321 | 637 | 1330 | 218 | 26 | 193 | 732 | 517 | 90 | .308 |

# Wallace Johnson

**Birth Date:** 12/25/56
**Bats:** Right and Left
**Throws:** Right
**1989 Club:**
**Montreal Expos**
**Contest Code #:** 113

**Rating: 1**

As a baseball player, Wallace Johnson, who in 1979 received his accounting degree from Indiana State University, is an example of the "highest and best use" ecomonics principle. Expos manager Buck Rodgers relies on Johnson as his top pinch-hitter and reserve first baseman, and whenever he's called on, he delivers. Last year Johnson batted .272, fifth-best on the Expos, and drove in a career-high 17 ribbies.

Johnson, who won the Class-A Florida State League batting title with a .334 average in 1980, made his major-league debut in September 1981. He was Montreal's Opening Day second baseman in 1982, but was demoted to Triple A shortly after and released following the season. After a pit stop with the Giants, Johnson was re-signed by the Expos in 1984 and has been with the big club since 1987.

As an added contribution to his team, Johnson helps players in the Expos organization, particularly those from Latin countries, with their tax returns.

| Year | Team | G | AB | R | H | 2B | 3B | HR | RBI | BB | SB | AVG |
|---|---|---|---|---|---|---|---|---|---|---|---|---|
| 1981 | Mon.... | 11 | 9 | 1 | 2 | 0 | 1 | 0 | 3 | 1 | 1 | .222 |
| 1982 | Mon.... | 36 | 57 | 5 | 11 | 0 | 2 | 0 | 2 | 5 | 4 | .193 |
| 1983 | Mon.... | 3 | 2 | 1 | 1 | 0 | 0 | 0 | 0 | 1 | 1 | .500 |
| 1983 | SF ..... | 7 | 8 | 0 | 1 | 0 | 0 | 0 | 1 | 0 | 0 | .125 |
| 1984 | Mon.... | 17 | 24 | 3 | 5 | 0 | 0 | 0 | 4 | 5 | 0 | .208 |
| 1986 | Mon.... | 61 | 127 | 13 | 36 | 3 | 1 | 1 | 10 | 7 | 6 | .283 |
| 1987 | Mon.... | 75 | 85 | 7 | 21 | 5 | 0 | 1 | 14 | 7 | 5 | .247 |
| 1988 | Mon.... | 86 | 94 | 7 | 29 | 5 | 1 | 0 | 3 | 12 | 0 | .309 |
| 1989 | Mon.... | 85 | 114 | 9 | 31 | 3 | 1 | 2 | 17 | 7 | 1 | .272 |
| | | 381 | 520 | 46 | 137 | 16 | 6 | 4 | 54 | 45 | 18 | .263 |

# Ricky Jordan

**Birth Date:** 5/26/65
**Bats:** Right
**Throws:** Right
**1989 Club:**
**Philadelphia Phillies**
**Contest Code #:** 114

**Rating: 3**

Paul Scott Jordan, better known as "Ricky," is a good hitter for average, but the Phillies expect him to hit for power. So far, Jordan's fallen below expectations.

After hitting 11 home runs in 69 games in 1988, Jordan hit 12 all of last year. At times the Phillies dropped him down in the order, as if a respite from the clean-up spot might energize his bat.

I say to the Phillies, don't force the issue. If Mr. Jordan can develop more power without affecting his batting average, fine. If not, then move Jordan into the number-three hole, where his high average and run production will satisfy your needs.

| Year | Team | G | AB | R | H | 2B | 3B | HR | RBI | BB | SB | AVG |
|---|---|---|---|---|---|---|---|---|---|---|---|---|
| 1988 | Phi .... | 69 | 273 | 41 | 84 | 15 | 1 | 11 | 43 | 7 | 1 | .308 |
| 1989 | Phi .... | 144 | 523 | 63 | 149 | 22 | 3 | 12 | 75 | 23 | 4 | .285 |
| | | 213 | 796 | 104 | 233 | 37 | 4 | 23 | 118 | 30 | 5 | .293 |

# Jeff King

Birth Date: 12/26/64
Bats: Right
Throws: Right
1989 Club:
Pittsburgh Pirates
Contest Code #: 115

Rating: 2

**J**eff King, the first player chosen in the June 1986 draft, had three and a half rocky seasons in the Pirates' system. He had trouble each time he advanced a level, and last summer, after a few months at Triple A, King groped with the pitching on the major-league level.

Because of a shoulder problem, the Pirates played King at first base (replacing the injured Sid Bream). When Jose Lind couldn't pull out of a slump, the Pirates kicked around the idea of making King into a power-hitting second baseman. What they should do is put King at third, his natural position, and move Bobby "The Butcher Boy" Bonilla from third to first.

Another suggestion: Bat King seventh or eighth. Let him continue to adjust to major-league pitching.

| Year | Team | G | AB | R | H | 2B | 3B | HR | RBI | BB | SB | AVG |
|------|------|---|----|---|---|----|----|----|----|----|----|-----|
| 1989 | Pit..... | 75 | 215 | 31 | 42 | 13 | 3 | 5 | 19 | 20 | 4 | .195 |
|      |      | 75 | 215 | 31 | 42 | 13 | 3 | 5 | 19 | 20 | 4 | .195 |

# Dave Magadan

Birth Date: 9/30/62
Bats: Left
Throws: Right
1989 Club:
New York Mets
Contest Code #: 116

Rating: 3

**D**ave Magadan's 1989 performance convinced the Mets' brass they could live without Keith Hernandez. In 374 at-bats, Magadan batted .286, fourth best on the Mets. He also drove in a career-high 41 RBI's.

Magadan is a slow-footed line-drive hitter in the mold of fellow Tampan Wade Boggs of the Red Sox. If Magadan is going to stand out, however, he's got to learn how to pull the ball for power. At 6'3"and 195 pounds, he's big enough and strong enough to handle it. At age twenty-seven, it's time for him to start doing it.

Even if he doesn't learn to pull the ball, Magadan can still be a productive run producer by emulating his cousin, former major-leaguer Lou Piniella, now the Reds' manager, who made a living driving in the key runs by slashing opportune line drives.

| Year | Team | G | AB | R | H | 2B | 3B | HR | RBI | BB | SB | AVG |
|------|------|---|----|---|---|----|----|----|-----|----|----|-----|
| 1986 | NYN ... | 10 | 18 | 3 | 8 | 0 | 0 | 0 | 3 | 3 | 0 | .444 |
| 1987 | NYN ... | 85 | 192 | 21 | 61 | 13 | 1 | 3 | 24 | 22 | 0 | .318 |
| 1988 | NYN ... | 112 | 314 | 39 | 87 | 15 | 0 | 1 | 35 | 60 | 0 | .277 |
| 1989 | NYN ... | 127 | 374 | 47 | 107 | 22 | 3 | 4 | 41 | 49 | 1 | .286 |
|      |      | 334 | 898 | 110 | 263 | 50 | 4 | 8 | 103 | 134 | 1 | .293 |

# Carmelo Martinez

Birth Date: 7/28/60
Bats: Right
Throws: Right
1989 Club:
San Diego Padres
Contest Code #: 117

Rating: 1

**C**armelo Martinez looks the part of a slugger. As he takes his stance, Martinez bunches his confining sleeves at his shoulders to free his biceps. He's got the big swing of a power hitter. If only he could make contact with any sort of consistency.

Martinez, a highly touted minor-leaguer who belted 31 home runs at Triple A in 1983, has proven to be a one-dimensional player. Fitting him into the everyday lineup has been a chore, since Martinez has hands of stone. As a platoon player and occasional regular, his seasonal batting averages, home runs, and RBI's have fallen well below expectations.

Last spring, with Jack Clark on board, the Padres had toyed with putting Martinez at third base, but Carmelo couldn't cut it at the hot corner. During the season Bip Roberts' batting left Martinez without a position. Seems the only spot open for Carmelo is as a designated hitter for an American League club.

| Year | Team | G | AB | R | H | 2B | 3B | HR | RBI | BB | SB | AVG |
|---|---|---|---|---|---|---|---|---|---|---|---|---|
| 1983 | ChN.... | 29 | 89 | 8 | 23 | 3 | 0 | 6 | 16 | 4 | 0 | .258 |
| 1984 | SD..... | 149 | 488 | 64 | 122 | 28 | 2 | 13 | 66 | 68 | 1 | .250 |
| 1985 | SD..... | 150 | 514 | 64 | 130 | 28 | 1 | 21 | 72 | 87 | 0 | .253 |
| 1986 | SD..... | 113 | 244 | 28 | 58 | 10 | 0 | 9 | 25 | 35 | 1 | .238 |
| 1987 | SD..... | 139 | 447 | 59 | 122 | 21 | 2 | 15 | 70 | 70 | 5 | .273 |
| 1988 | SD..... | 121 | 365 | 48 | 86 | 12 | 0 | 18 | 65 | 35 | 1 | .236 |
| 1989 | SD..... | 111 | 267 | 23 | 59 | 12 | 2 | 6 | 39 | 32 | 0 | .221 |
| | | 812 | 2414 | 294 | 600 | 114 | 7 | 88 | 353 | 331 | 8 | .249 |

# Lloyd McClendon

Birth Date: 1/11/59
Bats: Right
Throws: Right
1989 Club:
Chicago Cubs
Contest Code #: 118

Rating: 2

**U**ntil last season, Lloyd McClendon's claim to fame in baseball was that in 1982 he was one of three Mets' players traded to the Reds for Tom Seaver. In 1989, however, the stocky McClendon made a name for himself by coming through when injuries sidelined Andre Dawson and Mark Grace.

McClendon, who hit for power in the minor leagues (18 home runs in 1982, 15 in 1983, 16 in 1985, and 24 in 1986), rapped 12 home runs, 12 doubles, and 1 triple in 259 at-bats last season. McClendon's .479 slugging average was third on the Cubs behind Ryne Sandberg and Dwight Smith.

McClendon's value to the Cubs is his versatility; he can catch, play the corners, left field and right. His value to you is as a nice little run producer.

| Year | Team | G | AB | R | H | 2B | 3B | HR | RBI | BB | SB | AVG |
|---|---|---|---|---|---|---|---|---|---|---|---|---|
| 1987 | Cin .... | 45 | 72 | 8 | 15 | 5 | 0 | 2 | 13 | 4 | 1 | .208 |
| 1988 | Cin .... | 72 | 137 | 9 | 30 | 4 | 0 | 3 | 14 | 15 | 4 | .219 |
| 1989 | ChN.... | 92 | 259 | 47 | 74 | 12 | 1 | 12 | 40 | 37 | 6 | .286 |
| | | 209 | 468 | 64 | 119 | 21 | 1 | 17 | 67 | 56 | 11 | .254 |

# Eddie Murray

Birth Date: 2/24/56
Bats: Right and Left
Throws: Right
1989 Club:
Los Angeles Dodgers
Contest Code #: 119

Rating: 4

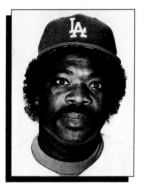

Twenty home runs and 88 RBI's is a pretty good season for many players, but below par for Eddie Murray. Murray, who in his 13-year career has hit 25 or more home runs 10 times and driven in more than 90 runners 8 times, hit just 9 home runs and drove in only 47 RBI's by the 1989 All-Star break.

But the most glaring statistic is Murray's measly 1989 batting average, a career low .247. Consider that Murray's previous career-low was .277 in 1987. If he'd been able to match his previous career average of 168 hits a season, he'd have hit .283. Imagine how much more productive he would have been.

I suspect that Murray will improve in 1990 because he'll have had a year to adjust to the National League's hard-throwing pitchers and more spacious ball parks.

| Year | Team | G | AB | R | H | 2B | 3B | HR | RBI | BB | SB | AVG |
|------|------|---|-----|-----|------|-----|----|-----|------|-----|----|------|
| 1977 | Bal .... | 160 | 611 | 81 | 173 | 29 | 2 | 27 | 88 | 48 | 0 | .283 |
| 1978 | Bal .... | 161 | 610 | 85 | 174 | 32 | 3 | 27 | 95 | 70 | 6 | .285 |
| 1979 | Bal .... | 159 | 606 | 90 | 179 | 30 | 2 | 25 | 99 | 72 | 10 | .295 |
| 1980 | Bal .... | 158 | 621 | 100 | 186 | 36 | 2 | 32 | 116 | 54 | 7 | .300 |
| 1981 | Bal .... | 99 | 378 | 57 | 111 | 21 | 2 | 22 | 78 | 40 | 2 | .294 |
| 1982 | Bal .... | 151 | 550 | 87 | 174 | 30 | 1 | 32 | 110 | 70 | 7 | .316 |
| 1983 | Bal .... | 156 | 582 | 115 | 178 | 30 | 3 | 33 | 111 | 86 | 5 | .306 |
| 1984 | Bal .... | 162 | 588 | 97 | 180 | 26 | 3 | 29 | 110 | 107 | 10 | .306 |
| 1985 | Bal .... | 156 | 583 | 111 | 173 | 37 | 1 | 31 | 124 | 84 | 5 | .297 |
| 1986 | Bal .... | 137 | 495 | 61 | 151 | 25 | 1 | 17 | 84 | 78 | 3 | .305 |
| 1987 | Bal .... | 160 | 618 | 89 | 171 | 28 | 3 | 30 | 91 | 73 | 1 | .277 |
| 1988 | Bal .... | 161 | 603 | 75 | 171 | 27 | 2 | 28 | 84 | 75 | 5 | .284 |
| 1989 | LA ..... | 160 | 594 | 66 | 147 | 29 | 1 | 20 | 88 | 87 | 7 | .247 |
| | | 1980 | 7439 | 1114 | 2168 | 380 | 26 | 353 | 1278 | 944 | 68 | .291 |

# Gerald Perry

Birth Date: 10/30/60
Bats: Left
Throws: Right
1989 Club:
Atlanta Braves
Contest Code #: 120

Rating: 2

Yesterday's hero, today's spare part. That's Gerald Perry's fate with the Braves in 1990.

Perry, who can hit for average and power, and can steal bases, had climbed the Braves' minor-league ladder beginning in 1978, and finally made it to the big leagues for good in 1987. That year, Perry batted .270, hit 12 home runs, drove in 74 runs, scored 77 runs, and stole 42 bases. In 1988, Perry earned National League All-Star honors, and wound up batting .300, with 74 RBIs.

Last season, Perry was dogged by shoulder problems that eventually required surgery. During his absence, the Braves tested Tommy Gregg at the position. During the offseason, the Braves signed power-hitting free agent Nick Esasky to take over the starting role in 1990. Whither Perry? Expect the Braves to showcase him during spring training and trade him to any interested party.

| Year | Team | G | AB | R | H | 2B | 3B | HR | RBI | BB | SB | AVG |
|------|------|---|-----|-----|-----|----|----|----|-----|-----|-----|------|
| 1983 | Atl .... | 27 | 39 | 5 | 14 | 2 | 0 | 1 | 6 | 5 | 0 | .359 |
| 1984 | Atl .... | 122 | 347 | 52 | 92 | 12 | 2 | 7 | 47 | 61 | 15 | .265 |
| 1985 | Atl .... | 110 | 238 | 22 | 51 | 5 | 0 | 3 | 13 | 23 | 9 | .214 |
| 1986 | Atl .... | 29 | 70 | 6 | 19 | 2 | 0 | 2 | 11 | 8 | 0 | .271 |
| 1987 | Atl .... | 142 | 533 | 77 | 144 | 35 | 2 | 12 | 74 | 48 | 42 | .270 |
| 1988 | Atl .... | 141 | 547 | 61 | 164 | 29 | 1 | 8 | 74 | 36 | 29 | .300 |
| 1989 | Atl .... | 72 | 266 | 24 | 67 | 11 | 0 | 4 | 21 | 32 | 10 | .252 |
| | | 643 | 2040 | 247 | 551 | 96 | 5 | 37 | 246 | 213 | 105 | .270 |

# Harry Spilman

Birth Date: 7/18/54
Bats: Left
Throws: Right
1989 Club:
Houston Astros
Contest Code #: 121

Rating: 1

**H**arry Spilman seems to be on an Astros lend-lease program. After leaving the Astros as a free agent following the 1985 season, Spilman signed with the Tigers, was released in June 1986, and immediately signed with the Giants. On August 11, 1988, the Giants released him. Seven days later, the Astros re-signed him.

William Harry Spilman, whose father, Harry, was a catcher in the Brooklyn Dodgers organization in 1952, has been a pinch-hitter for most of his major-league career. In 1978, Spilman made his major-league debut with the Reds by pinch-hitting four times. He was traded to the Astros in 1981 for shortstop Rafael Landestoy.

Last season, Spilman, who can fill in at third base, in the outfield, and behind the plate, was called up from Triple A to bolster the Astros' bench. He came to bat 36 times—19 as a pinch-hitter—and got 10 hits—4 as a pinch-hitter.

| Year | Team | G | AB | R | H | 2B | 3B | HR | RBI | BB | SB | AVG |
|------|------|---|-----|---|-----|----|----|----|-----|----|----|------|
| 1978 | Cin .... | 4 | 4 | 1 | 1 | 0 | 0 | 0 | 0 | 0 | 0 | .250 |
| 1979 | Cin .... | 43 | 56 | 7 | 12 | 3 | 0 | 0 | 5 | 7 | 0 | .214 |
| 1980 | Cin .... | 65 | 101 | 14 | 27 | 4 | 0 | 4 | 19 | 9 | 0 | .267 |
| 1981 | Cin .... | 23 | 24 | 4 | 4 | 1 | 0 | 0 | 3 | 3 | 0 | .167 |
| 1981 | Hou.... | 28 | 34 | 5 | 10 | 0 | 0 | 0 | 1 | 2 | 0 | .294 |
| 1982 | Hou.... | 38 | 61 | 7 | 17 | 2 | 0 | 3 | 11 | 5 | 0 | .279 |
| 1983 | Hou.... | 42 | 78 | 7 | 13 | 3 | 0 | 1 | 9 | 5 | 0 | .167 |
| 1984 | Hou.... | 32 | 72 | 14 | 19 | 2 | 0 | 2 | 15 | 12 | 0 | .264 |
| 1985 | Hou.... | 44 | 66 | 3 | 9 | 1 | 0 | 1 | 4 | 3 | 0 | .136 |
| 1986 | Det .... | 24 | 49 | 6 | 12 | 2 | 0 | 3 | 8 | 3 | 0 | .245 |
| 1986 | SF ..... | 58 | 94 | 12 | 27 | 7 | 0 | 2 | 22 | 12 | 0 | .287 |
| 1987 | SF ..... | 83 | 90 | 5 | 24 | 5 | 0 | 1 | 14 | 9 | 1 | .267 |
| 1988 | SF ..... | 40 | 40 | 4 | 7 | 1 | 1 | 1 | 3 | 4 | 0 | .175 |
| 1988 | Hou.... | 7 | 5 | 0 | 0 | 0 | 0 | 0 | 0 | 0 | 0 | .000 |
| 1989 | Hou.... | 32 | 36 | 7 | 10 | 3 | 0 | 0 | 3 | 7 | 0 | .278 |
| | | 563 | 810 | 96 | 192 | 34 | 1 | 18 | 117 | 81 | 1 | .237 |

# Denny Walling

Birth Date: 4/17/54
Bats: Left
Throws: Right
1989 Club:
St. Louis Cardinals
Contest Code #: 122

Rating: 2

**D**enny Walling is Cardinals' manager Whitey Herzog's kind of bench player: He can play first base, third base, and the outfield; he's a veteran who accepts his role; and he's always mentally prepared to pinch-hit.

Last season, Walling, a career .276 hitter, batted .304, second-best on the Cards. Walling compiled a .430 slugging average, as 8 of his 24 hits were for extra bases. He also walked 14 times, boosting his on-base average to .409.

| Year | Team | G | AB | R | H | 2B | 3B | HR | RBI | BB | SB | AVG |
|------|------|---|-----|----|-----|-----|----|----|-----|----|----|------|
| 1975 | Oak .... | 6 | 8 | 0 | 1 | 1 | 0 | 0 | 2 | 0 | 0 | .125 |
| 1976 | Oak .... | 3 | 11 | 1 | 3 | 0 | 0 | 0 | 0 | 0 | 0 | .273 |
| 1977 | Hou.... | 6 | 21 | 1 | 6 | 0 | 1 | 0 | 6 | 2 | 0 | .286 |
| 1978 | Hou.... | 120 | 247 | 30 | 62 | 11 | 3 | 3 | 36 | 30 | 9 | .251 |
| 1979 | Hou.... | 82 | 147 | 21 | 48 | 8 | 4 | 3 | 31 | 17 | 3 | .327 |
| 1980 | Hou.... | 100 | 284 | 30 | 85 | 6 | 5 | 3 | 29 | 35 | 4 | .299 |
| 1981 | Hou.... | 65 | 158 | 23 | 37 | 6 | 0 | 5 | 23 | 28 | 2 | .234 |
| 1982 | Hou.... | 85 | 146 | 22 | 30 | 4 | 1 | 1 | 14 | 23 | 4 | .205 |
| 1983 | Hou.... | 100 | 135 | 24 | 40 | 5 | 3 | 3 | 19 | 15 | 2 | .296 |
| 1984 | Hou.... | 87 | 249 | 37 | 70 | 11 | 5 | 3 | 31 | 16 | 7 | .281 |
| 1985 | Hou.... | 119 | 345 | 44 | 93 | 20 | 1 | 7 | 45 | 25 | 5 | .270 |
| 1986 | Hou.... | 130 | 382 | 54 | 119 | 23 | 1 | 13 | 58 | 36 | 1 | .312 |
| 1987 | Hou.... | 110 | 325 | 45 | 92 | 21 | 4 | 5 | 33 | 39 | 5 | .283 |
| 1988 | Hou.... | 65 | 176 | 19 | 43 | 10 | 2 | 1 | 20 | 15 | 1 | .244 |
| 1988 | StL .... | 19 | 58 | 3 | 13 | 3 | 0 | 0 | 1 | 2 | 1 | .224 |
| 1989 | StL .... | 69 | 79 | 9 | 24 | 7 | 0 | 1 | 11 | 14 | 0 | .304 |
| | | 1166 | 2771 | 363 | 766 | 136 | 30 | 48 | 359 | 297 | 44 | .276 |

# Jeff Wetherby

**Birth Date: 10/18/63**
**Bats: Left**
**Throws: Left**
**1989 Club:**
**Atlanta Braves**
**Contest Code #: 123**

**Rating: 1**

Jeff Wetherby, the Braves' twentieth selection in the June 1985 draft, has been a fairly good run producer during his minor-league career. At Class A in 1986 he drove in a combined 91 RBI's and scored 108 for Durham and Sumter. A year later, Wetherby led the Double A Greenville Braves in batting (.303, sixth-best in the Southern League), hits (148), and doubles (31), was second in RBI's (78), and third in home runs (12). In 1988, Wetherby's 61 RBI's were second on the Triple A Richmond Braves.

Wetherby advanced to the majors during the 1989 season when Braves first baseman Gerald Perry hurt his shoulder. Playing sporadically, Wetherby managed to amass a .364 slugging average.

Wetherby's future with the Braves is cloudy, because the team converted outfielder Tommy Gregg to first when it was learned that Perry would miss the rest of the 1989 season.

| Year | Team | G | AB | R | H | 2B | 3B | HR | RBI | BB | SB | AVG |
|------|------|---|----|----|----|----|----|----|-----|----|----|-----|
| 1989 | Atl..... | 52 | 48 | 5 | 10 | 2 | 1 | 1 | 7 | 4 | 1 | .208 |
|      |      | 52 | 48 | 5 | 10 | 2 | 1 | 1 | 7 | 4 | 1 | .208 |

# SECOND BASEMEN

# SECOND BASEMEN

## Roberto Alomar

**Birth Date: 2/3/68**
**Bats: Right and Left**
**Throws: Right**
**1989 Club:**
**San Diego Padres**
**Contest Code #: 125**

**Rating: 5**

**R**oberto Alomar gives the Padres all they can ask for in a leadoff hitter. He hits from both sides of the plate; hits for a high average (his .295 mark last season was sixth-best in the National League); often gets 2 or more hits a game (last season he was second in the league with 54 multiple-hit games); and steals bases (tied with Juan Samuel for second in the league).

What's more, Alomar should only get better with experience. He improved each year in his minor-league career, upping his batting average from .207 in 1985 to .240 in 1986 to .307 in 1987. In 1988, Alomar was named by *Baseball America* as the Triple A Player of the Year. Playing for the Las Vegas Star, he batted .297, hit 16 home runs, drove in 71 RBI's and stole 31 bases. Those numbers could have been better had Alomar not missed the final month of that season with a knee injury.

Alomar, the son of Padres coach Sandy Alomar and brother of catching phenom Sandy Alomar, Jr., has the pedigree for success. As long as he minimizes his strikeouts (last year he fanned 76 times), Alomar will soon challenge Ryne Sandberg for perennial All-Star status.

| Year | Team | G | AB | R | H | 2B | 3B | HR | RBI | BB | SB | AVG |
|------|------|---|-----|----|-----|----|----|----|-----|-----|----|------|
| 1988 | SD..... | 143 | 545 | 84 | 145 | 24 | 6 | 9 | 41 | 47 | 24 | .266 |
| 1989 | SD..... | 158 | 623 | 82 | 184 | 27 | 1 | 7 | 56 | 53 | 42 | .295 |
| | | 301 | 1168 | 166 | 329 | 51 | 7 | 16 | 97 | 100 | 66 | .282 |

## Jeff Blauser

**Birth Date: 11/8/65**
**Bats: Right**
**Throws: Right**
**1989 Club:**
**Atlanta Braves**
**Contest Code #: 126**

**Rating: 3**

**B**aby-faced Jeff Blauser showed real power in his first full season with the Braves. Shifting between second base (against lefthanders) and third base (when Ronnie Gant lost the job), Blauser rapped 12 home runs, third-best on the team, knocked in 46 runs, and had a slugging percentage of .412. Mercy!

Only once before in his pro career has the 6'1", 180-pound Blauser approached such power numbers: in 1986, he hit 13 dingers and drove in 52 runs for Double A Durham.

For Blauser's sake, he'd be better off focusing on making consistent contact (he whiffed 101 times last season) and let the home runs fall where they may. He has the speed to be a good number-two hitter (he swiped 36 bags for Class A Sumter in 1985), but he lacks the strength to be a middle-of-the-order man.

| Year | Team | G | AB | R | H | 2B | 3B | HR | RBI | BB | SB | AVG |
|------|------|---|-----|----|-----|----|----|----|-----|-----|----|------|
| 1987 | Atl..... | 51 | 165 | 11 | 40 | 6 | 3 | 2 | 15 | 18 | 7 | .242 |
| 1988 | Atl..... | 18 | 67 | 7 | 16 | 3 | 1 | 2 | 7 | 2 | 0 | .239 |
| 1989 | Atl..... | 142 | 456 | 63 | 123 | 24 | 2 | 12 | 46 | 38 | 5 | .270 |
| | | 211 | 688 | 81 | 179 | 33 | 6 | 16 | 68 | 58 | 12 | .260 |

# Bill Doran

Birth Date: 5/28/58
Bats: Right and Left
Throws: Right
1989 Club:
Houston Astros
Contest Code #: 127

Rating: 2

**B**ill Doran is maddening. Baseball observers have been touting him as the National League's next great second baseman, but all I've seen is a player who, when not injured (he's played a full, healthy season just once in eight major-league seasons), is hot for half a season and cold for the other.

The past two seasons, Doran has been dogged by a torn left rotator cuff that required surgery; an injured right knee that required surgery; and a chronically bad back that has been difficult to treat.

Dare we predict how Doran will fare this season?

| Year | Team | G | AB | R | H | 2B | 3B | HR | RBI | BB | SB | AVG |
|------|------|------|------|-----|------|-----|----|----|-----|-----|-----|------|
| 1982 | Hou.... | 26 | 97 | 11 | 27 | 3 | 0 | 0 | 6 | 4 | 5 | .278 |
| 1983 | Hou.... | 154 | 535 | 70 | 145 | 12 | 7 | 8 | 39 | 86 | 12 | .271 |
| 1984 | Hou.... | 147 | 548 | 92 | 143 | 18 | 11 | 4 | 41 | 66 | 21 | .261 |
| 1985 | Hou.... | 148 | 578 | 84 | 166 | 31 | 6 | 14 | 59 | 71 | 23 | .287 |
| 1986 | Hou.... | 145 | 550 | 92 | 152 | 29 | 3 | 6 | 37 | 81 | 42 | .276 |
| 1987 | Hou.... | 162 | 625 | 82 | 177 | 23 | 3 | 16 | 79 | 82 | 31 | .283 |
| 1988 | Hou.... | 132 | 480 | 66 | 119 | 18 | 1 | 7 | 53 | 65 | 17 | .248 |
| 1989 | Hou.... | 142 | 507 | 65 | 111 | 25 | 2 | 8 | 58 | 59 | 22 | .219 |
| | | 1056 | 3920 | 562 | 1040 | 159 | 33 | 63 | 372 | 514 | 173 | .265 |

# Tom Foley

Birth Date: 9/9/59
Bats: Left
Throws: Right
1989 Club:
Montreal Expos
Contest Code #: 128

Rating: 2

**I** thought I got a bargain at my 1989 fantasy draft in Tom Foley, platoon player at large. Foley plays second base, third base, and short, hits for a decent average, steals a base here and there, and drives in around 40 runs. Last season, in his platoon role as the Expos' left-handed-hitting platoon, Foley played more regularly than I expected and hit far worse than I expected.

With the Expos' infield prospects at Triple A almost ready to graduate to the big leagues, manager Buck Rodgers probably will return Foley to a roving role this season.

| Year | Team | G | AB | R | H | 2B | 3B | HR | RBI | BB | SB | AVG |
|------|------|-----|------|-----|-----|----|----|----|-----|-----|----|------|
| 1983 | Cin .... | 68 | 98 | 7 | 20 | 4 | 1 | 0 | 9 | 13 | 1 | .204 |
| 1984 | Cin .... | 106 | 277 | 26 | 70 | 8 | 3 | 5 | 27 | 24 | 3 | .253 |
| 1985 | Cin .... | 43 | 92 | 7 | 18 | 5 | 1 | 0 | 6 | 6 | 1 | .196 |
| 1985 | Phi .... | 46 | 158 | 17 | 42 | 8 | 0 | 3 | 17 | 13 | 1 | .266 |
| 1986 | Phi .... | 39 | 61 | 8 | 18 | 2 | 1 | 0 | 5 | 10 | 2 | .295 |
| 1986 | Mon.... | 64 | 202 | 18 | 52 | 13 | 2 | 1 | 18 | 20 | 8 | .257 |
| 1987 | Mon.... | 106 | 280 | 35 | 82 | 18 | 3 | 5 | 28 | 11 | 6 | .293 |
| 1988 | Mon.... | 127 | 377 | 33 | 100 | 21 | 3 | 5 | 43 | 30 | 2 | .265 |
| 1989 | Mon.... | 122 | 375 | 34 | 86 | 19 | 2 | 7 | 39 | 45 | 2 | .229 |
| | | 721 | 1920 | 185 | 488 | 98 | 16 | 26 | 192 | 172 | 26 | .254 |

# Damaso Garcia

**Birth Date:** 2/7/57
**Bats:** Right
**Throws:** Right
**1989 Club:**
**Montreal Expos**
**Contest Code #:** 129

**Rating: 1**

**D**amaso Garcia suffered the ultimate indignity last September: The Expos told the 11-year-veteran, who'd hinted at retirement following the season, to pack his bags and leave early, his services no longer required.

It wasn't that Garcia had a bad season. Used in 80 games, primarily as the right-handed-hitting platoon player at second base, Garcia batted .271, just 13 points below his previous career average. Rather, the Expos decided it was time to clear the way for young bloods Junior Noboa and Jeff Huson.

Garcia's career, once filled with promise, degenerated because of frequent injuries and occasional battles with his managers. Should he hook up with another National League club, Garcia remains capable of batting in the .270 range as a spot player.

| Year | Team | G | AB | R | H | 2B | 3B | HR | RBI | BB | SB | AVG |
|------|------|---|-----|---|-----|----|----|----|-----|----|----|------|
| 1978 | NYA.... | 18 | 41 | 5 | 8 | 0 | 0 | 0 | 1 | 2 | 1 | .195 |
| 1979 | NYA.... | 11 | 38 | 3 | 10 | 1 | 0 | 0 | 4 | 0 | 2 | .263 |
| 1980 | Tor..... | 140 | 543 | 50 | 151 | 30 | 7 | 4 | 46 | 12 | 13 | .278 |
| 1981 | Tor..... | 64 | 250 | 24 | 63 | 8 | 1 | 1 | 13 | 9 | 13 | .252 |
| 1982 | Tor..... | 147 | 597 | 89 | 185 | 32 | 3 | 5 | 42 | 21 | 54 | .310 |
| 1983 | Tor..... | 131 | 525 | 84 | 161 | 23 | 6 | 3 | 38 | 24 | 31 | .307 |
| 1984 | Tor..... | 152 | 633 | 79 | 180 | 32 | 5 | 5 | 46 | 16 | 46 | .284 |
| 1985 | Tor..... | 146 | 600 | 70 | 169 | 25 | 4 | 8 | 65 | 15 | 28 | .282 |
| 1986 | Tor..... | 122 | 424 | 57 | 119 | 22 | 0 | 6 | 46 | 13 | 9 | .281 |
| 1988 | Atl.... | 21 | 60 | 3 | 7 | 1 | 0 | 1 | 4 | 3 | 1 | .117 |
| 1989 | Mon.... | 80 | 203 | 26 | 55 | 9 | 1 | 3 | 18 | 15 | 5 | .271 |
| | | 1032 | 3914 | 490 | 1108 | 183 | 27 | 36 | 323 | 130 | 203 | .283 |

# Lenny Harris

**Birth Date:** 10/28/64
**Bats:** Left
**Throws:** Right
**1989 Club:**
**Los Angeles Dodgers**
**Contest Code #:** 130

**Rating: 1**

**I**n the Pete Rose regime, Reds' rookies who didn't produce immediately were replaced by veterans with whom Rose could relate better. So it wasn't surprising that rookie Lenny Harris, who opened the season as the Reds' starting second baseman, was benched in favor of old Ron Oester when his bat went cold, and was traded months later to the Dodgers.

The Dodgers, along with many other National League teams, still regard Harris as a prospect. In 1983, Harris stole 31 bases, sixth-best in the Midwest League. In 1984, he struggled at the plate, batting .246 for Class A Cedar Rapids. Though he wound up batting .259 for Tampa (Florida State League) in 1985, he did hit .320 that June and .294 that July. In 1988, Harris led the American Association with 45 stolen bases.

This season, Harris will be used as a reserve. Hopefully, the Dodgers will work with him and give him the time he needs to develop into a more consistent batter.

| Year | Team | G | AB | R | H | 2B | 3B | HR | RBI | BB | SB | AVG |
|------|------|---|-----|----|----|----|----|----|-----|----|----|------|
| 1988 | Cin .... | 16 | 43 | 7 | 16 | 1 | 0 | 0 | 8 | 5 | 4 | .372 |
| 1989 | Cin .... | 61 | 188 | 17 | 42 | 4 | 0 | 2 | 11 | 9 | 10 | .223 |
| 1989 | LA ..... | 54 | 147 | 19 | 37 | 6 | 1 | 1 | 15 | 11 | 4 | .252 |
| | | 131 | 378 | 43 | 95 | 11 | 1 | 3 | 34 | 25 | 18 | .251 |

# Tommy Herr

**Birth Date: 4/4/56**
**Bats: Left**
**Throws: Right**
**1989 Club:**
**Philadelphia Phillies**
**Contest Code #: 131**

## Rating: 3

Tommy Herr is a glamour name living off his 1985 numbers. After driving in 110 runs that season for the National League champion Cardinals, he's come close only once.

Herr hits for a moderate batting average, steals a few bases, but doesn't hit home runs. He does hit a lot of sacrifice flies; he led the league in that category in 1985 and 1987. Herr won't embarrass himself in any category, but he won't positively impact any, either.

One thing to keep in mind is Herr's batting average at Veteran's Stadium, which, going into the 1989 season, was .292 (77 for 264), his second-highest average in any stadium. His best average, by the way, is at Pittsburgh's Three Rivers Stadium (.299—64 for 214).

| Year | Team | G | AB | R | H | 2B | 3B | HR | RBI | BB | SB | AVG |
|------|------|---|----|----|---|----|----|----|-----|----|----|-----|
| 1979 | StL .... | 14 | 10 | 4 | 2 | 0 | 0 | 0 | 1 | 2 | 1 | .200 |
| 1980 | StL .... | 76 | 222 | 29 | 55 | 12 | 5 | 0 | 15 | 16 | 9 | .248 |
| 1981 | StL .... | 103 | 411 | 50 | 110 | 14 | 9 | 0 | 46 | 39 | 23 | .268 |
| 1982 | StL .... | 135 | 493 | 83 | 131 | 19 | 4 | 0 | 36 | 57 | 25 | .266 |
| 1983 | StL .... | 89 | 313 | 43 | 101 | 14 | 4 | 2 | 31 | 43 | 6 | .323 |
| 1984 | StL .... | 145 | 558 | 67 | 154 | 23 | 2 | 4 | 49 | 49 | 13 | .276 |
| 1985 | StL .... | 159 | 596 | 97 | 180 | 38 | 3 | 8 | 110 | 80 | 31 | .302 |
| 1986 | StL .... | 152 | 559 | 48 | 141 | 30 | 4 | 2 | 61 | 73 | 22 | .252 |
| 1987 | StL .... | 141 | 510 | 73 | 134 | 29 | 0 | 2 | 83 | 68 | 19 | .263 |
| 1988 | Min .... | 86 | 304 | 42 | 80 | 16 | 0 | 1 | 21 | 40 | 10 | .263 |
| 1988 | StL .... | 15 | 50 | 4 | 13 | 0 | 0 | 1 | 3 | 11 | 3 | .260 |
| 1989 | Phi .... | 151 | 561 | 65 | 161 | 25 | 6 | 2 | 37 | 54 | 10 | .287 |
| | | 1266 | 4587 | 605 | 1262 | 220 | 37 | 22 | 493 | 532 | 172 | .275 |

# Gregg Jefferies

**Birth Date: 8/1/67**
**Bats: Right and Left**
**Throws: Right**
**1989 Club:**
**New York Mets**
**Contest Code #: 132**

## Rating: 4

I hesitate to say this, only because I traded away Greg Jefferies during the middle of last year, when his batting average matched his weight, but he is definitely a star in the making. When he's in stride, he hits with line-drive power to all fields, he can pull the ball against any pitcher, and, as Mets radio voice Bob Murphy would say, he's "got a world of speed."

What accounted for Jefferies' slow start was that manager Davey Johnson switched him to a new position—second base, one of the hardest positions to learn and master—during the 1989 spring camp. Jefferies, an intense fellow with a burning desire to succeed, pressed himself like a well-starched shirt and his overall game became stiff.

Jefferies is not the most beloved Met. During a late-season game against the Phillies, former Met Roger McDowell wrestled with Jefferies on the field. Phils manager Nick Leyva didn't know what to make of the ensuing fracas; following the game, he told reporters that 30 Phillies rushed to McDowell's aid—and that 20 Mets did, too.

| Year | Team | G | AB | R | H | 2B | 3B | HR | RBI | BB | SB | AVG |
|------|------|---|----|----|---|----|----|----|-----|----|----|-----|
| 1987 | NYN ... | 6 | 6 | 0 | 3 | 1 | 0 | 0 | 2 | 0 | 0 | .500 |
| 1988 | NYN ... | 29 | 109 | 19 | 35 | 8 | 2 | 6 | 17 | 8 | 5 | .321 |
| 1989 | NYN ... | 141 | 508 | 72 | 131 | 28 | 2 | 12 | 56 | 39 | 21 | .258 |
| | | 176 | 623 | 91 | 169 | 37 | 4 | 18 | 75 | 47 | 26 | .271 |

# Tim Jones

Birth Date: 12/1/62
Bats: Left
Throws: Right
1989 Club:
St. Louis Cardinals
Contest Code #: 133

Rating: 1

**T**im knows the infield. Tim knows catching. Tim really knows the bench. Jones, the Cardinals' second-round pick in the June 1985 draft, sat on the bench for 120 games last season.

In his rare and infrequent appearances, he batted 75 times. Thanks to his 22 hits, his batting, slugging, and on-base averages were mighty handsome. Jones was supposed to take over Jose Oquendo's roving role, but the Cardinals didn't need a rover last season. Next time you go to a Cardinals game, look for Tim in the bullpen warming up relief pitchers.

| Year | Team | G | AB | R | H | 2B | 3B | HR | RBI | BB | SB | AVG |
|------|------|---|-----|----|----|----|----|----|-----|----|----|------|
| 1988 | StL .... | 31 | 52 | 2 | 14 | 0 | 0 | 0 | 3 | 4 | 4 | .269 |
| 1989 | StL .... | 42 | 75 | 11 | 22 | 6 | 0 | 0 | 7 | 7 | 1 | .293 |
| | | 73 | 127 | 13 | 36 | 6 | 0 | 0 | 10 | 11 | 5 | .283 |

# Jose Lind

Birth Date: 5/1/64
Bats: Right
Throws: Right
1989 Club:
Pittsburgh Pirates
Contest Code #: 134

Rating: 1

**N**ational League sources have a few opinions on Jose Lind's dramatic decline last season. Some scouts complained that Lind didn't take good care of his body.

Lind has great athletic gifts—remember when, on an NBC pre-game show, Lind took a running jump over a standing Joe Garagiola?—but if he can't hit for average, he won't steal enough bases to have value as a fantasy player. He struck out 64 times last season, and walked only 39 times.

The Pirates' coaches got so disenchanted with Lind last year that they considered moving a plodding Jeff King to second base. Lind is capable of a better average—in 1988 he batted .262—and can drive in some runs. It's all up to him.

| Year | Team | G | AB | R | H | 2B | 3B | HR | RBI | BB | SB | AVG |
|------|------|-----|------|-----|-----|----|----|----|-----|----|----|------|
| 1987 | Pit..... | 35 | 143 | 21 | 46 | 8 | 4 | 0 | 11 | 8 | 2 | .322 |
| 1988 | Pit..... | 154 | 611 | 82 | 160 | 24 | 4 | 2 | 49 | 42 | 15 | .262 |
| 1989 | Pit..... | 153 | 578 | 52 | 134 | 21 | 3 | 2 | 48 | 39 | 15 | .232 |
| | | 342 | 1332 | 155 | 340 | 53 | 11 | 4 | 108 | 89 | 32 | .255 |

# Keith Miller

Birth Date: 6/12/63
Bats: Right
Throws: Right
1989 Club:
New York Mets
Contest Code #: 135

Rating: 1

**T**he Mets' front office really messed with Keith Miller's head last year. During the 1988 winter meetings, they proclaimed Miller as "untouchable" to the many teams that inquired about his availability. Mets vice-president Joe McIlvaine said Miller would likely be the team's starting second baseman in 1989.

When Miller arrived at spring training, he was told that Gregg Jefferies was going to be the starting second sacker. So not only did Miller lose a job he never had, but his place on the team was in jeopardy. Later in camp, Miller pulled a hamstring muscle, but didn't tell the team because he couldn't afford any down time. The injury prevented him from breaking camp with the Mets.

Weeks later, Miller ripped a hamstring and was side-lined for nearly a month. The Mets' brass in New York told the media they were disappointed with him. Very nice.

Miller later rejoined the Mets as a roving infielder and outfielder. In a key series against the Cubs, he hit a home run, filling in for the real team disappointment, Darryl Strawberry.

| Year | Team | G | AB | R | H | 2B | 3B | HR | RBI | BB | SB | AVG |
|------|------|---|----|---|---|----|----|----|-----|----|----|-----|
| 1987 | NYN ... | 25 | 51 | 14 | 19 | 2 | 2 | 0 | 1 | 2 | 8 | .373 |
| 1988 | NYN ... | 40 | 70 | 9 | 15 | 1 | 1 | 1 | 5 | 6 | 0 | .214 |
| 1989 | NYN ... | 57 | 143 | 15 | 33 | 7 | 0 | 1 | 7 | 5 | 6 | .231 |
| | | 122 | 264 | 38 | 67 | 10 | 3 | 2 | 13 | 13 | 14 | .254 |

# Ron Oester

**Birth Date: 5/5/56**
**Bats: Left**
**Throws: Right**
**1989 Club:**
**Cincinnati Reds**
**Contest Code #: 136**

**Rating: 1**

With Pete Rose deposed, the party's over for Ron Oester. A good second baseman in his day, Oester suffered a serious knee injury in 1987—former Met Mookie Wilson barreled into him while trying to break up a double play—and he hasn't been the same player since.

Youngsters Jeff Treadway and Lenny Harris took their turns at the position, but Rose's impatience—combined with his affinity for older players—resulted in Oester's return.

Oester isn't fast, hits for a moderate average, and no longer drives in runs. Should the Reds be strapped for help at second, Oester will serve as their stopgap regular.

| Year | Team | G | AB | R | H | 2B | 3B | HR | RBI | BB | SB | AVG |
|------|------|---|----|---|---|----|----|----|-----|----|----|-----|
| 1978 | Cin .... | 6 | 8 | 1 | 3 | 0 | 0 | 0 | 1 | 0 | 0 | .375 |
| 1979 | Cin .... | 6 | 3 | 0 | 0 | 0 | 0 | 0 | 0 | 0 | 0 | .000 |
| 1980 | Cin .... | 100 | 303 | 40 | 84 | 16 | 2 | 2 | 20 | 26 | 6 | .277 |
| 1981 | Cin .... | 105 | 354 | 45 | 96 | 16 | 7 | 5 | 42 | 42 | 2 | .271 |
| 1982 | Cin .... | 151 | 549 | 63 | 143 | 19 | 4 | 9 | 47 | 35 | 5 | .260 |
| 1983 | Cin .... | 157 | 549 | 63 | 145 | 23 | 5 | 11 | 58 | 49 | 2 | .264 |
| 1984 | Cin .... | 150 | 553 | 54 | 134 | 26 | 3 | 3 | 38 | 41 | 7 | .242 |
| 1985 | Cin .... | 152 | 526 | 59 | 155 | 26 | 3 | 1 | 34 | 51 | 5 | .295 |
| 1986 | Cin .... | 153 | 523 | 52 | 135 | 23 | 2 | 8 | 44 | 52 | 9 | .258 |
| 1987 | Cin .... | 69 | 237 | 28 | 60 | 9 | 6 | 2 | 23 | 22 | 2 | .253 |
| 1988 | Cin .... | 54 | 150 | 20 | 42 | 7 | 0 | 0 | 10 | 9 | 0 | .280 |
| 1989 | Cin .... | 109 | 305 | 23 | 75 | 15 | 0 | 1 | 14 | 32 | 1 | .246 |
| | | 1212 | 4060 | 448 | 1072 | 180 | 32 | 42 | 331 | 359 | 39 | .264 |

# Jose Oquendo

**Birth Date: 7/4/63**
**Bats: Right and Left**
**Throws: Right**
**1989 Club:**
**St. Louis Cardinals**
**Contest Code #: 137**

**Rating: 4**

Jose Oquendo is the most improved player in the National League. Once a patsy at the plate, Oquendo has become a consistent, high-average batter through better technique and hours and hours of practice. Interestingly, Oquendo uses two markedly different batting stances. From the left side of the plate, he's a Rod Carew lookalike: a pronounced crouch; front foot pointing toward the pitcher; bat held flat. From the right side, he's more upright, with his bat held at a 45-degree angle.

Once the quintessential roving player, Oquendo hit so well in 1988 that Cardinals manager Whitey Herzog installed him as the starting second baseman.

As a trivia footnote, Oquendo, once a Mets' draft choice, was involved in what may have been Mets' gen-

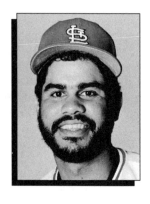

eral manager Frank Cashen's worst trade ever. On April 2, 1985, Cashen sent Oquendo and pitcher Mark Jason Davis to the Cards for shortstop Argenis Salazar and pitcher John Young.

| Year | Team | G | AB | R | H | 2B | 3B | HR | RBI | BB | SB | AVG |
|------|------|---|----|---|---|----|----|----|-----|----|----|-----|
| 1983 | NYN ... | 120 | 328 | 29 | 70 | 7 | 0 | 1 | 17 | 19 | 8 | .213 |
| 1984 | NYN ... | 81 | 189 | 23 | 42 | 5 | 0 | 0 | 10 | 15 | 10 | .222 |
| 1986 | StL .... | 76 | 138 | 20 | 41 | 4 | 1 | 0 | 13 | 15 | 2 | .297 |
| 1987 | StL .... | 116 | 248 | 43 | 71 | 9 | 0 | 1 | 24 | 54 | 4 | .286 |
| 1988 | StL .... | 148 | 451 | 36 | 125 | 10 | 1 | 7 | 46 | 52 | 4 | .277 |
| 1989 | StL .... | 163 | 556 | 59 | 162 | 28 | 7 | 1 | 48 | 79 | 3 | .291 |
| | | 704 | 1910 | 210 | 511 | 63 | 9 | 10 | 158 | 234 | 31 | .268 |

# Willie Randolph

**Birth Date: 6/6/54**
**Bats: Right**
**Throws: Right**
**1989 Club:**
**Los Angeles Dodgers**
**Contest Code #: 138**

**Rating: 2**

Willie Randolph is a fine gentleman who carried himself with grace and dignity through 13 years under George Steinbrenner. In his best seasons, Randolph was a .280 hitter who stole around 30 bases a season. Toward the tail end of his Yankees tenure, knee injuries slowed him down and diminished his batting average.

The question I have is whether Randolph was over-rated all those years solely because he played in New York. A cold, hard look at his stats shows Randolph actually had three strong seasons—1978, 1979, and 1980—in his prime, but, except for 1987, he has been on the decline.

Last year, the Dodgers signed Randolph as a free agent when they lost Steve Sax to the Yankees. Sax comes out far ahead in a comparison between the two. Randolph was not the type of leadoff hitter the Dodgers had hoped for.

| Year | Team | G | AB | R | H | 2B | 3B | HR | RBI | BB | SB | AVG |
|------|------|---|----|---|---|----|----|----|-----|----|----|-----|
| 1975 | Pit ..... | 30 | 61 | 9 | 10 | 1 | 0 | 0 | 3 | 7 | 1 | .164 |
| 1976 | NYA.... | 125 | 430 | 59 | 115 | 15 | 4 | 1 | 40 | 58 | 37 | .267 |
| 1977 | NYA.... | 147 | 551 | 91 | 151 | 28 | 11 | 4 | 40 | 64 | 13 | .274 |
| 1978 | NYA.... | 134 | 499 | 87 | 139 | 18 | 6 | 3 | 42 | 82 | 36 | .279 |
| 1979 | NYA.... | 153 | 574 | 98 | 155 | 15 | 13 | 5 | 61 | 95 | 33 | .270 |
| 1980 | NYA.... | 138 | 513 | 99 | 151 | 23 | 7 | 7 | 46 | 119 | 30 | .294 |
| 1981 | NYA.... | 93 | 357 | 59 | 83 | 14 | 3 | 2 | 24 | 57 | 14 | .232 |
| 1982 | NYA.... | 144 | 553 | 85 | 155 | 21 | 4 | 3 | 36 | 75 | 16 | .280 |
| 1983 | NYA.... | 104 | 420 | 73 | 117 | 21 | 1 | 2 | 38 | 53 | 12 | .279 |
| 1984 | NYA.... | 142 | 564 | 86 | 162 | 24 | 2 | 2 | 31 | 86 | 10 | .287 |
| 1985 | NYA.... | 143 | 497 | 75 | 137 | 21 | 2 | 5 | 40 | 85 | 16 | .276 |
| 1986 | NYA.... | 141 | 492 | 76 | 136 | 15 | 2 | 5 | 50 | 94 | 15 | .276 |
| 1987 | NYA.... | 120 | 449 | 96 | 137 | 24 | 2 | 7 | 67 | 82 | 11 | .305 |
| 1988 | NYA.... | 110 | 404 | 43 | 93 | 20 | 1 | 2 | 34 | 55 | 8 | .230 |
| 1989 | LA ..... | 145 | 549 | 62 | 155 | 18 | 0 | 2 | 36 | 71 | 7 | .282 |
| | | 1869 | 6913 | 1098 | 1896 | 278 | 58 | 50 | 588 | 1083 | 259 | .274 |

# Jeff Richardson

**Birth Date:** 8/26/65
**Bats:** Right
**Throws:** Right
**1989 Club:**
Cincinnati Reds
**Contest Code #:** 139

**Rating: 1**

Jeff Richardson was called up toward the end of last season to help fill the holes created by the injuries to Chris Sabo and Barry Larkin, the trade of Lenny Harris, and the futility of Scotti Madison.

Richardson's minor-league stats are not bad and not great. The Reds' seventh-round pick in the June 1986 draft, he played his first pro season with Class-A Billings in 1986. In 47 games, he batted .315, with no home runs, had 20 RBI's and 12 stolen bases. In 1987, he split time between Class A Tampa and Double A Vermont; he batted .299 in 100 games with Tampa, .209 in 35 games with Vermont, and stole a combined 15 bases. In 1988, Richardson batted .251 at Double A Chattanooga, with 1 home run—his first as a pro—37 RBI's and 8 steals.

| Year | Team | G | AB | R | H | 2B | 3B | HR | RBI | BB | SB | AVG |
|------|------|-----|-----|----|----|----|----|----|-----|----|----|------|
| 1989 | Cin .... | 53 | 125 | 10 | 21 | 4 | 0 | 2 | 11 | 10 | 1 | .168 |
| | | 53 | 125 | 10 | 21 | 4 | 0 | 2 | 11 | 10 | 1 | .168 |

# Ryne Sandberg

**Birth Date:** 9/18/59
**Bats:** Right
**Throws:** Right
**1989 Club:**
Chicago Cubs
**Contest Code #:** 140

**Rating: 5**

If you're looking for one reason why the Cubs won the National League Eastern Division championship last year, look no further than Ryne Sandberg. "Ryno," who was batting .262, with 11 home runs and 34 RBI's at the All-Star break, went on a rampage the second half—.321 (94 for 293), 19 home runs, 42 RBI's and 60 runs scored. Between August 7 and 11, he tied Hack Wilson's 1928 club record by hitting 6 home runs in 5 straight games.

Those numbers scratch the surface. In all, Sandberg tied Will Clark for first in the league in runs scored (104); was fifth in hits (176), home runs (30), and total bases (301); sixth in slugging average (.497); tied with Pedro Guerrero for sixth in extra-base hits (60); and was tenth in batting (.290).

And to think that after the 1988 season, some in baseball wondered whether Sandberg, regarded as the league's best second baseman since 1984, was showing signs of wear.

| Year | Team | G | AB | R | H | 2B | 3B | HR | RBI | BB | SB | AVG |
|------|------|-----|-----|-----|------|-----|----|-----|-----|-----|-----|------|
| 1981 | Phi .... | 13 | 6 | 2 | 1 | 0 | 0 | 0 | 0 | 0 | 0 | .167 |
| 1982 | ChN.... | 156 | 635 | 103 | 172 | 33 | 5 | 7 | 54 | 36 | 32 | .271 |
| 1983 | ChN.... | 158 | 633 | 94 | 165 | 25 | 4 | 8 | 48 | 51 | 37 | .261 |
| 1984 | ChN.... | 156 | 636 | 114 | 200 | 36 | 19 | 19 | 84 | 52 | 32 | .314 |
| 1985 | ChN.... | 153 | 609 | 113 | 186 | 31 | 6 | 26 | 83 | 57 | 54 | .305 |
| 1986 | ChN.... | 154 | 627 | 68 | 178 | 28 | 5 | 14 | 76 | 46 | 34 | .284 |
| 1987 | ChN.... | 132 | 523 | 81 | 154 | 25 | 2 | 16 | 59 | 59 | 21 | .294 |
| 1988 | ChN.... | 155 | 618 | 77 | 163 | 23 | 8 | 19 | 69 | 54 | 25 | .264 |
| 1989 | ChN.... | 157 | 606 | 104 | 176 | 25 | 5 | 30 | 76 | 59 | 15 | .290 |
| | | 1234 | 4893 | 756 | 1395 | 226 | 54 | 139 | 549 | 414 | 250 | .285 |

# Mike Sharperson

**Birth Date:** 10/4/61
**Bats:** Right
**Throws:** Right
**1989 Club:**
**Los Angeles Dodgers**
**Contest Code #:** 141

## Rating: 1

**M**ike Sharperson was selected by three teams—the Pirates, Expos, and Tigers—in three separate drafts, but didn't sign until he was drafted by the Blue Jays in June 1981.

In the Toronto system, Sharperson was twice named their minor-league player of the year. In 1984 at Double-A Knoxville, Sharperson batted .304 (best in the Southern League) with 20 stolen bases, and was named by *Baseball America* as their top prospect in the American League. In 1986 at Triple A Syracuse, he batted .289, with 4 home runs, 45 RBI's, stole 17 bases, and was named to the International League All-Star Team.

Sharperson was involved in a bit of controversy last season when recalled from Triple A. Seems that long-time Dodgers' prospect Tracy Woodson was so displeased about Sharperson's promotion over him that he quit the Albuquerque team. The Dodgers eventually persuaded Woodson to return and traded him to the White Sox last November.

| Year | Team | G | AB | R | H | 2B | 3B | HR | RBI | BB | SB | AVG |
|------|------|----|-----|----|----|----|----|----|-----|----|----|------|
| 1987 | Tor..... | 32 | 96 | 4 | 20 | 4 | 1 | 0 | 9 | 7 | 2 | .208 |
| 1987 | LA..... | 10 | 33 | 7 | 9 | 2 | 0 | 0 | 1 | 4 | 0 | .273 |
| 1988 | LA..... | 46 | 59 | 8 | 16 | 1 | 0 | 0 | 4 | 1 | 0 | .271 |
| 1989 | LA..... | 27 | 28 | 2 | 7 | 3 | 0 | 0 | 5 | 4 | 0 | .250 |
| | | 115 | 216 | 21 | 52 | 10 | 1 | 0 | 19 | 16 | 2 | .241 |

# Tim Teufel

**Birth Date:** 7/7/58
**Bats:** Right
**Throws:** Right
**1989 Club:**
**New York Mets**
**Contest Code #:** 142

## Rating: 2

**T**he most shocking Mets' news last November was that the team re-signed Tim Teufel for two more seasons. Who would ever have thought that after playing in just 83 games last season—often stuck deep on the bench—Teufel would want to return to the Mets? Apparently, Teufel, who used to beef long and loudly about his lack of playing time, has discovered that money may not buy happiness, but it can buy a lot of other things.

When Teufel plays, he slashes line drives to the gaps and hits for some power; in 1987, he hit 14 home runs and drove in 61 runs in only 299 at-bats. He had those same power numbers with the Twins in 1984 in 568 at-bats. Teufel's biggest problem with the Mets was that every time he won a starting job, he got hurt shortly thereafter.

| Year | Team | G | AB | R | H | 2B | 3B | HR | RBI | BB | SB | AVG |
|------|------|-----|------|-----|-----|-----|----|----|-----|-----|----|------|
| 1983 | Min.... | 21 | 78 | 11 | 24 | 7 | 1 | 3 | 6 | 2 | 0 | .308 |
| 1984 | Min.... | 157 | 568 | 76 | 149 | 30 | 3 | 14 | 61 | 76 | 1 | .262 |
| 1985 | Min.... | 138 | 434 | 58 | 113 | 24 | 3 | 10 | 50 | 48 | 4 | .260 |
| 1986 | NYN ... | 93 | 279 | 35 | 69 | 20 | 1 | 4 | 31 | 32 | 1 | .247 |
| 1987 | NYN ... | 97 | 299 | 55 | 92 | 29 | 0 | 14 | 61 | 44 | 3 | .308 |
| 1988 | NYN ... | 90 | 273 | 35 | 64 | 20 | 0 | 4 | 31 | 29 | 0 | .234 |
| 1989 | NYN ... | 83 | 219 | 27 | 56 | 7 | 2 | 2 | 15 | 32 | 1 | .256 |
| | | 679 | 2150 | 297 | 567 | 137 | 10 | 51 | 255 | 263 | 10 | .264 |

# Robby Thompson

**Birth Date:** 5/10/62
**Bats:** Right
**Throws:** Right
**1989 Club:**
**San Francisco Giants**
**Contest Code #:** 143

### Rating: 3

**R**obby Thompson is recognized by the Giants' players as one of their team leaders. In the field, he makes all the plays. He's been slowed but not stopped by a chronically sore back. He shows good power and run production for a second baseman.

There's just one teeny-weeny problem with Thompson: He strikes out like crazy! In 1986, he whiffed 112 times in 549 at-bats; in 1987, 91 times in 420 at-bats; in 1988, 111 times in 477 at-bats; and last season, 133 times in 547 at-bats. Meanwhile, Thompson has hit 37 home runs in his four major league seasons, so the tradeoff isn't worth it.

Thompson, selected by the Giants in the June 1983 draft, jumped from Double A to the majors, and in 1986 was named rookie of the year by *Sporting News*. He holds one dubious major-league record: In 1986, he was caught stealing four times in one game.

| Year | Team | G | AB | R | H | 2B | 3B | HR | RBI | BB | SB | AVG |
|---|---|---|---|---|---|---|---|---|---|---|---|---|
| 1986 | SF ..... | 149 | 549 | 73 | 149 | 27 | 3 | 7 | 47 | 42 | 12 | .271 |
| 1987 | SF ..... | 132 | 420 | 62 | 110 | 26 | 5 | 10 | 44 | 40 | 16 | .262 |
| 1988 | SF ..... | 138 | 477 | 66 | 126 | 24 | 6 | 7 | 48 | 40 | 14 | .264 |
| 1989 | SF ..... | 148 | 547 | 91 | 132 | 26 | 11 | 13 | 50 | 51 | 12 | .241 |
| | | 567 | 1993 | 292 | 517 | 103 | 25 | 37 | 189 | 173 | 54 | .259 |

# Jeff Treadway

**Birth Date:** 1/22/63
**Bats:** Left
**Throws:** Right
**1989 Club:**
**Atlanta Braves**
**Contest Code #:** 144

### Rating: 2

**J**eff Treadway, a .300 hitter throughout his four minor-league seasons, has had a long, strange trip in the bigs the past two years. In 1988, he started the season as the Reds' starting baseman, but his laid-back attitude bugged Pete Rose, and so he was benched. In 1989, the Reds released Treadway during spring training. He walked into the Braves' camp, went four for seven in two games, and was signed on the spot.

For most of the season, Treadway platooned with Jeff Blauser at second base and had a pretty good season. Granted, he doesn't hit for power and is as slow as a snail, but he batted in the .290 range for most of the season. But in September the Braves went with (yet again) their youth movement, meaning that Treadway, among others, was displaced from his job. As Mark Lemke manned second, Treadway was used as the Braves' top left-handed pinch-hitter off the bench. The poor guy was only twenty-six years old and being treated like Darrell Evans.

I still think Treadway can play, but if the Braves don't use him, what major-league team will?

| Year | Team | G | AB | R | H | 2B | 3B | HR | RBI | BB | SB | AVG |
|---|---|---|---|---|---|---|---|---|---|---|---|---|
| 1987 | Cin .... | 23 | 84 | 9 | 28 | 4 | 0 | 2 | 4 | 2 | 1 | .333 |
| 1988 | Cin .... | 103 | 301 | 30 | 76 | 19 | 4 | 2 | 23 | 27 | 2 | .252 |
| 1989 | Atl ..... | 134 | 473 | 58 | 131 | 18 | 3 | 8 | 40 | 30 | 3 | .277 |
| | | 260 | 858 | 97 | 235 | 41 | 7 | 12 | 67 | 59 | 6 | .274 |

# THIRD BASEMEN

# THIRD BASEMEN

## Bobby Bonilla

Birth Date: 2/23/63
Bats: Right and Left
Throws: Right
1989 Club:
Pittsburgh Pirates
Contest Code #: 151

Rating: 5

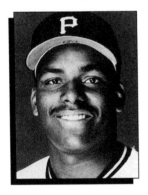

The Pirates' pathetic 1989 season almost obscured Bobby Bonilla's outstanding performance. Bonilla was second in the National League in triples (10); third in extra base hits (71); fourth in total bases (302); fifth in doubles (37); sixth in hits (173); tied for sixth in runs scored (96); eighth in slugging average (.490); and ninth in home runs (24) and RBI's (86).

The only flaw in Bonilla's offense was his .226 batting average (50 for 221) as a right-handed batter.

The biggest flaw in Bonilla's game is defense. Former Pirates general manager Syd Thrift initially signed Bonilla in 1981; he reacquired him by trade (Thrift's predecessor, Harding Peterson, left Bonilla off the Pirates' 1985 40-man roster), and shifted Bonilla to the infield because his mind wandered in the outfield. The current Pirate management is planning to move Bonilla back to the outfield. Let's hope Bonilla doesn't succumb to his earlier problem.

| Year | Team | G | AB | R | H | 2B | 3B | HR | RBI | BB | SB | AVG |
|------|------|---|----|----|----|----|----|----|-----|----|----|-----|
| 1986 | ChA.... | 75 | 234 | 27 | 63 | 10 | 2 | 2 | 26 | 33 | 4 | .269 |
| 1986 | Pit..... | 63 | 192 | 28 | 46 | 6 | 2 | 1 | 17 | 29 | 4 | .240 |
| 1987 | Pit..... | 141 | 466 | 58 | 140 | 33 | 3 | 15 | 77 | 39 | 3 | .300 |
| 1988 | Pit..... | 159 | 584 | 87 | 160 | 32 | 7 | 24 | 100 | 85 | 3 | .274 |
| 1989 | Pit..... | 163 | 616 | 96 | 173 | 37 | 10 | 24 | 86 | 76 | 8 | .281 |
| | | 601 | 2092 | 296 | 582 | 118 | 24 | 66 | 306 | 262 | 22 | .278 |

## Ken Caminiti

Birth Date: 4/21/63
Bats: Right and Left
Throws: Right
1989 Club:
Houston Astros
Contest Code #: 152

Rating: 4

Ken Caminiti, rushed to the major leagues from Double A in 1987, aroused hopes by hitting a triple and home run in his first game. He hit .500 in his first four games and was named the National League's Player of the Week. But he cooled significantly the rest of the way, and in 1988 he couldn't make the Astros' big-league club. Caminiti got his confidence back at Triple A Tucson, batting .272 and driving in 66 runs. But in a late-season return to Houston, he did not fulfill expectations.

Last season, Caminiti put it all together, hitting 10 home runs (fourth on the Astros) and driving in 72 runs (second on the team). He and Craig Biggio came through in the clutch so often that they are now regarded along with Glenn Davis as the team leaders.

Caminiti, whom National League scouts have long compared to former Cardinals' third baseman Ken Boyer, should hit for a higher average this season.

| Year | Team | G | AB | R | H | 2B | 3B | HR | RBI | BB | SB | AVG |
|------|------|---|----|----|----|----|----|----|-----|----|----|-----|
| 1987 | Hou.... | 63 | 203 | 10 | 50 | 7 | 1 | 3 | 23 | 12 | 0 | .246 |
| 1988 | Hou.... | 30 | 83 | 5 | 15 | 2 | 0 | 1 | 7 | 5 | 0 | .181 |
| 1989 | Hou.... | 161 | 585 | 71 | 149 | 31 | 3 | 10 | 72 | 51 | 4 | .255 |
| | | 254 | 871 | 86 | 214 | 40 | 4 | 14 | 102 | 68 | 4 | .246 |

# Tim Flannery

**Birth Date:** 9/29/57
**Bats:** Left
**Throws:** Right
**1989 Club:**
**San Diego Padres**
**Contest Code #:** 153

**Rating: 1**

Tim Flannery, who talked about retiring following the 1989 season, is known more for his glove than his bat. Last year, *Sports Illustrated* wrote about Flannery's attachment to his beat-up glove, the same one he's used for most of his career.

Used sparingly by the Padres, Flannery pinch-hits, and fills in at second base, shortstop, and third. Flannery, the nephew of former major-league third baseman Hal Smith, had his best seasons in 1985 and 1986, when he hit .281 and .280, respectively. He's the only remaining player from the Padres' 1980 club.

| Year | Team | G | AB | R | H | 2B | 3B | HR | RBI | BB | SB | AVG |
|------|------|-----|------|-----|-----|----|----|----|-----|-----|----|------|
| 1979 | SD..... | 22 | 65 | 2 | 10 | 0 | 1 | 0 | 4 | 4 | 0 | .154 |
| 1980 | SD..... | 95 | 292 | 15 | 70 | 12 | 0 | 0 | 25 | 18 | 2 | .240 |
| 1981 | SD..... | 37 | 67 | 4 | 17 | 4 | 1 | 0 | 6 | 2 | 1 | .254 |
| 1982 | SD..... | 122 | 379 | 40 | 100 | 11 | 7 | 0 | 30 | 30 | 1 | .264 |
| 1983 | SD..... | 92 | 214 | 24 | 50 | 7 | 3 | 0 | 19 | 20 | 2 | .234 |
| 1984 | SD..... | 86 | 128 | 24 | 35 | 3 | 3 | 2 | 10 | 12 | 4 | .273 |
| 1985 | SD..... | 126 | 384 | 50 | 108 | 14 | 3 | 1 | 40 | 58 | 2 | .281 |
| 1986 | SD..... | 134 | 368 | 48 | 103 | 11 | 2 | 3 | 28 | 54 | 3 | .280 |
| 1987 | SD..... | 106 | 276 | 23 | 63 | 5 | 1 | 0 | 20 | 42 | 2 | .228 |
| 1988 | SD..... | 79 | 170 | 16 | 45 | 5 | 4 | 0 | 19 | 24 | 3 | .265 |
| 1989 | SD..... | 73 | 130 | 9 | 30 | 5 | 0 | 0 | 8 | 13 | 2 | .231 |
| | | 972 | 2473 | 255 | 631 | 77 | 25 | 9 | 209 | 277 | 22 | .255 |

# Jeff Hamilton

**Birth Date:** 3/19/64
**Bats:** Right
**Throws:** Right
**1989 Club:**
**Los Angeles Dodgers**
**Contest Code #:** 154

**Rating: 2**

Slowly, Jeff Hamilton is showing himself to be the kind of fantasy-league player who will be a bargain at a low price but overpaid at a moderate price. Last season, the laid-back third baseman quietly hit 12 home runs and drove in 56 runs.

The 6'3", 205-pound Hamilton has to improve his on-base average if he's ever going to be more than a low-priced bargain. In 1988, he walked just 10 times in 111 games, and last year he walked 20 times in 151 games.

As a minor leaguer, Hamilton enjoyed the inflated numbers—.313 in 1986; .360 batting, .493 on-base, and .593 slugging averages in 1987—that most Albuquerque players accumulate in the rarified air of the Pacific Coast League. If he can hit .270 in the major leagues, he'll be a success.

| Year | Team | G | AB | R | H | 2B | 3B | HR | RBI | BB | SB | AVG |
|------|------|-----|------|-----|-----|----|----|----|-----|----|----|------|
| 1986 | LA..... | 71 | 147 | 22 | 33 | 5 | 0 | 5 | 19 | 2 | 0 | .224 |
| 1987 | LA..... | 35 | 83 | 5 | 18 | 3 | 0 | 0 | 1 | 7 | 0 | .217 |
| 1988 | LA..... | 111 | 309 | 34 | 73 | 14 | 2 | 6 | 33 | 10 | 0 | .236 |
| 1989 | LA..... | 151 | 548 | 45 | 134 | 35 | 1 | 12 | 56 | 20 | 0 | .245 |
| | | 368 | 1087 | 106 | 258 | 57 | 3 | 23 | 109 | 39 | 0 | .237 |

# Charlie Hayes

**Birth Date:** 5/29/65
**Bats:** Right
**Throws:** Right
**1989 Clubs:**
San Francisco Giants &
Philadelphia Phillies
**Contest Code #:** 155

**Rating: 4**

Charlie Hayes arrived in Philadelphia last summer as part of the Steve Bedrosian trade, and before long Hayes showed he is about to arrive as a major-league player. Hayes put up stellar numbers in his five-plus seasons in the Giants' system. Drafted in the fourth round of the June 1983 draft, the 6-foot, 195-pound Hayes pounded Double-A pitching in 1987. Playing for Shreveport, Hayes led the team in runs scored (66), hits (148), home runs (14) and RBI's (75).

Hayes was a member of the 1977 Hattiesburg, Mississippi, team that reached the Little League World Series. One of his opponents during the Little League regional playoffs was Dwight Gooden. Today, Hayes has staked his claim as Mike Schmidt's successor and should only get better with experience.

| Year | Team | G | AB | R | H | 2B | 3B | HR | RBI | BB | SB | AVG |
|------|------|---|----|----|----|----|----|----|-----|----|----|-----|
| 1988 | SF..... | 7 | 11 | 0 | 1 | 0 | 0 | 0 | 0 | 0 | 0 | .091 |
| 1989 | SF..... | 3 | 5 | 0 | 1 | 0 | 0 | 0 | 0 | 0 | 0 | .200 |
| 1989 | Phi .... | 84 | 299 | 26 | 77 | 15 | 1 | 8 | 43 | 11 | 3 | .258 |
| | | 94 | 315 | 26 | 79 | 15 | 1 | 8 | 43 | 11 | 3 | .251 |

# Howard Johnson

**Birth Date:** 11/29/60
**Bats:** Right and Left
**Throws:** Right
**1989 Club:**
New York Mets
**Contest Code #:** 156

**Rating: 5**

Howard Johnson is not only the premier third baseman in the National League, but has become one of the best players in baseball. In the past two seasons, Hojo has twice hit more than 30 home runs and stolen more than 30 bases. Last season, he was 4 home runs shy of joining the 40-40 club.

Besides ranking second in the league in home runs and tied (with Tim Raines) for fourth in stolen bases, Johnson also tied Will Clark and Ryne Sandberg for the lead in runs scored (104); finished second in slugging average (.559) and extra base hits (80); third in doubles (41) and total bases (319); tied Eric Davis for fourth in RBI's (101); and was eighth in hits (164).

Darryl Strawberry may be the Met who grabs all the headlines, but Hojo has become New York's most indispensable player.

| Year | Team | G | AB | R | H | 2B | 3B | HR | RBI | BB | SB | AVG |
|------|------|-----|------|-----|-----|-----|----|-----|-----|-----|-----|------|
| 1982 | Det .... | 54 | 155 | 23 | 49 | 5 | 0 | 4 | 14 | 16 | 7 | .316 |
| 1983 | Det .... | 27 | 66 | 11 | 14 | 0 | 0 | 3 | 5 | 7 | 0 | .212 |
| 1984 | Det .... | 116 | 355 | 43 | 88 | 14 | 1 | 12 | 50 | 40 | 10 | .248 |
| 1985 | NYN ... | 126 | 389 | 38 | 94 | 18 | 4 | 11 | 46 | 34 | 6 | .242 |
| 1986 | NYN ... | 88 | 220 | 30 | 54 | 14 | 0 | 10 | 39 | 31 | 8 | .245 |
| 1987 | NYN ... | 157 | 554 | 93 | 147 | 22 | 1 | 36 | 99 | 83 | 32 | .265 |
| 1988 | NYN ... | 148 | 495 | 85 | 114 | 21 | 1 | 24 | 68 | 86 | 23 | .230 |
| 1989 | NYN ... | 153 | 571 | 104 | 164 | 41 | 3 | 36 | 101 | 77 | 41 | .287 |
| | | 869 | 2805 | 427 | 724 | 135 | 10 | 136 | 422 | 374 | 127 | .258 |

# Vance Law

**Birth Date:** 10/1/56
**Bats:** Right
**Throws:** Right
**1989 Club:**
**Chicago Cubs**
**Contest Code #:** 157

**Rating: 2**

**V**ance Law picked the wrong time to have an off year. Last season, he was the Cubs' starting third baseman for most of the season. But his batting average was stuck in the .230 range. In September, with the Cubs in a four-team battle for first, Law was benched in favor of recently acquired Luis Salazar. So this spring, not only does Law have to battle Salazar for the job, but if young Ty Griffin is ready to take over at third, Law may have to battle to stay with the team.

Just two years ago, Law had his best season ever, playing in 151 games, driving in 78 runs (second on the team), batting .293 (eighth-best in the National League), and earning his first All-Star berth.

Should the Cubs decide to move Law, there are many teams who would take him. Though his fielding range is not what it used to be, Law can play third, first, and, when needed, second base. Despite his poor batting average last season, Law still knows how to hit. If he can't start somewhere, he'd be an excellent reserve infielder for a contending team.

| Year | Team | G | AB | R | H | 2B | 3B | HR | RBI | BB | SB | AVG |
|------|------|-----|------|-----|-----|-----|-----|-----|------|-----|-----|------|
| 1980 | Pit..... | 25 | 74 | 11 | 17 | 2 | 2 | 0 | 3 | 3 | 2 | .230 |
| 1981 | Pit..... | 30 | 67 | 1 | 9 | 0 | 1 | 0 | 3 | 2 | 1 | .134 |
| 1982 | ChA.... | 114 | 359 | 40 | 101 | 20 | 1 | 5 | 54 | 26 | 4 | .281 |
| 1983 | ChA.... | 145 | 408 | 55 | 99 | 21 | 5 | 4 | 42 | 51 | 3 | .243 |
| 1984 | ChA.... | 151 | 481 | 60 | 121 | 18 | 2 | 17 | 59 | 41 | 4 | .252 |
| 1985 | Mon.... | 147 | 519 | 75 | 138 | 30 | 6 | 10 | 52 | 86 | 6 | .266 |
| 1986 | Mon.... | 112 | 360 | 37 | 81 | 17 | 2 | 5 | 44 | 37 | 3 | .225 |
| 1987 | Mon.... | 133 | 436 | 52 | 119 | 27 | 1 | 12 | 56 | 51 | 8 | .273 |
| 1988 | ChN.... | 151 | 556 | 73 | 163 | 29 | 2 | 11 | 78 | 55 | 1 | .293 |
| 1989 | ChN.... | 130 | 408 | 38 | 96 | 22 | 3 | 7 | 42 | 38 | 2 | .235 |
| | | 1138 | 3668 | 442 | 944 | 186 | 25 | 71 | 433 | 390 | 34 | .257 |

# Greg Litton

**Birth Date:** 7/13/64
**Bats:** Right
**Throws:** Right
**1989 Club:**
**San Francisco Giants**
**Contest Code #:** 158

**Rating: 2**

**L**ast summer the Giants called up Triple A infielder Greg Litton, who was their first pick in the January 1984 draft, and told the media he would become the team's starting third baseman. So when I had an infield opening on my fantasy team, I grabbed him. A few days later, the Giants changed their minds; they recalled Matt Williams and benched Litton.

During his four-plus seasons in the Giants' farm system, Litton has hit about .260 but has shown some line-drive power. In Class-A Fresno in 1985, he smacked a league-high 33 doubles and knocked in 103 runs. The following season, he hit 30 doubles for Double-A Shreveport. Litton struggled at Triple A in 1987, so he returned for a Double A encore in 1988.

Last season, Litton hit four home runs for the Giants during the regular season and a big three-run shot against the Cubs during the National League Championship Series.

| Year | Team | G | AB | R | H | 2B | 3B | HR | RBI | BB | SB | AVG |
|------|------|-----|-----|-----|-----|-----|-----|-----|------|-----|-----|------|
| 1989 | SF..... | 71 | 143 | 12 | 36 | 5 | 3 | 4 | 17 | 7 | 0 | .252 |
| | | 71 | 143 | 12 | 36 | 5 | 3 | 4 | 17 | 7 | 0 | .252 |

# Scotti Madison

**Birth Date:** 9/12/59
**Bats:** Right and Left
**Throws:** Right
**1989 Club:**
**Cincinnati Reds**
**Contest Code #:** 159

**Rating: 1**

**B**ecause of the rash of injuries to the Reds' infielders last season, catcher Scotti Madison, who was a non-roster player last spring, was called up to the big leagues last summer and saw time at third base. Chris Sabo, he wasn't. In 40 games, Madison had more strike-outs (9) than RBI's (7).

Madison was a two-sport star at Vanderbilt University. He was a quarterback on the football team, and in 1980 he was the second-leading home-run hitter in all of college baseball. In June 1980, the Twins chose him in the third round of the amateur draft.

In 1981, Madison led the California League in doubles (32), and was among the league's top five players in batting average (.342) and RBI's (110). He was traded to the Dodgers in 1982 and sold to the Detroit Tigers in 1984. In 1985, he led the American Association in batting (.341) and slugging average. He made his major-league debut with the Tigers in 1985; he signed with the Royals in 1986, and with the Reds in 1988.

| Year | Team | G | AB | R | H | 2B | 3B | HR | RBI | BB | SB | AVG |
|------|------|---|----|---|---|----|----|----|-----|----|----|-----|
| 1985 | Det .... | 6 | 11 | 0 | 0 | 0 | 0 | 0 | 1 | 2 | 0 | .000 |
| 1986 | Det .... | 2 | 7 | 0 | 0 | 0 | 0 | 0 | 1 | 0 | 0 | .000 |
| 1987 | KC..... | 7 | 15 | 4 | 4 | 3 | 0 | 0 | 0 | 1 | 0 | .267 |
| 1988 | KC..... | 16 | 35 | 4 | 6 | 2 | 0 | 0 | 2 | 4 | 1 | .171 |
| 1989 | Cin .... | 40 | 98 | 13 | 17 | 7 | 0 | 1 | 7 | 8 | 0 | .173 |
| | | 71 | 166 | 21 | 27 | 12 | 0 | 1 | 11 | 15 | 1 | .163 |

# Ken Oberkfell

**Birth Date:** 5/4/56
**Bats:** Left
**Throws:** Right
**1989 Clubs:**
**Pittsburgh Pirates &**
**San Francisco Giants**
**Contest Code #:** 160

**Rating: 1**

**D**uring his years with the Braves, Ken Oberkfell's teammates gave him the nickname "5-0-2-0," which resembled his typical box score line: five at-bats, no runs scored, two hits, no RBI's. While Oberkfell has never been a run producer of note, he hits the ball where it's pitched and makes good contact. If only Oberkfell had average running speed, he'd be an excellent number-two hitter.

Last season, Oberkfell was acquired by the Giants to bolster their bench and add his post-season experience. As a pinch-hitter, Oberkfell hit .360 (18 for 50).

You'll probably pass on Obie, who signed with Houston in the off-season, but keep in mind that this season he'll pinch-hit often in crucial situations. If he comes through as he did last year, you'll pick up quite a few unexpected ribbies.

| Year | Team | G | AB | R | H | 2B | 3B | HR | RBI | BB | SB | AVG |
|------|------|---|----|---|---|----|----|----|-----|----|----|-----|
| 1977 | StL .... | 9 | 9 | 0 | 1 | 0 | 0 | 0 | 1 | 0 | 0 | .111 |
| 1978 | StL .... | 24 | 50 | 7 | 6 | 1 | 0 | 0 | 0 | 3 | 0 | .120 |
| 1979 | StL .... | 135 | 369 | 53 | 111 | 19 | 5 | 1 | 35 | 57 | 4 | .301 |
| 1980 | StL .... | 116 | 422 | 58 | 128 | 27 | 6 | 3 | 46 | 51 | 4 | .303 |
| 1981 | StL .... | 102 | 376 | 43 | 110 | 12 | 6 | 2 | 45 | 37 | 13 | .293 |
| 1982 | StL .... | 137 | 470 | 55 | 136 | 22 | 5 | 2 | 34 | 40 | 11 | .289 |
| 1983 | StL .... | 151 | 488 | 62 | 143 | 26 | 5 | 3 | 38 | 61 | 12 | .293 |
| 1984 | StL .... | 50 | 152 | 17 | 47 | 11 | 1 | 0 | 11 | 16 | 1 | .309 |
| 1984 | Atl..... | 50 | 172 | 21 | 40 | 8 | 1 | 1 | 10 | 15 | 1 | .233 |
| 1985 | Atl..... | 134 | 412 | 30 | 112 | 19 | 4 | 3 | 35 | 51 | 1 | .272 |
| 1986 | Atl..... | 151 | 503 | 62 | 136 | 24 | 3 | 5 | 48 | 83 | 7 | .270 |
| 1987 | Atl..... | 135 | 508 | 59 | 142 | 29 | 2 | 3 | 48 | 48 | 3 | .280 |
| 1988 | Atl..... | 120 | 422 | 42 | 117 | 20 | 4 | 3 | 40 | 32 | 4 | .277 |

| | | | | | | | | | | | |
|---|---|---|---|---|---|---|---|---|---|---|---|
| 1988 | Pit..... | 20 | 54 | 7 | 12 | 2 | 0 | 0 | 2 | 5 | 0 | .222 |
| 1989 | Pit..... | 14 | 40 | 2 | 5 | 1 | 0 | 0 | 2 | 2 | 0 | .125 |
| 1989 | SF..... | 83 | 116 | 17 | 37 | 5 | 1 | 2 | 15 | 8 | 0 | .319 |
| | | 1431 | 4563 | 535 | 1283 | 226 | 43 | 28 | 410 | 509 | 61 | .281 |

# Mike Pagliarulo

**Birth Date: 3/15/60**
**Bats: Left**
**Throws: Right**
**1989 Clubs:**
**New York Yankees &**
**San Diego Padres**
**Contest Code #: 161**

**Rating: 2**

Yankees' owner George Steinbrenner has ground many a player into chopped meat. Mike Pagliarulo was perhaps his worst victim.

"Pags," the Yankees sixth-round choice in the June 1981 draft, rose through the minor leagues with a reputation for power hitting and hard-nosed team play. In 1985, his first full season in the big ball yard in the Bronx, Pags hit 19 home runs and drove in 62 RBI's. The next two seasons he pounded out a combined 60 home runs and 158 RBI's. Then Pags dared to do what most Yankees feared—following a contract impasse, he took Steinbrenner to arbitration.

Steinbrenner sicced a team of lawyers on Pags during the hearings, grilling him mercilessly and convincing him that he was not a good player. Pagliarulo's on-field performance suffered, and the harder he drove himself, the more failure he encountered. Finally, Syd Thrift, the Yankees' senior vice-president in 1989, traded Pags to the Padres, where manager Jack McKeon could take him under his wing and restore his confidence.

Pags still has lots of mileage left, and McKeon is just the man to bring out the best in him.

| Year | Team | G | AB | R | H | 2B | 3B | HR | RBI | BB | SB | AVG |
|---|---|---|---|---|---|---|---|---|---|---|---|---|
| 1984 | NYA.... | 67 | 201 | 24 | 48 | 15 | 3 | 7 | 34 | 15 | 0 | .239 |
| 1985 | NYA.... | 138 | 380 | 55 | 91 | 16 | 2 | 19 | 62 | 45 | 0 | .239 |
| 1986 | NYA.... | 149 | 504 | 71 | 120 | 24 | 3 | 28 | 71 | 54 | 4 | .238 |
| 1987 | NYA.... | 150 | 522 | 76 | 122 | 26 | 3 | 32 | 87 | 53 | 1 | .234 |
| 1988 | NYA.... | 125 | 444 | 46 | 96 | 20 | 1 | 15 | 67 | 37 | 1 | .216 |
| 1989 | NYA.... | 74 | 223 | 19 | 44 | 10 | 0 | 4 | 16 | 19 | 1 | .197 |
| 1989 | SD..... | 50 | 148 | 12 | 29 | 7 | 0 | 3 | 14 | 18 | 2 | .196 |
| | | 753 | 2422 | 303 | 550 | 118 | 12 | 108 | 351 | 241 | 9 | .227 |

# Terry Pendleton

**Birth Date: 7/16/60**
**Bats: Right and Left**
**Throws: Right**
**1989 Club:**
**St. Louis Cardinals**
**Contest Code #: 162**

**Rating: 4**

You never know when thickly muscled Terry Pendleton, the best fielding third baseman in the game, will succumb to injury. He's been disabled three times in the past seven years with wrist, hamstring, arm, and knee problems.

Last season, Pendleton stayed healthy all year and batted .264, hit 13 home runs, and drove in 74 runs. He also stole 9 bases (prior to 1988, he'd averaged 20 steals a season).

Pendleton has a flair for the dramatic. He hits quite a few of his home runs in the late innings, and has been a thorn in the Mets' side for many seasons. In 1987, he dashed the Mets' hope of catching the World Series-bound Cards by crushing a ninth-inning home run off Roger McDowell.

| Year | Team | G | AB | R | H | 2B | 3B | HR | RBI | BB | SB | AVG |
|---|---|---|---|---|---|---|---|---|---|---|---|---|
| 1984 | StL .... | 67 | 262 | 37 | 85 | 16 | 3 | 1 | 33 | 16 | 20 | .324 |

| Year | Team | G | AB | R | H | 2B | 3B | HR | RBI | BB | SB | AVG |
|------|------|----|-----|-----|-----|-----|-----|-----|-----|-----|-----|------|
| 1985 | StL .... | 149 | 559 | 56 | 134 | 16 | 3 | 5 | 69 | 37 | 17 | .240 |
| 1986 | StL .... | 159 | 578 | 56 | 138 | 26 | 5 | 1 | 59 | 34 | 24 | .239 |
| 1987 | StL .... | 159 | 583 | 82 | 167 | 29 | 4 | 12 | 96 | 70 | 19 | .286 |
| 1988 | StL .... | 110 | 391 | 44 | 99 | 20 | 2 | 6 | 53 | 21 | 3 | .253 |
| 1989 | StL .... | 162 | 613 | 83 | 162 | 28 | 5 | 13 | 74 | 44 | 9 | .264 |
| | | 806 | 2986 | 358 | 785 | 135 | 22 | 38 | 384 | 222 | 92 | .263 |

## Luis Quinones

**Birth Date:** 4/28/62
**Bats:** Right and Left
**Throws:** Right
**1989 Club:**
**Cincinnati Reds**
**Contest Code #:** 163

**Rating: 2**

Not to be confused with Rey Quinones, the vagabond shortstop who wore out his welcome with the Pirates in only 71 games, Luis Quinones (no relation) found a home with the Reds last season.

Luis, who made his major-league debut with the A's in 1983, spent parts of the next five seasons in the minor leagues. But last season, when the Reds needed infield help, Quinones batted .244, with 12 home runs. He tied Chris James for the league's fourth-longest batting streak—18 games, from August 22 through September 10.

Quinones is a good role player. This season, however, he may take over Chris Sabo's job as the Reds' everyday third baseman.

| Year | Team | G | AB | R | H | 2B | 3B | HR | RBI | BB | SB | AVG |
|------|------|----|-----|-----|-----|-----|-----|-----|-----|-----|-----|------|
| 1983 | Oak .... | 19 | 42 | 5 | 8 | 2 | 1 | 0 | 4 | 1 | 1 | .190 |
| 1986 | SF ..... | 71 | 106 | 13 | 19 | 1 | 3 | 0 | 11 | 3 | 3 | .179 |
| 1987 | ChN.... | 49 | 101 | 12 | 22 | 6 | 0 | 0 | 8 | 10 | 0 | .218 |
| 1988 | Cin .... | 23 | 52 | 4 | 12 | 3 | 0 | 1 | 11 | 2 | 1 | .231 |
| 1989 | Cin .... | 97 | 340 | 43 | 83 | 13 | 4 | 12 | 34 | 25 | 2 | .244 |
| | | 259 | 641 | 77 | 144 | 25 | 8 | 13 | 68 | 41 | 7 | .225 |

## Domingo Ramos

**Birth Date:** 3/29/58
**Bats:** Right
**Throws:** Right
**1989 Club:**
**Chicago Cubs**
**Contest Code #:** 164

**Rating: 1**

Ramos is a versatile pro who's been with six organizations (Yankees, Blue Jays, Mariners, Indians, Angels, and Cubs) in 15 years. Last season, his tenth in the major leagues, Ramos played in 85 games and batted 179 times; both totals were career highs.

Ramos made the Cubs as a non-roster invitee to spring training. The year before, he'd begun the season with the Indians' Triple A team in Colorado Springs; came up to Cleveland in June and was released after playing 22 games; signed with the Angels' Triple-A team in Edmonton; and was called up to the Angels in September. His numbers aren't great, but you've got to salute his stick-to-itiveness.

| Year | Team | G | AB | R | H | 2B | 3B | HR | RBI | BB | SB | AVG |
|------|------|----|-----|-----|-----|-----|-----|-----|-----|-----|-----|------|
| 1978 | NYA.... | 1 | 0 | 0 | 0 | 0 | 0 | 0 | 0 | 0 | 0 | .000 |
| 1980 | Tor..... | 5 | 16 | 0 | 2 | 0 | 0 | 0 | 0 | 2 | 0 | .125 |
| 1982 | Sea .... | 8 | 26 | 3 | 4 | 2 | 0 | 0 | 1 | 3 | 0 | .154 |
| 1983 | Sea .... | 53 | 127 | 14 | 36 | 4 | 0 | 2 | 10 | 7 | 3 | .283 |
| 1984 | Sea .... | 59 | 81 | 6 | 15 | 2 | 0 | 0 | 2 | 5 | 2 | .185 |
| 1985 | Sea .... | 75 | 168 | 19 | 33 | 6 | 0 | 1 | 15 | 17 | 0 | .196 |
| 1986 | Sea .... | 49 | 99 | 8 | 18 | 2 | 0 | 0 | 5 | 8 | 0 | .182 |
| 1987 | Sea .... | 42 | 103 | 9 | 32 | 6 | 0 | 2 | 11 | 3 | 0 | .311 |
| 1988 | Cle..... | 22 | 46 | 7 | 12 | 1 | 0 | 0 | 5 | 3 | 0 | .261 |
| 1988 | Cal..... | 10 | 15 | 3 | 2 | 0 | 0 | 0 | 0 | 0 | 0 | .133 |
| 1989 | ChN.... | 85 | 179 | 18 | 47 | 6 | 2 | 1 | 19 | 17 | 1 | .263 |
| | | 409 | 860 | 87 | 201 | 29 | 2 | 6 | 68 | 65 | 6 | .234 |

# Ernest Riles

**Birth Date:** 10/2/60
**Bats:** Left
**Throws:** Right
**1989 Club:**
**San Francisco Giants**
**Contest Code #:** 165

**Rating: 2**

The Giants must have wanted to get rid of outfielder Jeffrey "Hac Man" Leonard pretty badly if they took the Brewers' Ernest Riles for him. Riles, who in 1987 was third in the American League Rookie of the Year voting, is a versatile infielder who makes contact, but he's not a run producer like Leonard.

Last year, Riles played third base while Matt Williams was demoted; shortstop when Jose Uribe was pinch-hit for; second base when Robby Thompson was rested; and right field when the the Sheraton/Maldonado/Nixon platoon didn't work. In 122 games (302 at-bats), Riles hit close to his major-league average.

| Year | Team | G | AB | R | H | 2B | 3B | HR | RBI | BB | SB | AVG |
|------|------|---|----|----|----|----|----|----|----|----|----|------|
| 1985 | Mil..... | 116 | 448 | 54 | 128 | 12 | 7 | 5 | 45 | 36 | 2 | .286 |
| 1986 | Mil..... | 145 | 524 | 69 | 132 | 24 | 2 | 9 | 47 | 54 | 7 | .252 |
| 1987 | Mil..... | 83 | 276 | 38 | 72 | 11 | 1 | 4 | 38 | 30 | 3 | .261 |
| 1988 | Mil..... | 41 | 127 | 7 | 32 | 6 | 1 | 1 | 9 | 7 | 2 | .252 |
| 1988 | SF ..... | 79 | 187 | 26 | 55 | 7 | 2 | 3 | 28 | 10 | 1 | .294 |
| 1989 | SF ..... | 122 | 302 | 43 | 84 | 13 | 2 | 7 | 40 | 28 | 0 | .278 |
| | | 586 | 1864 | 237 | 503 | 73 | 15 | 29 | 207 | 165 | 15 | .270 |

# Chris Sabo

**Birth Date:** 1/19/62
**Bats:** Right
**Throws:** Right
**1989 Club:**
**Cincinnati Reds**
**Contest Code #:** 166

**Rating: 2**

The following sentence is from the Reds' 1989 media guide: "[Chris] Sabo went to spring training [in 1988] with the prospect of winning a backup job and became the National League Rookie of the Year." In 1990, the Reds' media guide may say "Chris Sabo, the 1988 National league Rookie of the Year, came to spring training looking to win a backup job."

Sabo fooled everyone in 1988. Until then, he'd been languishing in the Reds' system for five years. During the first half of the 1988 campaign, Sabo, beloved for his resemblance to beer dog Spuds Mackenzie, batted .312 (97 for 311) with 10 home runs and 35 RBI's. His average was boosted by a 41-for-110 (.373) spree in June, including 4 home runs and 13 RBI's. During the second half, he batted .216 (49 for 227), with 1 home run (hit in July) and 9 ribbies.

Last season, Sabo was having a utility-infielder type of season—.260, with 6 home runs, 29 RBI's and 14 steals—and on June 27 hyperextended his left knee, which kept him out of action for all but 13 of the remaining games.

| Year | Team | G | AB | R | H | 2B | 3B | HR | RBI | BB | SB | AVG |
|------|------|---|----|----|----|----|----|----|----|----|----|------|
| 1988 | Cin .... | 137 | 538 | 74 | 146 | 40 | 2 | 11 | 44 | 29 | 46 | .271 |
| 1989 | Cin .... | 82 | 304 | 40 | 79 | 21 | 1 | 6 | 29 | 25 | 14 | .260 |
| | | 219 | 842 | 114 | 225 | 61 | 3 | 17 | 73 | 54 | 60 | .267 |

# Luis Salazar

**Birth Date:** 5/19/56
**Bats:** Right
**Throws:** Right
**1989 Clubs:**
**San Diego Padres &**
**Chicago Cubs**
**Contest Code #:** 167

**Rating: 2**

**W**ell-traveled Luis Salazar has carved out a 10-year major-league career by manning whatever position his managers need to fill. Originally signed as a free-agent shortstop by the Royals in 1973, Salazar was released in 1974 and signed a year later with the Pirates. In 1979, Salazar played third and the outfield, batted .323, hit 27 home runs, drove in 86 runs, and led the Eastern League in games (139), at-bats (561), and hits (181). A year later, he was traded to the Padres.

In his first tour of duty with San Diego, Salazar was the team's third baseman until the arrival of Graig Nettles in 1984. The next season, he was part of a six-player trade, going to the Chicago White Sox with shortstop Ozzie Guillen, pitchers Tim Lollar and Bill Long, for pitchers LaMarr Hoyt, Kevin Kristan, and Todd Simmons. When the White Sox released Salazar following the 1986 season, the Padres re-signed him on the eve of the 1987 season. That summer, Salazar played third, short, first, and the outfield, and pitched in two games. In 1988, he signed as a free agent with the Detroit Tigers and enjoyed his best season. The Padres reacquired him in 1989, then sent him to the Cubs last August.

Salazar, the Cubs' starting third baseman during the League Championship Series, will probably roam the diamond once more in 1990.

| Year | Team | G | AB | R | H | 2B | 3B | HR | RBI | BB | SB | AVG |
|------|------|---|----|----|----|----|----|----|-----|----|----|-----|
| 1980 | SD.... | 44 | 169 | 28 | 57 | 4 | 7 | 1 | 25 | 9 | 11 | .337 |
| 1981 | SD.... | 109 | 400 | 37 | 121 | 19 | 6 | 3 | 38 | 16 | 11 | .303 |
| 1982 | SD.... | 145 | 524 | 55 | 127 | 15 | 5 | 8 | 62 | 23 | 32 | .242 |
| 1983 | SD.... | 134 | 481 | 52 | 124 | 16 | 2 | 14 | 45 | 17 | 24 | .258 |
| 1984 | SD.... | 93 | 228 | 20 | 55 | 7 | 2 | 3 | 17 | 6 | 11 | .241 |
| 1985 | ChA.... | 122 | 327 | 39 | 80 | 18 | 2 | 10 | 45 | 12 | 14 | .245 |
| 1986 | ChA.... | 4 | 7 | 1 | 1 | 0 | 0 | 0 | 0 | 1 | 0 | .143 |
| 1987 | SD.... | 84 | 189 | 13 | 48 | 5 | 0 | 3 | 17 | 14 | 3 | .254 |
| 1988 | Det.... | 130 | 452 | 61 | 122 | 14 | 1 | 12 | 62 | 21 | 6 | .270 |
| 1989 | SD.... | 95 | 246 | 27 | 66 | 7 | 2 | 8 | 22 | 11 | 1 | .268 |
| 1989 | ChN.... | 26 | 80 | 7 | 26 | 5 | 0 | 1 | 12 | 4 | 0 | .325 |
| | | 986 | 3103 | 340 | 827 | 110 | 27 | 63 | 345 | 134 | 113 | .267 |

# Tim Wallach

**Birth Date:** 9/14/57
**Bats:** Right
**Throws:** Right
**1989 Club:**
**Montreal Expos**
**Contest Code #:** 168

**Rating: 3**

**F**antasy owners waiting for Tim Wallach to duplicate his career year of 1987 are wasting time. Wallach is a good player who'll reach double figures in home runs and drive in around 75 runs. That's nothing to be disappointed about.

One of Wallach's virtues is his power down the lines and to the gaps. Wallach led the National League in two-base hits in 1987 and tied Pedro Guerrero for the lead last year.

Known by teammates as "Eli," Wallach seems to perform best when he's not in the spotlight. But in 1988, when the Expos said good-bye to Andre Dawson, Wallach tried to hit every pitch for a five-run homer. The results? His worst career power numbers.

| Year | Team | G | AB | R | H | 2B | 3B | HR | RBI | BB | SB | AVG |
|------|------|---|----|----|----|----|----|----|-----|----|----|-----|
| 1980 | Mon.... | 5 | 11 | 1 | 2 | 0 | 0 | 1 | 2 | 1 | 0 | .182 |
| 1981 | Mon.... | 71 | 212 | 19 | 50 | 9 | 1 | 4 | 13 | 15 | 0 | .236 |
| 1982 | Mon.... | 158 | 596 | 89 | 160 | 31 | 3 | 28 | 97 | 36 | 6 | .268 |
| 1983 | Mon.... | 156 | 581 | 54 | 156 | 33 | 3 | 19 | 70 | 55 | 0 | .269 |

| 1984 | Mon.... | 160 | 582 | 55 | 143 | 25 | 4 | 18 | 72 | 50 | 3 | .246 |
| 1985 | Mon.... | 155 | 569 | 70 | 148 | 36 | 3 | 22 | 81 | 38 | 9 | .260 |
| 1986 | Mon.... | 134 | 480 | 50 | 112 | 22 | 1 | 18 | 71 | 44 | 8 | .233 |
| 1987 | Mon.... | 153 | 593 | 89 | 177 | 42 | 4 | 26 | 123 | 37 | 9 | .298 |
| 1988 | Mon.... | 159 | 592 | 52 | 152 | 32 | 5 | 12 | 69 | 38 | 2 | .257 |
| 1989 | Mon.... | 154 | 573 | 76 | 159 | 42 | 0 | 13 | 77 | 58 | 3 | .277 |
| | | 1305 | 4789 | 555 | 1259 | 272 | 24 | 161 | 675 | 372 | 40 | .263 |

# Matt Williams

**Birth Date: 11/28/65**
**Bats: Right**
**Throws: Right**
**1989 Club:**
**San Francisco Giants**
**Contest Code #: 169**

**Rating: 3**

In 1989, Kevin Mitchell led baseball with 47 home runs. Which player had the game's second-best total? Matt Williams, who hit 44 home runs—18 for the Giants, and 26 for Triple A Phoenix.

Two of Williams' statistics with the Giants seem contradictory: a .400 slugging average and a .202 batting average. How did he manage that? In 292 at-bats, Williams had 59 hits—22 singles, 18 doubles, 1 triple, 18 home runs—and struck out 72 times.

Williams has power to all fields and can turn on a fastball like nobody's business. But his major weakness is the curveball. Until he learns to hit the curve when it's in his hitting zone—and stops chasing curves in the dirt—Williams will duplicate his 1989 slugging and batting averages again and again.

| Year | Team | G | AB | R | H | 2B | 3B | HR | RBI | BB | SB | AVG |
|------|------|---|-----|----|-----|----|----|----|-----|----|----|------|
| 1987 | SF..... | 84 | 245 | 28 | 46 | 9 | 2 | 8 | 21 | 16 | 4 | .188 |
| 1988 | SF..... | 52 | 156 | 17 | 32 | 6 | 1 | 8 | 19 | 8 | 0 | .205 |
| 1989 | SF..... | 84 | 292 | 31 | 59 | 18 | 1 | 18 | 50 | 14 | 1 | .202 |
| | | 220 | 693 | 76 | 137 | 33 | 4 | 34 | 90 | 38 | 5 | .198 |

# SHORTSTOPS

# SHORTSTOPS

## Dave Anderson

**Birth Date:** 8/1/60
**Bats:** Right
**Throws:** Right
**1989 Club:**
**Los Angeles Dodgers**
**Contest Code #:** 175

**Rating: 1**

Back in the 1970s and early 1980s, when the Dodgers' farm system churned out youngsters who were worked into the major-league lineup one at a time, Dave Anderson was groomed as the successor to long-time shortstop Bill Russell. Anderson has been a capable defensive shortstop, but injuries and ineffective hitting cost him his starting job years ago.

Anderson, whom the Dodgers selected in the first round of the June 1981 draft, aroused the Dodgers' hopes by batting .343 at Triple A Albuquerque in 1982. Unfortunately, he has been overmatched by major-league pitching. In his best season (1984), all Anderson could muster was a .251 average.

| Year | Team | G | AB | R | H | 2B | 3B | HR | RBI | BB | SB | AVG |
|------|------|---|----|----|----|----|----|----|-----|----|----|-----|
| 1983 | LA..... | 61 | 115 | 12 | 19 | 4 | 2 | 1 | 2 | 12 | 6 | .165 |
| 1984 | LA..... | 121 | 374 | 51 | 94 | 16 | 2 | 3 | 34 | 45 | 15 | .251 |
| 1985 | LA..... | 77 | 221 | 24 | 44 | 6 | 0 | 4 | 18 | 35 | 5 | .199 |
| 1986 | LA..... | 92 | 216 | 31 | 53 | 9 | 0 | 1 | 15 | 22 | 5 | .245 |
| 1987 | LA..... | 108 | 265 | 32 | 62 | 12 | 3 | 1 | 13 | 24 | 9 | .234 |
| 1988 | LA..... | 116 | 285 | 31 | 71 | 10 | 2 | 2 | 20 | 32 | 4 | .249 |
| 1989 | LA..... | 87 | 140 | 15 | 32 | 2 | 0 | 1 | 14 | 17 | 2 | .229 |
| | | 662 | 1616 | 196 | 375 | 59 | 9 | 13 | 116 | 187 | 46 | .232 |

## Jay Bell

**Birth Date:** 12/11/65
**Bats:** Right
**Throws:** Right
**1989 Club:**
**Pittsburgh Pirates**
**Contest Code #:** 176

**Rating: 1**

Jay Bell is another good-fielding, slap-hitting short-stop. True, he batted a career-high .258 last season, but I think that was mostly a matter of good fortune. My contention is based on two things: Bell's previous career statistics, which you can scan; and from visual observations of his batting stance. The essence of a good batting stance is one that allows the hitter to wait on a pitch—so that he can identify it more easily—and, once he's read it, turn his hips, midsection, and hands quickly. You can't wait on a pitch and expect to hit it if you have too many unnecessary movements in your swing. For example, as the pitcher winds up, most hitters hold the bat in different positions, but as they coil, most hitters bring the bat to the same spot—above their front shoulder at a 45-degree angle—uncoil, and hit.

Bell holds his bat perpendicular to the ground. His hands are low and real close to his body. When the pitch is thrown, Bell has to bring his hands up to shoulder height and away from his body to get into hitting position. He's wasting the precious time other hitters use to read the pitch, and all these movements prevent him from hitting the ball sharply.

| Year | Team | G | AB | R | H | 2B | 3B | HR | RBI | BB | SB | AVG |
|------|------|---|----|----|----|----|----|----|-----|----|----|-----|
| 1986 | Cle..... | 5 | 14 | 3 | 5 | 2 | 0 | 1 | 4 | 2 | 0 | .357 |
| 1987 | Cle..... | 38 | 125 | 14 | 27 | 9 | 1 | 2 | 13 | 8 | 2 | .216 |

| | | | | | | | | | | | |
|---|---|---|---|---|---|---|---|---|---|---|---|
| 1988 | Cle..... | 73 | 211 | 23 | 46 | 5 | 1 | 2 | 21 | 21 | 4 | .218 |
| 1989 | Pit..... | 78 | 271 | 33 | 70 | 13 | 3 | 2 | 27 | 19 | 5 | .258 |
| | | 194 | 621 | 73 | 148 | 29 | 5 | 7 | 65 | 50 | 11 | .238 |

# Rafael Belliard

Birth Date: 10/24/61
Bats: Right
Throws: Right
1989 Club:
Pittsburgh Pirates
Contest Code #: 177

Rating: 1

In real baseball, a team needs a good fielding shortstop to contend. In fantasy baseball contests, a team with a good hitting shortstop will contend, since there are so few good-hitting shortstops.

Rafael Belliard is a delight to watch in the field. He makes all the plays, smoothly and efficiently. In 1988, he led all National League shortstops with a .977 fielding percentage. But at the plate, Belliard is an easy out. It's not that he strikes out a lot; he just doesn't hit the ball with any authority.

| Year | Team | G | AB | R | H | 2B | 3B | HR | RBI | BB | SB | AVG |
|---|---|---|---|---|---|---|---|---|---|---|---|---|
| 1982 | Pit..... | 9 | 2 | 3 | 1 | 0 | 0 | 0 | 0 | 0 | 1 | .500 |
| 1983 | Pit..... | 4 | 1 | 1 | 0 | 0 | 0 | 0 | 0 | 0 | 0 | .000 |
| 1984 | Pit..... | 20 | 22 | 3 | 5 | 0 | 0 | 0 | 0 | 0 | 4 | .227 |
| 1985 | Pit..... | 17 | 20 | 1 | 4 | 0 | 0 | 0 | 1 | 0 | 0 | .200 |
| 1986 | Pit..... | 117 | 309 | 33 | 72 | 5 | 2 | 0 | 31 | 26 | 12 | .233 |
| 1987 | Pit..... | 81 | 203 | 26 | 42 | 4 | 3 | 1 | 15 | 20 | 5 | .207 |
| 1988 | Pit..... | 122 | 286 | 28 | 61 | 0 | 4 | 0 | 11 | 26 | 7 | .213 |
| 1989 | Pit..... | 67 | 154 | 10 | 33 | 4 | 0 | 0 | 8 | 8 | 5 | .214 |
| | | 437 | 997 | 105 | 218 | 13 | 9 | 1 | 66 | 80 | 34 | .219 |

# Mariano Duncan

Birth Date: 3/13/63
Bats: Right and Left
Throws: Right
1989 Clubs:
Los Angeles Dodgers &
Cincinnati Reds
Contest Code #: 178

Rating: 2

Former Reds' manager Pete Rose still has some admirers. When Rose appeared on "Donahue" last November to promote his book, Phil Donahue took a phone call from a woman who said that her husband, a professional player in the Reds' organization, had played for many managers but that Pete was the best. When Phil asked her to identify herself, she replied, "Jackie Duncan, the wife of Mariano Duncan."

I couldn't help but wonder if Rose was Duncan's favorite manager because of some virtue, or was Rose great compared to Tommy Lasorda, with whom Duncan often found fault?

Duncan, who in 1985 finished third in the National League Rookie-of-the-Year voting, escaped from Lasorda's doghouse late last season when the Reds picked him up along with Tim Leary for Kal Daniels and Lenny Harris. Duncan played well in place of injured Reds' shortstop Barry Larkin, and may get a shot at the second-base job this spring.

| Year | Team | G | AB | R | H | 2B | 3B | HR | RBI | BB | SB | AVG |
|---|---|---|---|---|---|---|---|---|---|---|---|---|
| 1985 | LA ..... | 142 | 562 | 74 | 137 | 24 | 6 | 6 | 39 | 38 | 38 | .244 |
| 1986 | LA ..... | 109 | 407 | 47 | 93 | 7 | 0 | 8 | 30 | 30 | 48 | .229 |
| 1987 | LA ..... | 76 | 261 | 31 | 56 | 8 | 1 | 6 | 18 | 17 | 11 | .215 |
| 1989 | LA ..... | 49 | 84 | 9 | 21 | 5 | 1 | 0 | 8 | 0 | 3 | .250 |
| 1989 | Cin .... | 45 | 174 | 23 | 43 | 10 | 1 | 3 | 13 | 8 | 6 | .247 |
| | | 421 | 1488 | 184 | 350 | 54 | 9 | 23 | 108 | 93 | 106 | .235 |

# Shawon Dunston

**Birth Date:** 3/21/63
**Bats:** Right
**Throws:** Right
**1989 Club:**
**Chicago Cubs**
**Contest Code #:** 179

**Rating: 4**

Shawon Dunston began the 1989 season in typical fashion: his great promise blurred by poor batting performance. Thirty games into the season, Dunston had no home runs and two RBI's. Twenty games later, Dunston had hit 4 home runs and driven in 15 more runs, but his average stood at .215.

The full season was going to be different, however. Over his next 50 games, Dunston batted .329 (56 for 170) and wound up the season at .278. But even that average belies Dunston's coming of age. Dunston hit safely in 10 consecutive games from May 28 through June 7; batted .356 in July (32 for 90) and hit safely in 20 of 27 games; batted .294 in August (32 for 109) and hit safely in 21 of 28 games; and closed with a 14-game hitting streak (.412, 21 for 51) in September 9.

One of the first public statements Don Zimmer made when he became the Cubs' manager was that he was going to make Dunston his personal project. Last year, the project was a success.

| Year | Team | G | AB | R | H | 2B | 3B | HR | RBI | BB | SB | AVG |
|---|---|---|---|---|---|---|---|---|---|---|---|---|
| 1985 | ChN.... | 74 | 250 | 40 | 65 | 12 | 4 | 4 | 18 | 19 | 11 | .260 |
| 1986 | ChN.... | 150 | 581 | 66 | 145 | 37 | 3 | 17 | 68 | 21 | 13 | .250 |
| 1987 | ChN.... | 95 | 346 | 40 | 85 | 18 | 3 | 5 | 22 | 10 | 12 | .246 |
| 1988 | ChN.... | 155 | 575 | 69 | 143 | 23 | 6 | 9 | 56 | 16 | 30 | .249 |
| 1989 | ChN.... | 138 | 471 | 52 | 131 | 20 | 6 | 9 | 60 | 30 | 19 | .278 |
| | | 612 | 2223 | 267 | 569 | 110 | 22 | 44 | 224 | 96 | 85 | .256 |

# Kevin Elster

**Birth Date:** 8/3/64
**Bats:** Right
**Throws:** Right
**1989 Club:**
**New York Mets**
**Contest Code #:** 180

**Rating: 2**

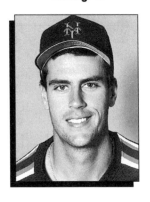

The Mets have always been high on Kevin Elster's fielding abilities, but have never been too sure of his hitting. Even though he joined the Mets as a replacement for injured shortstop Rafael Santana late in their 1986 championship season, the Mets sent him to Triple A in 1987 until he proved he could hit. When Elster batted .310 at Tidewater, they figured he was ready and traded Santana to the Yankees.

They were wrong. Elster floundered at the plate and often was used as a late-inning defensive replacement for Howard Johnson.

Last season, Elster looked lost during the early months. He stood so deep in the batter's box and so far from home that he was easy prey for outside pitches. Manager Davey Johnson was on the verge of moving Howard Johnson to short and playing Dave Magadan at third. But Elster got a reprieve when Keith Hernandez got hurt, and he made the most of it. By season's end, Elster improved his average to .231, with 10 home runs and 55 RBI's.

Elster hasn't fully answered the Mets' questions, just muted them.

| Year | Team | G | AB | R | H | 2B | 3B | HR | RBI | BB | SB | AVG |
|---|---|---|---|---|---|---|---|---|---|---|---|---|
| 1986 | NYN ... | 19 | 30 | 3 | 5 | 1 | 0 | 0 | 0 | 3 | 0 | .167 |
| 1987 | NYN ... | 5 | 10 | 1 | 4 | 2 | 0 | 0 | 1 | 0 | 0 | .400 |
| 1988 | NYN ... | 149 | 406 | 41 | 87 | 11 | 1 | 9 | 37 | 35 | 2 | .214 |
| 1989 | NYN ... | 151 | 458 | 52 | 106 | 25 | 2 | 10 | 55 | 34 | 4 | .231 |
| | | 324 | 904 | 97 | 202 | 39 | 3 | 19 | 93 | 72 | 6 | .223 |

# Alfredo Griffin

**Birth Date:** 3/6/57
**Bats:** Right and Left
**Throws:** Right
**1989 Club:**
**Los Angeles Dodgers**
**Contest Code #:** 181

## Rating: 1

**A**lfredo Griffin is one of the most undisciplined batters in the major leagues. Last year, the switch-hitting Griffin walked only 29 times in 506 at-bats. That might be acceptable for a slugger like Jose Canseco, but Griffin hit a grand total of 0 home runs and drove in a measly 29 runs.

Griffin broke into the bigs with the Indians in 1976, and has journeyed to Toronto, Oakland, and Los Angeles. At one time, he had some value as a base stealer, but since stealing 26 in 1987, he's stolen a total of 17 bases the past two seasons.

| Year | Team | G | AB | R | H | 2B | 3B | HR | RBI | BB | SB | AVG |
|------|------|------|------|-----|------|-----|-----|-----|-----|-----|-----|------|
| 1976 | Cle..... | 12 | 4 | 0 | 1 | 0 | 0 | 0 | 0 | 0 | 0 | .250 |
| 1977 | Cle..... | 14 | 41 | 5 | 6 | 1 | 0 | 0 | 3 | 3 | 2 | .146 |
| 1978 | Cle..... | 5 | 4 | 1 | 2 | 1 | 0 | 0 | 0 | 2 | 0 | .500 |
| 1979 | Tor..... | 153 | 624 | 81 | 179 | 22 | 10 | 2 | 31 | 40 | 21 | .287 |
| 1980 | Tor..... | 155 | 653 | 63 | 166 | 26 | 15 | 2 | 41 | 24 | 18 | .254 |
| 1981 | Tor..... | 101 | 388 | 30 | 81 | 19 | 6 | 0 | 21 | 17 | 8 | .209 |
| 1982 | Tor..... | 162 | 539 | 57 | 130 | 20 | 8 | 1 | 48 | 22 | 10 | .241 |
| 1983 | Tor..... | 162 | 528 | 62 | 132 | 22 | 9 | 4 | 47 | 27 | 8 | .250 |
| 1984 | Tor..... | 140 | 419 | 53 | 101 | 8 | 2 | 4 | 30 | 4 | 11 | .241 |
| 1985 | Oak.... | 162 | 614 | 75 | 166 | 18 | 7 | 2 | 64 | 20 | 24 | .270 |
| 1986 | Oak.... | 162 | 594 | 74 | 169 | 23 | 6 | 4 | 51 | 35 | 33 | .285 |
| 1987 | Oak.... | 144 | 494 | 69 | 130 | 23 | 5 | 3 | 60 | 28 | 26 | .263 |
| 1988 | LA..... | 95 | 316 | 39 | 63 | 8 | 3 | 1 | 27 | 24 | 7 | .199 |
| 1989 | LA..... | 136 | 506 | 49 | 125 | 27 | 2 | 0 | 29 | 29 | 10 | .247 |
| | | 1603 | 5724 | 658 | 1451 | 218 | 73 | 23 | 452 | 275 | 178 | .253 |

# Rex Hudler

**Birth Date:** 9/2/60
**Bats:** Right
**Throws:** Right
**1989 Club:**
**Montreal Expos**
**Contest Code #:** 182

## Rating: 1

**R**over infielder/outfielder Rex Hudler has been nick-named by teammates "The Wonder Dog" because he's always yapping. In 1988, Hudler howled at the plate (.273) and on the base paths (29 steals, the first 19 consecutively). But last year, with his playing time reduced, Hudler was a dog with fleas.

Hudler was originally Yankees property, but he was a second baseman and Willie Randolph was his competition. In December 1985, he was traded to the Orioles. Hudler's career line with Baltimore is unique: 14 games, 1 at-bat, 0 hits, 1 steal.

The Wonder Dog has to wonder what his role will be this season, now that the Expos' farm system is ready to yield a litter of middle infielders.

| Year | Team | G | AB | R | H | 2B | 3B | HR | RBI | BB | SB | AVG |
|------|------|-----|-----|-----|-----|-----|-----|-----|-----|-----|-----|------|
| 1984 | NYA.... | 9 | 7 | 2 | 1 | 1 | 0 | 0 | 0 | 1 | 0 | .143 |
| 1985 | NYA.... | 20 | 51 | 4 | 8 | 0 | 1 | 0 | 1 | 1 | 0 | .157 |
| 1986 | Bal .... | 14 | 1 | 1 | 0 | 0 | 0 | 0 | 0 | 0 | 1 | .000 |
| 1988 | Mon.... | 77 | 216 | 38 | 59 | 14 | 2 | 4 | 14 | 10 | 29 | .273 |
| 1989 | Mon.... | 92 | 155 | 21 | 38 | 7 | 0 | 6 | 13 | 6 | 15 | .245 |
| | | 212 | 430 | 66 | 106 | 22 | 3 | 10 | 28 | 18 | 45 | .247 |

# Steve Jeltz

Birth Date: 5/28/59
Bats: Right and Left
Throws: Right
1989 Club:
Philadelphia Phillies
Contest Code #: 183

Rating: 1

Steve Jeltz had a career year last season, batting 37 points above his previous major-league average and quintupling his career home-run total. Awesome. Unfortunately, his previous career average was .208 and home-run total was 1.

The key to Jeltz's "success" in 1989 was his performance from the right side of the plate. You'll no doubt recall that until last season Jeltz batted .200 as a right-handed hitter and .197 as a lefty. Last season, Jeltz jolted the baseball world by cracking a .268 average (19 for 71) from the right side and .234 (45 for 192) from the left.

| Year | Team | G | AB | R | H | 2B | 3B | HR | RBI | BB | SB | AVG |
|------|------|-----|------|-----|-----|----|----|----|-----|-----|----|------|
| 1983 | Phi .... | 13 | 8 | 0 | 1 | 0 | 1 | 0 | 1 | 1 | 0 | .125 |
| 1984 | Phi .... | 28 | 68 | 7 | 14 | 0 | 1 | 1 | 7 | 7 | 2 | .206 |
| 1985 | Phi .... | 89 | 196 | 17 | 37 | 4 | 1 | 0 | 12 | 26 | 1 | .189 |
| 1986 | Phi .... | 145 | 439 | 44 | 96 | 11 | 4 | 0 | 36 | 65 | 6 | .219 |
| 1987 | Phi .... | 114 | 293 | 37 | 68 | 9 | 6 | 0 | 12 | 39 | 1 | .232 |
| 1988 | Phi .... | 148 | 379 | 39 | 71 | 11 | 4 | 0 | 27 | 59 | 3 | .187 |
| 1989 | Phi .... | 116 | 263 | 28 | 64 | 7 | 3 | 4 | 25 | 45 | 4 | .243 |
| | | 653 | 1646 | 172 | 351 | 42 | 20 | 5 | 120 | 242 | 17 | .213 |

# Barry Larkin

Birth Date: 4/28/64
Bats: Right
Throws: Right
1989 Club:
Cincinnati Reds
Contest Code #: 184

Rating: 5

Barry Larkin, who in 1988 batted .296, with 12 home runs and 56 RBI's, and stole 40 bases, was off to a spectacular start last season. During the first half, Larkin was batting a torrid .340 in 315 at-bats. Then he injured his right elbow, went on the disabled list for two and a half months, and batted only 10 more times in September.

When healthy, Larkin is the best offensive shortstop in the National League. He blends a keen batting stroke with power and speed. The Reds' number-one pick (fourth overall) in the June 1985 draft, Larkin was a two-time all-American and two-time MVP of the Big Ten during his collegiate career at the University of Michigan. Larkin also hit .311 for the 1984 U.S. Olympic Baseball Team.

Larkin jumped from Double A to Triple A to the majors within a year's time, and immediately took over as the Reds' starting shortstop. The Cincinnati native, a crowd favorite, is the most recognized performer in a family of gifted athletes. His brother, Mike, played football at Notre Dame, and another brother, Byron, was an all-American guard at Xavier University.

There are those in baseball who believe that Larkin may one day be recognized as the game's best player.

| Year | Team | G | AB | R | H | 2B | 3B | HR | RBI | BB | SB | AVG |
|------|------|-----|------|-----|-----|----|----|----|-----|-----|----|------|
| 1986 | Cin .... | 41 | 159 | 27 | 45 | 4 | 3 | 3 | 19 | 9 | 8 | .283 |
| 1987 | Cin .... | 125 | 439 | 64 | 107 | 16 | 2 | 12 | 43 | 36 | 21 | .244 |
| 1988 | Cin .... | 151 | 588 | 91 | 174 | 32 | 5 | 12 | 56 | 41 | 40 | .296 |
| 1989 | Cin .... | 97 | 325 | 47 | 111 | 14 | 4 | 4 | 36 | 20 | 10 | .342 |
| | | 414 | 1511 | 229 | 437 | 66 | 14 | 31 | 154 | 106 | 79 | .289 |

# Spike Owen

Birth Date: 4/19/61
Bats: Both
Throws: Right
1989 Club:
Montreal Expos
Contest Code #: 185

Rating: 3

The Expos acquired Spike Owen during the 1988 winter meetings to be the captain of a porous middle infield. What surprised the Expos' decision-makers was the punch in Owen's bat.

Last season, he knocked in 41 runs in 437 at-bats. As a left-handed hitter, he batted just .216 (66 for 306), but from the right side he hit .275 (36 for 131). Owen's total of six home runs matched his single-season high of 1985, and was one better than his output in 1988.

Owen broke in with the Mariners, who drafted him in the June 1982 first round. During his collegiate career at the University of Texas, Owen was a teammate of Roger Clemens and Calvin Schiraldi. Owen holds school career records for walks (247), runs (250), and stolen bases (95). As a major leaguer, he's driven in more than 40 runs four times.

| Year | Team | G | AB | R | H | 2B | 3B | HR | RBI | BB | SB | AVG |
|------|------|---|-----|---|---|----|----|----|-----|----|----|-----|
| 1983 | Sea .... | 80 | 306 | 36 | 60 | 11 | 3 | 2 | 21 | 24 | 10 | .196 |
| 1984 | Sea .... | 152 | 530 | 67 | 130 | 18 | 8 | 3 | 43 | 46 | 16 | .245 |
| 1985 | Sea .... | 118 | 352 | 41 | 91 | 10 | 6 | 6 | 37 | 34 | 11 | .259 |
| 1986 | Sea .... | 112 | 402 | 46 | 99 | 22 | 6 | 0 | 35 | 34 | 1 | .246 |
| 1986 | Bos .... | 42 | 126 | 21 | 23 | 2 | 1 | 1 | 10 | 17 | 3 | .183 |
| 1987 | Bos .... | 132 | 437 | 50 | 113 | 17 | 7 | 2 | 48 | 53 | 11 | .259 |
| 1988 | Bos .... | 89 | 257 | 40 | 64 | 14 | 1 | 5 | 18 | 27 | 0 | .249 |
| 1989 | Mon.... | 142 | 437 | 52 | 102 | 17 | 4 | 6 | 41 | 76 | 3 | .233 |
| | | 867 | 2847 | 353 | 682 | 111 | 36 | 25 | 253 | 311 | 55 | .240 |

# Rafael Ramirez

Birth Date: 2/18/59
Bats: Right
Throws: Right
1989 Club:
Houston Astros
Contest Code #: 186

Rating: 3

Since 1984, Rafael Ramirez has produced virtually the same season over and again: .245–.260 batting average, 6 home runs, 50 to 60 RBI's. Years back, he used to steal 15 to 20 bases a season, but over the past three years he's slowed to a crawl.

At the start of his big-league career, Ramirez, who was signed as a free agent by the Braves in 1976, was viewed as the up-and-coming shortstop of his day. His blend of speed and power were most evident in 1982 and 1983. In 1984, Ramirez, batting .304 over the first half of the season, was selected to the National League All-Star team, but did not play.

Should Ramirez not hold on to the Astros' starting job (see Eric Yelding), he has plenty of mileage as a reserve shortstop/third baseman, or can still hold the fort for another team waiting for a prospect to complete his minor-league development.

| Year | Team | G | AB | R | H | 2B | 3B | HR | RBI | BB | SB | AVG |
|------|------|---|-----|---|---|----|----|----|-----|----|----|-----|
| 1980 | Atl ..... | 50 | 165 | 17 | 44 | 6 | 1 | 2 | 11 | 2 | 2 | .267 |
| 1981 | Atl ..... | 95 | 307 | 30 | 67 | 16 | 2 | 2 | 20 | 24 | 7 | .218 |
| 1982 | Atl ..... | 157 | 609 | 74 | 169 | 24 | 4 | 10 | 52 | 36 | 27 | .278 |
| 1983 | Atl ..... | 152 | 622 | 82 | 185 | 13 | 5 | 7 | 58 | 36 | 16 | .297 |
| 1984 | Atl ..... | 145 | 591 | 51 | 157 | 22 | 4 | 2 | 48 | 26 | 14 | .266 |
| 1985 | Atl ..... | 138 | 568 | 54 | 141 | 25 | 4 | 5 | 58 | 20 | 2 | .248 |
| 1986 | Atl ..... | 134 | 496 | 57 | 119 | 21 | 1 | 8 | 33 | 21 | 19 | .240 |
| 1987 | Atl ..... | 56 | 179 | 22 | 47 | 12 | 0 | 1 | 21 | 8 | 6 | .263 |
| 1988 | Hou .... | 155 | 566 | 51 | 156 | 30 | 5 | 6 | 59 | 18 | 3 | .276 |
| 1989 | Hou .... | 151 | 537 | 46 | 132 | 20 | 2 | 6 | 54 | 29 | 3 | .246 |
| | | 1233 | 4640 | 484 | 1217 | 189 | 28 | 49 | 414 | 220 | 99 | .262 |

# Craig Reynolds

**Birth Date:** 12/27/52
**Bats:** Left
**Throws:** Right
**1989 Club:**
**Houston Astros**
**Contest Code #:** 188

**Rating: 1**

**C**raig Reynolds has remained with the Astros the past six seasons as infield insurance. Once the starting shortstop, Reynolds has since filled in at second base, short, third, and the outfield.

Reynolds was so highly regarded early in his career that in 1978 he was traded to the Astros even-up for pitcher Floyd Bannister. The following season, Reynolds made his lone All-Star game appearance. In 1981, he led the major leagues with 12 triples. Last season, Reynolds batted .201 in 101 games. As a pinch-hitter, he went 5 for 37.

| Year | Team | G | AB | R | H | 2B | 3B | HR | RBI | BB | SB | AVG |
|------|------|-----|------|-----|------|-----|-----|-----|------|------|-----|------|
| 1975 | Pit..... | 31 | 76 | 8 | 17 | 3 | 0 | 0 | 4 | 3 | 0 | .224 |
| 1976 | Pit..... | 7 | 4 | 1 | 1 | 0 | 0 | 1 | 1 | 0 | 0 | .250 |
| 1977 | Sea.... | 135 | 420 | 41 | 104 | 12 | 3 | 4 | 28 | 15 | 6 | .248 |
| 1978 | Sea.... | 148 | 548 | 57 | 160 | 16 | 7 | 5 | 44 | 36 | 9 | .292 |
| 1979 | Hou.... | 146 | 555 | 63 | 147 | 20 | 9 | 0 | 39 | 21 | 12 | .265 |
| 1980 | Hou.... | 137 | 381 | 34 | 86 | 9 | 6 | 3 | 28 | 20 | 2 | .226 |
| 1981 | Hou.... | 87 | 323 | 43 | 84 | 10 | 12 | 4 | 31 | 12 | 3 | .260 |
| 1982 | Hou.... | 54 | 118 | 16 | 30 | 2 | 3 | 1 | 7 | 11 | 3 | .254 |
| 1983 | Hou.... | 65 | 98 | 10 | 21 | 3 | 0 | 1 | 6 | 6 | 0 | .214 |
| 1984 | Hou.... | 146 | 527 | 61 | 137 | 15 | 11 | 6 | 60 | 22 | 7 | .260 |
| 1985 | Hou.... | 107 | 379 | 43 | 103 | 18 | 8 | 4 | 32 | 12 | 4 | .272 |
| 1986 | Hou.... | 114 | 313 | 32 | 78 | 7 | 3 | 6 | 41 | 12 | 3 | .249 |
| 1987 | Hou.... | 135 | 374 | 35 | 95 | 17 | 3 | 4 | 28 | 30 | 5 | .254 |
| 1988 | Hou.... | 78 | 161 | 20 | 41 | 7 | 0 | 1 | 14 | 8 | 3 | .255 |
| 1989 | Hou.... | 101 | 189 | 16 | 38 | 4 | 0 | 2 | 14 | 19 | 1 | .201 |
| | | 1491 | 4466 | 480 | 1142 | 143 | 65 | 42 | 377 | 227 | 58 | .256 |

# Ozzie Smith

**Birth Date:** 12/26/54
**Bats:** Right and Left
**Throws:** Right
**1989 Club:**
**St. Louis Cardinals**
**Contest Code #:** 187

**Rating: 5**

**S**ure, Ozzie Smith is the best glove man in this group, but how does he rate as one of the the best offensive shortstops? Easy. In the past three seasons his batting average has ranged between .270 and .300; his stolen bases between 29 and 57; and his RBI's between 50 and 75.

A nine-time All Star, Ozzie came into his own as a hitter in 1985 after working with noted conditioning coach and nutritionist Mackie Shilstone of New Orleans. Under Shilstone's guidance, Smith developed the strength to drive the ball to the gaps without sacrificing speed or quickness. His endurance also improved.

Though Smith turned thirty-five in December, he still takes good care of himself. He should continue his productivity in three categories in 1990 and beyond.

| Year | Team | G | AB | R | H | 2B | 3B | HR | RBI | BB | SB | AVG |
|------|------|-----|------|-----|------|-----|-----|-----|------|------|-----|------|
| 1978 | SD..... | 159 | 590 | 69 | 152 | 17 | 6 | 1 | 46 | 47 | 40 | .258 |
| 1979 | SD..... | 156 | 587 | 77 | 124 | 18 | 6 | 0 | 27 | 37 | 28 | .211 |
| 1980 | SD..... | 158 | 609 | 67 | 140 | 18 | 5 | 0 | 35 | 71 | 57 | .230 |
| 1981 | SD..... | 110 | 450 | 53 | 100 | 11 | 2 | 0 | 21 | 41 | 22 | .222 |
| 1982 | StL .... | 140 | 488 | 58 | 121 | 24 | 1 | 2 | 43 | 68 | 25 | .248 |
| 1983 | StL .... | 159 | 552 | 69 | 134 | 30 | 6 | 3 | 50 | 64 | 34 | .243 |
| 1984 | StL .... | 124 | 412 | 53 | 106 | 20 | 5 | 1 | 44 | 56 | 35 | .257 |
| 1985 | StL .... | 158 | 537 | 70 | 148 | 22 | 3 | 6 | 54 | 65 | 31 | .276 |
| 1986 | StL .... | 153 | 514 | 67 | 144 | 19 | 4 | 0 | 54 | 79 | 31 | .280 |
| 1987 | StL .... | 158 | 600 | 104 | 182 | 40 | 4 | 0 | 75 | 89 | 43 | .303 |
| 1988 | StL .... | 153 | 575 | 80 | 155 | 27 | 1 | 3 | 51 | 74 | 57 | .270 |
| 1989 | StL .... | 155 | 593 | 82 | 162 | 30 | 8 | 2 | 50 | 55 | 29 | .273 |
| | | 1783 | 6507 | 849 | 1668 | 276 | 51 | 18 | 550 | 746 | 432 | .256 |

# Garry Templeton

**Birth Date: 3/24/56**
**Bats: Right and Left**
**Throws: Right**
**1989 Club:**
**San Diego Padres**
**Contest Code #: 189**

**Rating: 1**

**G**arry Templeton has been around so long that it's hard to believe he's only thirty-three years old. And because of his chronic knee problems, it's hard to believe that Templeton was once so good—bursting with speed and batting for high average—that he was traded even-up for Ozzie Smith in 1982.

Templeton's knee problems have so dramatically changed his game that his options as a batter are limited. With St. Louis, Templeton beat the ball onto Busch Stadium's artificial surface and legged out hits. Now his speed is gone and his ground balls are slowed by the natural grass at San Diego/Jack Murphy Stadium. Over the years, Templeton has become an undisciplined hitter, earning few walks and striking out too often. Templeton will continue as the Padres' shortstop until San Diego develops one in their system.

| Year | Team | G | AB | R | H | 2B | 3B | HR | RBI | BB | SB | AVG |
|---|---|---|---|---|---|---|---|---|---|---|---|---|
| 1976 | StL .... | 53 | 213 | 32 | 62 | 8 | 2 | 1 | 17 | 7 | 11 | .291 |
| 1977 | StL .... | 153 | 621 | 94 | 200 | 19 | 18 | 8 | 79 | 15 | 28 | .322 |
| 1978 | StL .... | 155 | 647 | 82 | 181 | 31 | 13 | 2 | 47 | 22 | 34 | .280 |
| 1979 | StL .... | 154 | 672 | 105 | 211 | 32 | 19 | 9 | 62 | 18 | 26 | .314 |
| 1980 | StL .... | 118 | 504 | 83 | 161 | 19 | 9 | 4 | 43 | 18 | 31 | .319 |
| 1981 | StL .... | 80 | 333 | 47 | 96 | 16 | 8 | 1 | 33 | 14 | 8 | .288 |
| 1982 | SD..... | 141 | 563 | 76 | 139 | 25 | 8 | 6 | 64 | 26 | 27 | .247 |
| 1983 | SD..... | 126 | 460 | 39 | 121 | 20 | 2 | 3 | 40 | 21 | 16 | .263 |
| 1984 | SD..... | 148 | 493 | 40 | 127 | 19 | 3 | 2 | 35 | 39 | 8 | .258 |
| 1985 | SD..... | 148 | 546 | 63 | 154 | 30 | 2 | 6 | 55 | 41 | 16 | .282 |
| 1986 | SD..... | 147 | 510 | 42 | 126 | 21 | 2 | 2 | 44 | 35 | 10 | .247 |
| 1987 | SD..... | 148 | 510 | 42 | 113 | 13 | 5 | 5 | 48 | 42 | 14 | .222 |
| 1988 | SD..... | 110 | 362 | 35 | 90 | 15 | 7 | 3 | 36 | 20 | 8 | .249 |
| 1989 | SD..... | 142 | 506 | 43 | 129 | 26 | 3 | 6 | 40 | 23 | 1 | .255 |
| | | 1823 | 6940 | 823 | 1910 | 294 | 101 | 58 | 643 | 341 | 238 | .275 |

# Andres Thomas

**Birth Date: 11/10/63**
**Bats: Right**
**Throws: Right**
**1989 Club:**
**Atlanta Braves**
**Contest Code #: 190**

**Rating: 2**

**E**very dog has his day, and some have their half-season. During the first half of the 1989 season, Andres Thomas, who reportedly has provided handfuls of headaches for Braves' managers, came into the All-Star break with 10 home runs, 43 RBI's and a .243 batting average. The Braves were so enthused that they moved Thomas into the number-four slot.

His second half was another story entirely: 3 home runs, 14 RBI's and a .135 batting average.

Overall, Thomas, who holds his bat above his head as if it were a television antenna in search of better reception, walked only 12 times in 554 at-bats. He posted a .213 batting average, a .316 slugging average, and a less-than-stellar .228 on-base average. So much for Thomas' future as a clean-up hitter.

| Year | Team | G | AB | R | H | 2B | 3B | HR | RBI | BB | SB | AVG |
|---|---|---|---|---|---|---|---|---|---|---|---|---|
| 1985 | Atl ..... | 15 | 18 | 6 | 5 | 0 | 0 | 0 | 2 | 0 | 0 | .278 |
| 1986 | Atl ..... | 102 | 323 | 26 | 81 | 17 | 2 | 6 | 32 | 8 | 4 | .251 |
| 1987 | Atl ..... | 82 | 324 | 29 | 75 | 11 | 0 | 5 | 39 | 14 | 6 | .231 |
| 1988 | Atl ..... | 153 | 606 | 54 | 153 | 22 | 2 | 13 | 68 | 14 | 7 | .252 |
| 1989 | Atl ..... | 141 | 554 | 41 | 118 | 18 | 0 | 13 | 57 | 12 | 3 | .213 |
| | | 493 | 1825 | 156 | 432 | 68 | 4 | 37 | 198 | 48 | 20 | .237 |

# Dickie Thon

Birth Date: 6/20/58
Bats: Right
Throws: Right
1989 Club:
Philadelphia Phillies
Contest Code #: 191

Rating: 3

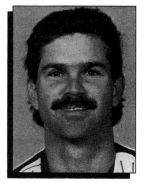

Lonnie Smith of the Braves may have had the finest comeback season in the National League, but Dickie Thon came pretty darned close.

You'll remember that in 1984 Thon nearly lost the sight in one eye after being hit in the face by a Mike Torrez pitch. Thon healed, rehabilitated, and returned, but at nowhere near the level he'd played before. He grew so frustrated that on July 4, 1987, he walked out on the Astros and was placed on the disqualified list for the rest of the season. In 1988, he signed as a free agent with the Padres and played in a utility role.

Last season, he joined the Phillies and resembled the hot tuna of old. Playing in 136 games, Thon batted .271, thwacked 15 home runs, and drove in 60 runs. His power numbers were second-best on the Phillies.

| Year | Team | G | AB | R | H | 2B | 3B | HR | RBI | BB | SB | AVG |
|------|------|---|----|---|---|----|----|----|-----|----|----|-----|
| 1979 | Cal..... | 35 | 56 | 6 | 19 | 3 | 0 | 0 | 8 | 5 | 0 | .339 |
| 1980 | Cal..... | 80 | 267 | 32 | 68 | 12 | 2 | 0 | 15 | 10 | 7 | .255 |
| 1981 | Hou.... | 49 | 95 | 13 | 26 | 6 | 0 | 0 | 3 | 9 | 6 | .274 |
| 1982 | Hou.... | 136 | 496 | 73 | 137 | 31 | 10 | 3 | 36 | 37 | 37 | .276 |
| 1983 | Hou.... | 154 | 619 | 81 | 177 | 28 | 9 | 20 | 79 | 54 | 34 | .286 |
| 1984 | Hou.... | 5 | 17 | 3 | 6 | 0 | 1 | 0 | 1 | 0 | 0 | .353 |
| 1985 | Hou.... | 84 | 251 | 26 | 63 | 6 | 1 | 6 | 29 | 18 | 8 | .251 |
| 1986 | Hou.... | 106 | 278 | 24 | 69 | 13 | 1 | 3 | 21 | 29 | 6 | .248 |
| 1987 | Hou.... | 32 | 66 | 6 | 14 | 1 | 0 | 1 | 3 | 16 | 3 | .212 |
| 1988 | SD..... | 95 | 258 | 36 | 68 | 12 | 2 | 1 | 18 | 33 | 19 | .264 |
| 1989 | Phi .... | 136 | 435 | 45 | 118 | 18 | 4 | 15 | 60 | 33 | 6 | .271 |
| | | 912 | 2838 | 345 | 765 | 130 | 30 | 49 | 273 | 244 | 126 | .270 |

# Jose Uribe

Birth Date: 1/21/60
Bats: Right and Left
Throws: Right
1989 Club:
San Francisco Giants
Contest Code #: 192

Rating: 1

What can you say about Jose Uribe? Only once in six years has this slick-fielding shortstop hit for average. He's another shortstop whose appetite for pitches (74 strikeouts) far exceeds his patience (34 walks in 453 at-bats).

Uribe, who made his professional debut with the Cardinals' Class-A St. Petersburg club in 1981, was traded to the Giants with pitcher Dave LaPoint and outfielders David Green and Gary Rajsich for Jack Clark. Uribe's best hitting—.291—came during the Giants' 1987 Western Division championship season.

This year, Uribe must find his 1987 form or face losing the starting job to Matt Williams, who may move over from third to make room for Greg Litton.

| Year | Team | G | AB | R | H | 2B | 3B | HR | RBI | BB | SB | AVG |
|------|------|---|----|---|---|----|----|----|-----|----|----|-----|
| 1984 | StL .... | 8 | 19 | 4 | 4 | 0 | 0 | 0 | 3 | 0 | 1 | .211 |
| 1985 | SF..... | 147 | 476 | 46 | 113 | 20 | 4 | 3 | 26 | 30 | 8 | .237 |
| 1986 | SF..... | 157 | 453 | 46 | 101 | 15 | 1 | 3 | 43 | 61 | 22 | .223 |
| 1987 | SF..... | 95 | 309 | 44 | 90 | 16 | 5 | 5 | 30 | 24 | 12 | .291 |
| 1988 | SF..... | 141 | 493 | 47 | 124 | 10 | 7 | 3 | 35 | 36 | 14 | .252 |
| 1989 | SF..... | 151 | 453 | 34 | 100 | 12 | 6 | 1 | 30 | 34 | 6 | .221 |
| | | 699 | 2203 | 221 | 532 | 73 | 23 | 15 | 167 | 185 | 63 | .241 |

# Curtis Wilkerson

**Birth Date:** 4/26/61
**Bats:** Right and Left
**Throws:** Right
**1989 Club:**
**Chicago Cubs**
**Contest Code #:** 193

**Rating: 1**

**C**urtis Wilkerson gives the Cubs a good utility infielder off the bench. But in fantasy baseball, he gives your team little to get excited about. With the Cubs' middle infield manned by Ryne Sandberg and Shawon Dunston, Wilkerson doesn't see a lot of daylight there. And with hot prospect Ty Griffin being groomed in the minors as a third baseman, Wilkerson won't see much time there, either.

During his six seasons with the Texas Rangers, Wilkerson, who came to the Cubs in December 1988 as part of the Mitch Williams trade, lost a starting job and became a roving substitute. Last season, Wilkerson's shining moment came on June 8. In a nationally televised game against the Mets, Wilkerson, subbing for Sandberg, had four hits in the Cubs' 5–4 victory.

| Year | Team | G | AB | R | H | 2B | 3B | HR | RBI | BB | SB | AVG |
|------|------|-----|------|-----|-----|----|----|----|-----|----|----|------|
| 1983 | Tex .... | 16 | 35 | 7 | 6 | 0 | 1 | 0 | 1 | 2 | 3 | .171 |
| 1984 | Tex .... | 153 | 484 | 47 | 120 | 12 | 0 | 1 | 26 | 22 | 12 | .248 |
| 1985 | Tex .... | 129 | 360 | 35 | 88 | 11 | 6 | 0 | 22 | 22 | 14 | .244 |
| 1986 | Tex .... | 110 | 236 | 27 | 56 | 10 | 3 | 0 | 15 | 11 | 9 | .237 |
| 1987 | Tex .... | 85 | 138 | 28 | 37 | 5 | 3 | 2 | 14 | 6 | 6 | .268 |
| 1988 | Tex .... | 117 | 338 | 41 | 99 | 12 | 5 | 0 | 28 | 26 | 9 | .293 |
| 1989 | ChN.... | 77 | 160 | 18 | 39 | 4 | 2 | 1 | 10 | 8 | 4 | .244 |
| | | 687 | 1751 | 203 | 445 | 54 | 20 | 4 | 116 | 97 | 57 | .254 |

# Eric Yelding

**Birth Date:** 2/22/65
**Bats:** Right
**Throws:** Right
**1989 Club:**
**Houston Astros**
**Contest Code #:** 194

**Rating: 3**

**D**on't be deceived by Eric Yelding's 1989 numbers. Yelding, originally drafted by the Toronto Blue Jays in the first round of the January 1984 draft, probably could have used another season at Triple A, but baseball's winter draft rules complicated matters. The Cubs drafted Yelding, who was left unprotected by the Blue Jays, in the December 1988 draft. In the last days of spring training, the Cubs decided Yelding would not make their major-league squad, which meant they'd have to return him to Toronto. Houston general manager Bill Wood acted quickly, removing outfielder Greg Gross from the Astros' roster and picking up Yelding. Remember, the same rules apply to a third party; if the Astros didn't keep Yelding in their major-league club for a full season, they'd have to send him back to Toronto. So Yelding rode the pines for most of his first big-league season.

The Astros used him at second base, shortstop, and in the outfield last season. This year, he may unseat Rafael Ramirez and become the team's regular shortstop.

| Year | Team | G | AB | R | H | 2B | 3B | HR | RBI | BB | SB | AVG |
|------|------|----|----|----|----|----|----|----|-----|----|----|------|
| 1989 | Hou.... | 70 | 90 | 19 | 21 | 2 | 0 | 0 | 9 | 7 | 11 | .233 |
| | | 70 | 90 | 19 | 21 | 2 | 0 | 0 | 9 | 7 | 11 | .233 |

# CATCHERS

# CATCHERS

## Damon Berryhill

**Birth Date:** 12/3/63
**Bats:** Right and Left
**Throws:** Right
**1989 Club:**
**Chicago Cubs**
**Contest Code #:** 201

**Rating:** 3

In May 1988, Damon Berryhill was recalled from Triple A Iowa to fill in for injured starter Jody Davis. From that point on, Berryhill batted .259, with 7 home runs and 38 RBI's in 309 at-bats. Because of his timely hitting and superior defense, the Cubs' brass gave him the starting job and traded Davis to the Braves that September.

In 1989, injuries cheated Berryhill out of a successful encore. He opened the season on the disabled list, returned in May, but a rotator-cuff injury in August sidelined him for the rest of the season. When Berryhill did play, he put up almost the same numbers that he had in 1988.

Berryhill is slated to return as the Cubs' number-one catcher this season. If he continues to play well, the Cubs may consider trading him now that Joe Girardi, who'd been considered the catcher of the future, got his feet wet in the bigs.

| Year | Team | G | AB | R | H | 2B | 3B | HR | RBI | BB | SB | AVG |
|------|------|---|----|---|---|----|----|----|-----|----|----|-----|
| 1987 | ChN.... | 12 | 28 | 2 | 5 | 1 | 0 | 0 | 1 | 3 | 0 | .179 |
| 1988 | ChN.... | 95 | 309 | 19 | 80 | 19 | 1 | 7 | 38 | 17 | 1 | .259 |
| 1989 | ChN.... | 91 | 334 | 37 | 86 | 13 | 0 | 5 | 41 | 16 | 1 | .257 |
| | | 198 | 671 | 58 | 171 | 33 | 1 | 12 | 80 | 36 | 2 | .255 |

## Craig Biggio

**Birth Date:** 12/14/65
**Bats:** Right
**Throws:** Right
**1989 Club:**
**Houston Astros**
**Contest Code #:** 202

**Rating:** 5

Craig Biggio (pronounced Bee-gee-o), selected in the first round of the June 1987 draft, was the first position player in that draft to reach the majors. Actually, the Astros rushed him up in 1988 when incumbent Alan Ashby got hurt. But last season Biggio proved himself ready, batting .257, with 13 home runs, 60 RBI's and 21 steals.

Biggio, a standout in his collegiate career with Seton Hall University, helped lead his team to a berth in the College Baseball World Series in 1987 and was named to *The Sporting News* All-America team.

Because of his power potential and stolen-base ability, Biggio is about to become the best catcher in fantasy baseball. Be warned, however, that the Astros are thinking of moving Biggio to second base or center field.

| Year | Team | G | AB | R | H | 2B | 3B | HR | RBI | BB | SB | AVG |
|------|------|---|----|---|---|----|----|----|-----|----|----|-----|
| 1988 | Hou.... | 50 | 123 | 14 | 26 | 6 | 1 | 3 | 5 | 7 | 6 | .211 |
| 1989 | Hou.... | 134 | 443 | 64 | 114 | 21 | 2 | 13 | 60 | 49 | 21 | .257 |
| | | 184 | 566 | 78 | 140 | 27 | 3 | 16 | 65 | 56 | 27 | .247 |

# Gary Carter

Birth Date: 4/8/54
Bats: Right
Throws: Right
1989 Club:
New York Mets
Contest Code #: 203

Rating: 1

After the 1989 season, Gary Carter wisely decided not to declare himself a free-agent when the Mets said they would not re-sign him. Had he gone the free agent route, any team that would have signed Carter—classified as "Type A" free agent under the confusing formulas used by the Major League Baseball Players Association and the owners' Player Relations Committee—would have had to give up a first-round pick in the June 1990 draft. Instead, Carter asked for—and was granted—his release, which opened up his future employment possibilities.

It's a shame Carter's wisdom doesn't transfer to his batting style. Throughout his career, Carter takes he-man cuts with what was once described by Joe Klein of *New York* magazine as a "lumberjack swing." Carter's swing depends entirely on his upper body. That sufficed nicely when he was young and strong, but the time has come for Carter to bring his legs into the action. His knees are so stiff, his legs so upright, that he doesn't generate all the force he's capable of.

Perhaps he can't bench his knees and pivot into the pitch because those joints are chronically sore. If that's the case, then Carter may consider retirement.

| Year | Team | G | AB | R | H | 2B | 3B | HR | RBI | BB | SB | AVG |
|------|------|---|-----|----|------|-----|----|-----|------|-----|----|------|
| 1974 | Mon.... | 9 | 27 | 5 | 11 | 0 | 1 | 1 | 6 | 1 | 2 | .407 |
| 1975 | Mon.... | 144 | 503 | 58 | 136 | 20 | 1 | 17 | 68 | 72 | 5 | .270 |
| 1976 | Mon.... | 91 | 311 | 31 | 68 | 8 | 1 | 6 | 38 | 30 | 0 | .219 |
| 1977 | Mon.... | 154 | 522 | 86 | 148 | 29 | 2 | 31 | 84 | 58 | 5 | .284 |
| 1978 | Mon.... | 157 | 533 | 76 | 136 | 27 | 1 | 20 | 72 | 62 | 10 | .255 |
| 1979 | Mon.... | 141 | 505 | 74 | 143 | 26 | 5 | 22 | 75 | 40 | 3 | .283 |
| 1980 | Mon.... | 154 | 549 | 76 | 145 | 25 | 5 | 29 | 101 | 58 | 3 | .264 |
| 1981 | Mon.... | 100 | 374 | 48 | 94 | 20 | 2 | 16 | 68 | 35 | 1 | .251 |
| 1982 | Mon.... | 154 | 557 | 91 | 163 | 32 | 1 | 29 | 97 | 78 | 2 | .293 |
| 1983 | Mon.... | 145 | 541 | 63 | 146 | 37 | 3 | 17 | 79 | 51 | 1 | .270 |
| 1984 | Mon.... | 159 | 596 | 75 | 175 | 32 | 1 | 27 | 106 | 64 | 2 | .294 |
| 1985 | NYN ... | 149 | 555 | 83 | 156 | 17 | 1 | 32 | 100 | 69 | 1 | .281 |
| 1986 | NYN ... | 132 | 490 | 81 | 125 | 14 | 2 | 24 | 105 | 62 | 1 | .255 |
| 1987 | NYN ... | 139 | 523 | 55 | 123 | 18 | 2 | 20 | 83 | 42 | 0 | .235 |
| 1988 | NYN ... | 130 | 455 | 39 | 110 | 16 | 2 | 11 | 46 | 34 | 0 | .242 |
| 1989 | NYN ... | 50 | 153 | 14 | 28 | 8 | 0 | 2 | 15 | 12 | 0 | .183 |
| | | 2008 | 7194 | 955 | 1907 | 329 | 30 | 304 | 1143 | 768 | 36 | .265 |

# Darren Daulton

Birth Date: 1/3/62
Bats: Left
Throws: Right
1989 Club:
Philadelphia Phillies
Contest Code #: 204

Rating: 1

Darren Daulton has had so many severe injuries over his pro career that he could double as the poster boy for the Mayo Clinic. Beyond the routine bumps and bruises every backstop collects, Daulton suffered tendinitis and nerve irritation in his right shoulder in 1984; strained his right shoulder in 1985 and missed half the season; tore the anterior cruciate ligament in his right knee in 1986 and missed the last three months of the season; had surgery to remove adhesions in his right knee in December 1986, and didn't return to action until April 16, 1987.

In 1988, he played regularly until August 27. On that day, he lost his temper, punched a wall in the clubhouse and broke his right hand, putting him out of action for the rest of the season.

In his guest-starring role as a major-league catcher,

Daulton hits for power but not for average. Last season, he collected six home runs during the first two months, but two thereafter. He had a reasonable ratio of walks to strikeouts, but had he sprayed the ball around he might have batted higher.

| Year | Team | G | AB | R | H | 2B | 3B | HR | RBI | BB | SB | AVG |
|------|------|-----|-----|----|-----|----|----|----|-----|-----|----|------|
| 1983 | Phi .... | 2 | 3 | 1 | 1 | 0 | 0 | 0 | 0 | 1 | 0 | .333 |
| 1985 | Phi .... | 36 | 103 | 14 | 21 | 3 | 1 | 4 | 11 | 16 | 3 | .204 |
| 1986 | Phi .... | 49 | 138 | 18 | 31 | 4 | 0 | 8 | 21 | 38 | 2 | .225 |
| 1987 | Phi .... | 53 | 129 | 10 | 25 | 6 | 0 | 3 | 13 | 16 | 0 | .194 |
| 1988 | Phi .... | 58 | 144 | 13 | 30 | 6 | 0 | 1 | 12 | 17 | 2 | .208 |
| 1989 | Phi .... | 131 | 368 | 29 | 74 | 12 | 2 | 8 | 44 | 52 | 2 | .201 |
| | | 329 | 885 | 85 | 182 | 31 | 3 | 24 | 101 | 140 | 9 | .206 |

# Jody Davis

Birth Date: 11/12/56
Bats: Right
Throws: Right
1989 Club:
Atlanta Braves
Contest Code #: 205

Rating: 1

Go figure this one: In 1988, the Braves talked and talked about their youth movement, but late that season they traded two pitching prospects to the Cubs for fading catcher Jody Davis.

Back in 1983, Davis was considered among the National League's best backstops. That year, he batted .271, with 24 home runs and 84 RBI's. Though he remained a power threat, his numbers would never be as strong again. Each season, he succumbed to a new injury that hampered his output. In 1988, Cubs manager Don Zimmer benched Davis and installed rookie Damon Berryhill as his regular catcher.

In 1989, Davis was atrocious at the plate. Things got so bad that he wound up splitting time with Bruce (.194) Benedict and John (.182) Russell.

| Year | Team | G | AB | R | H | 2B | 3B | HR | RBI | BB | SB | AVG |
|------|------|-----|------|-----|-----|-----|----|-----|-----|-----|----|------|
| 1981 | ChN.... | 56 | 180 | 14 | 46 | 5 | 1 | 4 | 21 | 21 | 0 | .256 |
| 1982 | ChN.... | 130 | 418 | 41 | 109 | 20 | 2 | 12 | 52 | 36 | 0 | .261 |
| 1983 | ChN.... | 151 | 510 | 56 | 138 | 31 | 2 | 24 | 84 | 33 | 0 | .271 |
| 1984 | ChN.... | 150 | 523 | 55 | 134 | 25 | 2 | 19 | 94 | 47 | 5 | .256 |
| 1985 | ChN.... | 142 | 482 | 47 | 112 | 30 | 0 | 17 | 58 | 48 | 1 | .232 |
| 1986 | ChN.... | 148 | 528 | 61 | 132 | 27 | 2 | 21 | 74 | 41 | 0 | .250 |
| 1987 | ChN.... | 125 | 428 | 57 | 106 | 12 | 2 | 19 | 51 | 52 | 1 | .248 |
| 1988 | ChN.... | 88 | 249 | 19 | 57 | 9 | 0 | 6 | 33 | 29 | 0 | .229 |
| 1988 | Atl ..... | 2 | 8 | 2 | 2 | 0 | 0 | 1 | 3 | 0 | 0 | .250 |
| 1989 | Atl ..... | 78 | 231 | 12 | 39 | 5 | 0 | 4 | 19 | 23 | 0 | .169 |
| | | 1070 | 3557 | 364 | 875 | 164 | 11 | 127 | 489 | 330 | 7 | .246 |

# Rick Dempsey

Birth Date: 9/13/49
Bats: Right
Throws: Right
1989 Club:
Los Angeles Dodgers
Contest Code #: 206

Rating: 1

Rick Dempsey has done a nice job as the Dodgers' backup catcher the last two seasons. In his rare appearances, the 21-year veteran has chipped in with some clutch hits.

Nonetheless, his role with the Dodgers is tenuous; as soon as they can develop a catcher for their future, Dempsey will be forced into retirement. But Dempsey, a funny guy who works hard, seems to have fit in well with the Dodgers, so if he doesn't land a full-time broadcasting job (he's done radio and television commentary in the past), the Dodgers may offer him a coaching position.

| Year | Team | G | AB | R | H | 2B | 3B | HR | RBI | BB | SB | AVG |
|------|------|---|----|---|---|----|----|----|-----|----|----|------|
| 1969 | Min .... | 5 | 6 | 1 | 3 | 1 | 0 | 0 | 0 | 1 | 0 | .500 |

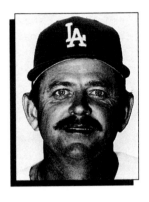

| Year | Team | G | AB | R | H | 2B | 3B | HR | RBI | BB | SB | AVG |
|---|---|---|---|---|---|---|---|---|---|---|---|---|
| 1970 | Min .... | 5 | 7 | 1 | 0 | 0 | 0 | 0 | 0 | 1 | 0 | .000 |
| 1971 | Min .... | 6 | 13 | 2 | 4 | 1 | 0 | 0 | 0 | 1 | 0 | .308 |
| 1972 | Min .... | 25 | 40 | 0 | 8 | 1 | 0 | 0 | 0 | 6 | 0 | .200 |
| 1973 | NYA.... | 6 | 11 | 0 | 2 | 0 | 0 | 0 | 0 | 1 | 0 | .182 |
| 1974 | NYA.... | 43 | 109 | 12 | 26 | 3 | 0 | 2 | 12 | 8 | 1 | .239 |
| 1975 | NYA.... | 71 | 145 | 18 | 38 | 8 | 0 | 1 | 11 | 21 | 0 | .262 |
| 1976 | Bal .... | 59 | 174 | 11 | 37 | 2 | 0 | 0 | 10 | 13 | 1 | .213 |
| 1976 | NYA.... | 21 | 42 | 1 | 5 | 0 | 0 | 0 | 2 | 5 | 0 | .119 |
| 1977 | Bal .... | 91 | 270 | 27 | 61 | 7 | 4 | 3 | 34 | 34 | 2 | .226 |
| 1978 | Bal .... | 136 | 441 | 41 | 114 | 25 | 0 | 6 | 32 | 48 | 7 | .259 |
| 1979 | Bal .... | 124 | 368 | 48 | 88 | 23 | 0 | 6 | 41 | 38 | 0 | .239 |
| 1980 | Bal .... | 119 | 362 | 51 | 95 | 26 | 3 | 9 | 40 | 36 | 3 | .262 |
| 1981 | Bal .... | 92 | 251 | 24 | 54 | 10 | 1 | 6 | 15 | 32 | 0 | .215 |
| 1982 | Bal .... | 125 | 344 | 35 | 88 | 15 | 1 | 5 | 36 | 46 | 0 | .256 |
| 1983 | Bal .... | 128 | 347 | 33 | 80 | 16 | 2 | 4 | 32 | 40 | 1 | .231 |
| 1984 | Bal .... | 109 | 330 | 37 | 76 | 11 | 0 | 11 | 34 | 40 | 1 | .230 |
| 1985 | Bal .... | 132 | 362 | 54 | 92 | 19 | 0 | 12 | 52 | 50 | 0 | .254 |
| 1986 | Bal .... | 122 | 327 | 42 | 68 | 15 | 1 | 13 | 29 | 45 | 1 | .208 |
| 1987 | Cle..... | 60 | 141 | 16 | 25 | 10 | 0 | 1 | 9 | 23 | 0 | .177 |
| 1988 | LA .... | 77 | 167 | 25 | 42 | 13 | 0 | 7 | 30 | 25 | 1 | .251 |
| 1989 | LA .... | 79 | 151 | 16 | 27 | 7 | 0 | 4 | 16 | 30 | 1 | .179 |
| | | 1635 | 4408 | 495 | 1033 | 213 | 12 | 90 | 435 | 544 | 19 | .234 |

# Mike Fitzgerald

**Birth Date: 7/13/60**
**Bats: Right**
**Throws: Right**
**1989 Club:**
**Montreal Expos**
**Contest Code #: 207**

**Rating: 1**

Mike Fitzgerald has the look of a journeyman catcher, even though he's played for only two pro teams. It seems as if he's been around for ages because he was noticed early in his career—in the nation's biggest media market—but has since popped in and out of box scores north of the U.S. border.

Fitzy's a nice guy whose best attributes as a player—he calls a good game, handles the pitchers well, blocks home plate aggressively—are of no interest to fantasy-team owners.

Though Fitzy doesn't have many major-league home runs, when he's hot he'll hit them in bunches. The assorted injuries to his fingers and hands have kept him from improving as a hitter.

| Year | Team | G | AB | R | H | 2B | 3B | HR | RBI | BB | SB | AVG |
|---|---|---|---|---|---|---|---|---|---|---|---|---|
| 1983 | NYN ... | 8 | 20 | 1 | 2 | 0 | 0 | 1 | 2 | 3 | 0 | .100 |
| 1984 | NYN ... | 112 | 360 | 20 | 87 | 15 | 1 | 2 | 33 | 24 | 1 | .242 |
| 1985 | Mon.... | 108 | 295 | 25 | 61 | 7 | 1 | 5 | 34 | 38 | 5 | .207 |
| 1986 | Mon.... | 73 | 209 | 20 | 59 | 13 | 1 | 6 | 37 | 27 | 3 | .282 |
| 1987 | Mon.... | 107 | 287 | 32 | 69 | 11 | 0 | 3 | 36 | 42 | 3 | .240 |
| 1988 | Mon.... | 63 | 155 | 17 | 42 | 6 | 1 | 5 | 23 | 19 | 2 | .271 |
| 1989 | Mon.... | 100 | 290 | 33 | 69 | 18 | 2 | 7 | 42 | 35 | 3 | .238 |
| | | 571 | 1616 | 148 | 389 | 70 | 6 | 29 | 207 | 188 | 17 | .241 |

# Joe Girardi

**Birth Date: 10/14/64**
**Bats: Right**
**Throws: Right**
**1989 Club:**
**Chicago Cubs**
**Contest Code #: 208**

**Rating: 2**

Joe Girardi, the pride of East Peoria, Illinois, jumped from Double A in 1988 to the bigs on Opening Day 1989, the first rookie catcher to start a Cubs opener since Randy Hundley in 1966. Actually, Girardi was on hand only because the incumbent, Damon Berryhill, was on the disabled list. When Berryhill returned, Girardi was sent to Triple A. But he returned for good on June 13, and took over the starting role when Berryhill tore his rotator cuff muscles.

Girardi, who received a degree in industrial engineering from Northwestern University in 1986, was chosen by the Cubs in the fifth round of the June draft. At Class A Peoria, Girardi batted .309. The following year, he batted .280 for Class A Winston-Salem and was named to

the mid-season and post-season Carolina League All-Star team. In August 1988, Girardi was batting .272 at Double A Pittsfield when he suffered a separated shoulder and was through for the season.

Before the 1988 season, National League sources told me the Cubs regarded Girardi as their catcher of the future. Berryhill's injuries accelerated the timetable, so Girardi may need another year of experience before he can establish himself among the league's top catchers.

| Year | Team | G | AB | R | H | 2B | 3B | HR | RBI | BB | SB | AVG |
|------|------|---|----|---|---|----|----|----|-----|----|----|-----|
| 1989 | ChN.... | 59 | 157 | 15 | 39 | 10 | 0 | 1 | 14 | 11 | 2 | .248 |
| | | 59 | 157 | 15 | 39 | 10 | 0 | 1 | 14 | 11 | 2 | .248 |

# Terry Kennedy

**Birth Date: 6/4/56**
**Bats: Left**
**Throws: Right**
**1989 Club:**
**San Francisco Giants**
**Contest Code #: 209**

**Rating: 3**

Terry Kennedy is still riding his 1982 season for all it's worth. Mention Kennedy to fantasy-team owners, and many will talk about his ability to produce runs. Wake up and smell the coffee, folks: Since the start of 1984, Kennedy has hit 14, 10, 12, 18, 3, and 5 home runs, and driven in 57, 74, 57, 62, 16 and 34. Last season, Kennedy had more walks (35) than RBI's.

But Kennedy needn't lose any sleep over this. First, his backup, Kirk Manwaring, can't hit much better. Second, there are few catchers in the National League who can hit much better. Third, Kennedy's father, Bob, is the Giants' vice-president of baseball operations.

| Year | Team | G | AB | R | H | 2B | 3B | HR | RBI | BB | SB | AVG |
|------|------|---|----|---|---|----|----|----|-----|----|----|-----|
| 1978 | StL .... | 10 | 29 | 0 | 5 | 0 | 0 | 0 | 2 | 4 | 0 | .172 |
| 1979 | StL .... | 33 | 109 | 11 | 31 | 7 | 0 | 2 | 17 | 6 | 0 | .284 |
| 1980 | StL .... | 84 | 248 | 28 | 63 | 12 | 3 | 4 | 34 | 28 | 0 | .254 |
| 1981 | SD..... | 101 | 382 | 32 | 115 | 24 | 1 | 2 | 41 | 22 | 0 | .301 |
| 1982 | SD..... | 153 | 562 | 75 | 166 | 42 | 1 | 21 | 97 | 26 | 1 | .295 |
| 1983 | SD..... | 149 | 549 | 47 | 156 | 27 | 2 | 17 | 98 | 51 | 1 | .284 |
| 1984 | SD..... | 148 | 530 | 54 | 127 | 16 | 1 | 14 | 57 | 33 | 1 | .240 |
| 1985 | SD..... | 143 | 532 | 54 | 139 | 27 | 1 | 10 | 74 | 31 | 0 | .261 |
| 1986 | SD..... | 141 | 432 | 46 | 114 | 22 | 1 | 12 | 57 | 37 | 0 | .264 |
| 1987 | Bal .... | 143 | 512 | 51 | 128 | 13 | 1 | 18 | 62 | 35 | 1 | .250 |
| 1988 | Bal .... | 85 | 265 | 20 | 60 | 10 | 0 | 3 | 16 | 15 | 0 | .226 |
| 1989 | SF ..... | 125 | 355 | 19 | 85 | 15 | 0 | 5 | 34 | 35 | 1 | .239 |
| | | 1315 | 4505 | 437 | 1189 | 215 | 11 | 108 | 589 | 323 | 5 | .264 |

# Mike LaValliere

**Birth Date: 8/18/60**
**Bats: Left**
**Throws: Right**
**1989 Club:**
**Pittsburgh Pirates**
**Contest Code #: 210**

**Rating: 3**

Who's the only player in baseball whose first and last names mean audio amplification equipment? Mike (as in microphone) LaValliere (a lavalier—two l's, not three—is a clip-on microphone).

LaValliere, who vies for the title of Roundest Man in the National League, is a slashing, line-drive hitter who has made his name with the Pirates as a producer in the clutch. Since leaving the Cardinals, he's become a good hitter by being more selective and hitting the ball where it's pitched.

He missed a lot of time last season because of a knee injury, but he came back strong, leading the team in batting (.316, 60 for 190). Under normal circumstances, he plays virtually every day because he's an outstanding defensive catcher; his pitchers just love him.

| Year | Team | G | AB | R | H | 2B | 3B | HR | RBI | BB | SB | AVG |
|---|---|---|---|---|---|---|---|---|---|---|---|---|
| 1984 | Phi .... | 6 | 7 | 0 | 0 | 0 | 0 | 0 | 0 | 2 | 0 | .000 |
| 1985 | StL .... | 12 | 34 | 2 | 5 | 1 | 0 | 0 | 6 | 7 | 0 | .147 |
| 1986 | StL .... | 110 | 303 | 18 | 71 | 10 | 2 | 3 | 30 | 36 | 0 | .234 |
| 1987 | Pit ..... | 121 | 340 | 33 | 102 | 19 | 0 | 1 | 36 | 43 | 0 | .300 |
| 1988 | Pit ..... | 120 | 352 | 24 | 92 | 18 | 0 | 2 | 47 | 50 | 3 | .261 |
| 1989 | Pit ..... | 68 | 190 | 15 | 60 | 10 | 0 | 2 | 23 | 29 | 0 | .316 |
| | | 437 | 1226 | 92 | 330 | 58 | 2 | 8 | 142 | 167 | 3 | .269 |

# Barry Lyons

Birth Date: 6/3/60
Bats: Right
Throws: Right
1989 Club:
New York Mets
Contest Code #: 211

Rating: 2

**B**arry Lyons, president of the Steve Balboni Look-alike Club, climbed the Mets' catching ladder last season, rising from third string to top banana. Some of it was his doing; he batted .247 in 235 at-bats. Mostly, his ascension was due to Gary Carter's injuries and ineffectiveness, Mackey Sasser's inability to throw the ball back to the pitcher (*see* Mackey Sasser), and the inexperience of minor-leaguer Phil Lombardi.

Lyons missed some time himself because of injury, but since he is the Mets' best defensive catcher, he goes into the 1990 season as the front runner for the starting job.

Already, Lyons has outlasted Carter, Mike Fitzgerald, and John Gibbons in tenure with the Mets' organization.

| Year | Team | G | AB | R | H | 2B | 3B | HR | RBI | BB | SB | AVG |
|---|---|---|---|---|---|---|---|---|---|---|---|---|
| 1986 | NYN ... | 6 | 9 | 1 | 0 | 0 | 0 | 0 | 2 | 1 | 0 | .000 |
| 1987 | NYN ... | 53 | 130 | 15 | 33 | 4 | 1 | 4 | 24 | 8 | 0 | .254 |
| 1988 | NYN ... | 50 | 91 | 5 | 21 | 7 | 1 | 0 | 11 | 3 | 0 | .231 |
| 1989 | NYN ... | 79 | 235 | 15 | 58 | 13 | 0 | 3 | 27 | 11 | 0 | .247 |
| | | 188 | 465 | 36 | 112 | 24 | 2 | 7 | 64 | 23 | 0 | .241 |

# Kirt Manwaring

Birth Date: 7/16/65
Bats: Right
Throws: Right
1989 Club:
San Francisco Giants
Contest Code #: 212

Rating: 1

**I**f you could sew Terry Kennedy's bat onto Kirt Manwaring's body, you'd have a good major-league catcher, one who could hit and field.

Manwaring, the Giants' best defensive catcher, batted .210 last season, with 18 RBI's in 200 at-bats. Manwaring once batted .282 in Triple A (1988), but he's never hit more than two home runs or driven in more than 35 runs in the four seasons of his professional career.

| Year | Team | G | AB | R | H | 2B | 3B | HR | RBI | BB | SB | AVG |
|---|---|---|---|---|---|---|---|---|---|---|---|---|
| 1987 | SF ..... | 6 | 7 | 0 | 1 | 0 | 0 | 0 | 0 | 0 | 0 | .143 |
| 1988 | SF ..... | 40 | 116 | 12 | 29 | 7 | 0 | 1 | 15 | 2 | 0 | .250 |
| 1989 | SF ..... | 85 | 200 | 14 | 42 | 4 | 2 | 0 | 18 | 11 | 2 | .210 |
| | | 131 | 323 | 26 | 72 | 11 | 2 | 1 | 33 | 13 | 2 | .223 |

# Tom Nieto

Birth Date: 10/27/60
Bats: Right
Throws: Right
1989 Club:
Philadelphia Phillies
Contest Code #: 213

### Rating: 1

**B**aseball has a cottage industry of Triple A catchers. Backstops like Tom Nieto easily qualify for the major-league pension by willingly shuttling up and down and all around whenever a big-league catching position opens up.

Nieto (who may be the only guy on the Phillies whom Steve Jeltz can laugh at) arrived in Philadelphia from Minnesota in 1989 with Tom Herr and outfielder Eric Bullock for pitcher Shane Rawley. Prior to his two seasons with the Twins, he'd played for the Expos and the Cardinals.

Last season, Nieto was called up in August to replace injured catcher Steve Lake. In 20 at-bats, he managed 3 hits and 6 walks. If he doesn't make the Phils this season, he'll play with another big-league club at another point in the season. He always seems to.

| Year | Team | G | AB | R | H | 2B | 3B | HR | RBI | BB | SB | AVG |
|------|------|---|-----|----|-----|----|----|----|-----|----|----|------|
| 1984 | StL .... | 33 | 86 | 7 | 24 | 4 | 0 | 3 | 12 | 5 | 0 | .279 |
| 1985 | StL .... | 95 | 253 | 15 | 57 | 10 | 2 | 0 | 34 | 26 | 0 | .225 |
| 1986 | Mon.... | 30 | 65 | 5 | 13 | 3 | 1 | 1 | 7 | 6 | 0 | .200 |
| 1987 | Min.... | 41 | 105 | 7 | 21 | 7 | 1 | 1 | 12 | 8 | 0 | .200 |
| 1988 | Min.... | 24 | 60 | 1 | 4 | 0 | 0 | 0 | 0 | 1 | 0 | .067 |
| 1989 | Phi .... | 11 | 20 | 1 | 3 | 0 | 0 | 0 | 0 | 6 | 0 | .150 |
| | | 234 | 589 | 36 | 122 | 24 | 4 | 5 | 65 | 52 | 0 | .207 |

# Joe Oliver

Birth Date: 7/25/65
Bats: Right
Throws: Right
1989 Club:
Cincinnati Reds
Contest Code #: 214

### Rating: 2

**T**he Reds have been high on Joe Oliver's defensive prowess since selecting him in the June 1982 draft. In 1983, Oliver was the top fielding catcher in the Pioneer League, leading the league in assists and making only five errors. In 1984, he finished second in the Midwest League with 85 assists, and the league managers voted him the catcher with the best arm. In 1985, Florida State League managers echoed that assessment.

So why haven't you heard about him? Because his bat had been stone silent until 1987. Playing for Double A Vermont that season, Oliver batted .305 with 10 home runs and 60 RBI's in only 236 at-bats (a broken finger shelved him for two months).

Last season, he made his major-league debut, thanks in part to Bo Diaz's injuries and Terry McGriff's feeble batting. Oliver batted .272, with 3 home runs and 23 RBI's in 151 at-bats. He is still considered the Reds' catcher of the future.

| Year | Team | G | AB | R | H | 2B | 3B | HR | RBI | BB | SB | AVG |
|------|------|---|-----|----|----|----|----|----|-----|----|----|------|
| 1989 | Cin .... | 49 | 151 | 13 | 41 | 8 | 0 | 3 | 23 | 6 | 0 | .272 |
| | | 49 | 151 | 13 | 41 | 8 | 0 | 3 | 23 | 6 | 0 | .272 |

# Junior Ortiz

Birth Date: 10/24/59
Bats: Right
Throws: Right
1989 Club:
Pittsburgh Pirates
Contest Code #: 215

Rating: 1

**J**unior Ortiz is one of the most spirited and well-liked players on the Pirates. He also has accepted his role as Mike LaValliere's caddy, and performs fairly well when called upon.

At the plate, Junior does the best he can. Last season, he had an off year, but in 1988 he batted .280, with 18 RBI's in 49 games. Oritz, a lifetime .268 hitter, has been with the Pirates longer than any current member.

Ortiz had originally signed with the Pirates in 1977, played in their system for five-plus seasons, and joined the big club in 1982. In 1983, he was traded to the Mets with pitcher Art Ray for Marvell Wynne and Steve Senteney. In December 1984, the Pirates drafted Ortiz from the Mets' unprotected list.

| Year | Team | G | AB | R | H | 2B | 3B | HR | RBI | BB | SB | AVG |
|------|------|---|----|---|---|----|----|----|-----|----|----|-----|
| 1982 | Pit..... | 7 | 15 | 1 | 3 | 1 | 0 | 0 | 0 | 1 | 0 | .200 |
| 1983 | NYN ... | 68 | 185 | 10 | 47 | 5 | 0 | 0 | 12 | 3 | 1 | .254 |
| 1983 | Pit..... | 5 | 8 | 1 | 1 | 0 | 0 | 0 | 0 | 1 | 0 | .125 |
| 1984 | NYN ... | 40 | 91 | 6 | 18 | 3 | 0 | 0 | 11 | 5 | 1 | .198 |
| 1985 | Pit..... | 23 | 72 | 4 | 21 | 2 | 0 | 1 | 5 | 3 | 1 | .292 |
| 1986 | Pit..... | 49 | 110 | 11 | 37 | 6 | 0 | 0 | 14 | 9 | 0 | .336 |
| 1987 | Pit..... | 75 | 192 | 16 | 52 | 8 | 1 | 1 | 22 | 15 | 0 | .271 |
| 1988 | Pit..... | 49 | 118 | 8 | 33 | 6 | 0 | 2 | 18 | 9 | 1 | .280 |
| 1989 | Pit..... | 91 | 230 | 16 | 50 | 6 | 1 | 1 | 22 | 20 | 2 | .217 |
| | | 407 | 1021 | 73 | 262 | 37 | 2 | 5 | 104 | 66 | 6 | .257 |

# Tom Pagnozzi

Birth Date: 7/30/62
Bats: Right
Throws: Right
1989 Club:
St. Louis Cardinals
Contest Code #: 216

Rating: 2

**T**om Pagnozzi once had a bright future with the Cardinals. Pagnozzi, drafted by the Cards in June 1983, had a fine season for Class A Springfield in 1984, batting .283 with 10 home runs and 68 RBI's. His 90 assists led all Midwest League catchers. In 1986, Pagnozzi was considered the Cardinals' best prospect and was included on their December 40-man roster. But on April 1, 1987, the Cards played a bad April Fools' Day joke on Pagnozzi; they traded for four-time All-Star Tony Pena.

Pagnozzi, demoted to Triple A Louisville, seemed to take it well. That season, he batted .313, with 14 home runs and 71 RBI's. In 1988, Pagnozzi played well in a backup role, and also saw time at first base and third. But last year, Pagnozzi hardly played, and, as a result, he hardly hit. Now the Cardinals see him as an understudy to their new catcher of the future, Todd Zeile.

| Year | Team | G | AB | R | H | 2B | 3B | HR | RBI | BB | SB | AVG |
|------|------|---|----|---|---|----|----|----|-----|----|----|-----|
| 1987 | StL .... | 27 | 48 | 8 | 9 | 1 | 0 | 2 | 9 | 4 | 1 | .188 |
| 1988 | StL .... | 81 | 195 | 17 | 55 | 9 | 0 | 0 | 15 | 11 | 0 | .282 |
| 1989 | StL .... | 52 | 80 | 3 | 12 | 2 | 0 | 0 | 3 | 6 | 0 | .150 |
| | | 160 | 323 | 28 | 76 | 12 | 0 | 2 | 27 | 21 | 1 | .235 |

# Mark Parent

Birth Date: 9/16/61
Bats: Right
Throws: Right
1989 Club:
San Diego Padres
Contest Code #: 217

Rating: 1

**M**ark Parent is easy to overlook. His backup status with the Padres limits his playing time, and his batting average is well below average. But if you're running low on ratings points as you fill out your roster, Parent might be a wise choice because of his home-run percentage.

In the past two seasons, 26 percent of Parent's hits have been home runs. Let's compare that percentage to the National League's top five home-run hitters in 1989: Kevin Mitchell, 30 percent; Howard Johnson, 22 percent; Eric Davis, 26 percent; Glenn Davis, 22 percent; and Ryne Sanberg, 17 percent.

In no way am I saying that Parent belongs in the class of those gentlemen, but he certainly merits consideration as your backup backstop.

| Year | Team | G | AB | R | H | 2B | 3B | HR | RBI | BB | SB | AVG |
|------|------|---|----|---|---|----|----|----|-----|----|----|-----|
| 1986 | SD..... | 8 | 14 | 1 | 2 | 0 | 0 | 0 | 0 | 1 | 0 | .143 |
| 1987 | SD..... | 12 | 25 | 0 | 2 | 0 | 0 | 0 | 2 | 0 | 0 | .080 |
| 1988 | SD..... | 41 | 118 | 9 | 23 | 3 | 0 | 6 | 15 | 6 | 0 | .195 |
| 1989 | SD..... | 52 | 141 | 12 | 27 | 4 | 0 | 7 | 21 | 8 | 1 | .191 |
| | | 113 | 298 | 22 | 54 | 7 | 0 | 13 | 38 | 15 | 1 | .181 |

# Jeff Reed

Birth Date: 11/12/62
Bats: Left
Throws: Right
1989 Club:
Cincinnati Reds
Contest Code #: 219

Rating: 1

**B**y now, you're probably as weary of reading about weak-hitting catchers as I am of writing about them. It's a dirty job, but someone has to do it. So let's get this over with quickly, shall we?

Jeff Reed is a .220 hitter. Last year, he hit three home runs, bringing his six-year major-league total to seven. He drove in 23 runs, hiking his career total to 70. Another member of the Triple A catchers' cottage industry, Reed was once traded for industry president Tom Nieto in 1987.

Reed broke in with the Twins, spending seven years in their organization, and was in the Expo organization for a year and a half. Jeff and his wife, Karen, live in Elizabethton, Tennessee, with their daughter, Lynzie, age two.

| Year | Team | G | AB | R | H | 2B | 3B | HR | RBI | BB | SB | AVG |
|------|------|---|----|---|---|----|----|----|-----|----|----|-----|
| 1984 | Min .... | 18 | 21 | 3 | 3 | 3 | 0 | 0 | 1 | 2 | 0 | .143 |
| 1985 | Min .... | 7 | 10 | 2 | 2 | 0 | 0 | 0 | 0 | 0 | 0 | .200 |
| 1986 | Min .... | 68 | 165 | 13 | 39 | 6 | 1 | 2 | 9 | 16 | 1 | .236 |
| 1987 | Mon.... | 75 | 207 | 15 | 44 | 11 | 0 | 1 | 21 | 12 | 0 | .213 |
| 1988 | Mon.... | 43 | 123 | 10 | 27 | 3 | 2 | 0 | 9 | 13 | 1 | .220 |
| 1988 | Cin .... | 49 | 142 | 10 | 33 | 6 | 0 | 1 | 7 | 15 | 0 | .232 |
| 1989 | Cin .... | 102 | 287 | 16 | 64 | 11 | 0 | 3 | 23 | 34 | 0 | .223 |
| | | 362 | 955 | 69 | 212 | 40 | 3 | 7 | 70 | 92 | 2 | .222 |

# John Russell

**Birth Date:** 9/2/61
**Bats:** Right
**Throws:** Right
**1989 Club:**
**Atlanta Braves**
**Contest Code #:** 220

**Rating: 1**

**B**ut wait, there's one more catcher to dispose of: Big John Russell. Last season, Russell caught and played the outfield. He batted .182 in 74 games, with 2 home runs, 9 RBI's and 53 strikeouts in 159 at-bats.

Russell has been a prodigious strikeout artist throughout his career. For example, in 1986 he struck out 103 times and had 25 walks—a 4-to-1 ratio—in only 315 at-bats. Look at it this way: He struck out once in every 3 at-bats. And that was during his best big-league season, a year in which he hit 13 home runs and drove in 60 runs.

Judging by his numbers, you'll find it hard to believe that Russell was the Phillies' Opening Day first baseman in 1985.

| Year | Team | G | AB | R | H | 2B | 3B | HR | RBI | BB | SB | AVG |
|------|------|---|----|----|----|----|----|----|-----|----|----|-----|
| 1984 | Phi .... | 39 | 99 | 11 | 28 | 8 | 1 | 2 | 11 | 12 | 0 | .283 |
| 1985 | Phi .... | 81 | 216 | 22 | 47 | 12 | 0 | 9 | 23 | 18 | 2 | .218 |
| 1986 | Phi .... | 93 | 315 | 35 | 76 | 21 | 2 | 13 | 60 | 25 | 0 | .241 |
| 1987 | Phi .... | 24 | 62 | 5 | 9 | 1 | 0 | 3 | 8 | 3 | 0 | .145 |
| 1988 | Phi .... | 22 | 49 | 5 | 12 | 1 | 0 | 2 | 4 | 3 | 0 | .245 |
| 1989 | Atl ..... | 74 | 159 | 14 | 29 | 2 | 0 | 2 | 9 | 8 | 0 | .182 |
| | | 333 | 900 | 92 | 201 | 45 | 3 | 31 | 115 | 69 | 2 | .223 |

# Benito Santiago

**Birth Date:** 3/9/65
**Bats:** Right
**Throws:** Right
**1989 Club:**
**San Diego Padres**
**Contest Code #:** 221

**Rating: 2**

**S**ome teams still have a high regard for Benito Santiago, the 1987 National League Rookie of the Year, who's been in a slump the past two seasons. I have devalued him among the league's catchers because of his attitude.

In 1988 and 1989, Santiago swung at pitches that weren't close to the strike zone. Last season, he was so sour, so unwilling to listen to his manager, so unreceptive to the suggestions of his batting coach to try hitting the ball to right field, that he wore out his welcome with the Padres.

When Santiago realizes that he's a high-average, line-drive hitter and not a power hitter, he'll be on the road to career recovery. And once he adopts a positive attitude, he'll be an asset on many teams. Until then, he's little more than a caustic player and .240 hitter.

| Year | Team | G | AB | R | H | 2B | 3B | HR | RBI | BB | SB | AVG |
|------|------|---|----|----|----|----|----|----|-----|----|----|-----|
| 1986 | SD ..... | 17 | 62 | 10 | 18 | 2 | 0 | 3 | 6 | 2 | 0 | .290 |
| 1987 | SD ..... | 146 | 546 | 64 | 164 | 33 | 2 | 18 | 79 | 16 | 21 | .300 |
| 1988 | SD ..... | 139 | 492 | 49 | 122 | 22 | 2 | 10 | 46 | 24 | 15 | .248 |
| 1989 | SD ..... | 129 | 462 | 50 | 109 | 16 | 3 | 16 | 62 | 26 | 11 | .236 |
| | | 431 | 1562 | 173 | 413 | 73 | 7 | 47 | 193 | 68 | 47 | .264 |

# Nelson Santovenia

Birth Date: 7/27/61
Bats: Right
Throws: Right
1989 Club:
Montreal Expos
Contest Code #: 222

Rating: 4

Early in his pro career, Nelson Santovenia hit like a 98-pound weakling. However, following the 1987 season, he embarked on a weightlifting and conditioning program that helped turn him into the catching stud he is today.

Playing for Double A Jacksonville in 1987, Santovenia (pronounced *San-toe-vayn-yuh*) batted .279, smacked 19 home runs, and knocked in 63 ribbies. He also reached personal highs in all defensive categories. There was no stopping this Goliath. In 1988, he came up to the big leagues for good, shoving Mike Fitzgerald aside and staking claim to the everyday catching job.

Last year, Santovenia batted .250 and drove in 31 runs in 97 games. His totals were hindered by injuries. With another winter of diligent physical training, Santovenia should be as good as new this season.

| Year | Team | G | AB | R | H | 2B | 3B | HR | RBI | BB | SB | AVG |
|------|------|---|-----|----|-----|----|----|----|-----|----|----|------|
| 1987 | Mon.... | 2 | 1 | 0 | 0 | 0 | 0 | 0 | 0 | 0 | 0 | .000 |
| 1988 | Mon.... | 92 | 309 | 26 | 73 | 20 | 2 | 8 | 41 | 24 | 2 | .236 |
| 1989 | Mon.... | 97 | 304 | 30 | 76 | 14 | 1 | 5 | 31 | 24 | 2 | .250 |
| | | 191 | 614 | 56 | 149 | 34 | 3 | 13 | 72 | 48 | 4 | .243 |

# Mackey Sasser

Birth Date: 8/3/62
Bats: Left
Throws: Right
1989 Club:
New York Mets
Contest Code #: 223

Rating: 3

Mackey Sasser could have—and should have—taken over as the Mets' full-time catcher when Gary Carter got hurt. Sasser hits line drives and runs the bases well. Someday, he may be a consistent .290 hitter. But Sasser had an odd mental block that put him on the bench: he couldn't throw the ball back to the pitcher.

Sasser would reach into his glove, pump-fake once, then lob the ball 60 feet, 6 inches. The word of his handicap spread like wildfire throughout the league, and before long even the slowest runners became brazen base stealers.

This spring, Mets' minor-league catching instructor Ven Hoscheit will spend countless hours helping Sasser correct his problem. If Sasser can overcome it, he should be able to wrest the starting job from Barry Lyons.

| Year | Team | G | AB | R | H | 2B | 3B | HR | RBI | BB | SB | AVG |
|------|------|---|-----|----|----|----|----|----|-----|----|----|------|
| 1987 | Pit..... | 12 | 23 | 2 | 5 | 0 | 0 | 0 | 2 | 0 | 0 | .217 |
| 1987 | SF..... | 2 | 4 | 0 | 0 | 0 | 0 | 0 | 0 | 0 | 0 | .000 |
| 1988 | NYN ... | 60 | 123 | 9 | 35 | 10 | 1 | 1 | 17 | 6 | 0 | .285 |
| 1989 | NYN ... | 72 | 182 | 17 | 53 | 14 | 2 | 1 | 22 | 7 | 0 | .291 |
| | | 146 | 332 | 28 | 93 | 24 | 3 | 2 | 41 | 13 | 0 | .280 |

# Mike Scioscia

Birth Date: 11/27/58
Bats: Left
Throws: Right
1989 Club:
Los Angeles Dodgers
Contest Code #: 224

Rating: 5

**M**ike Scioscia has been a solid performer for 10 major-league seasons. Last year, at age thirty, he had one of his finest seasons ever. In 133 games, Scoscia batted .250, with 10 home runs and 44 RBI's. He also walked 52 times and struck out only 29 times. Scioscia had such a good time that he even joined once-porcine manager Tom Lasorda on a liquid-diet television ad campaign.

Scioscia was originally chosen by the Dodgers in the first round of the June 1976 draft. Four years later, he was in L.A. to stay. Regarded as one of the league's toughest players, Scioscia is frequently involved in fierce collisions at home plate and has been disabled five times in 10 years.

Scioscia is so consistent that we can plug in his 1990 numbers right now: a .265 batting average, 7 home runs, and 50 RBI's.

| Year | Team | G | AB | R | H | 2B | 3B | HR | RBI | BB | SB | AVG |
|------|------|-----|------|-----|-----|-----|----|----|-----|-----|----|------|
| 1980 | LA..... | 54 | 134 | 8 | 34 | 5 | 1 | 1 | 8 | 12 | 1 | .254 |
| 1981 | LA..... | 93 | 290 | 27 | 80 | 10 | 0 | 2 | 29 | 36 | 0 | .276 |
| 1982 | LA..... | 129 | 365 | 31 | 80 | 11 | 1 | 5 | 38 | 44 | 2 | .219 |
| 1983 | LA..... | 12 | 35 | 3 | 11 | 3 | 0 | 1 | 7 | 5 | 0 | .314 |
| 1984 | LA..... | 114 | 341 | 29 | 93 | 18 | 0 | 5 | 38 | 52 | 2 | .273 |
| 1985 | LA..... | 141 | 429 | 47 | 127 | 26 | 3 | 7 | 53 | 77 | 3 | .296 |
| 1986 | LA..... | 122 | 374 | 36 | 94 | 18 | 1 | 5 | 26 | 62 | 3 | .251 |
| 1987 | LA..... | 142 | 461 | 44 | 122 | 26 | 1 | 6 | 38 | 55 | 7 | .265 |
| 1988 | LA..... | 130 | 408 | 29 | 105 | 18 | 0 | 3 | 35 | 38 | 0 | .257 |
| 1989 | LA..... | 133 | 408 | 40 | 102 | 16 | 0 | 10 | 44 | 52 | 0 | .250 |
|  |  | 1070 | 3245 | 294 | 848 | 151 | 7 | 45 | 316 | 433 | 18 | .261 |

# Don Slaught

Birth Date: 9/11/58
Bats: Right
Throws: Right
1989 Club:
New York Yankees
Contest Code #: 225

Rating: 3

**B**ack in 1986, Don Slaught was hitting .293 with 7 homers and 23 RBI's 23 games into the Texas Rangers' season. Then an Oil Can Boyd fastball fractured his nose and cheekbone, requiring surgery and two months on the disabled list. Slaught's offense has never returned to those levels.

The 6'1", 190-pound Slaught is a blue-collar worker behind the plate. He's tough, works hard, and is a real student of the game. He can handle the pitching staff, a big help to any manager. Still, he's really no better than adequate as a backstop, taking fullest advantage of the tools available to him. Offensively, Slaught failed to reach the higher standards he set for himself in 1988, when he hit around .300 for most of the season before slipping to .283 with 25 doubles and 9 homers. In 1989, the one-time Royal and Ranger hit .251 with 21 doubles and 5 round-trippers. Traded to the Pirates during the off-season, he will contribue to the club—it's just a question of how much.

| Year | Team | G | AB | R | H | 2B | 3B | HR | RBI | BB | SB | AVG |
|------|------|-----|------|-----|-----|-----|----|----|-----|-----|----|------|
| 1982 | KC..... | 43 | 115 | 14 | 32 | 6 | 0 | 3 | 8 | 9 | 0 | .278 |
| 1983 | KC..... | 83 | 276 | 21 | 86 | 13 | 4 | 0 | 28 | 11 | 3 | .312 |
| 1984 | KC..... | 124 | 409 | 48 | 108 | 27 | 4 | 4 | 42 | 20 | 0 | .264 |
| 1985 | Tex .... | 102 | 343 | 34 | 96 | 17 | 4 | 8 | 35 | 20 | 5 | .280 |
| 1986 | Tex .... | 95 | 314 | 39 | 83 | 17 | 1 | 13 | 46 | 16 | 3 | .264 |
| 1987 | Tex .... | 95 | 237 | 25 | 53 | 15 | 2 | 8 | 16 | 24 | 0 | .224 |
| 1988 | NYA.... | 97 | 322 | 33 | 91 | 25 | 1 | 9 | 43 | 24 | 1 | .283 |
| 1989 | NYA.... | 117 | 350 | 34 | 88 | 21 | 3 | 5 | 38 | 30 | 1 | .251 |
|  |  | 756 | 2366 | 248 | 637 | 141 | 19 | 50 | 256 | 154 | 13 | .269 |

# Alex Trevino

**Birth Date: 8/26/57**
**Bats: Right**
**Throws: Right**
**1989 Club:**
**Houston Astros**
**Contest Code #: 226**

**Rating: 2**

Alex Trevino was the right man for the Astros' backup catching job last season. When starter Craig Biggio rested, Trevino chimed in with a .290 batting average, with 2 home runs and 16 RBI's in only 131 at-bats.

Trevino, who first played in the Mexican League before being sold to the Mets in 1974, has since played with every National League West team except the Padres (no chance of that happening anytime soon). He's always had a good glove, but can't generate even line-drive power. In his early years with the Mets, he looked overmatched at the plate, but today he can hold his own against major-league pitching.

| Year | Team | G | AB | R | H | 2B | 3B | HR | RBI | BB | SB | AVG |
|------|------|---|----|----|----|----|----|----|-----|----|----|------|
| 1978 | NYN ... | 6 | 12 | 3 | 3 | 0 | 0 | 0 | 0 | 1 | 0 | .250 |
| 1979 | NYN ... | 79 | 207 | 24 | 56 | 11 | 1 | 0 | 20 | 20 | 2 | .271 |
| 1980 | NYN ... | 106 | 355 | 26 | 91 | 11 | 2 | 0 | 37 | 13 | 0 | .256 |
| 1981 | NYN ... | 56 | 149 | 17 | 39 | 2 | 0 | 0 | 10 | 13 | 3 | .262 |
| 1982 | Cin .... | 120 | 355 | 24 | 89 | 10 | 3 | 1 | 33 | 34 | 3 | .251 |
| 1983 | Cin .... | 74 | 167 | 14 | 36 | 8 | 1 | 1 | 13 | 17 | 0 | .216 |
| 1984 | Cin .... | 6 | 6 | 0 | 1 | 0 | 0 | 0 | 0 | 0 | 0 | .167 |
| 1984 | Atl ..... | 79 | 266 | 36 | 65 | 16 | 1 | 3 | 28 | 16 | 5 | .244 |
| 1985 | SF ..... | 57 | 157 | 17 | 34 | 10 | 1 | 6 | 19 | 20 | 0 | .217 |
| 1986 | LA ..... | 89 | 202 | 31 | 53 | 13 | 0 | 4 | 26 | 27 | 0 | .262 |
| 1987 | LA ..... | 72 | 144 | 16 | 32 | 7 | 1 | 3 | 16 | 6 | 1 | .222 |
| 1988 | Hou.... | 78 | 193 | 19 | 48 | 17 | 0 | 2 | 13 | 24 | 5 | .249 |
| 1989 | Hou.... | 59 | 131 | 15 | 38 | 7 | 1 | 2 | 16 | 7 | 0 | .290 |
| | | 881 | 2344 | 242 | 585 | 112 | 10 | 22 | 231 | 198 | 19 | .250 |

# Rick Wrona

**Birth Date: 12/10/63**
**Bats: Right**
**Throws: Right**
**1989 Club:**
**Chicago Cubs**
**Contest Code #: 227**

**Rating: 1**

Rick Wrona turned out to be a pleasant surprise for the Cubs last season. After three undistinguished minor-league seasons, Wrona, the Cubs' fifth-round pick in the June 1985 draft, was left off the team's 40-man roster. But the Cubs invited him to spring training last season, and he made the big club as Damon Berryhill's backup. Wrona was sent to Triple A in June when Joe Girardi was recalled, but he returned to Chicago in August as Girardi's caddie when Berryhill suffered a season-ending injury.

In 38 games, Wrona hit a perky .283 and was involved in some of the division-winning Cubs' season highlights. On June 8, in a nationally televised game against the Mets, Wrona delivered a game-winning squeeze bunt in the bottom of the twelfth inning. On August 25, in his first game back after being recalled from Iowa, Wrona singled and scored the winning run in the twelfth inning of a 4–3 victory over the Braves. And on September 26, Wrona's triple drove in the Cubs' first run in their division-clinching victory over Montreal.

What more can you ask from a backup catcher?

| Year | Team | G | AB | R | H | 2B | 3B | HR | RBI | BB | SB | AVG |
|------|------|---|----|----|----|----|----|----|-----|----|----|------|
| 1988 | ChN.... | 4 | 6 | 0 | 0 | 0 | 0 | 0 | 0 | 0 | 0 | .000 |
| 1989 | ChN.... | 38 | 92 | 11 | 26 | 2 | 1 | 2 | 14 | 2 | 0 | .283 |
| | | 42 | 98 | 11 | 26 | 2 | 1 | 2 | 14 | 2 | 0 | .265 |

# Todd Zeile

**Birth Date:** 9/9/65
**Bats:** Right
**Throws:** Right
**1989 Club:**
**St. Louis Cardinals**
**Contest Code #:** 228

**Rating: 4**

**T**odd Zeile has been hailed by scouts, minor-league officials, and Cardinals' manager Whitey Herzog as the best catching prospect in baseball.

Zeile, who in his collegiate career at the University of Southern California had been selected team MVP and twice named to the all-PAC 10 team, was chosen by the Cards in the third round of the June 1986 draft. That summer, Zeile earned All-Star honors in the New York-Penn League by hitting 14 home runs and amassing 122 total bases in 70 games. In 1987, Zeile hit .292, with 25 home runs and 106 RBI's for Class A Springfield and shared the Midwest League MVP award with Beloit's Greg Vaughn. Following that season, Zeile broke a bone in his hand in winter ball and struggled during the early stages of the 1988 season. When his hand healed, Zeile went on a tear playing for Double A Arkansas, and was named to the Texas League All-Star team.

Last August, Zeile was promoted to the majors after batting .292, with 19 home runs and 84 RBI's for Triple-A Louisville. It's only a matter of time before Zeile becomes the Cards' full-time catcher.

| Year | Team | G | AB | R | H | 2B | 3B | HR | RBI | BB | SB | AVG |
|------|------|---|----|----|---|----|----|----|-----|----|----|-----|
| 1989 | StL .... | 28 | 82 | 7 | 21 | 3 | 1 | 1 | 8 | 9 | 0 | .256 |
| | | 28 | 82 | 7 | 21 | 3 | 1 | 1 | 8 | 9 | 0 | .256 |

# Ernie Whitt

**Birth Date:** 6/13/52
**Bats:** Left
**Throws:** Right
**1989 Club:**
**Toronto Blue Jays**
**Contest Code #:** 229

**Rating: 4**

**Y**ou start to worry when you have a thirty-seven-year-old catcher, but not if he's Ernie Whitt. An original Toronto Blue Jay, selected off the Boston Red Sox roster during the 1976 expansion draft, Whitt is the Jays' all-time backstop. Fact is, Whitt has retained most of his skills at an age when most players have gone backward. His .261 batting average last year was 10 points better than his previous career mark. He's hitting better today than he did a decade ago. His 11 homers marked his eighth straight year in double-figures. Even better, the Michigan native can still do the job behind the plate. Throwing is an increasing problem, and he never could run. But he can handle pitchers, and they have confidence in him. A good glove, solid catching savvy, a decent bat with decent power...all plusses for one of Toronto's leading lights.

| Year | Team | G | AB | R | H | 2B | 3B | HR | RBI | BB | SB | AVG |
|------|------|----|-----|----|-----|-----|----|-----|-----|-----|----|------|
| 1976 | Bos .... | 8 | 18 | 4 | 4 | 2 | 0 | 1 | 3 | 2 | 0 | .222 |
| 1977 | Tor..... | 23 | 41 | 4 | 7 | 3 | 0 | 0 | 6 | 2 | 0 | .171 |
| 1978 | Tor..... | 2 | 4 | 0 | 0 | 0 | 0 | 0 | 0 | 1 | 0 | .000 |
| 1980 | Tor..... | 106 | 295 | 23 | 70 | 12 | 2 | 6 | 34 | 22 | 1 | .237 |
| 1981 | Tor..... | 74 | 195 | 16 | 46 | 9 | 0 | 1 | 16 | 20 | 5 | .236 |
| 1982 | Tor..... | 105 | 284 | 28 | 74 | 14 | 2 | 11 | 42 | 26 | 3 | .261 |
| 1983 | Tor..... | 123 | 344 | 53 | 88 | 15 | 2 | 17 | 56 | 50 | 1 | .256 |
| 1984 | Tor..... | 124 | 315 | 35 | 75 | 12 | 1 | 15 | 46 | 43 | 0 | .238 |
| 1985 | Tor..... | 139 | 412 | 55 | 101 | 21 | 2 | 19 | 64 | 47 | 3 | .245 |
| 1986 | Tor..... | 131 | 395 | 48 | 106 | 19 | 2 | 16 | 56 | 35 | 0 | .268 |
| 1987 | Tor..... | 135 | 446 | 57 | 120 | 24 | 1 | 19 | 75 | 44 | 0 | .269 |
| 1988 | Tor..... | 127 | 398 | 63 | 100 | 11 | 2 | 16 | 70 | 61 | 4 | .251 |
| 1989 | Tor..... | 129 | 385 | 42 | 101 | 24 | 1 | 11 | 53 | 52 | 5 | .262 |
| | | 1226 | 3532 | 428 | 892 | 166 | 15 | 132 | 521 | 405 | 22 | .253 |

# OUTFIELDERS

# OUTFIELDERS

## Shawn Abner

Birth Date: 6/17/66
Bats: Right
Throws: Right
1989 Club:
San Diego Padres
Contest Code #: 251

Rating: 1

In 1986, the worst-kept secret in the Mets' organization was that Shawn Abner, the team's number-one choice (and first player selected) in the June 1984 draft, couldn't hit a curveball. Teammates knew it, the media wrote about it. It seemed that only one person in baseball didn't know it: Ballard Smith, the son-in-law of Padres' owner Joan Kroc.

Back then, Smith was in charge of San Diego's trades. When the Mets wanted Kevin McReynolds, Smith countered by asking for Abner. I wish I could have seen the looks on the faces of the Mets' brass. In short order, McReynolds and Abner became the principles in an eight-player trade. Four years have gone by—and Abner still can't hit a curveball.

| Year | Team | G | AB | R | H | 2B | 3B | HR | RBI | BB | SB | AVG |
|------|------|---|----|----|----|----|----|----|-----|----|----|-----|
| 1987 | SD..... | 16 | 47 | 5 | 13 | 3 | 1 | 2 | 7 | 2 | 1 | .277 |
| 1988 | SD..... | 37 | 83 | 6 | 15 | 3 | 0 | 2 | 5 | 4 | 0 | .181 |
| 1989 | SD..... | 57 | 102 | 13 | 18 | 4 | 0 | 2 | 14 | 5 | 1 | .176 |
| | | 110 | 232 | 24 | 46 | 10 | 1 | 6 | 26 | 11 | 2 | .198 |

## Kevin Bass

Birth Date: 5/12/59
Bats: Right and Left
Throws: Right
1989 Club:
Houston Astros
Contest Code #: 252

Rating: 3

Despite a .300 batting average, Kevin Bass had a disappointing season last year. A bruised right shin limited him to 313 plate appearances. Once a dependable run producer, Bass managed only 5 home runs and 44 RBI's.

The shin bruise probably saved his career with Houston for the time being. Bass, who had had a sub-par 1988 season, was being shopped around both leagues at the start of 1989, but the injury kept him on the sidelines for two months.

During the off season, Bass signed a three-year contract with the Giants; he will be better off away from Houston.The Astros had been asking him to bat fifth, as protection for clean-up hitter Glenn Davis, but Bass' skills—line-drive hitting, speed on the bases—are more suited for the number-two or number-three spots in the order.

| Year | Team | G | AB | R | H | 2B | 3B | HR | RBI | BB | SB | AVG |
|------|------|---|----|----|----|----|----|----|-----|----|----|-----|
| 1982 | Mil.... | 18 | 9 | 4 | 0 | 0 | 0 | 0 | 0 | 1 | 0 | .000 |
| 1982 | Hou.... | 12 | 24 | 2 | 1 | 0 | 0 | 0 | 1 | 0 | 0 | .042 |
| 1983 | Hou.... | 88 | 195 | 25 | 46 | 7 | 3 | 2 | 18 | 6 | 2 | .236 |
| 1984 | Hou.... | 121 | 331 | 33 | 86 | 17 | 5 | 2 | 29 | 6 | 5 | .260 |
| 1985 | Hou.... | 150 | 539 | 72 | 145 | 27 | 5 | 16 | 68 | 31 | 19 | .269 |
| 1986 | Hou.... | 157 | 591 | 83 | 184 | 33 | 5 | 20 | 79 | 38 | 22 | .311 |
| 1987 | Hou.... | 157 | 592 | 83 | 168 | 31 | 5 | 19 | 85 | 53 | 21 | .284 |
| 1988 | Hou.... | 157 | 541 | 57 | 138 | 27 | 2 | 14 | 72 | 42 | 31 | .255 |
| 1989 | Hou.... | 87 | 313 | 42 | 94 | 19 | 4 | 5 | 44 | 29 | 11 | .300 |
| | | 947 | 3135 | 401 | 862 | 161 | 29 | 78 | 396 | 206 | 111 | .275 |

# Billy Bean

**Birth Date:** 5/11/64
**Bats:** Left
**Throws:** Left
**1989 Clubs:**
**Detroit Tigers &**
**Los Angeles Dodgers**
**Contest Code #:** 253

**Rating:** 1

**B**illy Bean arrived in the major leagues with a bang. On April 25, 1987, Bean started in the outfield for the Detroit Tigers and tied a modern-day record for most hits (four) in a major-league debut. Tigers manager Sparky Anderson must have thought this kid was Hall of Fame material. But since then Bean has done little to rave about.

Last season, when Dodgers outfielders were going down like the *Titanic*, L.A. acquired Bean and used him for 51 games. Bean managed only 14 hits, while striking out 10 times.

| Year | Team | G | AB | R | H | 2B | 3B | HR | RBI | BB | SB | AVG |
|------|------|---|----|---|---|----|----|----|-----|----|----|-----|
| 1987 | Det .... | 26 | 66 | 6 | 17 | 2 | 0 | 0 | 4 | 5 | 1 | .258 |
| 1988 | Det .... | 10 | 11 | 2 | 2 | 0 | 1 | 0 | 0 | 0 | 0 | .182 |
| 1989 | Det .... | 9 | 11 | 0 | 0 | 0 | 0 | 0 | 0 | 2 | 0 | .000 |
| 1989 | LA ..... | 51 | 71 | 7 | 14 | 4 | 0 | 0 | 3 | 4 | 0 | .197 |
| | | 96 | 159 | 15 | 33 | 6 | 1 | 0 | 7 | 11 | 1 | .208 |

# Geronimo Berroa

**Birth Date:** 3/18/65
**Bats:** Right
**Throws:** Right
**1989 Club:**
**Atlanta Braves**
**Contest Code #:** 254

**Rating:** 2

**T**he Braves drafted Geronimo Berroa from the Blue Jays' unprotected roster in December 1988 and were forced by draft rules to keep him on their major-league roster all season. Playing in 81 games, Berroa batted .265, with 2 home runs and 9 RBI's.

I can't understand why the Braves didn't play him more. They acted as if Berroa were a twenty-year-old prospect, when, in fact, he'd already played pro ball since 1984. What was he going to learn on the bench? And, since the Braves were going nowhere, why not give him a full shot?

Berroa's best minor-league seasons were in 1986, when he hit .298, with 21 home runs and 73 RBI's for Class A Ventura; and 1987, when he batted .287, with 36 home runs and 108 RBI's for Double A Knoxville. In 1988, he slumped to .260, with 8 home runs and 64 RBI's for Triple A Syracuse.

| Year | Team | G | AB | R | H | 2B | 3B | HR | RBI | BB | SB | AVG |
|------|------|---|----|---|---|----|----|----|-----|----|----|-----|
| 1989 | Atl ..... | 81 | 136 | 7 | 36 | 4 | 0 | 2 | 9 | 7 | 0 | .265 |
| | | 81 | 136 | 7 | 36 | 4 | 0 | 2 | 9 | 7 | 0 | .265 |

# Barry Bonds

**Birth Date:** 7/24/64
**Bats:** Left
**Throws:** Left
**1989 Club:**
**Pittsburgh Pirates**
**Contest Code #:** 255

**Rating:** 3

**B**arry Bonds is a gifted offensive player who may never live up to the early expectations. He has the speed of a lead-off hitter, the power of a number-three hitter, and the sculpted body of a fine athlete (only four percent of his body weight is fat). But as long as Bonds is fixated with hitting home runs, he'll never hit for the average of which he's capable.

Obviously, I'm being quite harsh. After all, last season Bonds was third in the National League in walks (93), tied with teammate Bobby Bonilla for sixth in runs scored (96), tied with Kevin Mitchell for seventh in doubles (34), and ninth in stolen bases (32). But Bonds can do more. Instead of accepting his 93 strikeouts, ask

what would happen if he had put the ball in play just 20 more times? He certainly would have driven in more than 58 runs. If 10 of those 20 balls had been hits, his average would have been 18 points better.

I'm sure you'll argue that Bonds can't be expected to drive in more than 65 runs a season because he bats leadoff. I've read scores of scouting reports on him; I've watched him extensively. I say he can do better.

| Year | Team | G | AB | R | H | 2B | 3B | HR | RBI | BB | SB | AVG |
|------|------|---|----|---|---|----|----|----|-----|----|----|-----|
| 1986 | Pit..... | 113 | 413 | 72 | 92 | 26 | 3 | 16 | 48 | 65 | 36 | .223 |
| 1987 | Pit..... | 150 | 551 | 99 | 144 | 34 | 9 | 25 | 59 | 54 | 32 | .261 |
| 1988 | Pit..... | 144 | 538 | 97 | 152 | 30 | 5 | 24 | 58 | 72 | 17 | .283 |
| 1989 | Pit..... | 159 | 580 | 96 | 144 | 34 | 6 | 19 | 58 | 93 | 32 | .248 |
| | | 566 | 2082 | 364 | 532 | 124 | 23 | 84 | 223 | 284 | 117 | .256 |

# Hubie Brooks

Birth Date: 9/24/56
Bats: Right
Throws: Right
1989 Club:
Montreal Expos
Contest Code #: 256

Rating: 3

While I expect more from Barry Bonds, I believe managers have expected too much from Hubie Brooks.

Brooks, a standout outfielder in his collegiate career at Arizona State University, was drafted by the Mets in June 1978 (the third player chosen in that draft) and converted to third base. Early in his major-league career, the Mets became frustrated with Brooks. Though he hit for average, Brooks didn't generate the power that teams expect from a corner man. When he tried to hit for power, he messed up his stroke.

In 1984, when Brooks began hitting for average and power, manager Davey Johnson fiddled with him some more, moving him to shortstop to beef up the Mets' offense. Following the season, while Brooks was in the Instructional League working on his shortstop play, the Mets traded him to Montreal in the Gary Carter deal.

In 1988, the Expos decided to move Brooks back to the outfield. Last season, Brooks was pulled so often during the late innings for a defensive replacement that he grew frustrated and let his dissatisfaction affect his offense. The Dodgers don't seem to be bothered by this—they signed Brooks during the off-season to a three-year, $6 million deal.

| Year | Team | G | AB | R | H | 2B | 3B | HR | RBI | BB | SB | AVG |
|------|------|---|----|---|---|----|----|----|-----|----|----|-----|
| 1980 | NYN ... | 24 | 81 | 8 | 25 | 2 | 1 | 1 | 10 | 5 | 1 | .309 |
| 1981 | NYN ... | 98 | 358 | 34 | 110 | 21 | 2 | 4 | 38 | 23 | 9 | .307 |
| 1982 | NYN ... | 126 | 457 | 40 | 114 | 21 | 2 | 2 | 40 | 28 | 6 | .249 |
| 1983 | NYN ... | 150 | 586 | 53 | 147 | 18 | 4 | 5 | 58 | 24 | 6 | .251 |
| 1984 | NYN ... | 153 | 561 | 61 | 159 | 23 | 2 | 16 | 73 | 48 | 6 | .283 |
| 1985 | Mon.... | 156 | 605 | 67 | 163 | 34 | 7 | 13 | 100 | 34 | 6 | .269 |
| 1986 | Mon.... | 80 | 306 | 50 | 104 | 18 | 5 | 14 | 58 | 25 | 4 | .340 |
| 1987 | Mon.... | 112 | 430 | 57 | 113 | 22 | 3 | 14 | 72 | 24 | 4 | .263 |
| 1988 | Mon.... | 151 | 588 | 61 | 164 | 35 | 2 | 20 | 90 | 35 | 7 | .279 |
| 1989 | Mon.... | 148 | 542 | 56 | 145 | 30 | 1 | 14 | 70 | 39 | 6 | .268 |
| | | 1198 | 4514 | 487 | 1244 | 224 | 29 | 103 | 609 | 285 | 55 | .276 |

# Tom Brunansky

Birth Date: 8/20/60
Bats: Right
Throws: Right
1989 Club:
St. Louis Cardinals
Contest Code #: 257

Rating: 3

**T**om Brunansky is a fantasy-evaluator's dream. You know he'll hit 20 or more home runs this season; he's done that for eight consecutive seasons. He'll drive in 75 or more runs; he's done that the past seven seasons. Those are excellent averages for any power-hitting fantasy player.

Just as impressive is the fact that Brunansky's numbers in the National League the past two seasons have held firm despite 81 home games at Busch Stadium, a power hitter's nightmare. Brunansky, a streak hitter, does what he can at home, then explodes on the road. It's not uncommon for him to hit five or six home runs during a six- or eight-game road trip.

Remember, too, that it's not uncommon for Bruno to go two weeks without a tater.

| Year | Team | G | AB | R | H | 2B | 3B | HR | RBI | BB | SB | AVG |
|------|------|----|-----|----|-----|-----|----|-----|-----|-----|----|------|
| 1981 | Cal..... | 11 | 33 | 7 | 5 | 0 | 0 | 3 | 6 | 8 | 1 | .152 |
| 1982 | Min .... | 127 | 463 | 77 | 126 | 30 | 1 | 20 | 46 | 71 | 1 | .272 |
| 1983 | Min .... | 151 | 542 | 70 | 123 | 24 | 5 | 28 | 82 | 61 | 2 | .227 |
| 1984 | Min .... | 155 | 567 | 75 | 144 | 21 | 0 | 32 | 85 | 57 | 4 | .254 |
| 1985 | Min .... | 157 | 567 | 71 | 137 | 28 | 4 | 27 | 90 | 71 | 5 | .242 |
| 1986 | Min .... | 157 | 593 | 69 | 152 | 28 | 1 | 23 | 75 | 53 | 12 | .256 |
| 1987 | Min .... | 155 | 532 | 83 | 138 | 22 | 2 | 32 | 85 | 74 | 11 | .259 |
| 1988 | Min .... | 14 | 49 | 5 | 9 | 1 | 0 | 1 | 6 | 7 | 1 | .184 |
| 1988 | StL .... | 143 | 523 | 69 | 128 | 22 | 4 | 22 | 79 | 79 | 16 | .245 |
| 1989 | StL .... | 158 | 556 | 67 | 133 | 29 | 3 | 20 | 85 | 59 | 5 | .239 |
| | | 1228 | 4425 | 593 | 1095 | 205 | 20 | 208 | 639 | 540 | 58 | .247 |

# Brett Butler

Birth Date: 6/15/57
Bats: Left
Throws: Left
1989 Club:
San Francisco Giants
Contest Code #: 258

Rating: 4

**S**peedy Brett Butler, chosen by the Braves in the June 1979 draft, dashed through the minor leagues and arrived in Atlanta on August 20, 1981, fresh off his International League MVP season. He seemed too good to be true: a prototypical lead off hitter with a name so similar to Margaret *(Gone With The Wind)* Mitchell's fictional Atlanta hero. Two years later, Butler set the Braves' single-season record for stolen bases (39) and led the majors in triples (13).

Alas, the Braves, in the thick of the 1983 National League Western Division race but short on pitching down the stretch, sent Butler, third-base prospect Brook Jacoby, and pitcher Rick Behenna to the Indians for pitcher Len Barker.

Since then, Butler has been quite a story. In 1984, he became the first player in Cleveland history to steal 50 or more bases and score 100 or more runs. In 1985, he batted a career-high .311 and scored 106 runs. In 1986, he led the majors with 14 triples. In 1987, he became the second player in the Indians' history to steal 30 or more bases in 4 consecutive seasons. After signing as a free agent with the Giants, in 1988 he led the National League in runs scored (109) and was second in on-base average (.393). Last year he was sixth in the league in hits (168), tenth in steals (31), and was four runs shy of tying for the lead.

| Year | Team | G | AB | R | H | 2B | 3B | HR | RBI | BB | SB | AVG |
|---|---|---|---|---|---|---|---|---|---|---|---|---|
| 1981 | Atl..... | 40 | 126 | 17 | 32 | 2 | 3 | 0 | 4 | 19 | 9 | .254 |
| 1982 | Atl..... | 89 | 240 | 35 | 52 | 2 | 0 | 0 | 7 | 25 | 21 | .217 |
| 1983 | Atl..... | 151 | 549 | 84 | 154 | 21 | 13 | 5 | 37 | 54 | 39 | .281 |
| 1984 | Cle..... | 159 | 602 | 108 | 162 | 25 | 9 | 3 | 49 | 86 | 52 | .269 |
| 1985 | Cle..... | 152 | 591 | 106 | 184 | 28 | 14 | 5 | 50 | 63 | 47 | .311 |
| 1986 | Cle..... | 161 | 587 | 92 | 163 | 17 | 14 | 4 | 51 | 70 | 32 | .278 |
| 1987 | Cle..... | 137 | 522 | 91 | 154 | 25 | 8 | 9 | 41 | 91 | 33 | .295 |
| 1988 | SF..... | 157 | 568 | 109 | 163 | 27 | 9 | 6 | 43 | 97 | 43 | .287 |
| 1989 | SF..... | 154 | 594 | 100 | 168 | 22 | 4 | 4 | 36 | 59 | 31 | .283 |
| | | 1200 | 4379 | 742 | 1232 | 169 | 74 | 36 | 318 | 564 | 307 | .281 |

# John Cangelosi

**Birth Date:** 3/10/63
**Bats:** Left
**Throws:** Left
**1989 Club:**
**Pittsburgh Pirates**
**Contest Code #:** 259

**Rating: 1**

John Cangelosi is the little engine who couldn't. Listed as 5'8" (but that's really stretching him), Cangelosi was acquired by the Pirates in 1987 to provide some spunk in the lead-off spot. But Cangelosi couldn't measure up.

Now a fourth outfielder, Cangelosi's batting suffers the less he plays. After long stretches of inactivity, he usually needs a week or two in Triple A to brush up his skills.

Cangelosi's sole offensive virtue is his ability to steal bases. He swiped 50 for the White Sox in 1986 and 21 for the Buccos in 1987. But if he doesn't get playing time, he doesn't hit when called on; when he doesn't hit, he can't steal bases.

| Year | Team | G | AB | R | H | 2B | 3B | HR | RBI | BB | SB | AVG |
|---|---|---|---|---|---|---|---|---|---|---|---|---|
| 1985 | ChA.... | 5 | 2 | 2 | 0 | 0 | 0 | 0 | 0 | 0 | 0 | .000 |
| 1986 | ChA.... | 137 | 438 | 65 | 103 | 16 | 3 | 2 | 32 | 71 | 50 | .235 |
| 1987 | Pit..... | 104 | 182 | 44 | 50 | 8 | 3 | 4 | 18 | 46 | 21 | .275 |
| 1988 | Pit..... | 75 | 118 | 18 | 30 | 4 | 1 | 0 | 8 | 17 | 9 | .254 |
| 1989 | Pit..... | 112 | 160 | 18 | 35 | 4 | 2 | 0 | 9 | 35 | 11 | .219 |
| | | 433 | 900 | 147 | 218 | 32 | 9 | 6 | 67 | 169 | 91 | .242 |

# Mark Carreon

**Birth Date:** 7/19/63
**Bats:** Right
**Throws:** Left
**1989 Club:**
**New York Mets**
**Contest Code #:** 260

**Rating: 1**

Mark Carreon is so brutal in the field—and "brutal" is a kind description—that he will never be an everyday player in the National League. He can't catch outfield flies and he can't move around the bag at first, but he can hit.

Carreon, the Mets' seventh selection in the June 1981 draft, hit .300 or better four times in eight minor-league seasons. He showed decent home-run power and a taste for RBI's. Last year, Carreon hit 4 home runs in 27 at-bats as a pinch-hitter, and 2 more in 106 regular at-bats.

If Carreon was an American Leaguer, he might earn a 3 rating as a designated hitter. But in the National League, man does not live by bat alone.

| Year | Team | G | AB | R | H | 2B | 3B | HR | RBI | BB | SB | AVG |
|---|---|---|---|---|---|---|---|---|---|---|---|---|
| 1987 | NYN ... | 9 | 12 | 0 | 3 | 0 | 0 | 0 | 1 | 1 | 0 | .250 |
| 1988 | NYN ... | 7 | 9 | 5 | 5 | 2 | 0 | 1 | 1 | 2 | 0 | .556 |
| 1989 | NYN ... | 68 | 133 | 20 | 41 | 6 | 0 | 6 | 16 | 12 | 2 | .308 |
| | | 84 | 154 | 25 | 49 | 8 | 0 | 7 | 18 | 15 | 2 | .318 |

# Joe Carter

**Birth Date:** 3/7/60
**Bats:** Right
**Throws:** Right
**1989 Club:**
**Cleveland Indians**
**Contest Code #:** 317

**Rating: 5**

**T**he switchboard at the Cleveland Indians' office must have been close to blowing on that day last November when the Tribe announced that Joe Carter would be on the trading block. The winner in the Carter sweepstakes? The San Diego Padres, who suddenly find themselves with several million-dollar men (Jack Clark, Bruce Hurst).

The powerfully-built, 6'3", 215-pounder is one of the biggest power threats in baseball. A team that has championship pretensions needs a guy who can jerk the ball out of the park—or at least threaten to do so. Carter has been that guy in Cleveland. Carter is the kind of player you can build a team around. An adequate player in left field, center field, or first base, he has enough speed to be a genuine base-stealing threat (despite only 13 last year). His batting average slipped to .243 in 1989, well off his career .274 mark and way off his .302 in 1986. But Carter should make the Padres very happy in 1990.

| Year | Team | G | AB | R | H | 2B | 3B | HR | RBI | BB | SB | AVG |
|------|------|-----|------|-----|-----|-----|-----|-----|-----|-----|-----|------|
| 1983 | ChN.... | 23 | 51 | 6 | 9 | 1 | 1 | 0 | 1 | 0 | 1 | .176 |
| 1984 | Cle..... | 66 | 244 | 32 | 67 | 6 | 1 | 13 | 41 | 11 | 2 | .275 |
| 1985 | Cle..... | 143 | 489 | 64 | 128 | 27 | 0 | 15 | 59 | 25 | 24 | .262 |
| 1986 | Cle..... | 162 | 663 | 108 | 200 | 36 | 9 | 29 | 121 | 32 | 29 | .302 |
| 1987 | Cle..... | 149 | 588 | 83 | 155 | 27 | 2 | 32 | 106 | 27 | 31 | .264 |
| 1988 | Cle..... | 157 | 621 | 85 | 168 | 36 | 6 | 27 | 98 | 35 | 27 | .271 |
| 1989 | Cle..... | 162 | 651 | 84 | 158 | 32 | 4 | 35 | 105 | 39 | 13 | .243 |
| | | 862 | 3307 | 462 | 885 | 165 | 23 | 151 | 531 | 169 | 127 | .268 |

# Vince Coleman

**Birth Date:** 9/22/61
**Bats:** Left
**Throws:** Left
**1989 Club:**
**St. Louis Cardinals**
**Contest Code #:** 261

**Rating: 3**

**T**he trade rumors emanating from St. Louis late last season involving Vince Coleman were another sign that he had exhausted the patience of the Cardinals' front office. How can one find fault with a player who's led the National League in stolen bases for five years running? Simple. Though he has speed to burn, Coleman's batting averages and on-base percentages in three of the past four seasons have been well below what is expected of a lead-off hitter.

Why? He strikes out too much (111 K's in 1988, 90 in 1989); he complains too much (he's notorious for nit-picking with National League umpires); he doesn't walk enough (49 in 1988, 50 in 1989). What's so surprising is that Coleman happens to be an excellent bunter. He could stop wasting so many at-bats on strikeouts by bunting more often—not just on the first pitch, but even when he's behind in the count by one strike.

Few players can dominate a fantasy-league category the way Coleman does in stolen bases. Trouble is, over five years he has shown himself to be little more than a one-category player.

| Year | Team | G | AB | R | H | 2B | 3B | HR | RBI | BB | SB | AVG |
|------|------|-----|------|-----|-----|-----|-----|-----|-----|-----|-----|------|
| 1985 | StL .... | 151 | 636 | 107 | 170 | 20 | 10 | 1 | 40 | 50 | 110 | .267 |
| 1986 | StL .... | 154 | 600 | 94 | 139 | 13 | 8 | 0 | 29 | 60 | 107 | .232 |
| 1987 | StL .... | 151 | 623 | 121 | 180 | 14 | 10 | 3 | 43 | 70 | 109 | .289 |
| 1988 | StL .... | 153 | 616 | 77 | 160 | 20 | 10 | 3 | 38 | 49 | 81 | .260 |
| 1989 | StL .... | 145 | 563 | 94 | 143 | 21 | 9 | 2 | 28 | 50 | 65 | .254 |
| | | 754 | 3038 | 493 | 792 | 88 | 47 | 9 | 178 | 279 | 472 | .261 |

# Dave Collins

**Birth Date:** 10/20/52
**Bats:** Left
**Throws:** Left
**1989 Club:**
**Cincinnati Reds**
**Contest Code #:** 262

## Rating: 1

Good-bye Pete Rose, good-bye Dave Collins. The thirty-seven-year-old Collins, who played with Rose in 1978 and 1979, was brought back to Cincinnati by Rose in 1987 as a backup outfielder. Once among baseball's best base stealers—he pilfered 79 in 1980 and 60 in 1984—Collins has stolen 19 in the past three seasons. Stick the fork in Collins. He's done.

| Year | Team | G | AB | R | H | 2B | 3B | HR | RBI | BB | SB | AVG |
|------|------|-----|------|-----|------|-----|----|----|-----|-----|-----|------|
| 1975 | Cal..... | 93 | 319 | 41 | 85 | 13 | 4 | 3 | 29 | 36 | 24 | .266 |
| 1976 | Cal..... | 99 | 365 | 45 | 96 | 12 | 1 | 4 | 28 | 40 | 32 | .263 |
| 1977 | Sea .... | 120 | 402 | 46 | 96 | 9 | 3 | 5 | 28 | 33 | 25 | .239 |
| 1978 | Cin .... | 102 | 102 | 13 | 22 | 1 | 0 | 0 | 7 | 15 | 7 | .216 |
| 1979 | Cin .... | 122 | 396 | 59 | 126 | 16 | 4 | 3 | 35 | 27 | 16 | .318 |
| 1980 | Cin .... | 144 | 551 | 94 | 167 | 20 | 4 | 3 | 35 | 53 | 79 | .303 |
| 1981 | Cin .... | 95 | 360 | 63 | 98 | 18 | 6 | 3 | 23 | 41 | 26 | .272 |
| 1982 | NYA.... | 111 | 348 | 41 | 88 | 12 | 3 | 3 | 25 | 28 | 13 | .253 |
| 1983 | Tor..... | 118 | 402 | 55 | 109 | 12 | 4 | 1 | 34 | 43 | 31 | .271 |
| 1984 | Tor..... | 128 | 441 | 59 | 136 | 24 | 15 | 2 | 44 | 33 | 60 | .308 |
| 1985 | Oak .... | 112 | 379 | 52 | 95 | 16 | 4 | 4 | 29 | 29 | 29 | .251 |
| 1986 | Det .... | 124 | 419 | 44 | 113 | 18 | 2 | 1 | 27 | 44 | 27 | .270 |
| 1987 | Cin .... | 57 | 85 | 19 | 25 | 5 | 0 | 0 | 5 | 11 | 9 | .294 |
| 1988 | Cin .... | 99 | 174 | 12 | 41 | 6 | 2 | 0 | 14 | 11 | 7 | .236 |
| 1989 | Cin .... | 78 | 106 | 12 | 25 | 4 | 0 | 0 | 7 | 10 | 3 | .236 |
| | | 1602 | 4849 | 655 | 1322 | 186 | 52 | 32 | 370 | 454 | 388 | .273 |

# Kal Daniels

**Birth Date:** 8/20/63
**Bats:** Left
**Throws:** Left
**1989 Clubs:**
**Cincinnati Reds &**
**Los Angeles Dodgers**
**Contest Code #:** 263

## Rating: 3

In Cincinnati, Kal Daniels was often unhappy with his spot in the batting order—sometimes leading off, sometimes batting third—and his salary. The Reds took care of both problems last season. Regarding the latter, owner Marge Schott agreed to flip a coin to decide on his raise (she lost). As for the former, the Reds sent Daniels to L.A. and let Tom Lasorda solve that problem.

But Daniels, who's had a history of knee problems, played a short time for the Dodgers before going on the disabled list in early August with an injured right knee. That injury cost him the rest of his season. He then underwent surgery—the sixth knee operation of his career.

When healthy, no achievement is beyond Daniels' reach. The concern among baseball people is whether Daniels has the desire and intensity needed for greatness.

| Year | Team | G | AB | R | H | 2B | 3B | HR | RBI | BB | SB | AVG |
|------|------|-----|------|-----|-----|----|----|----|-----|-----|----|------|
| 1986 | Cin .... | 74 | 181 | 34 | 58 | 10 | 4 | 6 | 23 | 22 | 15 | .320 |
| 1987 | Cin .... | 108 | 368 | 73 | 123 | 24 | 1 | 26 | 64 | 60 | 26 | .334 |
| 1988 | Cin .... | 140 | 495 | 95 | 144 | 29 | 1 | 18 | 64 | 87 | 27 | .291 |
| 1989 | Cin .... | 44 | 133 | 26 | 29 | 11 | 0 | 2 | 9 | 36 | 6 | .218 |
| 1989 | LA ..... | 11 | 38 | 7 | 13 | 2 | 0 | 2 | 8 | 7 | 3 | .342 |
| | | 377 | 1215 | 235 | 367 | 76 | 6 | 54 | 168 | 212 | 77 | .302 |

# Mark Davidson

Birth Date: 2/15/61
Bats: Right
Throws: Right
1989 Clubs:
Minnesota Twins &
Houston Astros
Contest Code #: 264

Rating: 1

Last season, the Astros acquired reserve outfielder Mark Davidson to fill in for an injured Kevin Bass and a slumping Billy Hatcher. Too bad Houston had no one to fill in for Davison.

The 6'2", 190-pound Davidson broke in with the Twins organization. His best minor-league season was 1984, in which he batted .302, with 25 home runs and 106 RBI's for Double-A Orlando. Since then, he played one year in Triple A before joining the Twins in 1986. He stuck around for most of 1988, and was sent packing thereafter. If Davidson makes the Astros this spring, it will be as a fifth outfielder.

| Year | Team | G | AB | R | H | 2B | 3B | HR | RBI | BB | SB | AVG |
|------|------|---|-----|----|----|----|----|----|-----|----|----|------|
| 1986 | Min .... | 36 | 68 | 5 | 8 | 3 | 0 | 0 | 2 | 6 | 2 | .118 |
| 1987 | Min .... | 102 | 150 | 32 | 40 | 4 | 1 | 1 | 14 | 13 | 9 | .267 |
| 1988 | Min .... | 100 | 106 | 22 | 23 | 7 | 0 | 1 | 10 | 10 | 3 | .217 |
| 1989 | Hou .... | 33 | 65 | 7 | 13 | 2 | 1 | 1 | 5 | 7 | 1 | .200 |
| | | 271 | 389 | 66 | 84 | 16 | 2 | 3 | 31 | 36 | 15 | .216 |

# Eric Davis

Birth Date: 5/29/62
Bats: Right
Throws: Right
1989 Club:
Cincinnati Reds
Contest Code #: 265

Rating: 5

A friend of mine has a saying: "Happy people produce." Whether you're a businessman or a bricklayer or a ballplayer, if you are happy with your working environment you will feel better—mentally and physically—and accomplish more.

Last season, Eric Davis was unhappy with the Reds management and unhappy with the rock-hard artificial surface in Cincinnati's Riverfront Stadium. With the Reds in a tailspin and his knees aching from the plastic turf, Davis asked to be traded; he'd consider staying, he added, if management installed a natural-grass field.

Despite his grievances, Davis had a better season last year than he did in 1988. But you have to wonder whether Davis' performance will diminish if the team can't satisfy the desires of its best player. Conversely, we can speculate that if Davis is traded to, say, the Padres, a team that plays on natural grass; in a hitter's park; near his home in Los Angeles; and for Jack McKeon, in the top echelon of baseball's managers and general managers, Davis would be the best player in baseball.

| Year | Team | G | AB | R | H | 2B | 3B | HR | RBI | BB | SB | AVG |
|------|------|---|-----|----|----|----|----|----|-----|----|----|------|
| 1984 | Cin .... | 57 | 174 | 33 | 39 | 10 | 1 | 10 | 30 | 24 | 10 | .224 |
| 1985 | Cin .... | 56 | 122 | 26 | 30 | 3 | 3 | 8 | 18 | 7 | 16 | .246 |
| 1986 | Cin .... | 132 | 415 | 97 | 115 | 15 | 3 | 27 | 71 | 68 | 80 | .277 |
| 1987 | Cin .... | 129 | 474 | 120 | 139 | 23 | 4 | 37 | 100 | 84 | 50 | .293 |
| 1988 | Cin .... | 135 | 472 | 81 | 129 | 18 | 3 | 26 | 93 | 65 | 35 | .273 |
| 1989 | Cin .... | 131 | 462 | 74 | 130 | 14 | 2 | 34 | 101 | 68 | 21 | .281 |
| | | 640 | 2119 | 431 | 582 | 83 | 16 | 142 | 413 | 316 | 212 | .275 |

# Andre Dawson

**Birth Date:** 7/10/54
**Bats:** Right
**Throws:** Right
**1989 Club:**
**Chicago Cubs**
**Contest Code #:** 266

**Rating: 4**

**A**ndre Dawson is awesome. He's a man's man, a leader by example, a multitalented, All-Star performer who plays as hard as he can through the constant throbbing from his arthritic knees.

You'll think I'm too emotional when I say that I like having players on my fantasy team like Dawson who have heart, character, and the will to excel—even though there are no categories for those qualities. Dawson may sometimes be forced to the sidelines by his arthritic knees, or he may be in a prolonged slump, but, on the whole, you know he'll find a way to come through for you.

To give you an example, following his prolific 1987 season, the pain in Dawson's knees hurt his ability to generate power from his legs. So Dawson focused on making contact and boosted his batting average to .303. Last year, knee problems limited Dawson to 118 games, yet he still hit 21 home runs.

I'd take "The Hawk" on my team any day.

| Year | Team | G | AB | R | H | 2B | 3B | HR | RBI | BB | SB | AVG |
|---|---|---|---|---|---|---|---|---|---|---|---|---|
| 1976 | Mon.... | 24 | 85 | 9 | 20 | 4 | 1 | 0 | 7 | 5 | 1 | .235 |
| 1977 | Mon.... | 139 | 525 | 64 | 148 | 26 | 9 | 19 | 65 | 34 | 21 | .282 |
| 1978 | Mon.... | 157 | 609 | 84 | 154 | 24 | 8 | 25 | 72 | 30 | 28 | .253 |
| 1979 | Mon.... | 155 | 639 | 90 | 176 | 24 | 12 | 25 | 92 | 27 | 35 | .275 |
| 1980 | Mon.... | 151 | 577 | 96 | 178 | 41 | 7 | 17 | 87 | 44 | 34 | .308 |
| 1981 | Mon.... | 103 | 394 | 71 | 119 | 21 | 3 | 24 | 64 | 35 | 26 | .302 |
| 1982 | Mon.... | 148 | 608 | 107 | 183 | 37 | 7 | 23 | 83 | 34 | 39 | .301 |
| 1983 | Mon.... | 159 | 633 | 104 | 189 | 36 | 10 | 32 | 113 | 38 | 25 | .299 |
| 1984 | Mon.... | 138 | 533 | 73 | 132 | 23 | 6 | 17 | 86 | 41 | 13 | .248 |
| 1985 | Mon.... | 139 | 529 | 65 | 135 | 27 | 2 | 23 | 91 | 29 | 13 | .255 |
| 1986 | Mon.... | 130 | 496 | 65 | 141 | 32 | 2 | 20 | 78 | 37 | 18 | .284 |
| 1987 | ChN.... | 153 | 621 | 90 | 178 | 24 | 2 | 49 | 137 | 32 | 11 | .287 |
| 1988 | ChN.... | 157 | 591 | 78 | 179 | 31 | 8 | 24 | 79 | 37 | 12 | .303 |
| 1989 | ChN.... | 118 | 416 | 62 | 105 | 18 | 6 | 21 | 77 | 35 | 8 | .252 |
| | | 1871 | 7256 | 1058 | 2037 | 368 | 83 | 319 | 1131 | 458 | 284 | .281 |

# Bob Dernier

**Birth Date:** 1/5/57
**Bats:** Right
**Throws:** Right
**1989 Club:**
**Philadelphia Phillies**
**Contest Code #:** 267

**Rating: 1**

**S**peedy Bob Dernier is running out of time. Once viewed by the Phillies as their center fielder of the future, Dernier couldn't hit big-league pitching and was traded to the Cubs in 1984.

That year, Dernier enjoyed his best season, batting .278 and stealing 45 bases. But his stolen-base totals dipped as his batting average sank. Following the 1987 season, Dernier re-signed with the Phillies.

In 1988, Dernier platooned in center with Milt Thompson, but lost five weeks because of two stints on the disabled list. Last year, Dernier was used in a reserve role. This year, he'll have to come into camp with Wonderboy in order to make the team.

| Year | Team | G | AB | R | H | 2B | 3B | HR | RBI | BB | SB | AVG |
|---|---|---|---|---|---|---|---|---|---|---|---|---|
| 1980 | Phi .... | 10 | 7 | 5 | 4 | 0 | 0 | 0 | 1 | 1 | 3 | .571 |
| 1981 | Phi .... | 10 | 4 | 0 | 3 | 0 | 0 | 0 | 0 | 0 | 2 | .750 |
| 1982 | Phi .... | 122 | 370 | 56 | 92 | 10 | 2 | 4 | 21 | 36 | 42 | .249 |
| 1983 | Phi .... | 122 | 221 | 41 | 51 | 10 | 0 | 1 | 15 | 18 | 35 | .231 |
| 1984 | ChN.... | 143 | 536 | 94 | 149 | 26 | 5 | 3 | 32 | 63 | 45 | .278 |
| 1985 | ChN.... | 121 | 469 | 63 | 119 | 20 | 3 | 1 | 21 | 40 | 31 | .254 |
| 1986 | ChN.... | 108 | 324 | 32 | 73 | 14 | 1 | 4 | 18 | 22 | 27 | .225 |
| 1987 | ChN.... | 93 | 199 | 38 | 63 | 4 | 4 | 8 | 21 | 19 | 16 | .317 |
| 1988 | Phi .... | 68 | 166 | 19 | 48 | 3 | 1 | 1 | 10 | 9 | 13 | .289 |
| 1989 | Phi .... | 107 | 187 | 26 | 32 | 5 | 0 | 1 | 13 | 14 | 4 | .171 |
| | | 904 | 2483 | 374 | 634 | 92 | 16 | 23 | 152 | 222 | 218 | .255 |

# Jim Dwyer

**Birth Date:** 1/3/50
**Bats:** Left
**Throws:** Left
**1989 Clubs:**
Minnesota Twins &
Montreal Expos
**Contest Code #:** 268

**Rating:** 1

The panic in Montreal to make a last-gasp division charge last season reached epic proportions when the Expos acquired Jim Dwyer from the Twins. Not that Dwyer played poorly—he notched 3 hits and 2 RBI's in 10 at-bats—but what National League team in its right mind would bring in a thirty-nine-year-old designated hitter?

A little traveling music: Dwyer, selected by the Cardinals in the June 1971 draft, reached the majors in 1973. He shuttled between the Cardinals and their Triple A affiliate for two seasons, and was traded to the Expos in 1975. A year later, he was sent to the Mets. Following the 1976 season, he was traded to the Cubs. The Cubbies cut him loose in 1977, but the Cardinals re-signed him a week later. In 1978, Dwyer was traded to the Giants. In 1979, the Giants sold him to Boston. In 1980, he signed as a free agent with the Orioles. In 1988, he was traded to the Twins. You think the Expos will keep him all season?

| Year | Team | G | AB | R | H | 2B | 3B | HR | RBI | BB | SB | AVG |
|------|------|---|----|----|----|----|----|----|-----|----|----|------|
| 1973 | StL .... | 28 | 57 | 7 | 11 | 1 | 1 | 0 | 0 | 1 | 0 | .193 |
| 1974 | StL .... | 74 | 86 | 13 | 24 | 1 | 0 | 2 | 11 | 11 | 0 | .279 |
| 1975 | StL .... | 21 | 31 | 4 | 6 | 1 | 0 | 0 | 1 | 4 | 0 | .194 |
| 1975 | Mon.... | 60 | 175 | 22 | 50 | 7 | 1 | 3 | 20 | 23 | 4 | .286 |
| 1976 | Mon.... | 50 | 92 | 7 | 17 | 3 | 1 | 0 | 5 | 11 | 0 | .185 |
| 1976 | NYN ... | 11 | 13 | 2 | 2 | 0 | 0 | 0 | 0 | 2 | 0 | .154 |
| 1977 | StL .... | 13 | 31 | 3 | 7 | 1 | 0 | 0 | 2 | 4 | 0 | .226 |
| 1978 | SF ..... | 73 | 173 | 22 | 39 | 9 | 2 | 5 | 22 | 28 | 6 | .225 |
| 1978 | StL .... | 34 | 65 | 8 | 14 | 3 | 0 | 1 | 4 | 9 | 1 | .215 |
| 1979 | Bos .... | 76 | 113 | 19 | 30 | 7 | 0 | 2 | 14 | 17 | 3 | .265 |
| 1980 | Bos .... | 93 | 260 | 41 | 74 | 11 | 1 | 9 | 38 | 28 | 3 | .285 |
| 1981 | Bal .... | 68 | 134 | 16 | 30 | 0 | 1 | 3 | 10 | 20 | 0 | .224 |
| 1982 | Bal .... | 71 | 148 | 28 | 45 | 4 | 3 | 6 | 15 | 27 | 2 | .304 |
| 1983 | Bal .... | 100 | 196 | 37 | 56 | 17 | 1 | 8 | 38 | 31 | 1 | .286 |
| 1984 | Bal .... | 76 | 161 | 22 | 41 | 9 | 1 | 2 | 21 | 23 | 0 | .255 |
| 1985 | Bal .... | 101 | 233 | 35 | 58 | 8 | 3 | 7 | 36 | 37 | 0 | .249 |
| 1986 | Bal .... | 94 | 160 | 18 | 39 | 13 | 1 | 8 | 31 | 23 | 0 | .244 |
| 1987 | Bal .... | 92 | 241 | 54 | 66 | 7 | 1 | 15 | 33 | 37 | 4 | .274 |
| 1988 | Bal .... | 35 | 53 | 3 | 12 | 0 | 0 | 0 | 3 | 12 | 0 | .226 |
| 1988 | Min .... | 20 | 41 | 6 | 12 | 1 | 0 | 2 | 15 | 13 | 0 | .293 |
| 1989 | Min .... | 88 | 225 | 34 | 71 | 11 | 0 | 3 | 23 | 28 | 2 | .316 |
| 1989 | Mon.... | 13 | 10 | 1 | 3 | 1 | 0 | 0 | 2 | 1 | 0 | .300 |
| | | 1291 | 2698 | 402 | 707 | 115 | 17 | 76 | 344 | 390 | 26 | .262 |

# Len Dykstra

**Birth Date:** 2/10/63
**Bats:** Left
**Throws:** Left
**1989 Clubs:**
New York Mets &
Philadelphia Phillies
**Contest Code #:** 269

**Rating:** 3

Is Lenny Dykstra an everyday player, or is he best suited for a platoon role? The Mets had decided the latter was true, while the Phillies believe the former. I side with the Mets on this call.

My reasoning? First, I don't think Dykstra is an intelligent enough batter. Because of his speed and line-drive power, he should be striving to be a top lead-off hitter. Instead, he fancies himself a long-ball threat. As a result, he hardly walks (30 in 429 at-bats in 1988, 60 in 511 at-bats last year). He negates his speed by trying to hit the ball in the air instead of on the ground. And by pumping iron to bulk his chest, pectorals, and forearms, he reinforces the misguided notion that he can be a power hitter.

Second, Dykstra is too reckless. He crashes into walls and opposing fielders instead of playing under control. He runs the bases with abandon; he has no stealing technique.

His do-or-die style may make him a favorite of baseball fans, but I think it will burn him out.

| Year | Team | G | AB | R | H | 2B | 3B | HR | RBI | BB | SB | AVG |
|------|------|---|----|----|----|----|----|----|-----|----|----|-----|
| 1985 | NYN ... | 83 | 236 | 40 | 60 | 9 | 3 | 1 | 19 | 30 | 15 | .254 |
| 1986 | NYN ... | 147 | 431 | 77 | 127 | 27 | 7 | 8 | 45 | 58 | 31 | .295 |
| 1987 | NYN ... | 132 | 431 | 86 | 123 | 37 | 3 | 10 | 43 | 40 | 27 | .285 |
| 1988 | NYN ... | 126 | 429 | 57 | 116 | 19 | 3 | 8 | 33 | 30 | 30 | .270 |
| 1989 | NYN ... | 56 | 159 | 27 | 43 | 12 | 1 | 3 | 13 | 23 | 13 | .270 |
| 1989 | Phi .... | 90 | 352 | 39 | 78 | 20 | 3 | 4 | 19 | 37 | 17 | .222 |
|  |  | 634 | 2038 | 326 | 547 | 124 | 20 | 34 | 172 | 218 | 133 | .268 |

# Curt Ford

**Birth Date: 11/11/60**
**Bats: Left**
**Throws: Right**
**1989 Club:**
**Philadelphia Phillies**
**Contest Code #: 270**

**Rating: 2**

I feel sorry for Curt Ford. He has the speed to be a good top-of-the-order man, but he never got a chance to be much more than a part-time, platoon outfielder for the Cardinals, the team that selected him in the fourth round of the June 1981 draft. Last season, at age twenty-eight, Ford was the Phillies' pinch-hitting specialist, batting .289 (11 for 62), with 3 RBI's in that role.

You may cite Ford's low batting averages the past two seasons as the reason he's played so little. I argue: How much can a player improve when he's had only 270 official plate appearances in the past two seasons? And it isn't as if Ford is devoid of talent. During the 1987 post-season, he batted .333 (3 for 9) in 4 playoff games versus the Giants and .308 (4 for 13), with 2 RBI's, in 5 World Series games against the Twins.

| Year | Team | G | AB | R | H | 2B | 3B | HR | RBI | BB | SB | AVG |
|------|------|---|----|----|----|----|----|----|-----|----|----|-----|
| 1985 | StL .... | 11 | 12 | 2 | 6 | 2 | 0 | 0 | 3 | 4 | 1 | .500 |
| 1986 | StL .... | 85 | 214 | 30 | 53 | 15 | 2 | 2 | 29 | 23 | 13 | .248 |
| 1987 | StL .... | 89 | 228 | 32 | 65 | 9 | 5 | 3 | 26 | 14 | 11 | .285 |
| 1988 | StL .... | 91 | 128 | 11 | 25 | 6 | 0 | 1 | 18 | 8 | 6 | .195 |
| 1989 | Phi .... | 108 | 142 | 13 | 31 | 5 | 1 | 1 | 13 | 16 | 5 | .218 |
|  |  | 384 | 724 | 88 | 180 | 37 | 8 | 7 | 89 | 65 | 36 | .249 |

# Kirk Gibson

**Birth Date: 5/28/57**
**Bats: Left**
**Throws: Left**
**1989 Club:**
**Los Angeles Dodgers**
**Contest Code #: 271**

**Rating: 4**

Kirk Gibson has been like a comet, bursting onto the major-league scene in 1980, playing with all-out abandon for the Tigers, then burning out the past two seasons with the Dodgers.

Gibson's aggressiveness has reduced his effectiveness in countless games and has landed him on the disabled list six times in his 11-year professional career. Gibson never learned to balance his aggression with discretion. In 1980, he suffered wrist and knee injuries; in 1982, he encountered knee, calf muscle, wrist, and stomach ailments; in 1983, more knee problems; in 1985, he was hit on the mouth by a Tim Birtsas fastball and needed 17 stitches—but he played the next day; in 1986, he severely injured his left ankle; in 1987, he pulled a rib-cage muscle; in 1988, he injured his right knee and left hamstring.

Who can forget Gibson limping to home plate, then straining to circle the bases after his ninth-inning home

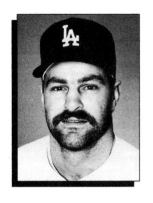

run in the first game of the 1988 World Series? But Gibson's 1988 injuries never healed properly, and by July of 1989 he was through for the season. Gibson has said that if he can't recover completely by this spring, he may retire.

| Year | Team | G | AB | R | H | 2B | 3B | HR | RBI | BB | SB | AVG |
|---|---|---|---|---|---|---|---|---|---|---|---|---|
| 1979 | Det .... | 12 | 38 | 3 | 9 | 3 | 0 | 1 | 4 | 1 | 3 | .237 |
| 1980 | Det .... | 51 | 175 | 23 | 46 | 2 | 1 | 9 | 16 | 10 | 4 | .263 |
| 1981 | Det .... | 83 | 290 | 41 | 95 | 11 | 3 | 9 | 40 | 18 | 17 | .328 |
| 1982 | Det .... | 69 | 266 | 34 | 74 | 16 | 2 | 8 | 35 | 25 | 9 | .278 |
| 1983 | Det .... | 128 | 401 | 60 | 91 | 12 | 9 | 15 | 51 | 53 | 14 | .227 |
| 1984 | Det .... | 149 | 531 | 92 | 150 | 23 | 10 | 27 | 91 | 63 | 29 | .282 |
| 1985 | Det .... | 154 | 581 | 96 | 167 | 37 | 5 | 29 | 97 | 71 | 30 | .287 |
| 1986 | Det .... | 119 | 441 | 84 | 118 | 11 | 2 | 28 | 86 | 68 | 34 | .268 |
| 1987 | Det .... | 128 | 487 | 95 | 135 | 25 | 3 | 24 | 79 | 71 | 26 | .277 |
| 1988 | LA .... | 150 | 542 | 106 | 157 | 28 | 1 | 25 | 76 | 73 | 31 | .290 |
| 1989 | LA .... | 71 | 253 | 35 | 54 | 8 | 2 | 9 | 28 | 35 | 12 | .213 |
| | | 1114 | 4005 | 669 | 1096 | 176 | 38 | 184 | 603 | 488 | 209 | .274 |

# Jose Gonzalez

Birth Date: 11/23/64
Bats: Right
Throws: Right
1989 Club:
Los Angeles Dodgers
Contest Code #: 272

Rating: 1

Jose Gonzalez is an example of the questionable moves that marked the later years of the Dodgers' Al Campanis' era. In 1980, the Dodgers signed the Dominican Republic native when he was fifteen. Early on, the Dodgers touted him as their star of the future, but by 1987 Gonzalez had still not been trained to hit a curveball or to run the bases efficiently.

Last season, Gonzalez had his longest stay in the majors. In 95 games (261 at-bats), he batted .268, with 3 home runs, 18 RBI's and 9 stolen bases. He'd been called up from Triple A Albuquerque only after injuries to Mike Marshall and Kirk Gibson. But the Dodgers subsequently traded for Kal Daniels, another outfielder, a sign of the little faith they had in Gonzalez. With Daniels back, Gonzalez should also be back—in Triple A.

| Year | Team | G | AB | R | H | 2B | 3B | HR | RBI | BB | SB | AVG |
|---|---|---|---|---|---|---|---|---|---|---|---|---|
| 1985 | LA ..... | 23 | 11 | 6 | 3 | 2 | 0 | 0 | 0 | 1 | 1 | .273 |
| 1986 | LA ..... | 57 | 93 | 15 | 20 | 5 | 1 | 2 | 6 | 7 | 4 | .215 |
| 1987 | LA ..... | 18 | 16 | 2 | 3 | 2 | 0 | 0 | 1 | 1 | 5 | .188 |
| 1988 | LA ..... | 37 | 24 | 7 | 2 | 1 | 0 | 0 | 0 | 2 | 3 | .083 |
| 1989 | LA ..... | 95 | 261 | 31 | 70 | 11 | 2 | 3 | 18 | 23 | 9 | .268 |
| | | 230 | 405 | 61 | 98 | 21 | 3 | 5 | 25 | 34 | 22 | .242 |

# Ken Griffey Sr.

Birth Date: 4/10/50
Bats: Left
Throws: Left
1989 Club:
Cincinnati Reds
Contest Code #: 273

Rating: 1

In 1989, Ken Griffey, Sr., showed he still had some life in his aging baseball body. Griffey batted .263, tied with Rolando Roomes for sixth-best on the Reds, with a .424 slugging average (third best) and a .346 on-base average (tied with Paul O'Neill for fourth-best). He hit 8 home runs, drove in 30 runs, and chipped in 4 stolen bases.

Griffey had almost as good a season as his twenty-year-old son, Ken, Jr., the Mariners' center fielder. Of course, Ken, Jr., was hurt the latter part of the season, so don't expect Pop to come as close this year.

| Year | Team | G | AB | R | H | 2B | 3B | HR | RBI | BB | SB | AVG |
|---|---|---|---|---|---|---|---|---|---|---|---|---|
| 1973 | Cin .... | 25 | 86 | 19 | 33 | 5 | 1 | 3 | 14 | 6 | 4 | .384 |
| 1974 | Cin .... | 88 | 227 | 24 | 57 | 9 | 5 | 2 | 19 | 27 | 9 | .251 |
| 1975 | Cin .... | 132 | 463 | 95 | 141 | 15 | 9 | 4 | 46 | 67 | 16 | .305 |

| Year | Team | | G | AB | R | H | 2B | 3B | HR | RBI | BB | SB | AVG |
|------|------|---|-----|------|------|------|-----|----|-----|-----|-----|-----|------|
| 1976 | Cin | .... | 148 | 562 | 111 | 189 | 28 | 9 | 6 | 74 | 62 | 34 | .336 |
| 1977 | Cin | .... | 154 | 585 | 117 | 186 | 35 | 8 | 12 | 57 | 69 | 17 | .318 |
| 1978 | Cin | .... | 158 | 614 | 90 | 177 | 33 | 8 | 10 | 63 | 54 | 23 | .288 |
| 1979 | Cin | .... | 95 | 380 | 62 | 120 | 27 | 4 | 8 | 32 | 36 | 12 | .316 |
| 1980 | Cin | .... | 146 | 544 | 89 | 160 | 28 | 10 | 13 | 85 | 62 | 23 | .294 |
| 1981 | Cin | .... | 101 | 396 | 65 | 123 | 21 | 6 | 2 | 34 | 39 | 12 | .311 |
| 1982 | NYA | .... | 127 | 484 | 70 | 134 | 23 | 2 | 12 | 54 | 39 | 10 | .277 |
| 1983 | NYA | .... | 118 | 458 | 60 | 140 | 21 | 3 | 11 | 46 | 34 | 6 | .306 |
| 1984 | NYA | .... | 120 | 399 | 44 | 109 | 20 | 1 | 7 | 56 | 29 | 2 | .273 |
| 1985 | NYA | .... | 127 | 438 | 68 | 120 | 28 | 4 | 10 | 69 | 41 | 7 | .274 |
| 1986 | NYA | .... | 59 | 198 | 33 | 60 | 7 | 0 | 9 | 26 | 15 | 2 | .303 |
| 1986 | Atl | .... | 80 | 292 | 36 | 90 | 15 | 3 | 12 | 32 | 20 | 12 | .308 |
| 1987 | Atl | .... | 122 | 399 | 65 | 114 | 24 | 1 | 14 | 64 | 46 | 4 | .286 |
| 1988 | Atl | .... | 69 | 193 | 21 | 48 | 5 | 0 | 2 | 19 | 17 | 1 | .249 |
| 1988 | Cin | .... | 25 | 50 | 5 | 14 | 1 | 0 | 2 | 4 | 2 | 0 | .280 |
| 1989 | Cin | .... | 106 | 236 | 26 | 62 | 8 | 3 | 8 | 30 | 29 | 4 | .263 |
| | | | 2000 | 7004 | 1100 | 2077 | 353 | 77 | 147 | 824 | 694 | 198 | .297 |

# Marquis Grissom

**Birth Date: 4/17/67**
**Bats: Right**
**Throws: Right**
**1989 Club:**
**Montreal Expos**
**Contest Code #: 274**

**Rating: 4**

You may not have heard much about Marquis (pronounced *Mar-cus)* Grissom before this spring, but by now you've been inundated by pre-season magazines heralding Grissom as the leading candidate for 1990 National League Rookie of the Year honors. Believe it; Grissom is going to be a superstar for years to come.

Grissom, selected by the Expos in the third round of the June 1988 draft, was a star at Florida A & M. As a sophomore, he batted .448 with 12 home runs as an outfielder, and was 9-3 with a 2.40 ERA as a pitcher. In 1988, he sizzled in the Class A league, batting .323, with 8 home runs, 39 RBI's and 23 stolen bases. Last season, he was promoted to the majors at the end of August and hit a respectable .257 in 26 games (74 at-bats).

Unless he has an atrocious spring, Grissom will be starting in the Expos' outfield this season. If you can afford him, he's well worth the risk.

| Year | Team | | G | AB | R | H | 2B | 3B | HR | RBI | BB | SB | AVG |
|------|------|---|----|----|----|----|----|----|----|-----|----|----|------|
| 1989 | Mon | .... | 26 | 74 | 16 | 19 | 2 | 0 | 1 | 2 | 12 | 1 | .257 |
| | | | 26 | 74 | 16 | 19 | 2 | 0 | 1 | 2 | 12 | 1 | .257 |

# Tony Gwynn

**Birth Date: 5/9/60**
**Bats: Left**
**Throws: Left**
**1989 Club:**
**San Diego Padres**
**Contest Code #: 275**

**Rating: 5**

Tony Gwynn is my favorite major-league player because he's never satisfied with his accomplishments; he always works hard to improve all facets of his game. During batting practice, he doesn't go for the downs like most players. He visualizes situations—hit and run, pulling the ball, going the other way, sacrifices—and practices his execution.

During the 1984 season, Gwynn stole 33 bases, but he realized he needed to improve his stealing technique (he told me that in 1984 he rode on lead-off hitter Alan Wiggins' coattails). Now he's a 40-to-50 stolen base man. In 1985, he thought he could do better on defense, so he worked on his outfield play and is now an annual Gold Glove winner.

Gwynn's batting accomplishments have been dazzling: 4 titles, including 3 in the past three seasons, and 4 200-hit seasons. Take Gwynn on your team, and he'll keep

you among the batting-average and stolen-base leaders, and he'll drive in 60 to 70 runs. Gwynn, who turns thirty in May, is just reaching his prime on his way to the Hall of Fame.

| Year | Team | G | AB | R | H | 2B | 3B | HR | RBI | BB | SB | AVG |
|------|------|----|-----|-----|------|-----|-----|-----|-----|-----|-----|------|
| 1982 | SD..... | 54 | 190 | 33 | 55 | 12 | 2 | 1 | 17 | 14 | 8 | .289 |
| 1983 | SD..... | 86 | 304 | 34 | 94 | 12 | 2 | 1 | 37 | 23 | 7 | .309 |
| 1984 | SD..... | 158 | 606 | 88 | 213 | 21 | 10 | 5 | 71 | 59 | 33 | .351 |
| 1985 | SD..... | 154 | 622 | 90 | 197 | 29 | 5 | 6 | 46 | 45 | 14 | .317 |
| 1986 | SD..... | 160 | 642 | 107 | 211 | 33 | 7 | 14 | 59 | 52 | 37 | .329 |
| 1987 | SD..... | 157 | 589 | 119 | 218 | 36 | 13 | 7 | 54 | 82 | 56 | .370 |
| 1988 | SD..... | 133 | 521 | 64 | 163 | 22 | 5 | 7 | 70 | 51 | 26 | .313 |
| 1989 | SD..... | 158 | 604 | 82 | 203 | 27 | 7 | 4 | 62 | 56 | 40 | .336 |
| | | 1060 | 4078 | 617 | 1354 | 192 | 51 | 45 | 416 | 382 | 221 | .332 |

# Billy Hatcher

**Birth Date: 10/4/60**
**Bats: Right**
**Throws: Right**
**1989 Clubs:**
**Houston Astros &**
**Pittsburgh Pirates**
**Contest Code #: 276**

**Rating: 2**

In 1987, Billy Hatcher's cork-stuffed bat split open during one game. The two halves resembled a meatball hero. Chef Hatcher was punished with a 10-day suspension. Since then, Hatcher's bat has been as flat as an overcooked crepe.

Last season, the Astros realized they needed another bat in the outfield, preferably one who had a strong right fielder's arm. Hatcher was disqualified because of his weak hitting and puny arm, so the Astros traded him to the Pirates for Glenn Wilson. The comical aspect of this trade is that the Pirates made Hatcher their right fielder.

If baseball ever makes the switch to aluminum bats, Hatcher will be in real trouble.

| Year | Team | G | AB | R | H | 2B | 3B | HR | RBI | BB | SB | AVG |
|------|------|----|-----|-----|-----|-----|-----|-----|-----|-----|-----|------|
| 1984 | ChN.... | 8 | 9 | 1 | 1 | 0 | 0 | 0 | 0 | 1 | 2 | .111 |
| 1985 | ChN.... | 53 | 163 | 24 | 40 | 12 | 1 | 2 | 10 | 8 | 2 | .245 |
| 1986 | Hou.... | 127 | 419 | 55 | 108 | 15 | 4 | 6 | 36 | 22 | 38 | .258 |
| 1987 | Hou.... | 141 | 564 | 96 | 167 | 28 | 3 | 11 | 63 | 42 | 53 | .296 |
| 1988 | Hou.... | 145 | 530 | 79 | 142 | 25 | 4 | 7 | 52 | 37 | 32 | .268 |
| 1989 | Hou.... | 108 | 395 | 49 | 90 | 15 | 3 | 3 | 44 | 30 | 22 | .228 |
| 1989 | Pit..... | 27 | 86 | 10 | 21 | 4 | 0 | 1 | 7 | 0 | 2 | .244 |
| | | 609 | 2166 | 314 | 569 | 99 | 15 | 30 | 212 | 140 | 151 | .263 |

# Mickey Hatcher

**Birth Date: 5/15/55**
**Bats: Right**
**Throws: Right**
**1989 Club:**
**Los Angeles Dodgers**
**Contest Code #: 277**

**Rating: 2**

I'll never forget a moment during the 1988 World Series, when Mickey Hatcher's face was shown in close-up on television. NBC's Vin Scully mentioned Hatcher's age, which at that time was thirty-two. My wife looked at Hatcher's silver hair and creased, weathered face and said, "No way he's thirty-two. He's got to be around thirty-five." I grabbed *The Sporting News Baseball Register*, found Hatcher's biography, and told her, "Hatcher was born in 1955, so he is thirty-two." My wife frowned. I asked her what was wrong. She said, "I was born in 1955, too. Do I look as old as he does? I'm so depressed."

Not only does Hatcher look old, but he runs like a duck and thrashes against outfield walls and into bases like a semi-pro player in a beer league. Yet in the past three seasons he's been one of the Dodgers' most consis-

tent hitters, posting batting averages of .282 in 1987, .293 in 1988, and a team-best .295 last year.

But Hatcher gets hurt a lot because of his rough-and-tumble style. He's been on the disabled list four times in the past seven seasons, including stints in 1988 and 1989.

| Year | Team | G | AB | R | H | 2B | 3B | HR | RBI | BB | SB | AVG |
|------|------|---|----|---|---|----|----|----|-----|----|----|-----|
| 1979 | LA..... | 33 | 93 | 9 | 25 | 4 | 1 | 1 | 5 | 7 | 1 | .269 |
| 1980 | LA..... | 57 | 84 | 4 | 19 | 2 | 0 | 1 | 5 | 2 | 0 | .226 |
| 1981 | Min.... | 99 | 377 | 36 | 96 | 23 | 2 | 3 | 37 | 15 | 3 | .255 |
| 1982 | Min.... | 84 | 277 | 23 | 69 | 13 | 2 | 3 | 26 | 8 | 0 | .249 |
| 1983 | Min.... | 106 | 375 | 50 | 119 | 15 | 3 | 9 | 47 | 14 | 2 | .317 |
| 1984 | Min.... | 152 | 576 | 61 | 174 | 35 | 5 | 5 | 69 | 37 | 0 | .302 |
| 1985 | Min.... | 116 | 444 | 46 | 125 | 28 | 0 | 3 | 49 | 16 | 0 | .282 |
| 1986 | Min.... | 115 | 317 | 40 | 88 | 13 | 3 | 3 | 32 | 19 | 2 | .278 |
| 1987 | LA..... | 101 | 287 | 27 | 81 | 19 | 1 | 7 | 42 | 20 | 2 | .282 |
| 1988 | LA..... | 88 | 191 | 22 | 56 | 8 | 0 | 1 | 25 | 7 | 0 | .293 |
| 1989 | LA..... | 94 | 224 | 18 | 66 | 9 | 2 | 2 | 25 | 13 | 1 | .295 |
| | | 1045 | 3245 | 336 | 918 | 169 | 19 | 38 | 362 | 158 | 11 | .283 |

# Von Hayes

**Birth Date: 8/31/58**
**Bats: Left**
**Throws: Right**
**1989 Club:**
**Philadelphia Phillies**
**Contest Code #: 278**

**Rating: 4**

**B**aseball Economics 102. In today's class, we'll study Von Hayes, who last season put together three strong months early on and was rewarded with a multi-year contract. The Phillies traded five players—including Julio Franco—to get Hayes from the Indians in December 1982. The 1983 season was a disappointment, but he had a great 1984, batting .292, with 16 home runs, 67 RBI's and 48 steals—an ideal season for a four-category fantasy player. In 1985, Hayes was more work-manlike, but in 1986 he was back among the best—a .305 average, 19 home runs, 98 RBI's and 24 steals. That season, Hayes led the National League with 46 doubles. In 1987, he reached a career high in home runs but was otherwise satisfactory, not superlative.

Considering his up-and-down performances, you'd have expected Hayes to have had a great 1988. But no: He missed most of July and August because of bone chips in his right elbow, and finished with six home runs. The critical Phillies' fans were lining up to lynch him. But Hayes, in the last year of his contract, played so well in the first half of the season that the Phillies re-signed him early. Then he cooled considerably.

No matter. Hayes still rates as a four-category star player in a good season and a three-category producer in an off year.

| Year | Team | G | AB | R | H | 2B | 3B | HR | RBI | BB | SB | AVG |
|------|------|---|----|---|---|----|----|----|-----|----|----|-----|
| 1981 | Cle..... | 43 | 109 | 21 | 28 | 8 | 2 | 1 | 17 | 14 | 8 | .257 |
| 1982 | Cle..... | 150 | 527 | 65 | 132 | 25 | 3 | 14 | 82 | 42 | 32 | .250 |
| 1983 | Phi.... | 124 | 351 | 45 | 93 | 9 | 5 | 6 | 32 | 36 | 20 | .265 |
| 1984 | Phi.... | 152 | 561 | 85 | 164 | 27 | 6 | 16 | 67 | 59 | 48 | .292 |
| 1985 | Phi.... | 152 | 570 | 76 | 150 | 30 | 4 | 13 | 70 | 61 | 21 | .263 |
| 1986 | Phi.... | 158 | 610 | 107 | 186 | 46 | 2 | 19 | 98 | 74 | 24 | .305 |
| 1987 | Phi.... | 158 | 556 | 84 | 154 | 36 | 5 | 21 | 84 | 121 | 16 | .277 |
| 1988 | Phi.... | 104 | 367 | 43 | 100 | 28 | 2 | 6 | 45 | 49 | 20 | .272 |
| 1989 | Phi.... | 154 | 540 | 93 | 140 | 27 | 2 | 26 | 78 | 101 | 28 | .259 |
| | | 1195 | 4191 | 619 | 1147 | 236 | 31 | 122 | 573 | 557 | 217 | .274 |

# Mike Huff

Birth Date: 8/11/63
Bats: Right
Throws: Right
1989 Club:
Los Angeles Dodgers
Contest Code #: 279

### Rating: 2

**M**ike Huff is the latest in a long line of Dodgers' outfield prospects who must prove his numbers were not a mirage.

Huff, selected by the Dodgers in the sixteenth round of the June 1985 draft, is a speedster who has hit for average and stolen quite a lot of stolen bases, in his minor-league career. In 1985, he batted .316 and stole 28 bases in 70 games for Great Falls (Rookie League); in 1986, he hit .293 and swiped 28 bags for Class A Vero Beach. Huff played only 31 games for Double-A San Antonio in 1987, but in his second Double A season hit .311 and stole 33 bases. Over those first four minor-league seasons, Huff hit a total of seven home runs.

The Dodgers summoned him to the big leagues late last season. In 25 at-bats, Huff had 5 hits—3 singles, 1 double, 1 home run—struck out 6 times, and was caught stealing once. He most likely will return to Triple A this season.

| Year | Team | G | AB | R | H | 2B | 3B | HR | RBI | BB | SB | AVG |
|------|------|---|----|---|---|----|----|----|-----|----|----|-----|
| 1989 | LA . . . . . | 12 | 25 | 4 | 5 | 1 | 0 | 1 | 2 | 3 | 0 | .200 |
| | | 12 | 25 | 4 | 5 | 1 | 0 | 1 | 2 | 3 | 0 | .200 |

# Darrin Jackson

Birth Date: 8/22/63
Bats: Right
Throws: Right
1989 Clubs:
Chicago Cubs &
San Diego Padres
Contest Code #: 280

### Rating: 1

**D**arrin Jackson, a good defensive outfielder, should see time as the Padres' fourth outfielder this season. Jackson was acquired from the Cubs last August with Calvin Schiraldi for Marvell Wynne, whose role he will take, and Luis Salazar.

Jackson, the Cubs' second-round pick in the June 1981 draft, developed in the minors into a .270 hitter with some pop. In 1986, he hit 15 home runs and drove in 64 runs for Double-A Pittsfield, and in 1987 hit 32 doubles, 23 taters, and knocked in 81 ribbies for Triple A Iowa. But Jackson's career came to an abrupt halt shortly after he was called up by the Cubs in September 1987; team doctors detected and removed a testicular tumor. Jackson returned at full strength in 1988. As the Cubs' fifth outfielder, he started 40 games, hit .266, drove in 20 runs, and committed only 2 errors.

| Year | Team | G | AB | R | H | 2B | 3B | HR | RBI | BB | SB | AVG |
|------|------|---|----|---|---|----|----|----|-----|----|----|-----|
| 1985 | ChN . . . . | 5 | 11 | 0 | 1 | 0 | 0 | 0 | 0 | 0 | 0 | .091 |
| 1987 | ChN . . . . | 7 | 5 | 2 | 4 | 1 | 0 | 0 | 0 | 0 | 0 | .800 |
| 1988 | ChN . . . . | 100 | 188 | 29 | 50 | 11 | 3 | 6 | 20 | 5 | 4 | .266 |
| 1989 | ChN . . . . | 45 | 83 | 7 | 19 | 4 | 0 | 1 | 8 | 6 | 1 | .229 |
| 1989 | SD . . . . . | 25 | 87 | 10 | 18 | 3 | 0 | 3 | 12 | 7 | 0 | .207 |
| | | 182 | 374 | 48 | 92 | 19 | 3 | 10 | 40 | 18 | 5 | .246 |

# John Kruk

**Birth Date: 2/9/61**
**Bats: Left**
**Throws: Left**
**1989 Clubs:**
**San Diego Padres &**
**Philadelphia Phillies**
**Contest Code #: 282**

**Rating: 3**

John Kruk has a taste for adventure and everything else in his path. Last season, Kruk, listed at 205 pounds, ate his way off the Padres. His incredible bulk was adding stress to his injured knees, yet he refused to miss a meal.

After not hitting his weight with the Padres, Kruk had a robust run of good fortune with the Phillies. By season's end, he batted .300, with 8 home runs and 44 RBI's.

In 1987, Kruk caught the attention of the National League by batting .313, fourth in the league, with 20 home runs (almost all of them to the opposite field), 91 RBI's, and 18 steals. In 1988, he picked up one injury after another and was a bigger man for the experience. Kruk's weight became a comical issue; teammates called him Curley Joe Howard.

Call Kruk anything you want, but don't call him late for dinner.

| Year | Team | G | AB | R | H | 2B | 3B | HR | RBI | BB | SB | AVG |
|------|------|---|----|----|----|----|----|----|-----|----|----|-----|
| 1986 | SD..... | 122 | 278 | 33 | 86 | 16 | 2 | 4 | 38 | 45 | 2 | .309 |
| 1987 | SD..... | 138 | 447 | 72 | 140 | 14 | 2 | 20 | 91 | 73 | 18 | .313 |
| 1988 | SD..... | 120 | 378 | 54 | 91 | 17 | 1 | 9 | 44 | 80 | 5 | .241 |
| 1989 | SD..... | 31 | 76 | 7 | 14 | 0 | 0 | 3 | 6 | 17 | 0 | .184 |
| 1989 | Phi .... | 81 | 281 | 46 | 93 | 13 | 6 | 5 | 38 | 27 | 3 | .331 |
| | | 492 | 1460 | 212 | 424 | 60 | 11 | 41 | 217 | 242 | 28 | .290 |

# Candy Maldonado

**Birth Date: 9/5/60**
**Bats: Right**
**Throws: Right**
**1989 Club:**
**San Francisco Giants**
**Contest Code #: 283**

**Rating: 1**

Candy Maldonado, an import from the Dodgers' system, strutted proudly in 1986 and 1987, first as a pinch-hitter extraordinaire and then as the Giants' everyday right fielder. But one little mistake reversed the fortunes of his entire career. During the 1987 National League Championship Series, Maldonado misplayed a catchable fly ball into a triple, which cost the Giants the series.

Since then, one imagines Maldonado replaying the episode in his head over and over again. Certainly, his mind doesn't seem to be on current events. Last season, Candy looked absolutely lost at the plate. He swing was so out of sync that it appeared he was tring to swat a gnat. With the signing of free agent Kevin Bass, expect Maldonado to find employment elsewhere.

| Year | Team | G | AB | R | H | 2B | 3B | HR | RBI | BB | SB | AVG |
|------|------|---|----|----|----|----|----|----|-----|----|----|-----|
| 1981 | LA..... | 11 | 12 | 0 | 1 | 0 | 0 | 0 | 0 | 0 | 0 | .083 |
| 1982 | LA..... | 6 | 4 | 0 | 0 | 0 | 0 | 0 | 0 | 1 | 0 | .000 |
| 1983 | LA..... | 42 | 62 | 5 | 12 | 1 | 1 | 1 | 6 | 5 | 0 | .194 |
| 1984 | LA..... | 116 | 254 | 25 | 68 | 14 | 0 | 5 | 28 | 19 | 0 | .268 |
| 1985 | LA..... | 121 | 213 | 20 | 48 | 7 | 1 | 5 | 19 | 19 | 1 | .225 |
| 1986 | SF..... | 133 | 405 | 49 | 102 | 31 | 3 | 18 | 85 | 20 | 4 | .252 |
| 1987 | SF..... | 118 | 442 | 69 | 129 | 28 | 4 | 20 | 85 | 34 | 8 | .292 |
| 1988 | SF..... | 142 | 499 | 53 | 127 | 23 | 1 | 12 | 68 | 37 | 6 | .255 |
| 1989 | SF..... | 129 | 345 | 39 | 75 | 23 | 0 | 9 | 41 | 37 | 4 | .217 |
| | | 818 | 2236 | 260 | 562 | 127 | 10 | 70 | 332 | 172 | 23 | .251 |

# Mike Marshall

**Birth Date:** 1/12/60
**Bats:** Right
**Throws:** Right
**1989 Club:**
**Los Angeles Dodgers**
**Contest Code #:** 284

**Rating:** 2

The Dodgers would be wise to do to Mike Marshall what singer Belinda Carlisle did to him several years back—dump him.

To say that Marshall has a low threshold for pain is like saying Zsa Zsa Gabor is a tad overbearing. From 1984 to 1987, Marshall was a regular on the disabled list. He's missed so many games that in 1988, his eighth year in the majors, he played a career-high 144 games—still 18 games short of a full season. Last year, Marshall was at it again, idle for 57 games. Is Marshall still a force to be reckoned with? The Mets, to whom he was traded during the off-season, are willing to find out.

| Year | Team | G | AB | R | H | 2B | 3B | HR | RBI | BB | SB | AVG |
|------|------|-----|------|-----|-----|-----|----|-----|-----|-----|-----|------|
| 1981 | LA . . . . . | 14 | 25 | 2 | 5 | 3 | 0 | 0 | 1 | 1 | 0 | .200 |
| 1982 | LA . . . . . | 49 | 95 | 10 | 23 | 3 | 0 | 5 | 9 | 13 | 2 | .242 |
| 1983 | LA . . . . . | 140 | 465 | 47 | 132 | 17 | 1 | 17 | 65 | 43 | 7 | .284 |
| 1984 | LA . . . . . | 134 | 495 | 68 | 127 | 27 | 0 | 21 | 65 | 40 | 4 | .257 |
| 1985 | LA . . . . . | 135 | 518 | 72 | 152 | 27 | 2 | 28 | 95 | 37 | 3 | .293 |
| 1986 | LA . . . . . | 103 | 330 | 47 | 77 | 11 | 0 | 19 | 53 | 27 | 4 | .233 |
| 1987 | LA . . . . . | 104 | 402 | 45 | 118 | 19 | 0 | 16 | 72 | 18 | 0 | .294 |
| 1988 | LA . . . . . | 144 | 542 | 63 | 150 | 27 | 2 | 20 | 82 | 24 | 4 | .277 |
| 1989 | LA . . . . . | 105 | 377 | 41 | 98 | 21 | 1 | 11 | 42 | 33 | 2 | .260 |
| | | 928 | 3249 | 395 | 882 | 155 | 6 | 137 | 484 | 236 | 26 | .271 |

# Dave Martinez

**Birth Date:** 9/26/64
**Bats:** Left
**Throws:** Left
**1989 Club:**
**Montreal Expos**
**Contest Code #:** 285

**Rating:** 2

In 1988, Cubs manager Don Zimmer berated center fielder Dave Martinez for not stealing enough bases. When Martinez came over to the Expos, team officials were amazed at how little Martinez had been taught about the fundamentals of base running. With proper tutelage, Martinez stole 57 bases last year. (So much for the Cubs' complaints.)

Our criticism of Martinez is his impatience at the plate. Last season, batting mostly in the lead-off spot, Martinez walked a mere 27 times—while striking out 57 times—in 361 at-bats. He's not a home-run hitter—18 in four seasons—so he shouldn't be swinging like one.

| Year | Team | G | AB | R | H | 2B | 3B | HR | RBI | BB | SB | AVG |
|------|------|-----|------|-----|-----|-----|----|-----|-----|-----|-----|------|
| 1986 | ChN . . . . | 53 | 108 | 13 | 15 | 1 | 1 | 1 | 7 | 6 | 4 | .139 |
| 1987 | ChN . . . . | 142 | 459 | 70 | 134 | 18 | 8 | 8 | 36 | 57 | 16 | .292 |
| 1988 | ChN . . . . | 75 | 256 | 27 | 65 | 10 | 1 | 4 | 34 | 21 | 7 | .254 |
| 1988 | Mon . . . . | 63 | 191 | 24 | 49 | 3 | 5 | 2 | 12 | 17 | 16 | .257 |
| 1989 | Mon . . . . | 126 | 361 | 41 | 99 | 16 | 7 | 3 | 27 | 27 | 57 | .274 |
| | | 459 | 1375 | 175 | 362 | 48 | 22 | 18 | 116 | 128 | 100 | .263 |

# Oddibe McDowell

**Birth Date:** 8/25/62
**Bats:** Left
**Throws:** Left
**1989 Clubs:**
**Cleveland Indians &**
**Atlanta Braves**
**Contest Code #:** 286

**Rating:** 2

I've never been impressed with Oddibe McDowell despite his credentials from his amateur career with Arizona State University and the 1984 U.S. Olympic baseball team. The 5′9″, 160-pound McDowell should concentrate on making contact—the more he gets on base, the more he can use his speed—and not on hitting home runs.

McDowell's power in his first three major-league seasons only reinforced his misguided notion that he can be the next Bobby Bonds. The Rangers, who'd drafted McDowell in June 1984 and promoted him to the big leagues within a year's time, became exasperated by his failure to reach base as often as he should. They farmed him out during the 1988 season, and following the season they traded him with first baseman Pete O'Brien and second baseman Jerry Browne to the Indians for second baseman Julio Franco. In short order, the Indians discovered what the Rangers already knew. In 69 games, McDowell batted .222 (53 for 239), with 3 home runs, 22 RBI's, and 12 stolen bases. McDowell struck out 36 times and walked only 25 times. His on-base average was a dismal .297.

McDowell seemed to revive himself after being traded to the Braves. Some National League fantasy-team owners now feel he's ready to deliver the promise he showed in college. I believe he was fortunate to have a good run of 76 games.

| Year | Team | G | AB | R | H | 2B | 3B | HR | RBI | BB | SB | AVG |
|---|---|---|---|---|---|---|---|---|---|---|---|---|
| 1985 | Tex .... | 111 | 406 | 63 | 97 | 14 | 5 | 18 | 42 | 36 | 25 | .239 |
| 1986 | Tex .... | 154 | 572 | 105 | 152 | 24 | 7 | 18 | 49 | 65 | 33 | .266 |
| 1987 | Tex .... | 128 | 407 | 65 | 98 | 26 | 4 | 14 | 52 | 51 | 24 | .241 |
| 1988 | Tex .... | 120 | 437 | 55 | 108 | 19 | 5 | 6 | 37 | 41 | 33 | .247 |
| 1989 | Cle..... | 69 | 239 | 33 | 53 | 5 | 2 | 3 | 22 | 25 | 12 | .222 |
| 1989 | Atl..... | 76 | 280 | 56 | 85 | 18 | 4 | 7 | 24 | 27 | 15 | .304 |
| | | 658 | 2341 | 377 | 593 | 106 | 27 | 66 | 226 | 245 | 142 | .253 |

# Willie McGee

**Birth Date: 11/2/58**
**Bats: Both**
**Throws: Right**
**1989 Club:**
**St. Louis Cardinals**
**Contest Code #: 287**

**Rating: 4**

Willie McGee did a foolish thing last season. After working with conditioning expert Mackie Shilstone prior to the season, McGee decided to supplement his regimen by pumping iron—without counseling or supervision. Instead of strengthening his body, McGee made it more susceptible to injury. Sure enough, McGee spent most of the season sidelined by rib-cage and hamstring injuries. In September, he called Shilstone and apologized; baseball observers, not aware of McGee's extracurricular activities, had assumed Shilstone's program contributed to McGee's nightmarish season.

Now that McGee has learned his lesson, he should rebound as a productive performer. He has excellent speed, good bat control, and shows occasional power.

One of the reasons McGee had originally sought out Shilstone was to help him develop more consistent power. If McGee can become a power hitter without sacrificing his health, he would be among the National League's finest all-around outfielders. But even if he stays as he is, McGee is an outstanding talent.

| Year | Team | G | AB | R | H | 2B | 3B | HR | RBI | BB | SB | AVG |
|---|---|---|---|---|---|---|---|---|---|---|---|---|
| 1982 | StL .... | 123 | 422 | 43 | 125 | 12 | 8 | 4 | 56 | 12 | 24 | .296 |
| 1983 | StL .... | 147 | 601 | 75 | 172 | 22 | 8 | 5 | 75 | 26 | 39 | .286 |
| 1984 | StL .... | 145 | 571 | 82 | 166 | 19 | 11 | 6 | 50 | 29 | 43 | .291 |
| 1985 | StL .... | 152 | 612 | 114 | 216 | 26 | 18 | 10 | 82 | 34 | 56 | .353 |
| 1986 | StL .... | 124 | 497 | 65 | 127 | 22 | 7 | 7 | 48 | 37 | 19 | .256 |
| 1987 | StL .... | 153 | 620 | 76 | 177 | 37 | 11 | 11 | 105 | 24 | 16 | .285 |
| 1988 | StL .... | 137 | 562 | 73 | 164 | 24 | 6 | 3 | 50 | 32 | 41 | .292 |
| 1989 | StL .... | 58 | 199 | 23 | 47 | 10 | 2 | 3 | 17 | 10 | 8 | .236 |
| | | 1039 | 4084 | 551 | 1194 | 172 | 71 | 49 | 483 | 204 | 246 | .292 |

# Kevin McReynolds

Birth Date: 10/16/59
Bats: Right
Throws: Right
1989 Club:
New York Mets
Contest Code #: 288

Rating: 4

**B**aseball is more of a job than a passion for Kevin McReynolds, which is why this shy outfielder sometimes appears to be disinterested and lackadaisical. During McReynolds' years in San Diego, former teammate Goose Gossage lambasted him in the media for his lack of emotion and character. And last season, McReynolds caught flak for being the fastest Met to dress and exit the clubhouse after games.

No question, McReynolds has an abundance of talent. He hits for average and for power, has speed, and plays left field exceptionally well. But in a way, he's the antithesis of Kirk Gibson. McReynolds plays with such restraint that he looks as if he's performing in slow motion. He's so ambivalent that his good performances don't inspire his teammates.

As a result, McReynolds fits in best on a team that has others who play with spark. In 1987 and 1988, McReynolds flourished when surrounded by the likes of Len Dykstra, Mookie Wilson, Keith Hernandez, Darryl Strawberry, and Howard Johnson. But when his teammates are slumping, McReynolds can't pick up the slack by himself.

| Year | Team | G | AB | R | H | 2B | 3B | HR | RBI | BB | SB | AVG |
|------|------|-----|------|-----|-----|-----|----|-----|-----|-----|----|------|
| 1983 | SD..... | 39 | 140 | 15 | 31 | 3 | 1 | 4 | 14 | 12 | 2 | .221 |
| 1984 | SD..... | 147 | 525 | 68 | 146 | 26 | 6 | 20 | 75 | 34 | 3 | .278 |
| 1985 | SD..... | 152 | 564 | 61 | 132 | 24 | 4 | 15 | 75 | 43 | 4 | .234 |
| 1986 | SD..... | 158 | 560 | 89 | 161 | 31 | 6 | 26 | 96 | 66 | 8 | .287 |
| 1987 | NYN ... | 151 | 590 | 86 | 163 | 32 | 5 | 29 | 95 | 39 | 14 | .276 |
| 1988 | NYN ... | 147 | 552 | 82 | 159 | 30 | 2 | 27 | 99 | 38 | 21 | .288 |
| 1989 | NYN ... | 148 | 545 | 74 | 148 | 25 | 3 | 22 | 85 | 46 | 15 | .272 |
| | | 942 | 3476 | 475 | 940 | 171 | 27 | 143 | 539 | 278 | 67 | .270 |

# Kevin Mitchell

Birth Date: 1/13/62
Bats: Right
Throws: Right
1989 Club:
San Francisco Giants
Contest Code #: 289

Rating: 5

**T**hroughout his pro career, Kevin Mitchell has always needed time to adjust to new surroundings. In the minor leagues, he didn't perform quite as well after a promotion as he had in a lower classification the previous seasons. And since he wasn't a good fielder at third base or in the outfield, by 1985 the Mets wondered whether he would be little more than a good Triple A player.

In 1986, Mitchell broke camp with the Mets as a utility player. He hit so well that manager Davey Johnson kept him in the lineup by rotating him at shortstop, third base, first base, and the outfield. After the season, the Mets included him in a package to obtain Kevin McReynolds from San Diego.

Mitchell struggled in San Diego, his hometown, because, insiders note, he was distracted by his playful friends and his disciplinarian grandmother. In midseason, the Padres sent him to the Giants with pitchers Dave Dravecky and Craig Lefferts for third baseman Chris Brown and pitchers Keith Comstock, Mark Davis, and Mark Grant.

After a satisfactory 1988 season, Mitchell busted loose last year, leading the major leagues in home runs and RBI's. If not for an injured left wrist, which robbed him

of his power over the second half, Mitchell might have challenged the all-time, single-season home-run record. In any case, his overall performance won him NL MVP honors. Now that he's comfortable with his role with the Giants, Mitchell should continue to produce.

| Year | Team | G | AB | R | H | 2B | 3B | HR | RBI | BB | SB | AVG |
|------|------|---|----|---|---|----|----|----|-----|----|----|-----|
| 1984 | NYN ... | 7 | 14 | 0 | 3 | 0 | 0 | 0 | 1 | 0 | 0 | .214 |
| 1986 | NYN ... | 108 | 328 | 51 | 91 | 22 | 2 | 12 | 43 | 33 | 3 | .277 |
| 1987 | SD ..... | 62 | 196 | 19 | 48 | 7 | 1 | 7 | 26 | 20 | 0 | .245 |
| 1987 | SF ..... | 69 | 268 | 49 | 82 | 13 | 1 | 15 | 44 | 28 | 9 | .306 |
| 1988 | SF ..... | 148 | 505 | 60 | 127 | 25 | 7 | 19 | 80 | 48 | 5 | .251 |
| 1989 | SF ..... | 154 | 543 | 100 | 158 | 34 | 6 | 47 | 125 | 87 | 3 | .291 |
| | | 548 | 1854 | 279 | 509 | 101 | 17 | 100 | 319 | 216 | 20 | .275 |

# John Morris

**Birth Date: 2/23/61**
**Bats: Left**
**Throws: Left**
**1989 Club:**
**St. Louis Cardinals**
**Contest Code #: 290**

**Rating: 1**

As a member of Seton Hall University's baseball team, John Morris was named to *The Sporting News* college baseball All-America team in 1982. In 1983, Morris, who was chosen by the Royals in the first round of the June 1982 draft, was named the Southern League MVP. That season, Morris batted .288, with 23 home runs and 92 RBI's. In 1985, the Royals sent him to the Cardinals for Lonnie Smith.

But injuries and ineffective hitting have marred Morris's major-league totals. In 1986, he was twice put on the disabled list because of elbow and back injuries. In 1987, the only season in which Morris played more than 100 games, he batted .261, with 3 home runs and 23 RBI's, as a platoon and backup outfielder. In 1988, he missed most of the season because of his slow recovery from pre-season back surgery. Last year, Morris was used as a pinch-hitter (9 for 41) and as a replacement for injured and resting Redbirds.

| Year | Team | G | AB | R | H | 2B | 3B | HR | RBI | BB | SB | AVG |
|------|------|---|----|---|---|----|----|----|-----|----|----|-----|
| 1986 | StL .... | 39 | 100 | 8 | 24 | 0 | 1 | 1 | 14 | 7 | 6 | .240 |
| 1987 | StL .... | 101 | 157 | 22 | 41 | 6 | 4 | 3 | 23 | 11 | 5 | .261 |
| 1988 | StL .... | 20 | 38 | 3 | 11 | 2 | 1 | 0 | 3 | 1 | 0 | .289 |
| 1989 | StL .... | 96 | 117 | 8 | 28 | 4 | 1 | 2 | 14 | 4 | 1 | .239 |
| | | 256 | 412 | 41 | 104 | 12 | 7 | 6 | 54 | 23 | 12 | .252 |

# Dale Murphy

**Birth Date: 3/12/56**
**Bats: Right**
**Throws: Right**
**1989 Club:**
**Atlanta Braves**
**Contest Code #: 291**

**Rating: 3**

Over the past two seasons, Dale Murphy's poor performances have been diagnosed by scores of scouts and hundreds of thousands of fans. The sideline practitioners offered such opinions as: Murphy's bat slowed; his feet slowed; he was burned out from the weight of dismal Braves baseball.

But during the middle of last season, Murphy's power came out of hiding. Always a streaky hitter, Murphy began launching monstrous home runs in bunches. By season's end, the Murph had totaled 20. Not bad for most, but not up to the standards Murphy had set in the past.

Murphy's most glaring weakness has been his failure to reach base with any consistency. Coming off a .226

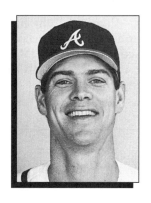

batting average in 1988, last season Murphy struck out 142 times and made 131 hits in 574 at-bats. Perhaps the grind—Murphy has played 150 or more games a season 9 times since 1980—and the years of losing have worn Murphy down. I believe that Murphy could come closer to his earlier form if he was not on a team that expected him to produce all the runs by himself.

| Year | Team | G | AB | R | H | 2B | 3B | HR | RBI | BB | SB | AVG |
|------|------|---|----|---|---|----|----|----|-----|----|----|-----|
| 1976 | Atl..... | 19 | 65 | 3 | 17 | 6 | 0 | 0 | 9 | 7 | 0 | .262 |
| 1977 | Atl..... | 18 | 76 | 5 | 24 | 8 | 1 | 2 | 14 | 0 | 0 | .316 |
| 1978 | Atl..... | 151 | 530 | 66 | 120 | 14 | 3 | 23 | 79 | 42 | 11 | .226 |
| 1979 | Atl..... | 104 | 384 | 53 | 106 | 7 | 2 | 21 | 57 | 38 | 6 | .276 |
| 1980 | Atl..... | 156 | 569 | 98 | 160 | 27 | 2 | 33 | 89 | 59 | 9 | .281 |
| 1981 | Atl..... | 104 | 369 | 43 | 91 | 12 | 1 | 13 | 50 | 44 | 14 | .247 |
| 1982 | Atl..... | 162 | 598 | 113 | 168 | 23 | 2 | 36 | 109 | 93 | 23 | .281 |
| 1983 | Atl..... | 162 | 589 | 131 | 178 | 24 | 4 | 36 | 121 | 90 | 30 | .302 |
| 1984 | Atl..... | 162 | 607 | 94 | 176 | 32 | 8 | 36 | 100 | 79 | 19 | .290 |
| 1985 | Atl..... | 162 | 616 | 118 | 185 | 32 | 2 | 37 | 111 | 90 | 10 | .300 |
| 1986 | Atl..... | 160 | 614 | 89 | 163 | 29 | 7 | 29 | 83 | 75 | 7 | .265 |
| 1987 | Atl..... | 159 | 566 | 115 | 167 | 27 | 1 | 44 | 105 | 115 | 16 | .295 |
| 1988 | Atl..... | 156 | 592 | 77 | 134 | 35 | 4 | 24 | 77 | 74 | 3 | .226 |
| 1989 | Atl..... | 154 | 574 | 60 | 131 | 16 | 0 | 20 | 84 | 65 | 3 | .228 |
| | | 1829 | 6749 | 1065 | 1820 | 292 | 37 | 354 | 1088 | 871 | 151 | .270 |

# Dwayne Murphy

**Birth Date: 3/18/55**
**Bats: Left**
**Throws: Right**
**1989 Club:**
**Philadelphia Phillies**
**Contest Code #: 292**

**Rating: 1**

Dwayne Murphy's long and winding road led him to the Phillies last year. Philadelphia may be the last stop in Murphy's odyssey.

Early in his major-league career, Murphy was a standout defensive center fielder with the A's. His batting average was usually sub-par, but he reached double figures in home runs seven straight seasons. In 1984, he swatted a career-high 33 dingers. But beginning in 1986, injuries have reduced his playing time, and the less he batted, the more conspicuous his anemic batting averages became. He's since bounced around in the minors, with the Tigers and now the Phillies.

Last year, Murphy hit .218, including 9 hits in 43 at-bats as a pinch-hitter. His slugging average was an impressive .423, though he participated in only 98 games.

| Year | Team | G | AB | R | H | 2B | 3B | HR | RBI | BB | SB | AVG |
|------|------|---|----|---|---|----|----|----|-----|----|----|-----|
| 1978 | Oak.... | 60 | 52 | 15 | 10 | 2 | 0 | 0 | 5 | 7 | 0 | .192 |
| 1979 | Oak.... | 121 | 388 | 57 | 99 | 10 | 4 | 11 | 40 | 84 | 15 | .255 |
| 1980 | Oak.... | 159 | 573 | 86 | 157 | 18 | 2 | 13 | 68 | 102 | 26 | .274 |
| 1981 | Oak.... | 107 | 390 | 58 | 98 | 10 | 3 | 15 | 60 | 73 | 10 | .251 |
| 1982 | Oak.... | 151 | 543 | 84 | 129 | 15 | 1 | 27 | 94 | 94 | 26 | .238 |
| 1983 | Oak.... | 130 | 471 | 55 | 107 | 17 | 2 | 17 | 75 | 62 | 7 | .227 |
| 1984 | Oak.... | 153 | 559 | 93 | 143 | 18 | 2 | 33 | 88 | 74 | 4 | .256 |
| 1985 | Oak.... | 152 | 523 | 77 | 122 | 21 | 3 | 20 | 59 | 84 | 4 | .233 |
| 1986 | Oak.... | 98 | 329 | 50 | 83 | 11 | 3 | 9 | 39 | 56 | 3 | .252 |
| 1987 | Oak.... | 82 | 219 | 39 | 51 | 7 | 0 | 8 | 35 | 58 | 4 | .233 |
| 1988 | Det .... | 49 | 144 | 14 | 36 | 5 | 0 | 4 | 19 | 24 | 1 | .250 |
| 1989 | Phi .... | 98 | 156 | 20 | 34 | 5 | 0 | 9 | 27 | 29 | 0 | .218 |
| | | 1360 | 4347 | 648 | 1069 | 139 | 20 | 166 | 609 | 747 | 100 | .246 |

# Donell Nixon

**Birth Date:** 12/31/61
**Bats:** Right
**Throws:** Right
**1989 Club:**
San Francisco Giants
**Contest Code #:** 293

**Rating: 1**

**D**onell Nixon had his turn in Giants' manager Roger Craig's musical-chairs contest for the right-field job, but his atrocious defense left him without a seat in the lineup.

At best, Nixon is a decent hitter who has little power but good speed. Nixon had been a speed merchant in the minors, leading the California League with 144 stolen bases in 1983; leading the Southern League with 102 thefts in 1984; and topping the Pacific Coast League with 46 in 1987. But in the major leagues, his defense has kept him chained to the bench.

The answer to Nixon's problems would be a trade to an American League team, where he could be used as a designated hitter near the top of the batting order.

| Year | Team | G | AB | R | H | 2B | 3B | HR | RBI | BB | SB | AVG |
|------|------|----|-----|----|-----|----|----|----|-----|----|----|------|
| 1987 | Sea .... | 46 | 132 | 17 | 33 | 4 | 0 | 3 | 12 | 13 | 21 | .250 |
| 1988 | SF ..... | 59 | 78 | 15 | 27 | 3 | 0 | 0 | 6 | 10 | 11 | .346 |
| 1989 | SF ..... | 95 | 166 | 23 | 44 | 2 | 0 | 1 | 15 | 11 | 10 | .265 |
| | | 200 | 376 | 55 | 104 | 9 | 0 | 4 | 33 | 34 | 42 | .277 |

# Otis Nixon

**Birth Date:** 1/9/59
**Bats:** Right & Left
**Throws:** Right
**1989 Club:**
Montreal Expos
**Contest Code #:** 294

**Rating: 2**

**O**tis Nixon, Donell Nixon's older brother, has found his niche with the Expos as a platoon outfielder who can steal bases by the bushels. In the past two seasons, Otis has stolen a combined 83 bases in 216 major-league games. Nixon's feeble batting averages may make him a one-dimensional player, but he's excellent in that dimension.

Nixon has spent a good portion of his 11 pro seasons in the minor leagues. Drafted by the Yankees in June 1979, Nixon was promoted to the majors at the end of the 1983 season, and was traded months later to the Indians. In 1988, after completing six years of pro service, Nixon was signed by the Expos to a minor-league contract. He arrived in Montreal 67 games later.

If you're looking for a low-rated outfielder who can help you in one category, this Nixon's the one.

| Year | Team | G | AB | R | H | 2B | 3B | HR | RBI | BB | SB | AVG |
|------|------|-----|-----|-----|-----|----|----|----|-----|----|-----|------|
| 1983 | NYA.... | 13 | 14 | 2 | 2 | 0 | 0 | 0 | 0 | 1 | 2 | .143 |
| 1984 | Cle..... | 49 | 91 | 16 | 14 | 0 | 0 | 0 | 1 | 8 | 12 | .154 |
| 1985 | Cle..... | 104 | 162 | 34 | 38 | 4 | 0 | 3 | 9 | 8 | 20 | .235 |
| 1986 | Cle..... | 105 | 95 | 33 | 25 | 4 | 1 | 0 | 8 | 13 | 23 | .263 |
| 1987 | Cle..... | 19 | 17 | 2 | 1 | 0 | 0 | 0 | 1 | 3 | 2 | .059 |
| 1988 | Mon.... | 90 | 271 | 47 | 66 | 8 | 2 | 0 | 15 | 28 | 46 | .244 |
| 1989 | Mon.... | 126 | 258 | 41 | 56 | 7 | 2 | 0 | 21 | 33 | 37 | .217 |
| | | 506 | 908 | 175 | 202 | 23 | 5 | 3 | 55 | 94 | 142 | .222 |

# Paul O'Neill

**Birth Date:** 2/25/63
**Bats:** Left
**Throws:** Left
**1989 Club:**
Cincinnati Reds
**Contest Code #:** 295

## Rating: 3

**D**espite putting up good numbers in the minor leagues for seven seasons, it took the Reds until 1988 to feel comfortable with Paul O'Neill in their everyday lineup. But once they installed him as a platoon player in the outfield and at first base, O'Neill delivered 16 home runs and 73 RBI's.

Last season, O'Neill started off nicely, batting .287, with 14 home runs, 62 RBI's, and 13 stolen bases. By July 21, he went on the disabled list with a fractured left thumb and did not return until September.

National League scouts say O'Neill, a good low-ball hitter, is capable of 20 home runs, 90 RBI's, a .300 batting average, and 15 stolen bases. Now that he's entering his tenth pro season, it would be timely for O'Neill to reach those expectations.

| Year | Team | G | AB | R | H | 2B | 3B | HR | RBI | BB | SB | AVG |
|------|------|---|-----|---|-----|----|----|----|-----|-----|----|------|
| 1985 | Cin .... | 5 | 12 | 1 | 4 | 1 | 0 | 0 | 1 | 0 | 0 | .333 |
| 1986 | Cin .... | 3 | 2 | 0 | 0 | 0 | 0 | 0 | 0 | 1 | 0 | .000 |
| 1987 | Cin .... | 84 | 160 | 24 | 41 | 14 | 1 | 7 | 28 | 18 | 2 | .256 |
| 1988 | Cin .... | 145 | 485 | 58 | 122 | 25 | 3 | 16 | 73 | 38 | 8 | .252 |
| 1989 | Cin .... | 117 | 428 | 49 | 118 | 24 | 2 | 15 | 74 | 46 | 20 | .276 |
| | | 354 | 1087 | 132 | 285 | 64 | 6 | 38 | 176 | 103 | 30 | .262 |

# Terry Puhl

**Birth Date:** 7/8/56
**Bats:** Left
**Throws:** Right
**1989 Club:**
Houston Astros
**Contest Code #:** 296

## Rating: 1

**I**n the world of fantasy baseball, Terry Puhl is the kind of player many owners have paid too much for at their drafts. In 1980, when fantasy leagues were in their infancy, Puhl had his most productive season, hitting a career-best 13 home runs. But over time Puhl's home-run and stolen-base totals have declined, and his batting average has fluctuated between .303 and .230.

Fortunately for Puhl, the Astros have never given up on him. In the past two seasons, he's rewarded them with a career-high .303 average and a respectable .271. But whatever power and speed he once possessed are long gone, making Puhl an unpredictable singles hitter.

| Year | Team | G | AB | R | H | 2B | 3B | HR | RBI | BB | SB | AVG |
|------|------|---|-----|---|-----|----|----|----|-----|-----|----|------|
| 1977 | Hou.... | 60 | 229 | 40 | 69 | 13 | 5 | 0 | 10 | 30 | 10 | .301 |
| 1978 | Hou.... | 149 | 585 | 87 | 169 | 25 | 6 | 3 | 35 | 48 | 32 | .289 |
| 1979 | Hou.... | 157 | 600 | 87 | 172 | 22 | 4 | 8 | 49 | 58 | 30 | .287 |
| 1980 | Hou.... | 141 | 535 | 75 | 151 | 24 | 5 | 13 | 55 | 60 | 27 | .282 |
| 1981 | Hou.... | 96 | 350 | 43 | 88 | 19 | 4 | 3 | 28 | 31 | 22 | .251 |
| 1982 | Hou.... | 145 | 507 | 64 | 133 | 17 | 9 | 8 | 50 | 51 | 17 | .262 |
| 1983 | Hou.... | 137 | 465 | 66 | 136 | 25 | 7 | 8 | 44 | 36 | 24 | .292 |
| 1984 | Hou.... | 132 | 449 | 66 | 135 | 19 | 7 | 9 | 55 | 59 | 13 | .301 |
| 1985 | Hou.... | 57 | 194 | 34 | 55 | 14 | 3 | 2 | 23 | 18 | 6 | .284 |
| 1986 | Hou.... | 81 | 172 | 17 | 42 | 10 | 0 | 3 | 14 | 15 | 3 | .244 |
| 1987 | Hou.... | 90 | 122 | 9 | 28 | 5 | 0 | 2 | 15 | 11 | 1 | .230 |
| 1988 | Hou.... | 113 | 234 | 42 | 71 | 7 | 2 | 3 | 19 | 35 | 22 | .303 |
| 1989 | Hou.... | 121 | 354 | 41 | 96 | 25 | 4 | 0 | 27 | 45 | 9 | .271 |
| | | 1479 | 4796 | 671 | 1345 | 225 | 56 | 62 | 424 | 497 | 216 | .280 |

# Tim Raines

**Birth Date: 9/16/59**
**Bats: Right & Left**
**Throws: Right**
**1989 Club:**
**Montreal Expos**
**Contest Code #: 297**

**Rating: 5**

Only Tim Raines can hit .286, with 9 home runs, 60 RBI's, and steal 41 bases, and have that characterized as an off year. In reality, Raines was asked to carry the Expos through their lean second half by moving from the lead-off spot to the number four hole; his left-handed bat balanced the excess of right-handed hitters in the middle of the Expos' batting order.

Raines is one of my favorite players and one of the best in baseball. He's a four-category player, pumping out home runs and ribbies, and shining in batting average and steals. He's hit higher than .309 for four consecutive seasons (1984 through 1987), has reached double figures in home runs four times, and stolen 70 or more bases six times.

Tim Raines is the National League's equivalent of Rickey Henderson, with a shade less power. There were rumors following the 1989 season that the Expos were toying with trading Raines. Wherever he winds up, he'll hit the ground running.

| Year | Team | G | AB | R | H | 2B | 3B | HR | RBI | BB | SB | AVG |
|------|------|---|----|---|---|----|----|----|-----|----|----|-----|
| 1979 | Mon.... | 6 | 0 | 3 | 0 | 0 | 0 | 0 | 0 | 0 | 2 | .000 |
| 1980 | Mon.... | 15 | 20 | 5 | 1 | 0 | 0 | 0 | 0 | 6 | 5 | .050 |
| 1981 | Mon.... | 88 | 313 | 61 | 95 | 13 | 7 | 5 | 37 | 45 | 71 | .304 |
| 1982 | Mon.... | 156 | 647 | 90 | 179 | 32 | 8 | 4 | 43 | 75 | 78 | .277 |
| 1983 | Mon.... | 156 | 615 | 133 | 183 | 32 | 8 | 11 | 71 | 97 | 90 | .298 |
| 1984 | Mon.... | 160 | 622 | 106 | 192 | 38 | 9 | 8 | 60 | 87 | 75 | .309 |
| 1985 | Mon.... | 150 | 575 | 115 | 184 | 30 | 13 | 11 | 41 | 81 | 70 | .320 |
| 1986 | Mon.... | 151 | 580 | 91 | 194 | 35 | 10 | 9 | 62 | 78 | 70 | .334 |
| 1987 | Mon.... | 139 | 530 | 123 | 175 | 34 | 8 | 18 | 68 | 90 | 50 | .330 |
| 1988 | Mon.... | 109 | 429 | 66 | 116 | 19 | 7 | 12 | 48 | 53 | 33 | .270 |
| 1989 | Mon.... | 145 | 517 | 76 | 148 | 29 | 6 | 9 | 60 | 93 | 41 | .286 |
| | | 1275 | 4848 | 869 | 1467 | 262 | 76 | 87 | 490 | 705 | 585 | .303 |

# Randy Ready

**Birth Date: 1/8/60**
**Bats: Right**
**Throws: Right**
**1989 Clubs:**
**San Diego Padres &**
**Philadelphia Phillies**
**Contest Code #: 298**

**Rating: 2**

National League fantasy-team owners appreciate Randy Ready for his versatility—he can play second base, third base, and the outfield. In this contest, you'll come to appreciate Ready's offensive contributions over the long haul.

Ready, who'll rove across the diamond for the Phillies this season, hits for a reasonable average, shows some power, brings home runners in RBI opportunities, and occasionally steals a base. Last year, Ready had a .368 on-base average and a .425 slugging average.

Once a highly touted prospect in the Brewers' organization, Ready batted .300 or better in seven minor-league seasons; his cumulative minor-league average was .341. Ready's best major-league season was 1987, in which he played 124 games, batted .309, hit 12 home runs, drove in 54 runs, and stole 7 bases.

| Year | Team | G | AB | R | H | 2B | 3B | HR | RBI | BB | SB | AVG |
|------|------|---|----|---|---|----|----|----|-----|----|----|-----|
| 1983 | Mil..... | 12 | 37 | 8 | 15 | 3 | 2 | 1 | 6 | 6 | 0 | .405 |
| 1984 | Mil..... | 37 | 123 | 13 | 23 | 6 | 1 | 3 | 13 | 14 | 0 | .187 |
| 1985 | Mil..... | 48 | 181 | 29 | 48 | 9 | 5 | 1 | 21 | 14 | 0 | .265 |
| 1986 | Mil..... | 23 | 79 | 8 | 15 | 4 | 0 | 1 | 4 | 9 | 2 | .190 |
| 1986 | SD..... | 1 | 3 | 0 | 0 | 0 | 0 | 0 | 0 | 0 | 0 | .000 |
| 1987 | SD..... | 124 | 350 | 69 | 108 | 26 | 6 | 12 | 54 | 67 | 7 | .309 |
| 1988 | SD..... | 114 | 331 | 43 | 88 | 16 | 2 | 7 | 39 | 39 | 6 | .266 |
| 1989 | SD..... | 28 | 67 | 4 | 17 | 2 | 1 | 0 | 5 | 11 | 0 | .254 |
| 1989 | Phi .... | 72 | 187 | 33 | 50 | 11 | 1 | 8 | 21 | 31 | 4 | .267 |
| | | 459 | 1358 | 207 | 364 | 77 | 18 | 33 | 163 | 191 | 19 | .268 |

# Gary Redus

Birth Date: 11/1/56
Bats: Right
Throws: Right
1989 Club:
Pittsburgh Pirates
Contest Code #: 299

### Rating: 2

**T**he Pirates acquired Gary Redus in August 1988 to fortify their bench for the stretch run. As it turned out, Redus became even more valuable in 1989 as Andy Van Slyke's replacement. In 98 games, Redus was second on the team in batting average (.283), slugging percentage (.462), and stolen bases (25).

Drafted by the Reds in June 1978, Redus was a star in the minor leagues, batting .301 or better in three of five seasons, including a .462 mark in his first pro season. But, as a platoon outfielder with the Reds' big club, Redus never came close to his lofty minor-league batting numbers.

Redus is in excellent physical condition; tests conducted by the Pirates in 1988 showed Redus, then thirty-one, to have the body of a twenty-five-year-old player.

| Year | Team | G | AB | R | H | 2B | 3B | HR | RBI | BB | SB | AVG |
|------|------|---|----|---|---|----|----|----|-----|----|----|-----|
| 1982 | Cin .... | 20 | 83 | 12 | 18 | 3 | 2 | 1 | 7 | 5 | 11 | .217 |
| 1983 | Cin .... | 125 | 453 | 90 | 112 | 20 | 9 | 17 | 51 | 71 | 39 | .247 |
| 1984 | Cin .... | 123 | 394 | 69 | 100 | 21 | 3 | 7 | 22 | 52 | 48 | .254 |
| 1985 | Cin .... | 101 | 246 | 51 | 62 | 14 | 4 | 6 | 28 | 44 | 48 | .252 |
| 1986 | Phi .... | 90 | 340 | 62 | 84 | 22 | 4 | 11 | 33 | 47 | 25 | .247 |
| 1987 | ChA.... | 130 | 475 | 78 | 112 | 26 | 6 | 12 | 48 | 69 | 52 | .236 |
| 1988 | ChA.... | 77 | 262 | 42 | 69 | 10 | 4 | 6 | 34 | 33 | 26 | .263 |
| 1988 | Pit..... | 30 | 71 | 12 | 14 | 2 | 0 | 2 | 4 | 15 | 5 | .197 |
| 1989 | Pit..... | 98 | 279 | 42 | 79 | 18 | 7 | 6 | 33 | 40 | 25 | .283 |
| | | 794 | 2603 | 458 | 650 | 136 | 39 | 68 | 260 | 376 | 279 | .250 |

# R. J. Reynolds

Birth Date: 4/19/60
Bats: Right & Left
Throws: Right
1989 Club:
Pittsburgh Pirates
Contest Code #: 300

### Rating: 2

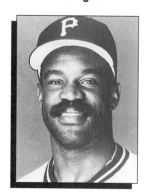

**W**ho does R. J. Reynolds have to appease in order to play every day?

Last season, Reynolds, a lifetime .264 hitter, batted .270—.263 (65 for 247) from the left side, .284 (33 for 116) from the right—and stole a career-high 22 bases. As a pinch-hitter, Reynolds batted .290 (9 for 31) and drove in 5 runs. More important, he played hard throughout the Pirates' horrendous season and set an example for his teammates. Because he was one of the team's most dependable players last year, it was surprising that the team traded right-fielder Glenn Wilson for another outfielder (Billy Hatcher).

Fortunately for Reynolds, his good humor carries him through such situations. Reynolds, a sensitive man, also happens to be one of the funniest, most quick-witted players in the National League.

| Year | Team | G | AB | R | H | 2B | 3B | HR | RBI | BB | SB | AVG |
|------|------|---|----|---|---|----|----|----|-----|----|----|-----|
| 1983 | LA ..... | 24 | 55 | 5 | 13 | 0 | 0 | 2 | 11 | 3 | 5 | .236 |
| 1984 | LA ..... | 73 | 240 | 24 | 62 | 12 | 2 | 2 | 24 | 14 | 7 | .258 |
| 1985 | LA ..... | 73 | 207 | 22 | 55 | 10 | 4 | 0 | 25 | 13 | 6 | .266 |
| 1985 | Pit ..... | 31 | 130 | 22 | 40 | 5 | 3 | 3 | 17 | 9 | 12 | .308 |
| 1986 | Pit ..... | 118 | 402 | 63 | 108 | 30 | 2 | 9 | 48 | 40 | 16 | .269 |
| 1987 | Pit ..... | 117 | 335 | 47 | 87 | 24 | 1 | 7 | 51 | 34 | 14 | .260 |
| 1988 | Pit ..... | 130 | 323 | 35 | 80 | 14 | 2 | 6 | 51 | 20 | 15 | .248 |
| 1989 | Pit ..... | 125 | 363 | 45 | 98 | 16 | 2 | 6 | 48 | 34 | 22 | .270 |
| | | 691 | 2055 | 263 | 543 | 111 | 16 | 35 | 275 | 167 | 97 | .264 |

# Bip Roberts

Birth Date: 10/27/63
Bats: Right & Left
Throws: Right
1989 Club:
San Diego Padres
Contest Code #: 301

### Rating: 3

**L**eon "Bip" Roberts had a truly impressive 1989 season. Playing in the infield and outfield, Roberts batted .301, had an on-base average of .391, a slugging average of .422, stole 21 bases, and was a factor in the Padres' late run at the National League's Western Division champion Giants.

Roberts, a good hitter in his first four minor-league seasons, was drafted off the Pirates' unprotected list in December 1985. In 1986, he joined the big club and platooned with Tim Flannery at second. Once the Padres fulfilled their draft obligation (remember, players drafted in December must stay in the majors a full season or be returned to their former club), Roberts spent two successful seasons at Triple A (.306 and .353, respectively) as a second baseman, third baseman, and outfielder.

With Jose Oquendo now a starting player, Roberts has become the league's best roving player.

| Year | Team | G | AB | R | H | 2B | 3B | HR | RBI | BB | SB | AVG |
|------|------|---|----|---|---|----|----|----|----|----|----|-----|
| 1986 | SD..... | 101 | 241 | 34 | 61 | 5 | 2 | 1 | 12 | 14 | 14 | .253 |
| 1988 | SD..... | 5 | 9 | 1 | 3 | 0 | 0 | 0 | 0 | 1 | 0 | .333 |
| 1989 | SD..... | 117 | 329 | 81 | 99 | 15 | 8 | 3 | 25 | 49 | 21 | .301 |
| | | 223 | 579 | 116 | 163 | 20 | 10 | 4 | 37 | 64 | 35 | .282 |

# Rolando Roomes

Birth Date: 2/15/62
Bats: Right
Throws: Right
1989 Club:
Cincinnati Reds
Contest Code #: 302

### Rating: 3

**I**'ll always have a warm spot in my heart for Rolando Roomes. I drafted him for my fantasy team in 1988—and endure the hearty laughter from my fellow owners, who said "Rolando who?" when I brought up his name—for two reasons. First, I'd been tipped by a Cubs' scout about Roomes' power and speed. Second, I figured Roomes would most likely be the player demoted when the Cubs felt Mark Grace was ready for promotion. A month later, I reserved Roomes, moved John Kruk to the outfield, and claimed Grace.

In December 1988, Cubs general manager Jim Frey, not as impressed with Roomes as one of his scouts was, traded him to the Reds for Lloyd McClendon. The Reds called up Roomes last summer and he responded with a .263 average, 7 home runs, 34 RBI's, and 12 stolen bases in 107 games. He platooned with Herm Winningham for a time, but showed himself ready to play on a full-time basis.

Early in his pro career, Roomes put up big numbers in 1982 (.319, 22 home runs, 59 RBI's in 65 games for Class-A Geneva) and 1987 (.308, 21 home runs, 95 RBI's and an Eastern League–leading 12 triples for Double-A Pittsfield).

| Year | Team | G | AB | R | H | 2B | 3B | HR | RBI | BB | SB | AVG |
|------|------|---|----|---|---|----|----|----|----|----|----|-----|
| 1988 | ChN.... | 17 | 16 | 3 | 3 | 0 | 0 | 0 | 0 | 0 | 0 | .188 |
| 1989 | Cin .... | 107 | 315 | 36 | 83 | 18 | 5 | 7 | 34 | 13 | 12 | .263 |
| | | 124 | 331 | 39 | 86 | 18 | 5 | 7 | 34 | 13 | 12 | .260 |

# Juan Samuel

**Birth Date:** 12/9/60
**Bats:** Right
**Throws:** Right
**1989 Clubs:**
**Philadelphia Phillies &**
**New York Mets**
**Contest Code #: 303**

## Rating: 3

Juan Samuel has some great gifts, but the sum of his parts does not equal a great player.

Samuel can hit for power (he's reached double figures in home runs every season since 1984), drive in runs (he's averaged 73 ribbies per year since 1984), and steal bases (an average of 46 a season since 1984). The problems: He doesn't hit for enough power to bat in the middle of the order, where his speed also would be wasted; and he doesn't make enough contact to be a good top-of-the-order hitter. Since 1984, he's averaged 147 strikeouts and only 38 walks a season.

Last, but not least, Samuel is a poor fielder. He led all National League second basemen in errors in 1984 (33), 1986 (25), and 1987 (18). As a center fielder, he has the speed to cover the position but lacks sure hands and a sense of awareness.

So where should Samuel bat, and which position should he play? If I were his manager, I'd consider batting him third to utilize his power and get into scoring position for my clean-up hitter. In 1990, it's Tommy Lasorda's problem; the Mets traded Samuel to the Dodgers during the off-season.

| Year | Team | G | AB | R | H | 2B | 3B | HR | RBI | BB | SB | AVG |
|------|------|-----|------|-----|-----|-----|-----|-----|-----|-----|-----|------|
| 1983 | Phi .... | 18 | 65 | 14 | 18 | 1 | 2 | 2 | 5 | 4 | 3 | .277 |
| 1984 | Phi .... | 160 | 701 | 105 | 191 | 36 | 19 | 15 | 69 | 28 | 72 | .272 |
| 1985 | Phi .... | 161 | 663 | 101 | 175 | 31 | 13 | 19 | 74 | 33 | 53 | .264 |
| 1986 | Phi .... | 145 | 591 | 90 | 157 | 36 | 12 | 16 | 78 | 26 | 42 | .266 |
| 1987 | Phi .... | 160 | 655 | 113 | 178 | 37 | 15 | 28 | 100 | 60 | 35 | .272 |
| 1988 | Phi .... | 157 | 629 | 68 | 153 | 32 | 9 | 12 | 67 | 39 | 33 | .243 |
| 1989 | Phi .... | 51 | 199 | 32 | 49 | 3 | 1 | 8 | 20 | 18 | 11 | .246 |
| 1989 | NYN ... | 86 | 333 | 37 | 76 | 13 | 1 | 3 | 28 | 24 | 31 | .228 |
| | | 938 | 3836 | 560 | 997 | 189 | 72 | 103 | 441 | 232 | 280 | .260 |

# Pat Sheridan

**Birth Date:** 12/4/57
**Bats:** Left
**Throws:** Right
**1989 Clubs:**
**Detroit Tigers &**
**San Francisco Giants**
**Contest Code #: 304**

## Rating: 1

I hate whiners like Pat Sheridan. During the lull between the second and third games of the 1989 World Series, Sheridan, a good-fielding/poor-hitting outfielder, campaigned in the media that he deserved to start in right field over his struggling teammate, Candy Maldonado. So Giants' manager Roger Craig obliged him. Sure enough, Sheridan misplayed the first ball hit his way—a catchable fly ball—into a triple, and the A's were on their way to another victory.

Sheridan should be thankful he's still a major leaguer. He's had only two good seasons in the bigs—a .270 batting average in 1983, and a .283 average in 1984. He has fair speed and very little power. His 11 home runs in 1988 were inflated by the friendly confines of Tiger Stadium.

Last year, he batted .205, with 3 home runs and 14 RBI's in 161 at-bats. His on-base average was a mediocre .264, and he stole only 4 bases. The Giants acted on Sheridan's complaints by signing free agent Kevin Bass in November.

| Year | Team | G | AB | R | H | 2B | 3B | HR | RBI | BB | SB | AVG |
|------|------|---|----|---|---|----|----|----|----|----|----|-----|
| 1981 | KC..... | 3 | 1 | 0 | 0 | 0 | 0 | 0 | 0 | 0 | 0 | .000 |
| 1983 | KC..... | 109 | 333 | 43 | 90 | 12 | 2 | 7 | 36 | 20 | 12 | .270 |
| 1984 | KC..... | 138 | 481 | 64 | 136 | 24 | 4 | 8 | 53 | 41 | 19 | .283 |
| 1985 | KC..... | 78 | 206 | 18 | 47 | 9 | 2 | 3 | 17 | 23 | 11 | .228 |
| 1986 | Det .... | 98 | 236 | 41 | 56 | 9 | 1 | 6 | 19 | 21 | 9 | .237 |
| 1987 | Det .... | 141 | 421 | 57 | 109 | 19 | 3 | 6 | 49 | 44 | 18 | .259 |
| 1988 | Det .... | 127 | 347 | 47 | 88 | 9 | 5 | 11 | 47 | 44 | 8 | .254 |
| 1989 | Det .... | 50 | 120 | 16 | 29 | 3 | 0 | 3 | 15 | 17 | 4 | .242 |
| 1989 | SF..... | 70 | 161 | 20 | 33 | 3 | 4 | 3 | 14 | 13 | 4 | .205 |
| | | 814 | 2306 | 306 | 588 | 88 | 21 | 47 | 250 | 223 | 85 | .255 |

# Dwight Smith

**Birth Date: 11/8/63**
**Bats: Left**
**Throws: Right**
**1989 Club:**
**Chicago Cubs**
**Contest Code #: 305**

**Rating: 4**

When Andre Dawson underwent arthroscopic surgery on his left knee last May, the Cubs reluctantly called up Dwight Smith to fill in. Smith had always hit well on the minor-league level, and was batting .325 at Triple A through April, but Smith's poor spring training performance still lingered in the minds of the Cubs' brass.

As it turned out, Dwight was quite ready for the major leagues. He batted .327 in May, .333 in June, and .362 in July. Smith slumped in August (.182), but batted .425 (17 for 40) between August 29 and September 19. Smith finished second to teammate Jerome Walton in the National League Rookie of the Year voting, the first time two teammates finished first and second in that voting since Fred Lynn and Jim Rice of the Red Sox in 1975.

In his minor-league career, Smith twice reached double figures in home runs. Once the Cubs let him play against left-handed pitchers as well as right-handers, he should become a double-digit dinger hitter. Right now, he's got the stroke that suggests a run at the 1990 National League batting crown.

| Year | Team | G | AB | R | H | 2B | 3B | HR | RBI | BB | SB | AVG |
|------|------|---|----|---|---|----|----|----|----|----|----|-----|
| 1989 | ChN.... | 109 | 343 | 52 | 111 | 19 | 6 | 9 | 52 | 31 | 9 | .324 |
| | | 109 | 343 | 52 | 111 | 19 | 6 | 9 | 52 | 31 | 9 | .324 |

# Lonnie Smith

**Birth Date: 12/22/55**
**Bats: Right**
**Throws: Right**
**1989 Club:**
**Atlanta Braves**
**Contest Code #: 306**

**Rating: 4**

Lonnie Smith deserved National League comeback-player-of-the-year honors for his excellent 1989 season. During the early 1980's, Smith was a speedy, high-average hitter. But substance abuse put his career in a downward spiral; Smith went from the Phillies to the Cardinals in 1982; to the Royals in 1985; and was demoted to Double A in 1987. Smith had successfully rehabilitated himself, but by 1988 only the Braves were willing to give Lonnie another shot.

Smith performed well at Triple A Richmond in 1988, batting .300, with 9 home runs and 51 RBI's. The Braves called him up for 43 games, but he looked rusty in his major-league return.

Last season, Smith won the Braves' left-field job and produced a league-leading on-base average of .415; a .315 batting average, third-best in the league; a .533 slugging average, fifth in the league; tied Barry Bonds and Kevin Mitchell for seventh in doubles (34); and tied Bonds for ninth in extra base hits (59). Smith might have put up better numbers had a knee injury not hampered his performance in the second half.

Smith should continue as a four-category player in 1990.

| Year | Team | G | AB | R | H | 2B | 3B | HR | RBI | BB | SB | AVG |
|------|------|----|-----|-----|------|-----|----|----|-----|-----|-----|------|
| 1978 | Phi .... | 17 | 4 | 6 | 0 | 0 | 0 | 0 | 0 | 4 | 4 | .000 |
| 1979 | Phi .... | 17 | 30 | 4 | 5 | 2 | 0 | 0 | 3 | 1 | 2 | .167 |
| 1980 | Phi .... | 100 | 298 | 69 | 101 | 14 | 4 | 3 | 20 | 26 | 33 | .339 |
| 1981 | Phi .... | 62 | 176 | 40 | 57 | 14 | 3 | 2 | 11 | 18 | 21 | .324 |
| 1982 | StL .... | 156 | 592 | 120 | 182 | 35 | 8 | 8 | 69 | 64 | 68 | .307 |
| 1983 | StL .... | 130 | 492 | 83 | 158 | 31 | 5 | 8 | 45 | 41 | 43 | .321 |
| 1984 | StL .... | 145 | 504 | 77 | 126 | 20 | 4 | 6 | 49 | 70 | 50 | .250 |
| 1985 | KC .... | 120 | 448 | 77 | 115 | 23 | 4 | 6 | 41 | 41 | 40 | .257 |
| 1985 | StL .... | 28 | 96 | 15 | 25 | 2 | 2 | 0 | 7 | 15 | 12 | .260 |
| 1986 | KC .... | 134 | 508 | 80 | 146 | 25 | 7 | 8 | 44 | 46 | 26 | .287 |
| 1987 | KC .... | 48 | 167 | 26 | 42 | 7 | 1 | 3 | 8 | 24 | 9 | .251 |
| 1988 | Atl .... | 43 | 114 | 14 | 27 | 3 | 0 | 3 | 9 | 10 | 4 | .237 |
| 1989 | Atl .... | 134 | 482 | 89 | 152 | 34 | 4 | 21 | 79 | 76 | 25 | .315 |
| | | 1134 | 3911 | 700 | 1136 | 210 | 42 | 68 | 385 | 436 | 337 | .290 |

# Darryl Strawberry

**Birth Date: 3/12/62**
**Bats: Left**
**Throws: Left**
**1989 Club:**
**New York Mets**
**Contest Code #: 307**

**Rating: 4**

Until last season, Darryl Strawberry was a better fantasy player than real-life player. In fantasy ball, his papers were always in order at the end of the season. In real ball, he went through incredible peaks and valleys, typically slumping for a month or two, then effortlessly pounding out home runs and stealing bases.

Last season, Darryl disappointed baseball people in both worlds. During spring training, he demanded a contract extension, calling his $1.4 million salary "a disgrace." It was, judging by his 1989 numbers. Despite 29 home runs, he drove in only 77 runs; subtract those home runs and you'll find that Darryl plated only 48 teammates. The Straw Man had 10 stolen bases at the All-Star break, but then he hurt a toe and decided base stealing was no longer for him. In the first half, he batted .236 (56 for 237); in the second half, when the Mets needed him most, .213 (51 for 239), with 35 RBI's.

Strawberry, who's always talked a good game, was a staple in the New York papers last year, making headlines for his frequent trade demands; his pre-season fistfight with Keith Hernandez; and his unpreparedness for a ninth-inning at-bat in a key late-season road game against the Cubs. In that last episode, Darryl, changing into his street threads, had to be summoned from the locker room to take his turn at the plate. Straw Man, representing the game-tying run, took three futile cuts against three Mitch Williams fastballs that were out of the strike zone.

Over a full season with Darryl, you'll find yourself whistling that old Supremes' song, "Nothing but Heartache."

| Year | Team | G | AB | R | H | 2B | 3B | HR | RBI | BB | SB | AVG |
|------|------|-----|-----|----|-----|----|----|----|-----|----|----|------|
| 1983 | NYN ... | 122 | 420 | 63 | 108 | 15 | 7 | 26 | 74 | 47 | 19 | .257 |
| 1984 | NYN ... | 147 | 522 | 75 | 131 | 27 | 4 | 26 | 97 | 75 | 27 | .251 |
| 1985 | NYN ... | 111 | 393 | 78 | 109 | 15 | 4 | 29 | 79 | 73 | 26 | .277 |
| 1986 | NYN ... | 136 | 475 | 76 | 123 | 27 | 5 | 27 | 93 | 72 | 28 | .259 |

| | | | | | | | | | | | |
|---|---|---|---|---|---|---|---|---|---|---|---|
| 1987 | NYN ... | 154 | 532 | 108 | 151 | 32 | 5 | 39 | 104 | 97 | 36 | .284 |
| 1988 | NYN ... | 153 | 543 | 101 | 146 | 27 | 3 | 39 | 101 | 85 | 29 | .269 |
| 1989 | NYN ... | 134 | 476 | 69 | 107 | 26 | 1 | 29 | 77 | 61 | 11 | .225 |
| | | 957 | 3361 | 570 | 875 | 169 | 29 | 215 | 625 | 510 | 176 | .260 |

# Milt Thompson

**Birth Date: 1/5/59**
**Bats: Left**
**Throws: Right**
**1989 Club:**
**St. Louis Cardinals**
**Contest Code #: 308**

**Rating: 4**

Last season, Milt Thompson showed up the Braves—who gave up on him in 1985, and the Phillies, who traded him away for Curt Ford and poor-hitting catcher Steve Lake—by having an outstanding year for the Cardinals.

Thompson, who was viewed as a reserve outfielder before the season began, seized his opportunity when Willie McGee got hurt and became an important part of the Cardinals' division drive. In a career-high 155 games, Thompson batted .2899 (158 for 545), just behind Ryne Sandberg's .2904 for tenth in the National League. Thompson's eight triples tied Ozzie Smith and Bip Roberts for sixth in the league. He posted a .393 slugging average, stole 27 bases in 35 attempts, and made only 8 errors in the field.

Thompson's emergence has made Vince Coleman and/or Willie McGee expendable.

| Year | Team | G | AB | R | H | 2B | 3B | HR | RBI | BB | SB | AVG |
|---|---|---|---|---|---|---|---|---|---|---|---|---|
| 1984 | Atl..... | 25 | 99 | 16 | 30 | 1 | 0 | 2 | 4 | 11 | 14 | .303 |
| 1985 | Atl..... | 73 | 182 | 17 | 55 | 7 | 2 | 0 | 6 | 7 | 9 | .302 |
| 1986 | Phi .... | 96 | 299 | 38 | 75 | 7 | 1 | 6 | 23 | 26 | 19 | .251 |
| 1987 | Phi .... | 150 | 527 | 86 | 159 | 26 | 9 | 7 | 43 | 42 | 46 | .302 |
| 1988 | Phi .... | 122 | 378 | 53 | 109 | 16 | 2 | 2 | 33 | 39 | 17 | .288 |
| 1989 | StL .... | 155 | 545 | 60 | 158 | 28 | 8 | 4 | 68 | 39 | 27 | .290 |
| | | 621 | 2030 | 270 | 586 | 85 | 22 | 21 | 177 | 164 | 132 | .289 |

# Andy Van Slyke

**Birth Date: 12/21/60**
**Bats: Left**
**Throws: Right**
**1989 Club:**
**Pittsburgh Pirates**
**Contest Code #: 309**

**Rating: 5**

The most common injury in baseball is the dreaded hamstring pull. But number two on the charts is the rib-cage muscle pull. As with the hamstring, the rib cage takes weeks to heal and can be reinjured easily. The pulled hamstring hurts when a player runs or sits down, but the pulled rib-cage muscle hurts when a player so much as coughs.

Andy Van Slyke's pulled rib-cage muscle sidelined him for 32 games and affected his swing even after he returned from the disabled list. It was a season he'd just as soon forget, and so should you.

When healthy, Van Slyke, the best defensive outfielder in baseball, is one of the premier offensive forces in the National League. He can hit, hit for power, drive in runs, and steal bases. The 1987 and 1988 seasons are true indications of his capabilities.

When asked in November what he remembered most about the 1989 season, Van Slyke answered, "Crickets chirping. Crickets chirp real loudly at two, three, four in the morning. I heard them, laying in bed, thinking." Van Slyke should rest easier this year.

| Year | Team | G | AB | R | H | 2B | 3B | HR | RBI | BB | SB | AVG |
|------|------|----|-----|-----|-----|-----|-----|-----|-----|-----|-----|------|
| 1983 | StL .... | 101 | 309 | 51 | 81 | 15 | 5 | 8 | 38 | 46 | 21 | .262 |
| 1984 | StL .... | 137 | 361 | 45 | 88 | 16 | 4 | 7 | 50 | 63 | 28 | .244 |
| 1985 | StL .... | 146 | 424 | 61 | 110 | 25 | 6 | 13 | 55 | 47 | 34 | .259 |
| 1986 | StL .... | 137 | 418 | 48 | 113 | 23 | 7 | 13 | 61 | 47 | 21 | .270 |
| 1987 | Pit..... | 157 | 564 | 93 | 165 | 36 | 11 | 21 | 82 | 56 | 34 | .293 |
| 1988 | Pit..... | 154 | 587 | 101 | 169 | 23 | 15 | 25 | 100 | 57 | 30 | .288 |
| 1989 | Pit..... | 130 | 476 | 64 | 113 | 18 | 9 | 9 | 53 | 47 | 16 | .237 |
| | | 962 | 3139 | 463 | 839 | 156 | 57 | 96 | 439 | 363 | 184 | .267 |

# Jerome Walton

**Birth Date: 7/8/65**
**Bats: Right**
**Throws: Right**
**1989 Club:**
**Chicago Cubs**
**Contest Code #: 310**

**Rating: 4**

Jerome Walton, the Double A Eastern League batting champion (.331) in 1988, established himself as one of the National League's finest young talents last year.

The National League Rookie of the Year opened the 1989 season with a seven-game hitting streak. Then a hamstring injury shelved him for a month. But he came back with a bang, hitting safely in 10 of his next 11 games and stealing 8 bases. On July 21, Walton, the Cubs' lead-off hitter, began a 30-game hitting streak, the longest in the major leagues last year. During the streak, he got 46 hits in 136 at-bats for a .338 average.

As a lead-off hitter, Walton, who stands at the plate with an exaggerated open stance, then closes his left foot as he starts his hitting action, opened 113 games by reaching base 40 times, and scoring the Cubs' first run 21 times. When Walton scored the first run, the Cubs went 16-5.

| Year | Team | G | AB | R | H | 2B | 3B | HR | RBI | BB | SB | AVG |
|------|------|-----|-----|----|-----|-----|-----|-----|-----|-----|-----|------|
| 1989 | ChN.... | 116 | 475 | 64 | 139 | 23 | 3 | 5 | 46 | 27 | 24 | .293 |
| | | 116 | 475 | 64 | 139 | 23 | 3 | 5 | 46 | 27 | 24 | .293 |

# Mitch Webster

**Birth Date: 5/16/59**
**Bats: Left**
**Throws: Left**
**1989 Club:**
**Chicago Cubs**
**Contest Code #: 311**

**Rating: 2**

Watching Mitch Webster over the years, I always got the impression that he was holding down a starting position until his team's hot outfield prospect was ready. That premonition came to pass in 1989, when Webster, who began the season as the Cubs' starting left fielder, gave way to Dwight Smith.

Webster is a competent, unspectacular player who hits around .275, steals a few bases and raps an occasional home run. Drafted by the Dodgers in the twenty-third round of the June 1977 draft, Webster was sent to the Blue Jays, then to the Expos. He enjoyed a career year in 1986, batting .290 with 36 stolen bases and a league-leading 13 triples. He hit a career-high 15 home runs in 1987, but has declined rapidly since.

Some batters relish the prospect of playing in Wrigley Field, but I think Webster's better off in a stadium where the games are at night and on artificial turf. Last season, Webster batted .271 at night but .248 in day games; and .299 on artificial surfaces but .246 on grass.

| Year | Team | G | AB | R | H | 2B | 3B | HR | RBI | BB | SB | AVG |
|------|------|----|-----|-----|-----|----|----|----|-----|-----|-----|------|
| 1983 | Tor..... | 11 | 11 | 2 | 2 | 0 | 0 | 0 | 0 | 1 | 0 | .182 |
| 1984 | Tor..... | 26 | 22 | 9 | 5 | 2 | 1 | 0 | 4 | 1 | 0 | .227 |
| 1985 | Tor..... | 4 | 1 | 0 | 0 | 0 | 0 | 0 | 0 | 0 | 0 | .000 |
| 1985 | Mon.... | 74 | 212 | 32 | 58 | 8 | 2 | 11 | 30 | 20 | 15 | .274 |
| 1986 | Mon.... | 151 | 576 | 89 | 167 | 31 | 13 | 8 | 49 | 57 | 36 | .290 |
| 1987 | Mon.... | 156 | 588 | 101 | 165 | 30 | 8 | 15 | 63 | 70 | 33 | .281 |
| 1988 | Mon.... | 81 | 259 | 33 | 66 | 5 | 2 | 2 | 13 | 36 | 12 | .255 |
| 1988 | ChN.... | 70 | 264 | 36 | 70 | 11 | 6 | 4 | 26 | 19 | 10 | .265 |
| 1989 | ChN.... | 98 | 272 | 40 | 70 | 12 | 4 | 3 | 19 | 30 | 14 | .257 |
| | | 671 | 2205 | 342 | 603 | 99 | 36 | 43 | 204 | 234 | 120 | .273 |

# Glenn Wilson

**Birth Date: 12/22/58**
**Bats: Right**
**Throws: Right**
**1989 Clubs:**
**Pittsburgh Pirates &**
**Houston Astros**
**Contest Code #: 312**

**Rating: 3**

Glenn Wilson was twice traded to the Astros last season—once through the media and once for a player. Early on, the Pirates decided to shop for a catcher when Mike LaValliere got hurt. They turned their attention to the Astros' Alan Ashby, who was in the twilight of his career. The Pirates decided Wilson was expendable because he was making $750,000. The proposed swap fell through when Ashby demanded a new contract. Days later, the Astros waived their veteran catcher, but, oddly, the Pirates didn't claim him.

The Astros knocked on the Pirates' door once more in August, and finally landed Wilson for Billy Hatcher.

Wilson, who grappled with a mysterious illness during the early months of the 1988 season, rebounded nicely last year, batting .266 with 11 home runs and 64 RBI's in 128 games. He can still be counted on to reach double figures in home runs and, batting behind Glenn Davis, should get many RBI opportunities this year.

| Year | Team | G | AB | R | H | 2B | 3B | HR | RBI | BB | SB | AVG |
|------|------|----|-----|-----|-----|----|----|----|-----|-----|-----|------|
| 1982 | Det .... | 84 | 322 | 39 | 94 | 15 | 1 | 12 | 34 | 15 | 2 | .292 |
| 1983 | Det .... | 144 | 503 | 55 | 135 | 25 | 6 | 11 | 65 | 25 | 1 | .268 |
| 1984 | Phi .... | 132 | 341 | 28 | 82 | 21 | 3 | 6 | 31 | 17 | 7 | .240 |
| 1985 | Phi .... | 161 | 608 | 73 | 167 | 39 | 5 | 14 | 102 | 35 | 7 | .275 |
| 1986 | Phi .... | 155 | 584 | 70 | 158 | 30 | 4 | 15 | 84 | 42 | 5 | .271 |
| 1987 | Phi .... | 154 | 569 | 55 | 150 | 21 | 2 | 14 | 54 | 38 | 3 | .264 |
| 1988 | Sea .... | 78 | 284 | 28 | 71 | 10 | 1 | 3 | 17 | 15 | 1 | .250 |
| 1988 | Pit..... | 37 | 126 | 11 | 34 | 8 | 0 | 2 | 15 | 3 | 0 | .270 |
| 1989 | Pit..... | 100 | 330 | 42 | 93 | 20 | 4 | 9 | 49 | 32 | 1 | .282 |
| 1989 | Hou.... | 28 | 102 | 8 | 22 | 6 | 0 | 2 | 15 | 5 | 0 | .216 |
| | | 1073 | 3769 | 409 | 1006 | 195 | 26 | 88 | 466 | 227 | 27 | .267 |

# Herm Winningham

**Birth Date: 12/1/61**
**Bats: Left**
**Throws: Right**
**1989 Club:**
**Cincinnati Reds**
**Contest Code #: 313**

**Rating: 1**

The Mets shrewdly promoted Herm Winningham late in the 1984 season and showcased him beautifully. Winningham, who'd hit .354 at Double A in 1983 and .281 at Triple A in 1984, batted a sizzling .407 for the Mets in 14 games. Three months later, Winningham was included in the Mets' package of Hubie Brooks, Mike Fitzgerald, and Floyd Youmans for Expos catcher Gary Carter.

Since then, Winningham has floundered against major-league pitching. He lost his job as Montreal's starting center fielder, and in 1988 was traded with Jeff Reed and pitcher Randy St. Claire to the Reds for outfielder Tracy Jones and pitcher Pat Pacillo.

With the Reds plagued by injuries last season, Winningham saw action in 115 games, batted .251, and stole 14 bases.

| Year | Team | G | AB | R | H | 2B | 3B | HR | RBI | BB | SB | AVG |
|------|------|---|----|----|----|----|----|----|-----|----|----|-----|
| 1984 | NYN ... | 14 | 27 | 5 | 11 | 1 | 1 | 0 | 5 | 1 | 2 | .407 |
| 1985 | Mon.... | 125 | 312 | 30 | 74 | 6 | 5 | 3 | 21 | 28 | 20 | .237 |
| 1986 | Mon.... | 90 | 185 | 23 | 40 | 6 | 3 | 4 | 11 | 18 | 12 | .216 |
| 1987 | Mon.... | 137 | 347 | 34 | 83 | 20 | 3 | 4 | 41 | 34 | 29 | .239 |
| 1988 | Mon.... | 47 | 90 | 10 | 21 | 2 | 1 | 0 | 6 | 12 | 4 | .233 |
| 1988 | Cin .... | 53 | 113 | 6 | 26 | 1 | 3 | 0 | 15 | 5 | 8 | .230 |
| 1989 | Cin .... | 115 | 251 | 40 | 63 | 11 | 3 | 3 | 13 | 24 | 14 | .251 |
| | | 581 | 1325 | 148 | 318 | 47 | 19 | 14 | 112 | 122 | 89 | .240 |

# Marvell Wynne

**Birth Date: 12/17/59**
**Bats: Left**
**Throws: Left**
**1989 Clubs:**
**San Diego Padres & Chicago Cubs**
**Contest Code #: 314**

**Rating: 2**

After the Mets picked up Marvell Wynne from the Kansas City Royals organization in 1981, the franchise, at the time barren of prospects, hailed him as "the next Mookie Wilson." Unfortunately, the Mets' instructors didn't school him well; when the Pirates acquired him two years later, they were startled by Wynne's lack of knowledge in the art of stolen bases.

Wynne has since taught himself to be a productive player. He's become a good fourth outfielder and pinch-hitter, capable of hitting the long ball on occasion. In 1989 Wynne batted .326 against left-handed pitching and .272 in late-inning pressure situations. Wynne, obtained last August by the Cubs for their stretch run, should see a fair amount of playing time this season when the regular outfielders need days off.

| Year | Team | G | AB | R | H | 2B | 3B | HR | RBI | BB | SB | AVG |
|------|------|---|----|----|----|----|----|----|-----|----|----|-----|
| 1983 | Pit ..... | 103 | 366 | 66 | 89 | 16 | 2 | 7 | 26 | 38 | 12 | .243 |
| 1984 | Pit ..... | 154 | 653 | 77 | 174 | 24 | 11 | 0 | 39 | 42 | 24 | .266 |
| 1985 | Pit ..... | 103 | 337 | 21 | 69 | 6 | 3 | 2 | 18 | 18 | 10 | .205 |
| 1986 | SD ..... | 137 | 288 | 34 | 76 | 19 | 2 | 7 | 37 | 15 | 11 | .264 |
| 1987 | SD ..... | 98 | 188 | 17 | 47 | 8 | 2 | 2 | 24 | 20 | 11 | .250 |
| 1988 | SD ..... | 128 | 333 | 37 | 88 | 13 | 4 | 11 | 42 | 31 | 3 | .264 |
| 1989 | SD ..... | 105 | 294 | 19 | 74 | 11 | 1 | 6 | 35 | 12 | 4 | .252 |
| 1989 | ChN.... | 20 | 48 | 8 | 9 | 2 | 1 | 1 | 4 | 1 | 2 | .188 |
| | | 848 | 2507 | 279 | 626 | 99 | 26 | 36 | 225 | 177 | 77 | .250 |

# Gerald Young

**Birth Date: 10/22/64**
**Bats: Left**
**Throws: Left**
**1989 Club:**
**Houston Astros**
**Contest Code #: 315**

**Rating: 3**

Young Gerald Young probably needs to change his batting approach if he's ever going to be a successful major leaguer. Blessed with great speed and bereft of power, Young wastes too many at-bats trying to hit the ball in the air. What's so maddening is that Young plays in Houston, where Astroturf was born. He can be a .300 hitter simply by chopping the ball on the carpet.

Last season, Young was hitting .189 in early June. The Astros got him to hit the ball on the ground, and his average soared to .232 at the All-Star break. But Young reverted to his earlier habits and finished the season only a point higher.

Young had a knee problem during the second half of the season that restricted his base stealing. Perhaps that's why he stole just three bases after the All-Star break. I'm sure that not getting on base hurt him, too.

| Year | Team | G | AB | R | H | 2B | 3B | HR | RBI | BB | SB | AVG |
|------|------|---|----|----|----|----|----|----|-----|----|----|-----|
| 1987 | Hou .... | 71 | 274 | 44 | 88 | 9 | 2 | 1 | 15 | 26 | 26 | .321 |
| 1988 | Hou .... | 149 | 576 | 79 | 148 | 21 | 9 | 0 | 37 | 66 | 65 | .257 |
| 1989 | Hou .... | 146 | 533 | 71 | 124 | 17 | 3 | 0 | 38 | 74 | 34 | .233 |
| | | 366 | 1383 | 194 | 360 | 47 | 14 | 1 | 90 | 166 | 125 | .260 |

# Joel Youngblood

**Birth Date: 8/28/51**
**Bats: Right**
**Throws: Right**
**1989 Club:**
**Cincinnati Reds**
**Contest Code #: 316**

**Rating: 1**

Joel Youngblood has carved a niche as a pinch-hitter and spot player who can sit on the bench for weeks at a clip and still be useful when called upon.

Early in his career, Youngblood may have been harmed by his ability to play every fielding position. Managers rotated him so frequently that Youngblood became a jack of all trades and master of none. Youngblood, selected by the Reds in the second round of the June 1970 draft, broke in as a shortstop, then was used at second and third as well. A season later, he played short, third, and the outfield. In 1976, he added catching and first base to his resume. He'd shown flashes of consistency as an everyday player, but could never quite put a good full season together.

| Year | Team | G | AB | R | H | 2B | 3B | HR | RBI | BB | SB | AVG |
|------|------|---|----|----|----|----|----|----|-----|----|----|------|
| 1976 | Cin .... | 55 | 57 | 8 | 11 | 1 | 1 | 0 | 1 | 2 | 1 | .193 |
| 1977 | NYN ... | 70 | 182 | 16 | 46 | 11 | 1 | 0 | 11 | 13 | 1 | .253 |
| 1977 | StL .... | 25 | 27 | 1 | 5 | 2 | 0 | 0 | 1 | 3 | 0 | .185 |
| 1978 | NYN ... | 113 | 266 | 40 | 67 | 12 | 8 | 7 | 30 | 16 | 4 | .252 |
| 1979 | NYN ... | 158 | 590 | 90 | 162 | 37 | 5 | 16 | 60 | 60 | 18 | .275 |
| 1980 | NYN ... | 146 | 514 | 58 | 142 | 26 | 2 | 8 | 69 | 52 | 14 | .276 |
| 1981 | NYN ... | 43 | 143 | 16 | 50 | 10 | 2 | 4 | 25 | 12 | 2 | .350 |
| 1982 | Mon.... | 40 | 90 | 16 | 18 | 2 | 0 | 0 | 8 | 9 | 2 | .200 |
| 1982 | NYN ... | 80 | 202 | 21 | 52 | 12 | 0 | 3 | 21 | 8 | 0 | .257 |
| 1983 | SF ..... | 124 | 373 | 59 | 109 | 20 | 3 | 17 | 53 | 33 | 7 | .292 |
| 1984 | SF ..... | 134 | 469 | 50 | 119 | 17 | 1 | 10 | 51 | 48 | 5 | .254 |
| 1985 | SF ..... | 95 | 230 | 24 | 62 | 6 | 0 | 4 | 24 | 30 | 3 | .270 |
| 1986 | SF ..... | 97 | 184 | 20 | 47 | 12 | 0 | 5 | 28 | 18 | 1 | .255 |
| 1987 | SF ..... | 69 | 91 | 9 | 23 | 3 | 0 | 3 | 11 | 5 | 1 | .253 |
| 1988 | SF ..... | 83 | 123 | 12 | 31 | 4 | 0 | 0 | 16 | 10 | 1 | .252 |
| 1989 | Cin .... | 76 | 118 | 13 | 25 | 5 | 0 | 3 | 13 | 13 | 0 | .212 |
| | | 1408 | 3659 | 453 | 969 | 180 | 23 | 80 | 422 | 332 | 60 | .265 |

# PITCHERS

# PITCHERS

## Don Aase

**Birth Date:** 9/8/54
**Throws:** Right
**1989 Club:**
**New York Mets**
**Contest Code #:** 325

**Rating: 1**

**D**on Aase was the Cinderella story in the Mets' 1989 spring training camp. Invited for a tryout, the often-injured 11-year veteran, who'd been released by the Baltimore Orioles following the 1988 season, won a spot on the National League's best pitching staff.

A month into the 1989 season, Aase, used in middle relief, sported a 1.59 ERA and one save in his first 11⅓ innings pitched. By June 6 Aase picked up his first win and his ERA was a tidy 1.72. The Mets were so impressed that a week later, when they traded Roger McDowell to the Philadelphia Phillies, they expanded Aase's role to include late-inning appearances.

Then the clock struck midnight, and Aase's fastball looked as big as a pumpkin. By July 4 his ERA climbed to 2.65; by August 8, 3.40; by September 5, 3.68; and, at season's end, 3.94. During the last month of the season Aase pitched only three innings, giving way to a promising, young right hander named Julio Machado, who'd also been a free agent during spring training.

| Year | Team | W | L | SV | ERA | IP | H | BB | K |
|------|------|---|---|----|-----|----|----|----|----|
| 1977 | Bos...... | 6 | 2 | 0 | 3.13 | 92.0 | 85 | 19 | 49 |
| 1978 | Cal ...... | 11 | 8 | 0 | 4.02 | 179.0 | 185 | 80 | 93 |
| 1979 | Cal ...... | 9 | 10 | 2 | 4.82 | 185.0 | 200 | 77 | 96 |
| 1980 | Cal ...... | 8 | 13 | 2 | 4.06 | 175.0 | 193 | 66 | 74 |
| 1981 | Cal ...... | 4 | 4 | 11 | 2.35 | 65.0 | 56 | 24 | 38 |
| 1982 | Cal ...... | 3 | 3 | 4 | 3.46 | 52.0 | 45 | 23 | 40 |
| 1984 | Cal ...... | 4 | 1 | 8 | 1.62 | 39.0 | 30 | 19 | 28 |
| 1985 | Bal ...... | 10 | 6 | 14 | 3.78 | 88.0 | 83 | 35 | 67 |
| 1986 | Bal ...... | 6 | 7 | 34 | 2.98 | 81.2 | 71 | 28 | 67 |
| 1987 | Bal ...... | 1 | 0 | 2 | 2.25 | 8.0 | 8 | 4 | 3 |
| 1988 | Bal ...... | 0 | 0 | 0 | 4.05 | 46.2 | 40 | 37 | 28 |
| 1989 | NYN ..... | 1 | 5 | 2 | 3.94 | 59.1 | 56 | 26 | 34 |
| | | 63 | 59 | 79 | 3.76 | 1070.2 | 1052 | 438 | 617 |

## Juan Agosto

**Birth Date:** 2/23/58
**Throws:** Left
**1989 Club:**
**Houston Astros**
**Contest Code #:** 326

**Rating: 1**

**I**n 1987 the Astros, desperate for left-handed relief pitchers, signed Juan Agosto, who pitched in 14 different cities over his first 14 pro seasons. A year later, Agosto was the unsung star of the staff, winning 10 games—doubling his major-league career total—and losing only 2, with a 2.26 ERA in 91⅔ innings. These are numbers a team's third starter would be proud of. Suddenly, this vagabond found a home on many fantasy-league teams.

But Agosto returned to reality in 1989: 4 victories, 5 defeats, and a 2.93 ERA.

There's a moral here. Effective middle relievers on good teams get lots of opportunities for victories (*see* Danny Darwin and Frank DiPino). Marginal middle relievers are pulled quickly, before their earned run averages take a beating. Agosto's 1989 ERA doesn't look too bad, but he allowed 81 hits and 32 walks in 83 innings. That's almost 1.4 runners per inning, close to Agosto's career average.

| Year | Team | W | L | SV | ERA | IP | H | BB | K |
|------|------|---|---|----|----|-----|-----|-----|-----|
| 1981 | ChA...... | 0 | 0 | 0 | 4.50 | 6.0 | 5 | 0 | 3 |
| 1982 | ChA...... | 0 | 0 | 0 | 18.00 | 2.0 | 7 | 0 | 1 |
| 1983 | ChA...... | 2 | 2 | 7 | 4.10 | 41.2 | 41 | 11 | 29 |
| 1984 | ChA...... | 2 | 1 | 7 | 3.09 | 55.1 | 54 | 34 | 26 |
| 1985 | ChA...... | 4 | 3 | 1 | 3.58 | 60.1 | 45 | 23 | 39 |
| 1986 | ChA...... | 0 | 2 | 0 | 7.73 | 4.2 | 6 | 4 | 3 |
| 1986 | Min...... | 1 | 2 | 1 | 8.85 | 20.1 | 43 | 14 | 9 |
| 1987 | Hou...... | 1 | 1 | 2 | 2.63 | 27.1 | 26 | 10 | 6 |
| 1988 | Hou...... | 10 | 2 | 4 | 2.26 | 91.2 | 74 | 30 | 33 |
| 1989 | Hou...... | 4 | 5 | 1 | 2.93 | 83.0 | 81 | 32 | 46 |
| | | 24 | 18 | 23 | 3.46 | 392.1 | 382 | 158 | 195 |

# Larry Andersen

**Birth Date: 5/6/53**
**Throws: Right**
**1989 Club:**
**Houston Astros**
**Contest Code #: 327**

**Rating: 3**

Like fine wine, Larry Andersen gets better—and funnier—with age. He has been the Astros' most dependable reliever since 1986. He's also the Andy Rooney of the National League—among his comic quips: "Why is there an expiration date on sour cream?" "Why do you drive on a parkway and park in a driveway?"

Andersen arrives on the scene between the sixth and eighth innings of tightly contested games and keeps the opposition at bay until closer Dave Smith comes in. Andersen's control is amazing. Last season, Andersen allowed only 15 earned runs, walked 24 batters, and struck out 85 in 87⅔ innings. He doesn't get many wins or saves, but he gives you a truckload of quality innings.

| Year | Team | W | L | SV | ERA | IP | H | BB | K |
|------|------|---|---|----|----|-----|-----|-----|-----|
| 1975 | Cle ...... | 0 | 0 | 0 | 4.50 | 6.0 | 4 | 2 | 4 |
| 1977 | Cle ...... | 0 | 1 | 0 | 3.21 | 14.0 | 10 | 9 | 8 |
| 1979 | Cle ...... | 0 | 0 | 0 | 7.41 | 17.0 | 25 | 4 | 7 |
| 1981 | Sea...... | 3 | 3 | 5 | 2.65 | 68.0 | 57 | 18 | 40 |
| 1982 | Sea...... | 0 | 0 | 1 | 5.99 | 79.2 | 100 | 23 | 32 |
| 1983 | Phi ...... | 1 | 0 | 0 | 2.39 | 26.1 | 19 | 9 | 14 |
| 1984 | Phi ...... | 3 | 7 | 4 | 2.38 | 90.2 | 85 | 25 | 54 |
| 1985 | Phi ...... | 3 | 3 | 3 | 4.32 | 73.0 | 78 | 26 | 50 |
| 1986 | Phi ...... | 0 | 0 | 0 | 4.27 | 12.2 | 19 | 3 | 9 |
| 1986 | Hou...... | 2 | 1 | 1 | 2.78 | 64.2 | 64 | 23 | 33 |
| 1987 | Hou...... | 9 | 5 | 5 | 3.45 | 101.2 | 95 | 41 | 94 |
| 1988 | Hou...... | 2 | 4 | 5 | 2.94 | 82.2 | 82 | 20 | 66 |
| 1989 | Hou...... | 4 | 4 | 3 | 1.54 | 87.2 | 63 | 24 | 85 |
| | | 27 | 28 | 27 | 3.33 | 724.0 | 701 | 227 | 496 |

# Paul Assenmacher

**Birth Date: 12/10/60**
**Throws: Left**
**1989 Clubs:**
**Atlanta Braves &**
**Chicago Cubs**
**Contest Code #: 328**

**Rating: 2**

We with available cable television get to see Atlanta Braves baseball, courtesy of Superstation WTBS. In recent years, that has allowed us to judge firsthand whether the Braves' annual crop of touted pitching prospects are as good as advertised; whether their arms won't fall off from overuse; and whether they have the mettle to endure annual last-place finishes.

Paul Assenmacher, a sidearm, breaking-ball pitcher, who worked in 79 games over three minor-league seasons, appeared in 61 games his first season with the Braves. Not coincidentally, Assenmacher spent time on the disabled list with arm trouble in both 1987 and 1988.

Moreover, Assenmacher developed a placid demeanor—his face expressionless, his baseball cap askew—that made it seem as if he didn't care. Last August the Braves gave up on their onetime closer and traded him to the Cubs.

If Assenmacher, who induces a lot of fly balls, had been traded to a team that plays in a larger ball park—like the Cardinals or the Astros—I'd project him as a good middle-inning reliever. But not in Wrigley Field. Consider that in 1988 Assenmacher's ERA away from Atlanta Fulton County Stadium, where home runs abound, was only 1.13.

| Year | Team | W | L | SV | ERA | IP | H | BB | K |
|---|---|---|---|---|---|---|---|---|---|
| 1986 | Atl....... | 7 | 3 | 7 | 2.50 | 68.1 | 61 | 26 | 56 |
| 1987 | Atl....... | 1 | 1 | 2 | 5.10 | 54.2 | 58 | 24 | 39 |
| 1988 | Atl....... | 8 | 7 | 5 | 3.06 | 79.1 | 72 | 32 | 71 |
| 1989 | Atl....... | 1 | 3 | 0 | 3.59 | 57.2 | 55 | 16 | 64 |
| 1989 | ChN...... | 2 | 1 | 0 | 5.21 | 19.0 | 19 | 12 | 15 |
| | | 19 | 15 | 14 | 3.58 | 279.0 | 265 | 110 | 245 |

# Doug Bair

Birth Date: 8/22/49
Throws: Right
1989 Club:
Pittsburgh Pirates
Contest Code #: 329

Rating: 1

How old is Doug Bair? Older than Bruce Kimm, Milt May, and Tommy Sandt, three of the Pirates' coaches, and only four years younger than pitching coach Ray Miller. He's so old that in 1989 Bair became the fourth pitcher in the last 30 years to win a game after his fortieth birthday.

It's not easy to know how Bair, who was originally signed by the Pirates in 1971, has managed to hang on this long. His best season came with the Cincinnati Reds 12 years ago, and since then he's bounced from St. Louis to Detroit, back to St. Louis, to Oakland, where he originally broke into the bigs in 1976, to Philadelphia, to Toronto, and back to the Pirates' organization. He pitched fairly well in 1989, but his addition to the staff had more to do with the Pirates' desperate attempts to plug a leaky bullpen.

| Year | Team | W | L | SV | ERA | IP | H | BB | K |
|---|---|---|---|---|---|---|---|---|---|
| 1976 | Pit....... | 0 | 0 | 0 | 6.00 | 6.0 | 4 | 5 | 4 |
| 1977 | Oak...... | 4 | 6 | 8 | 3.47 | 83.0 | 78 | 57 | 68 |
| 1978 | Cin ...... | 7 | 6 | 28 | 1.98 | 100.0 | 87 | 38 | 91 |
| 1979 | Cin ...... | 11 | 7 | 16 | 4.31 | 94.0 | 93 | 51 | 86 |
| 1980 | Cin ...... | 3 | 6 | 6 | 4.24 | 85.0 | 91 | 39 | 62 |
| 1981 | Cin ...... | 2 | 2 | 0 | 5.77 | 39.0 | 42 | 17 | 16 |
| 1981 | StL ...... | 2 | 0 | 1 | 3.45 | 15.2 | 13 | 2 | 14 |
| 1982 | StL ...... | 5 | 3 | 8 | 2.55 | 91.2 | 69 | 36 | 68 |
| 1983 | Det ...... | 7 | 3 | 4 | 3.88 | 55.2 | 51 | 19 | 39 |
| 1983 | StL ...... | 1 | 1 | 1 | 3.03 | 29.2 | 24 | 13 | 21 |
| 1984 | Det ...... | 5 | 3 | 4 | 3.75 | 93.2 | 82 | 36 | 57 |
| 1985 | Det ...... | 2 | 0 | 0 | 6.24 | 49.0 | 54 | 25 | 30 |
| 1985 | StL ...... | 0 | 0 | 0 | 0.00 | 2.0 | 1 | 2 | 0 |
| 1986 | Oak...... | 2 | 3 | 4 | 3.00 | 45.0 | 37 | 18 | 40 |
| 1987 | Phi...... | 2 | 0 | 0 | 5.93 | 13.2 | 17 | 5 | 10 |
| 1988 | Tor....... | 0 | 0 | 0 | 4.05 | 13.1 | 14 | 3 | 8 |
| 1989 | Pit....... | 2 | 3 | 1 | 2.27 | 67.1 | 52 | 28 | 56 |
| | | 55 | 43 | 81 | 3.61 | 883.2 | 809 | 394 | 670 |

# Steve Bedrosian

**Birth Date:** 12/6/57
**Throws:** Right
**1989 Clubs:**
**Philadelphia Phillies &**
**San Francisco Giants**
**Contest Code #:** 330

**Rating: 3**

To Steve Bedrosian's credit, he withstood all the damage an early 1980's Braves pitching prospect had to suffer. Bedrosian stumbled, after initial success as a closer, because of arm trouble, so then-Braves' manager Joe Torre had the notion of putting him into the starting rotation. In 1985, "Bedrock," pitching more innings than he had in the previous two years combined, set a major-league record: most games taken out as a starting pitcher, 37.

The Braves gave up on Bedrock in 1986 and traded him to the Phillies. In his first two seasons in Philadelphia, Bedrock, back in the pen, notched 69 saves. But in 1988 Bedrosian had more arm trouble, and he was shipped to the Giants during the 1989 season.

Toward the end of July, Bedrock's ERA was a puffy 3.47. However, once Giants manager Roger Craig rationed Bedrock's appearances and pitching coach Norm Sherry altered his motion, Bedrock lowered his ERA to 2.87.

Used judiciously—no more than one inning per game—Bedrosian should earn 20 saves in 1990. But, with his recent wildness, those saves won't come easily. Bedrock's heart may now be in San Francisco, but he left part of his right arm in Atlanta.

| Year | Team | W | L | SV | ERA | IP | H | BB | K |
|------|------|---|---|----|----|----|---|----|----|
| 1981 | Atl....... | 1 | 2 | 0 | 4.50 | 24.0 | 15 | 15 | 9 |
| 1982 | Atl....... | 8 | 6 | 11 | 2.42 | 137.2 | 102 | 57 | 123 |
| 1983 | Atl....... | 9 | 10 | 19 | 3.60 | 120.0 | 100 | 51 | 114 |
| 1984 | Atl....... | 9 | 6 | 11 | 2.37 | 83.2 | 65 | 33 | 81 |
| 1985 | Atl....... | 7 | 15 | 0 | 3.83 | 206.2 | 198 | 111 | 134 |
| 1986 | Phi ...... | 8 | 6 | 29 | 3.39 | 90.1 | 79 | 34 | 82 |
| 1987 | Phi ...... | 5 | 3 | 40 | 2.83 | 89.0 | 79 | 28 | 74 |
| 1988 | Phi ...... | 6 | 6 | 28 | 3.75 | 74.1 | 75 | 27 | 61 |
| 1989 | Phi ...... | 2 | 3 | 6 | 3.21 | 33.2 | 21 | 17 | 24 |
| 1989 | SF....... | 1 | 4 | 17 | 2.87 | 51.0 | 35 | 22 | 34 |
| | | 56 | 61 | 161 | 3.23 | 910.1 | 769 | 395 | 736 |

# Tim Belcher

**Birth Date:** 10/19/61
**Throws:** Right
**1989 Club:**
**Los Angeles Dodgers**
**Contest Code #:** 331

**Rating: 5**

Let's stop picking on the Braves (for now) and turn our critical attention to Tommy Lasorda and the Dodgers. The book on Lasorda's handling of young pitchers is that he gives them what many say is too many innings of work (*see* Alejandro Pena and Fernando Valenzuela). But last year Lasorda did an about-face with Tim Belcher, his most effective starter after Hershiser.

When John Tudor came off the disabled list, Lasorda pulled Belcher, who'd earned a starting role in 1988, from the rotation and stuck him in middle relief. Perhaps Lasorda felt Belcher was resilient enough to withstand the change. Whatever the reason, the move made little sense. Thankfully, Tudor's stay was short and Belcher regained his rightful place in the rotation.

Belcher has all the makings of a pitcher that Lasorda can count on for 240 innings or more. He has a fluid, effortless motion and exceptional velocity on his fastball (95 mph), which make him tough for batters to time. He's averaged an impressive eight strikeouts and a mere three walks per game, and has a career winning percent-

age of .607. Last year he led all National League pitchers with eight shutouts.

With reasonable offensive support, Belcher could win 20 games in 1990. I suspect Lasorda realizes that, too, so this season he'll probably give Belcher all the innings he can handle.

| Year | Team | W | L | SV | ERA | IP | H | BB | K |
|------|------|---|---|----|----|----|----|----|----|
| 1987 | LA....... | 4 | 2 | 0 | 2.38 | 34.0 | 30 | 7 | 23 |
| 1988 | LA....... | 12 | 6 | 4 | 2.91 | 179.2 | 143 | 51 | 152 |
| 1989 | LA....... | 15 | 12 | 1 | 2.82 | 230.0 | 182 | 80 | 200 |
| | | 31 | 20 | 5 | 2.82 | 443.2 | 355 | 138 | 375 |

# Andy Benes

Birth Date: 8/20/67
Throws: Right
1989 Club:
San Diego Padres
Contest Code #: 332

Rating: 4

In 1988 the San Diego Padres signed Andy Benes, their first pick in the June amateur draft, for $240,000, at the time the largest bonus in draft history.

The Padres are lucky that Benes has a great aptitude for pitching. Upon his call-up, Benes complained that he didn't receive enough instruction on his curveball and his pickoff move from the Padres' minor-league staff. But, thanks to a crash course from Padres' major-league pitching coach Pat Dobson, Benes learned to throw a hard slider and a slide-step from the stretch to keep base runners closer.

Once Benes gets a little more schooling on his curveball and learns from experience, he should join the National League's elite starters. That may take only half a season.

| Year | Team | W | L | SV | ERA | IP | H | BB | K |
|------|------|---|---|----|----|----|----|----|----|
| 1989 | SD....... | 6 | 3 | 0 | 3.51 | 66.2 | 51 | 31 | 66 |
| | | 6 | 3 | 0 | 3.51 | 66.2 | 51 | 31 | 66 |

# Mike Bielecki

Birth Date: 7/31/59
Throws: Right
1989 Club:
Chicago Cubs
Contest Code #: 333

Rating: 3

Mike Bielecki deserves a lot of credit for keeping his faith through the ups and downs of his career. At the start of 1985, Bielecki was one of the Pirates' top pitching prospects. In his first start that season, he earned his first major-league victory, limiting the Mets to 1 earned run and 7 hits in 6⅔ innings. He then lost three straight and was optioned to Triple A. Following that season, team doctors removed a portion of a ruptured disc between Bielecki's fourth and fifth lumbar vertebrae.

Considering how weak the Pirates were in 1986, Bielecki pitched reasonably well, leading all N.L. rookie pitchers in starts and innings pitched. Returned to Triple A in 1987, he finished second in the Pacific Coast League in innings pitched (181), strikeouts (140), and shutouts (3). However, in the spring of 1988 the Pirates' starting staff was filled by Doug Drabek, John Smiley, Bob Walk, Mike Dunne, and Brian Fisher, so former Pirates general manager Syd Thrift traded Bielecki to

the Cubs. When a spot in the Cubs' rotation opened in the spring of 1989, Bielecki made the most of it. The statistic that spoke best for Bielecki was that opponents batted only .226 against him with runners on base, the lowest average among Cubs starters.

Some may dismiss Bielecki's 1989 season as a fluke, a career year. One can also argue that a good pitcher looks like a great pitcher when he has a great team behind him. But I'm guessing that thirty-year-old Bielecki is good enough to win 14 games and post a 3.30 ERA this year.

| Year | Team | W | L | SV | ERA | IP | H | BB | K |
|------|------|---|---|----|----|----|----|----|----|
| 1984 | Pit...... | 0 | 0 | 0 | 0.00 | 4.1 | 4 | 0 | 1 |
| 1985 | Pit...... | 2 | 3 | 0 | 4.53 | 45.2 | 45 | 31 | 22 |
| 1986 | Pit...... | 6 | 11 | 0 | 4.66 | 148.2 | 149 | 83 | 83 |
| 1987 | Pit...... | 2 | 3 | 0 | 4.73 | 45.2 | 43 | 12 | 25 |
| 1988 | ChN..... | 2 | 2 | 0 | 3.35 | 48.1 | 55 | 16 | 33 |
| 1989 | ChN..... | 18 | 7 | 0 | 3.14 | 212.1 | 187 | 81 | 147 |
| | | 30 | 26 | 0 | 3.85 | 505.0 | 483 | 223 | 311 |

# Tim Birtsas

Birth Date: 4/13/62
Throws: Left
1989 Club:
Cincinnati Reds
Contest Code #: 334

Rating: 1

What does Tim Birtsas have in common with Rickey Henderson, Dave Parker, Jay Howell, Erik Plunk, Jose Rijo, and Stan Javier...? Time's up. In 1984 he was traded by the New York Yankees—along with Howell, Plunk and Rijo—to the A's for Henderson, and in 1987 he was traded with Rijo to the Reds for Dave Parker.

There was a time when Birtsas was viewed as a promising left-handed starter, but his lack of control has made him a fixture in games in which the Reds are behind.

| Year | Team | W | L | SV | ERA | IP | H | BB | K |
|------|------|---|---|----|----|----|----|----|----|
| 1985 | Oak...... | 10 | 6 | 0 | 4.01 | 141.1 | 124 | 91 | 94 |
| 1986 | Oak...... | 0 | 0 | 0 | 22.50 | 2.0 | 2 | 4 | 1 |
| 1988 | Cin ...... | 1 | 3 | 0 | 4.20 | 64.1 | 61 | 24 | 38 |
| 1989 | Cin ...... | 2 | 2 | 1 | 3.75 | 69.2 | 68 | 27 | 57 |
| | | 13 | 11 | 1 | 4.12 | 277.1 | 255 | 146 | 190 |

# Joe Boever

Birth Date: 10/4/60
Throws: Right
1989 Club:
Atlanta Braves
Contest Code #: 335

Rating: 2

Palm-ball specialist Joe Boever (pronounced *Bay-ver*) can fool some of the people some of the time, but over a full season he can't seem to fool all of the hitters all of the time.

In 1988 Boever, a middle reliever by trade, pitched well in a late season tryout as the Braves closer. He inherited the role in 1989 when Bruce Sutter could not come back from injury. Boever, whose offspeed pitches, wispy moustache, and pot belly give him the appearance of a young Rick Reuschel, earned 2 wins, 10 saves, and had a 2.28 ERA over the first three months of last season. By August 1, he'd notched a total of 18 saves. Then the hitters got wise to Boever's out-pitch, a change-up held in the palm. They waited for it, and when they saw it they hit it. Boever's numbers from August 1 to season's end were: no wins, 8 losses, a 7.12 ERA, with 19 hits and 13 walks in 24 innings pitched.

| Year | Team | W | L | SV | ERA | IP | H | BB | K |
|------|------|---|---|----|----|----|----|----|----|
| 1985 | StL ...... | 0 | 0 | 0 | 4.41 | 16.1 | 17 | 4 | 20 |
| 1986 | StL ...... | 0 | 1 | 0 | 1.66 | 21.2 | 19 | 11 | 8 |
| 1987 | Atl ...... | 1 | 0 | 0 | 7.36 | 18.1 | 29 | 12 | 18 |
| 1988 | Atl ...... | 0 | 2 | 1 | 1.77 | 20.1 | 12 | 1 | 7 |
| 1989 | Atl ...... | 4 | 11 | 21 | 3.94 | 82.1 | 78 | 34 | 68 |
| | | 5 | 14 | 22 | 3.79 | 159.0 | 155 | 62 | 121 |

# Jeff Brantley

**Birth Date:** 9/5/63
**Throws:** Right
**1989 Club:**
**San Francisco Giants**
**Contest Code #:** 336

**Rating: 2**

At the start of the 1989 season, with the Giants' bullpen in flux, I picked up Jeff Brantley, a free agent in my fantasy league, because I assumed that he might see some action as a closer. Not only didn't he close games, but he couldn't close an inning. From April 25 to June 27, Brantley, an offspeed pitcher who throws a split-fingered fastball, had no wins and no saves, a 4.70 ERA, with 26 hits and 11 walks in 23 innings.

Since I didn't see Brantley's name in the transaction lists in the daily newspapers, I didn't know Giants' president and general manager Al Rosen sent him to Triple A for an attitude readjustment. By the time I found this out, Brantley had been recalled. So I traded him, assuming anyone I'd acquire would be an improvement.

Brantley then reeled off four victories in a two-week period. I assumed he'd found himself, so I reacquired him. He won 3 games for me, but not without a hitch: 17 earned runs, 32 hits and 10 walks in 29 ⅓ innings. Ouch!

So when you look over Brantley's 1989 stats, don't assume he'll go 7-1 again this year.

| Year | Team | W | L | SV | ERA | IP | H | BB | K |
|------|------|---|---|----|----|----|----|----|----|
| 1988 | SF ...... | 0 | 1 | 1 | 5.66 | 20.2 | 22 | 6 | 11 |
| 1989 | SF ...... | 7 | 1 | 0 | 4.07 | 97.1 | 101 | 37 | 69 |
| | | 7 | 2 | 1 | 4.35 | 118.0 | 123 | 43 | 80 |

# Tom Browning

**Birth Date:** 4/28/60
**Throws:** Left
**1989 Club:**
**Cincinnati Reds**
**Contest Code #:** 337

**Rating: 4**

The dumbest phrase in the book of baseball cliches is the "sophomore jinx." Why did Tom Browning, who won 20 games in 1985, slide to 14-13 in 1986? "The sophomore jinx," crowed the crowd of baseball publications. Baseball isn't voodoo. There's no such thing as a jinx or a curse. Everything has a reason.

Browning's slump in 1986 and again in 1987 can be traced back to the spring of 1986. After beaning a few batters, he stopped pitching inside. Instead of using all 17 inches of home plate's width, he was using only 8 or 9. Once Browning overcame this phobia, he returned to his winning ways.

Browning is now one of the league's best and most durable left handed starters. He has excellent control of his fastball, change-up, curve, full-speed screwball, and offspeed screwball. Over the past two seasons he's walked only 128 batters in 500 ⅓ innings.

He's also a streaky pitcher. In 1988 he won 10 of his last 12 decisions, including a perfect game, and in 1989 he won 6 of his last 9 decisions. All told, he's averaged more than 15 victories per season in the last five years, and he should win at least as many in 1990.

| Year | Team | W | L | SV | ERA | IP | H | BB | K |
|------|------|---|---|----|----|----|---|----|---|
| 1984 | Cin ...... | 1 | 0 | 0 | 1.54 | 23.1 | 27 | 5 | 14 |
| 1985 | Cin ...... | 20 | 9 | 0 | 3.55 | 261.1 | 242 | 73 | 155 |
| 1986 | Cin ...... | 14 | 13 | 0 | 3.81 | 243.1 | 225 | 70 | 147 |
| 1987 | Cin ...... | 10 | 13 | 0 | 5.02 | 183.0 | 201 | 61 | 117 |
| 1988 | Cin ...... | 18 | 5 | 0 | 3.41 | 250.2 | 205 | 64 | 124 |
| 1989 | Cin ...... | 15 | 12 | 0 | 3.39 | 249.2 | 241 | 64 | 118 |
| | | 78 | 52 | 0 | 3.72 | 1211.1 | 1141 | 337 | 675 |

# Tim Burke

**Birth Date: 2/19/59**
**Throws: Right**
**1989 Club:**
**Montreal Expos**
**Contest Code #: 338**

**Rating: 5**

Tim Burke gives batters fits. He has an unusual pitching motion—reminiscent of "The Honeymooners" Ed Norton's fluttering his hands in a windup before tinkling "Swanee River" on the piano—making his release point on his fastball, slider, and change hard to pick up. And Burke issues few walks, a real plus for a closer.

Burke, who didn't break into the majors until the age of twenty-six, has only recently garnered the recognition he deserves. Originally drafted by the Pirates in 1979, Burke was traded to the Yankees in a package for outfielder Lee Mazzilli in 1982. One year later the Yankees shipped him to the Expos for an outfielder named Pat Rooney. (Nice trade, George.)

Burke was first used as part of Montreal's bullpen-by-committee, but in subsequent seasons he took on a greater role and is now the team's closer. He's won nine games three times, and his save totals have steadily increased each year. He would have had more than 22 saves last year had the Expos not gone into the tank in August and September.

In past years, owners in many fantasy leagues bid on Burke as their number-two or -three man in the pen. Not anymore. Burke, named to the 1989 N.L. All-Star team, has proven he belongs among the league's best closers.

| Year | Team | W | L | SV | ERA | IP | H | BB | K |
|------|------|---|---|----|----|----|---|----|---|
| 1985 | Mon ..... | 9 | 4 | 8 | 2.39 | 120.1 | 86 | 44 | 87 |
| 1986 | Mon ..... | 9 | 7 | 4 | 2.93 | 101.1 | 103 | 46 | 82 |
| 1987 | Mon ..... | 7 | 0 | 18 | 1.19 | 91.0 | 64 | 17 | 58 |
| 1988 | Mon ..... | 3 | 5 | 18 | 3.40 | 82.0 | 84 | 25 | 42 |
| 1989 | Mon ..... | 9 | 3 | 28 | 2.55 | 84.2 | 68 | 22 | 54 |
| | | 37 | 19 | 76 | 2.48 | 479.1 | 405 | 154 | 323 |

# John Candelaria

Birth Date: 11/6/53
Throws: Left
1989 Club:
New York Yankees &
Montreal Expos
Contest Code #: 339

Rating: 1

Just when you count John Candelaria out, "The Candy Man" hooks up with a new club and prolongs his 15-year career. Candelaria, who's spent time on the disabled list three of the past four seasons, was fresh off the D. L. when the Expos picked him up from the Yankees for the stretch run, giving up Mike Blowers, an excellent third-base prospect, in return.

True, Candelaria is a cagey veteran who, when healthy, is capable of six strong innings. His 84-mile-an-hour sidearm fastball has good movement in the hitting zone. He has a good curveball and changes speeds well. But he's never lived up to his sensational 1977 season because of injuries to his pitching elbow and his knees.

Controversy has also followed The Candy Man. He moaned loud enough to be traded from Pittsburgh, and, with the Yankees in 1988, he decided he didn't want to pitch for manager Lou Piniella.

The Expos used Candelaria out of their bullpen, but how frequently can one call on a pitcher with a history of elbow problems? If they have enough depth in their pen, the Expos could possibly wheel out Candy as a fifth starter to give them five or six innings.

| Year | Team | W | L | SV | ERA | IP | H | BB | K |
|------|------|---|---|----|-----|----|----|-----|---|
| 1975 | Pit....... | 8 | 6 | 0 | 2.75 | 121.0 | 95 | 36 | 95 |
| 1976 | Pit....... | 16 | 7 | 1 | 3.15 | 220.0 | 173 | 60 | 138 |
| 1977 | Pit....... | 20 | 5 | 0 | 2.34 | 231.0 | 197 | 50 | 133 |
| 1978 | Pit....... | 12 | 11 | 1 | 3.24 | 189.0 | 191 | 49 | 94 |
| 1979 | Pit....... | 14 | 9 | 0 | 3.22 | 207.0 | 201 | 41 | 101 |
| 1980 | Pit....... | 11 | 14 | 1 | 4.02 | 233.0 | 246 | 50 | 97 |
| 1981 | Pit....... | 2 | 2 | 0 | 3.51 | 41.0 | 42 | 11 | 14 |
| 1982 | Pit....... | 12 | 7 | 1 | 2.94 | 174.2 | 166 | 37 | 133 |
| 1983 | Pit....... | 15 | 8 | 0 | 3.23 | 197.2 | 191 | 45 | 157 |
| 1984 | Pit....... | 12 | 11 | 2 | 2.72 | 185.1 | 179 | 34 | 133 |
| 1985 | Cal ...... | 7 | 3 | 0 | 3.80 | 71.0 | 70 | 24 | 53 |
| 1985 | Pit....... | 2 | 4 | 9 | 3.64 | 54.1 | 57 | 14 | 47 |
| 1986 | Cal ...... | 10 | 2 | 0 | 2.55 | 91.2 | 68 | 26 | 81 |
| 1987 | Cal ...... | 8 | 6 | 0 | 4.71 | 116.2 | 127 | 20 | 74 |
| 1987 | NYN ..... | 2 | 0 | 0 | 5.84 | 12.1 | 17 | 3 | 10 |
| 1988 | NYA...... | 13 | 7 | 1 | 3.38 | 157.0 | 150 | 23 | 121 |
| 1989 | NYA...... | 3 | 3 | 0 | 5.14 | 49.0 | 49 | 12 | 37 |
| 1989 | Mon ..... | 0 | 2 | 0 | 3.31 | 16.1 | 17 | 4 | 14 |
| | | 167 | 107 | 16 | 3.27 | 2368.0 | 2236 | 539 | 1532 |

# Don Carman

Birth Date: 8/14/59
Throws: Left
1989 Club:
Philadelphia Phillies
Contest Code #: 340

Rating: 1

When a weak team lacks starters, anyone who can pitch and chew gum at the same time can make its staff. On a good team, one-pitch pitcher Don Carman would be in Triple A working to develop a change-up or knuckleball, anything beside his less-than-average fastball. But as long as there are weak teams, there's a spot in the majors for Carman.

Even worse, throughout his career Carman has allowed bad outings to linger in his mind into his next appearances. Last season he tied teammate Larry McWilliams and Zane Smith of the Braves and Expos for the league's longest losing streak (nine games).

If you were his manager, you might think the best course of action would be to put Carman in the bullpen, where he could get away with one pitch while not having four days between starts to dwell on his last outing. The

Phillies tried that. In fact, Carman broke in as a reliever. The problem is that his fastball isn't fast enough to get the key out.

| Year | Team | W | L | SV | ERA | IP | H | BB | K |
|------|------|---|---|----|----|-----|-----|-----|-----|
| 1983 | Phi ...... | 0 | 0 | 1 | 0.00 | 1.0 | 0 | 0 | 0 |
| 1984 | Phi ...... | 0 | 1 | 0 | 5.40 | 13.1 | 14 | 6 | 16 |
| 1985 | Phi ...... | 9 | 4 | 7 | 2.09 | 86.1 | 52 | 38 | 87 |
| 1986 | Phi ...... | 10 | 5 | 1 | 3.22 | 134.1 | 113 | 52 | 98 |
| 1987 | Phi ...... | 13 | 11 | 0 | 4.22 | 211.0 | 194 | 69 | 125 |
| 1988 | Phi ...... | 10 | 14 | 0 | 4.29 | 201.1 | 211 | 70 | 116 |
| 1989 | Phi ...... | 5 | 15 | 0 | 5.24 | 149.1 | 152 | 86 | 81 |
| | | 47 | 50 | 9 | 4.04 | 796.2 | 736 | 321 | 523 |

# Norm Charlton

**Birth Date: 1/6/63**
**Throws: Left**
**1989 Club:**
**Cincinnati Reds**
**Contest Code #: 341**

**Rating: 3**

The off-season shake-up in the Reds' front office may be a huge boost for Norm Charlton's career.

Charlton, an all-American starting pitcher at Rice University who became the Expos' first pick in the June 1984 draft, was acquired by the Reds in 1986. In Double A that year he went 8–1 in his last 11 starts with a 1.99 ERA, then won 3 games in the Eastern League playoffs. An arm injury sidelined him for most of the 1987 season, but in 1988 he joined the Reds' rotation in August. Though his record wasn't impressive, he allowed only 3 runs or less in 8 of his 10 starts, while the Reds were shut out in 3 of his 5 losses.

When the Reds traded lefty setup man Rob Murphy to the Boston Red Sox, Charlton, a hard thrower, moved into the pen. In his new role he struck out 98 batters in 95⅓ innings.

With Reds bullpen ace John Franco entering the option year of his contract, Charlton could move in as the closer should new general manager Bob Quinn opt to trade Franco. In my book, that makes Charlton worth a gamble.

| Year | Team | W | L | SV | ERA | IP | H | BB | K |
|------|------|---|---|----|----|-----|-----|-----|-----|
| 1988 | Cin ...... | 4 | 5 | 0 | 3.96 | 61.1 | 60 | 20 | 39 |
| 1989 | Cin ...... | 8 | 3 | 0 | 2.93 | 95.1 | 67 | 40 | 98 |
| | | 12 | 8 | 0 | 3.33 | 156.2 | 127 | 60 | 137 |

# Jim Clancy

**Birth Date: 12/18/55**
**Throws: Right**
**1989 Club:**
**Houston Astros**
**Contest Code #: 342**

**Rating: 1**

When Nolan Ryan signed as a free agent with the Texas Rangers last winter, the Astros acquired two pitchers—Rick Rhoden and Jim Clancy—to fill Ryan's boots. The bad news was that Rhoden came up lame and Clancy didn't.

Clancy, a 13-year veteran who was on the decline in 1988, was worse in 1989. Clancy was little more than a batting-practice pitcher in his 147 innings of work, spoon-feeding 155 hits and 66 walks—an average of 13.5 runners per game. The epitome of Clancy's futility came in August when he gave up the first 7 runs—all earned—in the Reds' record-setting 18-run first inning.

More bad news for the Astros: Ryan, who wound up 16–10 with a 3.20 ERA, was paid $1.8 million by the

Rangers last year, while Clancy, 7–14 with a 5.08 ERA, earned just $600,000 less.

| Year | Team | W | L | SV | ERA | IP | H | BB | K |
|------|------|---|---|----|-----|----|----|----|----|
| 1977 | Tor...... | 4 | 9 | 0 | 5.03 | 77.0 | 80 | 47 | 44 |
| 1978 | Tor...... | 10 | 12 | 0 | 4.08 | 194.0 | 199 | 91 | 106 |
| 1979 | Tor...... | 2 | 7 | 0 | 5.48 | 64.0 | 65 | 31 | 33 |
| 1980 | Tor...... | 13 | 16 | 0 | 3.30 | 251.0 | 217 | 128 | 152 |
| 1981 | Tor...... | 6 | 12 | 0 | 4.90 | 125.0 | 126 | 64 | 56 |
| 1982 | Tor...... | 16 | 14 | 0 | 3.71 | 266.2 | 251 | 77 | 139 |
| 1983 | Tor...... | 15 | 11 | 0 | 3.91 | 223.0 | 238 | 61 | 99 |
| 1984 | Tor...... | 13 | 15 | 0 | 5.12 | 219.2 | 249 | 88 | 118 |
| 1985 | Tor...... | 9 | 6 | 0 | 3.78 | 128.2 | 117 | 37 | 66 |
| 1986 | Tor...... | 14 | 14 | 0 | 3.94 | 219.1 | 202 | 63 | 126 |
| 1987 | Tor...... | 15 | 11 | 0 | 3.54 | 241.1 | 234 | 80 | 180 |
| 1988 | Tor...... | 11 | 13 | 0 | 4.49 | 196.1 | 207 | 47 | 118 |
| 1989 | Hou...... | 7 | 14 | 0 | 5.08 | 147.0 | 155 | 66 | 91 |
| | | 135 | 154 | 1 | 4.16 | 2353.0 | 2340 | 880 | 1328 |

# Marty Clary

**Birth Date: 4/3/62**
**Throws: Right**
**1989 Club:**
**Atlanta Braves**
**Contest Code #: 343**

**Rating: 2**

**M**arty Clary was called up to the majors in July, when the Braves were going nowhere and had nothing to lose. Clary, who possesses a 90-mile-an-hour fastball that doesn't move and a below-average curveball, didn't exactly have impeccable Triple A credentials. With Richmond in 1988 he was 6–11 with a 3.38 ERA, allowing 142 hits and 37 walks in 143⅔ innings. Surprise! Clary won three games for the Braves. No surprise: Clary lost three of four the rest of the way.

With pitching prospects Kent Mercker and Tommy Greene ready for prime time, we don't know if Clary will make the Braves' staff in 1990 or will be showcased in spring training for a possible trade. Two scouts I've spoken with feel Clary is, at best, a number-three-type starter.

| Year | Team | W | L | SV | ERA | IP | H | BB | K |
|------|------|---|---|----|-----|----|----|----|----|
| 1987 | Atl...... | 0 | 1 | 0 | 6.14 | 14.2 | 20 | 4 | 7 |
| 1989 | Atl...... | 4 | 3 | 0 | 3.15 | 108.2 | 103 | 31 | 30 |
| | | 4 | 4 | 0 | 3.50 | 123.1 | 123 | 35 | 37 |

# Pat Clements

**Birth Date: 2/2/62**
**Throws: Left**
**1989 Club:**
**San Diego Padres**
**Contest Code #: 344**

**Rating: 1**

**P**at Clements has always had the tools to be a good reliever. His motion is deceptive. His curveball has a bite to it. He doesn't allow many home runs. If he only had control...

Because of the paucity of left-handed relievers, four teams have tried Clements out of the pen, but only one—the California Angels—succeeded. That was Clements' best big-league season. Unfortunately, that was five years ago, Clements' first season. The Pirates gave him a shot as a closer. The Yankees tried him as a setup man and, later, as a starter. Now the Padres have him as middle relief.

Whichever league Clements has pitched in, he's consistently allowed 1.4 runners per inning. That's too high for any pitcher, particularly for a lefty like Clements, who's often called in to face one left-handed batter. He may pick up four or five wins for you, but your ERA will suffer.

| Year | Team | W | L | SV | ERA | IP | H | BB | K |
|------|------|---|---|----|----|----|----|----|----|
| 1985 | Cal ...... | 5 | 0 | 1 | 3.34 | 62.0 | 47 | 25 | 19 |
| 1985 | Pit. ...... | 0 | 2 | 2 | 3.67 | 34.1 | 39 | 15 | 17 |
| 1986 | Pit. ...... | 0 | 4 | 2 | 2.80 | 61.0 | 53 | 32 | 31 |
| 1987 | NYA. ..... | 3 | 3 | 7 | 4.95 | 80.0 | 91 | 30 | 36 |
| 1988 | NYA. ..... | 0 | 0 | 0 | 6.48 | 8.1 | 12 | 4 | 3 |
| 1989 | SD. ...... | 4 | 1 | 0 | 3.92 | 39.0 | 39 | 15 | 18 |
| | | 12 | 10 | 12 | 3.89 | 284.2 | 281 | 121 | 124 |

# David Cone

Birth Date: 1/2/63
Throws: Right
1989 Club:
New York Mets
Contest Code #: 345

Rating: 4

The one intangible attribute that separates David Cone from the National League's best starting pitchers is poise. Cone's face burns with anger when teammates make errors or when umpires call balls on pitches he thinks are strikes. When the Mets play well, he pitches well. When the chips are down, he sometimes succumbs to the pressure.

Last year Cone was the Mets' pitcher most affected by the loss of injured catcher Gary Carter and the subsequent rotation of backstops Barry Lyons, Mackey Sasser, and Phil Lombardi. Without a strong game caller to guide him, Cone, who normally has a three-quarter delivery, fell in love with a sidearm fastball; as soon as hitters saw his arm drop, they knew what was coming. Upon his return, Carter instructed Cone that he must mix in a sidearm curve if he was going to use a sidearm delivery. That simple suggestion pulled Cone out of a mid-season rut.

Cone's statistics indicate his value in three of our four pitching categories. If the Mets perform well in 1990, Cone should again win 20 games. If they play as they did in 1989, Cone's performances will tell us if he has grown up.

| Year | Team | W | L | SV | ERA | IP | H | BB | K |
|------|------|---|---|----|----|----|----|----|----|
| 1986 | KC. ....... | 0 | 0 | 0 | 5.56 | 22.2 | 29 | 13 | 21 |
| 1987 | NYN ..... | 5 | 6 | 1 | 3.71 | 99.1 | 87 | 44 | 68 |
| 1988 | NYN ..... | 20 | 3 | 0 | 2.22 | 231.1 | 178 | 80 | 213 |
| 1989 | NYN ..... | 14 | 8 | 0 | 3.52 | 219.2 | 183 | 74 | 190 |
| | | 39 | 17 | 1 | 3.11 | 573.0 | 477 | 211 | 492 |

# Dennis Cook

Birth Date: 10/4/62
Throws: Left
1989 Clubs:
San Francisco Giants &
Philadelphia Phillies
Contest Code #: 346

Rating: 3

Dennis Cook's first outing in 1989—a nationally televised complete game victory in June—was so good that the next day he was sent to the Phillies as part of the Steve Bedrosian trade.

Understand that left handed starters new to a league often do well their first time around because of two factors: Left-handers are in the minority, so the hitters are more accustomed to batting against right-handers; and their pitches have more natural movement than those of their right-handed counterparts. Cook made the most of these advantages, winning 2 of his next 3 starts with an ERA under 2.00. But like most left-handed pitching puppies, life was more difficult the second time around. The losses piled up and Cook's ERA ballooned as he overthrew and overthought. He also suffered back spasms. Phils manager Nick Leyva wisely moved Cook to the bullpen before his confidence was shot. Toward the end of the season Cook was put back into the rotation and showed his early form, including a complete-game shutout in his last start of the season.

Cook, a gifted athlete who has good running speed and line-drive batting power, may need another major-league season to help him grow. Nonetheless, he's capable of winning 15 games while the Phillies' coaching staff smooths out his rough edges.

| Year | Team | W | L | SV | ERA | IP | H | BB | K |
|------|------|---|---|----|-----|-----|---|----|---|
| 1988 | SF....... | 2 | 1 | 0 | 2.86 | 22.0 | 9 | 11 | 13 |
| 1989 | SF....... | 1 | 0 | 0 | 1.80 | 15.0 | 13 | 5 | 9 |
| 1989 | Phi ...... | 6 | 8 | 0 | 3.99 | 106.0 | 97 | 33 | 58 |
| | | 9 | 9 | 0 | 3.59 | 143.0 | 119 | 49 | 80 |

# John Costello

Birth Date: 12/24/60
Throws: Right
1989 Club:
St. Louis Cardinals
Contest Code #: 347

Rating: 3

In John Costello, the Cardinals have a relief pitcher who can take some of the closing workload from Todd Worrell. Costello is a smart pitcher with great stuff, a budding star capable of being a bullpen ace for any team in the league.

Costello, who in 1988 was selected as the best relief pitcher in the American Association in a *Baseball America* poll of managers, picked up the key outs in the sixth through eighth innings when called upon last year. When Worrell suffered a season-ending injury, Costello ably shared closing duties with left-hander Ken Dayley.

Costello's 1989 win and save totals were affected by the specific roles Cards manager Whitey Herzog delegates to his relievers, based on his belief in playing the percentages; Costello could be mowing them down, but if a left-handed batter stepped in with two outs in the ninth, Dayley would get the save opportunity. This year, if a right-handed batter steps in with two outs in the ninth, Costello may not give way.

| Year | Team | W | L | SV | ERA | IP | H | BB | K |
|------|------|---|---|----|-----|-----|---|----|---|
| 1988 | StL ...... | 5 | 2 | 1 | 1.81 | 49.2 | 44 | 25 | 38 |
| 1989 | StL ...... | 5 | 4 | 3 | 3.32 | 62.1 | 48 | 20 | 40 |
| | | 10 | 6 | 4 | 2.65 | 112.0 | 92 | 45 | 78 |

# Tim Crews

Birth Date: 4/3/61
Throws: Right
1989 Club:
Los Angeles Dodgers
Contest Code #: 348

Rating: 2

Middle reliever Tim Crews is the type of pitcher we call a sponge. He gets few wins and no saves, but his ERA is generally low enough to soak up the run-scoring mess that another pitcher may leave behind.

Crews, originally signed by the Milwaukee Brewers in 1980, was a promising starting pitcher until 1984, when he underwent surgery to correct an impingement in his right shoulder. Though he pitched well as a reliever, his career stalled at Triple A. Then Crews learned to throw the split-fingered fastball, and at the 1986 baseball winter meetings—the height of split-fingered fastball ma-

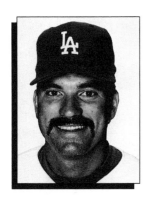

nia—the Dodgers acquired Crews and Tim Leary, another split-fingerer, for Greg Brock.

But the fate of a workmanlike pitcher is precarious on a star-studded pitching staff. Crews has spent parts of previous summers with the Dodgers' Triple A team in Albuquerque before, and, if some of the young prospects are ready, he could do so again this year.

| Year | Team | W | L | SV | ERA | IP | H | BB | K |
|------|------|---|---|----|-----|-----|---|----|---|
| 1987 | LA....... | 1 | 1 | 3 | 2.48 | 29.0 | 30 | 8 | 20 |
| 1988 | LA....... | 4 | 0 | 0 | 3.14 | 71.2 | 77 | 16 | 45 |
| 1989 | LA....... | 0 | 1 | 1 | 3.21 | 61.2 | 69 | 23 | 56 |
| | | 5 | 2 | 4 | 3.05 | 162.1 | 176 | 47 | 121 |

# Ron Darling

**Birth Date: 8/19/60**
**Throws: Right**
**1989 Club:**
**New York Mets**
**Contest Code #: 349**

**Rating: 3**

Meet Ron Darling: scholar, graceful athlete, fashion-magazine cover-boy, restaurateur, father, a star in New York's night life, a million-dollar pitcher on the National League team in the biggest media market. There's only one description Darling has yet to earn: clutch performer.

Last season provided an example of Darling's performance under pressure. When Dwight Gooden injured his right shoulder, Darling, the number-two man on the Mets' staff, faltered. The Mets acquired Frank Viola to anchor the staff, something Darling has failed to do when called upon previoulsy.

Does Darling let his off-the-field activities affect his performance? He says no, but last October New York-based *Spy* magazine built an interesting argument in a chart—"Batter Up, Pitcher Depressed"—correlating his emotional and athletic highs and lows from 1986 to the middle of 1989. Again and again, when Darling's personal life has flourished—his marriage to fashion model Toni O'Reilly; his appearance on the cover of *GQ*; his romance with actress Rae Dawn Chong after separating from Toni; and his marital reconciliation—he's pitched well. When off-the-field problems arise—his separation from Toni; the dissolution of his downtown Manhattan restaurant—Darling gets shelled.

| Year | Team | W | L | SV | ERA | IP | H | BB | K |
|------|------|---|---|----|-----|-----|---|----|---|
| 1983 | NYN ..... | 1 | 3 | 0 | 2.80 | 35.1 | 31 | 17 | 23 |
| 1984 | NYN ..... | 12 | 9 | 0 | 3.81 | 205.2 | 179 | 104 | 136 |
| 1985 | NYN ..... | 16 | 6 | 0 | 2.90 | 248.0 | 214 | 114 | 167 |
| 1986 | NYN ..... | 15 | 6 | 0 | 2.81 | 237.0 | 203 | 81 | 184 |
| 1987 | NYN ..... | 12 | 8 | 0 | 4.29 | 207.2 | 183 | 96 | 167 |
| 1988 | NYN ..... | 17 | 9 | 0 | 3.25 | 240.2 | 218 | 60 | 161 |
| 1989 | NYN ..... | 14 | 14 | 0 | 3.52 | 217.1 | 214 | 70 | 153 |
| | | 87 | 55 | 0 | 3.38 | 1391.2 | 1242 | 542 | 991 |

# Danny Darwin

**Birth Date:** 10/25/55
**Throws:** Right
**1989 Club:**
**Houston Astros**
**Contest Code #:** 350

**Rating: 3**

**E**very owner in my fantasy league congratulated me for having the wisdom to obtain Danny Darwin last year. Oh, baby, did he help me look like a genius! Darwin's 11 victories were the equivalent of having another starter; his 7 saves bolstered my bullpen; and his 2.36 ERA and .733 winning percentage were outstanding.

Now for a humbling confession. I was scared to death of Darwin. During the course of his career he usually wins between 8 and 10 games a season, but his loss totals have consistently been in the double digits since 1983. The raps on Darwin, the power hitter's best friend, were a lack of concentration and a tendency to get too fine with his pitches. But in 1989 he was on a streak too hot to ignore. After a while I stopped fretting about the day when Darwin would start thinking and stop doing.

Please don't tell this to my fellow game players, but I hope to trade Darwin before the 1990 season begins, while his value is inflated. Middle relievers get mileage on their meters. You get a Juan Agosto or a Terry Leach or an Andy McGaffigan on a hot streak and you milk them. Middle relief is important, but the truth is that teams often fill that role with failed starters and ineffective closers.

| Year | Team | W | L | SV | ERA | IP | H | BB | K |
|------|------|---|---|----|----|----|----|----|----|
| 1978 | Tex ...... | 1 | 0 | 0 | 4.00 | 9.0 | 11 | 1 | 8 |
| 1979 | Tex ...... | 4 | 4 | 0 | 4.04 | 78.0 | 50 | 30 | 58 |
| 1980 | Tex ...... | 13 | 4 | 8 | 2.62 | 110.0 | 98 | 50 | 104 |
| 1981 | Tex ...... | 9 | 9 | 0 | 3.64 | 146.0 | 115 | 57 | 98 |
| 1982 | Tex ...... | 10 | 8 | 7 | 3.44 | 89.0 | 95 | 37 | 61 |
| 1983 | Tex ...... | 8 | 13 | 0 | 3.49 | 183.0 | 175 | 62 | 92 |
| 1984 | Tex ...... | 8 | 12 | 0 | 3.94 | 223.2 | 249 | 54 | 123 |
| 1985 | Mil ...... | 8 | 18 | 2 | 3.80 | 217.2 | 212 | 65 | 125 |
| 1986 | Mil ...... | 6 | 8 | 0 | 3.52 | 130.1 | 120 | 35 | 80 |
| 1986 | Hou...... | 5 | 2 | 0 | 2.32 | 54.1 | 50 | 9 | 40 |
| 1987 | Hou...... | 9 | 10 | 0 | 3.59 | 195.2 | 184 | 69 | 134 |
| 1988 | Hou...... | 8 | 13 | 3 | 3.84 | 192.0 | 189 | 48 | 129 |
| 1989 | Hou...... | 11 | 4 | 7 | 2.36 | 122.0 | 92 | 33 | 104 |
| | | 100 | 105 | 27 | 3.51 | 1750.2 | 1640 | 550 | 1156 |

# Ken Dayley

**Birth Date:** 2/25/59
**Throws:** Left
**1989 Club:**
**St. Louis Cardinals**
**Contest Code #:** 352

**Rating: 3**

**K**en Dayley is the best number-two closer and number-one set-up man a team can have. Dayley's big-breaking curveball ties left-handed batters in knots. Last year, picking up the slack when Todd Worrell went down, he earned 12 saves and allowed only 3 home runs in 75 ⅓ innings.

Dayley is a fine athlete. In high school he lettered in baseball, basketball, and football. He played baseball and basketball at the University of Portland (Oregon), and in 1980 he was named to *The Sporting News* all-America team as a starting pitcher. That June Dayley was the third player chosen in the amateur draft.

The team that chose him, the Braves, couldn't wait for Dayley to develop, so in 1984 it sent him to the Cardinals with backup first baseman Mike Jorgensen for third baseman Ken Oberkfell. Whitey Herzog put Dayley in

his bullpen, where he's been a standout ever since, even after undergoing major elbow surgery before the 1987 season.

| Year | Team | W | L | SV | ERA | IP | H | BB | K |
|------|------|---|---|----|-----|-----|-----|-----|-----|
| 1982 | Atl....... | 5 | 6 | 0 | 4.54 | 71.1 | 79 | 25 | 34 |
| 1983 | Atl....... | 5 | 8 | 0 | 4.30 | 104.2 | 100 | 39 | 70 |
| 1984 | StL ...... | 0 | 2 | 0 | 18.00 | 5.0 | 16 | 5 | 0 |
| 1984 | Atl....... | 0 | 3 | 0 | 5.31 | 18.2 | 28 | 6 | 10 |
| 1985 | StL ...... | 4 | 4 | 11 | 2.76 | 65.1 | 65 | 18 | 62 |
| 1986 | StL ...... | 0 | 3 | 5 | 3.26 | 38.2 | 42 | 11 | 33 |
| 1987 | StL ...... | 9 | 5 | 4 | 2.66 | 61.0 | 52 | 33 | 63 |
| 1988 | StL ...... | 2 | 7 | 5 | 2.77 | 55.1 | 48 | 19 | 38 |
| 1989 | StL ...... | 4 | 3 | 12 | 2.87 | 75.1 | 63 | 30 | 40 |
| | | 29 | 41 | 37 | 3.63 | 495.1 | 493 | 186 | 350 |

# Jose DeLeon

**Birth Date: 12/20/60**
**Throws: Right**
**1989 Club:**
**St. Louis Cardinals**
**Contest Code #: 353**

**Rating: 4**

It's hard to believe, watching Jose DeLeon pitch so well the past two seasons, that in 1985 he was a 19-game loser. What happened? Five years ago DeLeon became so enamored of his forkball, which drops in the hitting zone like a two-ton weight, that he threw it too early in the count and got behind. Today he uses his fastball and slider early in the count to set up his nasty forkball.

Now that DeLeon's pitch sequence has improved, so has his ratio of strikeouts to walks. He's also permitted fewer base runners in the past two seasons—an average of 12 per game in 1988 and 10 in 1989. Last year he hurled three shutouts plus an 11-inning, no-run performance in which he didn't get a decision.

If the Cardinals are contenders in 1990, DeLeon, a mature pitcher in his physical prime, may post his first 20-win season.

| Year | Team | W | L | SV | ERA | IP | H | BB | K |
|------|------|---|---|----|-----|-----|-----|-----|-----|
| 1983 | Pit....... | 7 | 3 | 0 | 2.83 | 108.0 | 75 | 47 | 118 |
| 1984 | Pit....... | 7 | 13 | 0 | 3.74 | 192.1 | 147 | 92 | 153 |
| 1985 | Pit....... | 2 | 19 | 3 | 4.70 | 162.2 | 138 | 89 | 149 |
| 1986 | ChA...... | 4 | 5 | 0 | 2.96 | 79.0 | 49 | 42 | 68 |
| 1986 | Pit....... | 1 | 3 | 1 | 8.27 | 16.1 | 17 | 17 | 11 |
| 1987 | ChA...... | 11 | 12 | 0 | 4.02 | 206.0 | 177 | 97 | 153 |
| 1988 | StL ...... | 13 | 10 | 0 | 3.67 | 225.1 | 198 | 86 | 208 |
| 1989 | StL ...... | 16 | 12 | 0 | 3.05 | 244.2 | 173 | 80 | 201 |
| | | 61 | 77 | 4 | 3.70 | 1234.1 | 974 | 550 | 1061 |

# Jim Deshaies

**Birth Date: 6/23/60**
**Throws: Left**
**1989 Club:**
**Houston Astros**
**Contest Code #: 354**

**Rating: 4**

Jim Deshaies is one of my favorite pitchers. He is a master at pitching high in the strike zone—even though his fastball is in the 85-mile-an-hour range, helping disprove the longstanding notion that a pitcher must pitch low in the strike zone to be effective. The hitters see his high fastball and can't help but chase it, even if it's out of the strike zone. On September 23, 1986, Deshaies set a modern major-league record by striking out the first eight Dodgers he faced; only one of those batters didn't fan swinging.

Deshaies, who also throws a curve, slider, and change-up, has won in double digits for four years running. Last year, with the Astros batting .239 as a team, he won 15

games and struck out 153 batters, both career highs, with an ERA of 2.91.

In the past fans looked down on the 6'4", 222-pound Deshaies for not being strong enough to finish games—he completed only one in 1986 and one in 1987. But he completed three in 1988 and six last year, and in both seasons he pitched more than 200 innings.

Deshaies gets better each year, so expect him to close in on 20 victories in 1990.

| Year | Team | W | L | SV | ERA | IP | H | BB | K |
|------|------|---|---|----|----|----|----|----|----|
| 1984 | NYA...... | 0 | 1 | 0 | 11.57 | 7.0 | 14 | 7 | 5 |
| 1985 | Hou...... | 0 | 0 | 0 | 0.00 | 3.0 | 1 | 0 | 2 |
| 1986 | Hou...... | 12 | 5 | 0 | 3.25 | 144.0 | 124 | 59 | 128 |
| 1987 | Hou...... | 11 | 6 | 0 | 4.62 | 152.0 | 149 | 57 | 104 |
| 1988 | Hou...... | 11 | 14 | 0 | 3.00 | 207.0 | 164 | 72 | 127 |
| 1989 | Hou...... | 15 | 10 | 0 | 2.91 | 225.2 | 180 | 79 | 153 |
| | | 49 | 36 | 0 | 3.42 | 738.2 | 632 | 274 | 519 |

# Rob Dibble

**Birth Date: 1/24/64**
**Throws: Right**
**1989 Club:**
**Cincinnati Reds**
**Contest Code #: 355**

**Rating: 3**

Rob Dibble has an explosive fastball and a temper to match. Bill White, the first-year president of the National League, called in Dibble so many times for disciplinary reasons that he should have given Dibble an adjoining office. Two Dibble tantrums stand out: He ignited a brawl with the Mets by burying his heater into Tim Teufel's back; and, earlier, he had thrown a bat into the stands after a frustrating outing. When Dibble's in the game, no one is safe.

Dibble's fastball, which helped him pitch four no-hitters as a high-school starter, makes him a rising star. Last season, as the Reds' right-handed setup man for lefty John Franco, Dibble struck out 141 batters in 99 innings—an average of 3 K's every two innings—while earning 10 wins and 2 saves. Dibble showed excellent control, walking only 39 batters and giving up just 4 home runs.

The problem for Dibble is self-control. This season he could share or wrest the closing role from Franco, who's in the option year of his contract. But if he continues to act up, what manager would entrust him to be his everyday closer?

| Year | Team | W | L | SV | ERA | IP | H | BB | K |
|------|------|---|---|----|----|----|----|----|----|
| 1988 | Cin ...... | 1 | 1 | 0 | 1.82 | 59.1 | 43 | 21 | 59 |
| 1989 | Cin ...... | 10 | 5 | 2 | 2.09 | 99.0 | 62 | 39 | 141 |
| | | 11 | 6 | 2 | 1.99 | 158.1 | 105 | 60 | 200 |

# Frank DiPino

**Birth Date: 10/22/56**
**Throws: Left**
**1989 Club:**
**St. Louis Cardinals**
**Contest Code #: 356**

**Rating: 2**

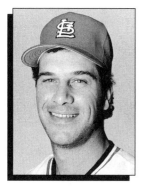

Last year Frank DiPino's typical work routine went like this: The left-handed middle reliever would hurl a scoreless inning or two when the Cardinals were tied or behind; the half-inning after DiPino's departure from the game, the Cards would rally, take the lead, and let their setup men and stoppers seal the victory. The decision would go to DiPino. Talk about being in the right place at the right time!

Let's not minimize DiPino's 1989 efforts. He did appear in 67 games and finish 8. He did lead the Cardinals in victories, winning percentage, and ERA. But Frank DiPino had 20 career victories and a winning percentage of .364 over his first eight seasons. He was a feared lefty closer six years ago, but in recent years has been little more than a middle-inning mop-up man.

| Year | Team | W | L | SV | ERA | IP | H | BB | K |
|------|------|---|---|----|----|----|----|----|----|
| 1981 | Mil ...... | 0 | 0 | 0 | 0.00 | 2.0 | 0 | 3 | 3 |
| 1982 | Hou...... | 2 | 2 | 0 | 6.04 | 28.1 | 32 | 11 | 25 |
| 1983 | Hou...... | 3 | 4 | 20 | 2.65 | 71.1 | 52 | 20 | 67 |
| 1984 | Hou...... | 4 | 9 | 14 | 3.35 | 75.1 | 74 | 36 | 65 |
| 1985 | Hou...... | 3 | 7 | 6 | 4.03 | 76.0 | 69 | 43 | 49 |
| 1986 | Hou...... | 1 | 3 | 3 | 3.57 | 40.1 | 27 | 16 | 27 |
| 1986 | ChN...... | 2 | 4 | 0 | 5.17 | 40.0 | 47 | 14 | 43 |
| 1987 | ChN...... | 3 | 3 | 4 | 3.15 | 80.0 | 75 | 34 | 61 |
| 1988 | ChN...... | 2 | 3 | 6 | 4.98 | 90.1 | 102 | 32 | 69 |
| 1989 | StL ...... | 9 | 0 | 0 | 2.45 | 88.1 | 73 | 20 | 44 |
| | | 29 | 35 | 53 | 3.69 | 592.0 | 551 | 229 | 453 |

# Kelly Downs

**Birth Date: 10/25/60**
**Throws: Right**
**1989 Club:**
**San Francisco Giants**
**Contest Code #: 357**

**Rating: 2**

The Giants have reason to worry about the future of once-promising right-hander Kelly Downs. In each of his last two seasons, Downs missed a lot of time because of problems in his throwing shoulder.

Suspecting that his shoulder problems stemmed from his delivery—Downs throws across his body—the Giants changed his delivery during a rehabilitative stint in the minors last year. However, his performance did not improve.

When healthy, Downs has good control of his 94-mile-an-hour fastball, split-fingered fastball, curveball, and change-up. But he's been healthy in only one of his three big-league seasons.

It took Downs until age twenty-six to reach the majors, and let's hope he can rebound at age thirty.

| Year | Team | W | L | SV | ERA | IP | H | BB | K |
|------|------|---|---|----|----|----|----|----|----|
| 1986 | SF....... | 4 | 4 | 0 | 2.75 | 88.1 | 78 | 30 | 64 |
| 1987 | SF....... | 12 | 9 | 1 | 3.63 | 186.0 | 185 | 67 | 137 |
| 1988 | SF....... | 13 | 9 | 0 | 3.32 | 168.0 | 140 | 47 | 118 |
| 1989 | SF....... | 4 | 8 | 0 | 4.79 | 82.2 | 82 | 26 | 49 |
| | | 33 | 30 | 1 | 3.57 | 525.0 | 485 | 170 | 368 |

# Doug Drabek

Birth Date: 7/25/62
Throws: Right
1989 Club:
Pittsburgh Pirates
Contest Code #: 358

Rating: 5

If I could choose any National League pitcher to start a crucial game for my team, I'd choose Doug Drabek. The twenty-seven-year-old right-hander has a great pitching repertoire—a two-seam fastball that sinks, a four-seamer that doesn't sink, a curveball, hard slider and forkball—and is the most intense competitor in the league.

Drabek may be the only pitcher who Pirates' manager Jim Leyland allows to talk him out of getting pulled from a game in progress. And when Drabek stays in, even if he's tired, he gets the job done.

Don't be deceived by Drabek's 1989 win-loss record; the pitiful Pirates had little offensive punch and were without a bullpen closer for the early months of the season. Despite this lack of support, Drabek hurled five shutouts in eight complete games, was fifth in innings pitched, sixth in ERA's, and, as in 1988, he permitted an average of only 10 batters to reach base per game.

| Year | Team | W | L | SV | ERA | IP | H | BB | K |
|------|------|---|---|----|----|----|----|----|----|
| 1986 | NYA...... | 7 | 8 | 0 | 4.10 | 131.2 | 126 | 50 | 76 |
| 1987 | Pit....... | 11 | 12 | 0 | 3.88 | 176.1 | 165 | 46 | 120 |
| 1988 | Pit....... | 15 | 7 | 0 | 3.08 | 219.1 | 194 | 50 | 127 |
| 1989 | Pit....... | 14 | 12 | 0 | 2.80 | 244.1 | 215 | 69 | 123 |
| | | 47 | 39 | 0 | 3.35 | 771.2 | 700 | 215 | 446 |

# Mark Eichhorn

Birth Date: 11/21/60
Throws: Right
1989 Club:
Atlanta Braves
Contest Code #: 359

Rating: 1

When one's career is on the decline, the Braves is the perfect way station before reaching the end of the line.

Mark Eichhorn (pronounced *Ike-horn*), who made his major-league debut for the Toronto Blue Jays in 1982, had his best season four years ago. Pitching in relief, Eichhorn played an important role in the Blue Jays' American League Eastern Division title by winning 14 games and saving 10, with a 1.72 ERA. In 1987, Eichhorn had a league-leading 89 appearances. He again won 10 games, but his save total dropped to 4 while his ERA rose to 3.17. In 1988 Eichhorn was so ineffective that, at age twenty-eight, he was shipped back to the minors. Last year he was sent to the home of the Braves, reunited with general manager Bobby Cox, who managed the Jays during Eichhorn's best season.

When Eichhorn was on the mound, it was like batting practice: 70 hits, 19 walks, and 33 earned runs in 68⅓ innings. As a testimonial to the Braves' ineptitude, Eichhorn managed to finish 13 games.

| Year | Team | W | L | SV | ERA | IP | H | BB | K |
|------|------|---|---|----|----|----|----|----|----|
| 1982 | Tor....... | 0 | 3 | 0 | 5.45 | 38.0 | 40 | 14 | 16 |
| 1986 | Tor....... | 14 | 6 | 10 | 1.72 | 157.0 | 105 | 45 | 166 |
| 1987 | Tor....... | 10 | 6 | 4 | 3.17 | 127.2 | 110 | 52 | 96 |
| 1988 | Tor....... | 0 | 3 | 1 | 4.19 | 66.2 | 79 | 27 | 28 |
| 1989 | Atl....... | 5 | 5 | 0 | 4.35 | 68.1 | 70 | 19 | 49 |
| | | 29 | 23 | 15 | 3.19 | 457.2 | 404 | 157 | 355 |

# Sid Fernandez

**Birth Date:** 10/12/62
**Throws:** Left
**1989 Club:**
**New York Mets**
**Contest Code #: 360**

## Rating: 5

**T**he Mets' patience with Sid Fernandez may finally have paid off. Going into the 1988 season, Fernandez was a first-half wonder: 24–12 with a 2.91 ERA before the All-Star break, 19–18, with a 3.38 ERA in the second half. In 1988 Fernandez was a second-half sensation: 5–6, 3.43 before the All-Star break, 7–4, 2.60 after the break. But last season Fernandez was 7–2, with a 2.83 ERA before the break and 7–3, with a 2.84 ERA, in the second half.

Fernandez's earlier "before and after" stats related to his body weights before the season and after the break. Until 1988, Fernandez would weigh in at around 230 pounds but balloon toward 260 months later. In 1988 Fernandez came in heavy and was ordered to lose weight during the season. His weight is an issue because of a chronic knee ailment; the heavier he is, the more weight his knee joint must carry. Last year, with his diet modified, Fernandez maintained his endurance from start to finish.

Fernandez's pitching motion, in which he pauses for a split-second into his coil before throwing home, makes his release point hard to pick up, giving the hitter less time and thereby making his 88-mile-an-hour fastball appear faster. He also has a wicked, roundhouse curveball. Last season Fernandez emerged as the staff's most consistent pitcher, and if he keeps his girth in check he could be the staff ace in 1990.

| Year | Team | W | L | SV | ERA | IP | H | BB | K |
|------|------|---|---|----|----|----|----|----|----|
| 1983 | LA....... | 0 | 1 | 0 | 6.00 | 6.0 | 7 | 7 | 9 |
| 1984 | NYN ..... | 6 | 6 | 0 | 3.50 | 90.0 | 74 | 34 | 62 |
| 1985 | NYN ..... | 9 | 9 | 0 | 2.80 | 170.1 | 108 | 80 | 180 |
| 1986 | NYN ..... | 16 | 6 | 1 | 3.52 | 204.1 | 161 | 91 | 200 |
| 1987 | NYN ..... | 12 | 8 | 0 | 3.81 | 156.0 | 130 | 67 | 134 |
| 1988 | NYN ..... | 12 | 10 | 0 | 3.03 | 187.0 | 127 | 70 | 189 |
| 1989 | NYN ..... | 14 | 5 | 0 | 2.83 | 219.1 | 157 | 75 | 198 |
| | | 69 | 45 | 1 | 3.22 | 1033.0 | 764 | 424 | 972 |

# Bob Forsch

**Birth Date:** 1/13/50
**Throws:** Right
**1989 Club:**
**Houston Astros**
**Contest Code #: 361**

## Rating: 1

**T**he question most every athlete faces in the latter part of his career is: When is it time to retire? The great Mike Schmidt knew. He called it quits a month into the 1989 season, the moment he realized his skills were irretrievable. Sadly, too often players continue past their productive, useful years, perhaps blinded by the great paychecks in baseball. Remember the pathetic end of Steve Carlton's career?

With all due respect, Bob Forsch, your time to retire has come. We'll remember your wise decision to stop being an infielder and become a pitcher in your third minor-league season. We'll remember your two no-hitters. We'll remember your consistency, even in 1987 at age thirty-seven. But, frankly, you started to lose it in 1988, and last year... well, we won't even talk about that.

I know, I'm only a baseball writer. Who am I to tell you to walk away from an annual salary of more than

$700,000? Sorry, I'm also a fan who hates to see a respectable ball player hanging on for dear life.

| Year | Team | W | L | SV | ERA | IP | H | BB | K |
|------|------|---|---|----|----|----|---|----|---|
| 1974 | StL . . . . . . | 7 | 4 | 0 | 2.97 | 100.0 | 84 | 34 | 39 |
| 1975 | StL . . . . . . | 15 | 10 | 0 | 2.86 | 230.0 | 213 | 70 | 108 |
| 1976 | StL . . . . . . | 8 | 10 | 0 | 3.94 | 194.0 | 209 | 71 | 76 |
| 1977 | StL . . . . . . | 20 | 7 | 0 | 3.48 | 217.0 | 210 | 69 | 95 |
| 1978 | StL . . . . . . | 11 | 17 | 0 | 3.69 | 234.0 | 205 | 97 | 114 |
| 1979 | StL . . . . . . | 11 | 11 | 0 | 3.82 | 219.0 | 215 | 52 | 92 |
| 1980 | StL . . . . . . | 11 | 10 | 0 | 3.77 | 215.0 | 225 | 33 | 87 |
| 1981 | StL . . . . . . | 10 | 5 | 0 | 3.19 | 124.0 | 106 | 29 | 41 |
| 1982 | StL . . . . . . | 15 | 9 | 1 | 3.48 | 233.0 | 238 | 54 | 69 |
| 1983 | StL . . . . . . | 10 | 12 | 0 | 4.28 | 187.0 | 190 | 54 | 56 |
| 1984 | StL . . . . . . | 2 | 5 | 0 | 6.02 | 52.1 | 64 | 19 | 21 |
| 1985 | StL . . . . . . | 9 | 6 | 2 | 3.90 | 136.0 | 132 | 47 | 48 |
| 1986 | StL . . . . . . | 14 | 10 | 0 | 3.25 | 230.0 | 211 | 68 | 104 |
| 1987 | StL . . . . . . | 11 | 7 | 0 | 4.32 | 179.0 | 189 | 45 | 89 |
| 1988 | StL . . . . . . | 9 | 4 | 0 | 3.73 | 108.2 | 111 | 38 | 40 |
| 1988 | Hou . . . . . . | 1 | 4 | 0 | 6.51 | 27.2 | 42 | 6 | 14 |
| 1989 | Hou . . . . . . | 4 | 5 | 0 | 5.32 | 108.1 | 133 | 46 | 40 |
| | | 168 | 136 | 3 | 3.76 | 2795.0 | 2777 | 832 | 1133 |

# John Franco

**Birth Date: 9/17/60**
**Throws: Left**
**1989 Club:**
**Cincinnati Reds**
**Contest Code #: 362**

**Rating: 5**

John Franco has been so consistently effective the past few seasons that 1989 has to be considered an off year, even if he did save 32 games.

Franco, who generally doesn't come into games unless the Reds have the lead, had a career-low four wins and a career-high eight defeats. He allowed an average of 1.4 batters to reach base per inning, high for any pitcher, let alone John Franco.

Why did Franco become more hittable? Talk with scouts and sources close to the Reds and one hears two schools of thought. One advance scout contends that hitters learned to lay off Franco's screwball, his out pitch, which usually drops out of the strike zone, and made him throw more pitches in the strike zone. Others who know Franco, a down-to-earth guy who's sensitive by nature, suggest that during the second half of last season he was deeply affected when his name was erroneously linked to Pete Rose's alleged betting activites. Interestingly, Franco, who was 2–2 with a 1.60 ERA and 23 saves by July 18, went 2–6 with a 5.04 ERA and 9 saves the rest of the way. This didn't seem to dampen the Mets' enthusiasm for Franco—they traded their number-one lefty, Randy Myers, to get Franco in December. They probably figure that Franco should be able to overcome these factors and get back to business as usual. He has every reason to, now that he's in the option year of his contract.

| Year | Team | W | L | SV | ERA | IP | H | BB | K |
|------|------|---|---|----|----|----|---|----|---|
| 1984 | Cin . . . . . . | 6 | 2 | 4 | 2.61 | 79.1 | 74 | 36 | 55 |
| 1985 | Cin . . . . . . | 12 | 3 | 12 | 2.18 | 99.0 | 83 | 40 | 61 |
| 1986 | Cin . . . . . . | 6 | 6 | 29 | 2.94 | 101.0 | 90 | 44 | 84 |
| 1987 | Cin . . . . . . | 8 | 5 | 32 | 2.52 | 82.0 | 76 | 27 | 61 |
| 1988 | Cin . . . . . . | 6 | 6 | 39 | 1.57 | 86.0 | 60 | 27 | 46 |
| 1989 | Cin . . . . . . | 4 | 8 | 32 | 3.12 | 80.2 | 77 | 36 | 60 |
| | | 42 | 30 | 148 | 2.49 | 528.0 | 460 | 210 | 367 |

# Todd Frohwirth

**Birth Date:** 9/28/62
**Throws:** Right
**1989 Club:**
**Philadelphia Phillies**
**Contest Code #:** 363

**Rating: 1**

Submariner Todd Frohwirth throws like former Phillies reliever Kent Tekulve. His 6'4", 195-pound string-bean frame is virtually the same as Tekulve's. And, like Tekulve, he's spent the better part of his first six seasons in the minor leagues.

Frohwirth, who in 1987 climbed from Double A to Triple A to the major leagues, shined in his short stint with the Phillies. Unfortunately, he couldn't carry that form into the next season. Frohwirth was left off the Phillies' 1988 40-man post-season roster and made available to any team that wished to claim him.

Frohwirth opened the 1989 season at Triple A. Upon his return to the majors, he was used in middle relief, appeared in 45 games and finished 11. His average of hits and walks allowed wasn't bad, though his ERA wasn't that good. Frohwirth is not yet Kent Tekulve.

| Year | Team | W | L | SV | ERA | IP | H | BB | K |
|------|------|---|---|----|----|----|----|----|----|
| 1987 | Phi ...... | 1 | 0 | 0 | 0.00 | 11.0 | 12 | 2 | 9 |
| 1988 | Phi ...... | 1 | 2 | 0 | 8.25 | 12.0 | 16 | 11 | 11 |
| 1989 | Phi ...... | 1 | 0 | 0 | 3.59 | 62.2 | 56 | 18 | 39 |
| | | 3 | 2 | 0 | 3.78 | 85.2 | 84 | 31 | 59 |

# Scott Garrelts

**Birth Date:** 10/30/61
**Throws:** Right
**1989 Club:**
**San Francisco Giants**
**Contest Code #:** 364

**Rating: 4**

Genius is sometimes accidental. Last season Roger Craig, the National League Western Division's smartest manager and father of the split-fingered fastball, decided to move his closer, Scott Garrelts, into the starting rotation. As a reliever, Garrelts too often fell behind in the count, forcing him to groove strikes. Craig, who needed healthy starters, figured that Garrelts couldwork out his problems in a starting role, where every pitch doesn't have to be perfect. Craig had once before moved Garrelts into his rotation (in 1986) and Garrelts won 13 games. The second time was a real charm: Garrelts allowed an average of just one base runner per inning, led the Giants in victories, and the National League in ERA.

Garrelts has always possessed the tools for success: a good fastball, a hard slider, and a splitter. His problems stemmed from a lack of control. In 1988 he walked 46 batters and threw 6 wild pitches in 98 innings, numbers a manager can't tolerate from his closer. But as a starter in 1989, he issued 46 walks in 193⅓ innings.

At least Craig never said he always knew Garrelts would be a first-rate starter.

| Year | Team | W | L | SV | ERA | IP | H | BB | K |
|------|------|---|---|----|----|----|----|----|----|
| 1982 | SF ...... | 0 | 0 | 0 | 13.50 | 2.0 | 3 | 2 | 4 |
| 1983 | SF ...... | 2 | 2 | 0 | 2.52 | 35.2 | 33 | 19 | 16 |
| 1984 | SF ...... | 2 | 3 | 0 | 5.65 | 43.0 | 45 | 34 | 32 |
| 1985 | SF ...... | 9 | 6 | 13 | 2.30 | 105.2 | 76 | 58 | 106 |
| 1986 | SF ...... | 13 | 9 | 10 | 3.11 | 173.2 | 144 | 74 | 125 |
| 1987 | SF ...... | 11 | 7 | 12 | 3.22 | 106.1 | 70 | 55 | 127 |
| 1988 | SF ...... | 5 | 9 | 13 | 3.58 | 98.0 | 80 | 46 | 86 |
| 1989 | SF ...... | 14 | 5 | 0 | 2.28 | 193.1 | 149 | 46 | 119 |
| | | 56 | 41 | 48 | 3.01 | 757.2 | 600 | 334 | 615 |

# Tom Glavine

**Birth Date:** 3/25/66
**Throws:** Left
**1989 Club:**
**Atlanta Braves**
**Contest Code #:** 365

**Rating: 4**

**I**t takes a strong constitution to overcome the treatment former Braves manager Chuck Tanner heaped upon Atlanta's young starters. Tanner damaged Tom Glavine's confidence by leaving him in games in which he was already getting pounded. But Glavine, a fine athlete who in 1984 had been drafted by the Braves and the NHL's Los Angeles Kings, survived. His career is back on a promising course.

Glavine had exceptional control last season. In 186 innings he gave up 172 hits (an average of 8 per 9 innings), just 40 walks (2 per 9 innings), and struck out 90. He hurled six complete games, including four shutouts.

If the Braves can strengthen their bullpen this season, Glavine, who is best when used for 7 innings a pop, could win 18 games.

| Year | Team | W | L | SV | ERA | IP | H | BB | K |
|------|------|---|---|----|----|-----|-----|-----|-----|
| 1987 | Atl...... | 2 | 4 | 0 | 5.54 | 50.1 | 55 | 33 | 20 |
| 1988 | Atl...... | 7 | 17 | 0 | 4.56 | 195.1 | 201 | 63 | 84 |
| 1989 | Atl...... | 14 | 8 | 0 | 3.68 | 186.0 | 172 | 40 | 90 |
| | | 23 | 29 | 0 | 4.30 | 431.2 | 428 | 136 | 194 |

# Dwight Gooden

**Birth Date:** 10/16/64
**Throws:** Right
**1989 Club:**
**New York Mets**
**Contest Code #:** 366

**Rating: 5**

**D**wight Gooden has racked up so many achievements in his short career that he occupies 10 pages in the Mets media guide; that's 4 percent of the entire 250-page book.

Here's the abridged version, starting with awards: Carolina League pitcher of the year, 1983; National League Rookie of the Year, 1984; National League Cy Young winner, 1985; and the Associated Press' Male Athlete of the Year, 1985.

Now the distinctions: led Carolina League in shutouts (6) and strikeouts (300) in 1983; established National League record for most strikeouts in 3 consecutive games (43), 1984; led National League in complete games (16), 1985; set team record for ERA (1.53), 1985.

From 1986 to 1988, Gooden continued his brilliance as the Mets' ace of the staff. Last season, a muscle tear in his shoulder—the first significant injury of his career—crippled the Mets' chances of catching the Cubs.

The best thing one can say about Gooden is that when he's on the mound, the Mets believe they will win the game.

| Year | Team | W | L | SV | ERA | IP | H | BB | K |
|------|------|---|---|----|----|-----|-----|-----|-----|
| 1984 | NYN ..... | 17 | 9 | 0 | 2.60 | 218.0 | 161 | 73 | 276 |
| 1985 | NYN ..... | 24 | 4 | 0 | 1.53 | 276.2 | 198 | 69 | 268 |
| 1986 | NYN ..... | 17 | 6 | 0 | 2.84 | 250.0 | 197 | 80 | 200 |
| 1987 | NYN ..... | 15 | 7 | 0 | 3.21 | 179.2 | 162 | 53 | 148 |
| 1988 | NYN ..... | 18 | 9 | 0 | 3.19 | 248.1 | 242 | 57 | 175 |
| 1989 | NYN ..... | 9 | 4 | 1 | 2.89 | 118.1 | 93 | 47 | 101 |
| | | 100 | 39 | 1 | 2.64 | 1291.0 | 1053 | 379 | 1168 |

# Jim Gott

**Birth Date: 8/3/59**
**Throws: Right**
**1989 Club:**
**Pittsburgh Pirates**
**Contest Code #: 451**

**Rating: 4**

Jim Gott, second in the National League in saves (34) in 1988, arrived in the Pirates' 1989 spring training camp with a sore right elbow. The Pirates' medical staff wrote off Gott's pain as simple muscle soreness. However, after he pitched in one regular season game, the pain was too great to ignore. Doctors diagnosed a more severe elbow condition and performed corrective surgery.

Gott was back in good health after the season, but we can't be sure the Pirates' decision-makers will restore him to his role as the closer. When Gott was out last year, the Pirates played "hot potato" in the pen. Now, with Bill Landrum on the scene, Gott may have to share his role.

Forget Gott's pre-1988 stats. He's a much-improved pitcher. I'd normally rate him among the league's best closers, but Gott may be wasted as a setup man or co-closer.

| Year | Team | W | L | SV | ERA | IP | H | BB | K |
|------|------|---|---|----|----|----|---|----|---|
| 1982 | Tor....... | 5 | 10 | 0 | 4.43 | 136.0 | 134 | 66 | 82 |
| 1983 | Tor....... | 9 | 14 | 0 | 4.74 | 176.2 | 195 | 68 | 121 |
| 1984 | Tor....... | 7 | 6 | 2 | 4.02 | 109.2 | 93 | 49 | 73 |
| 1985 | SF........ | 7 | 10 | 0 | 3.88 | 148.1 | 144 | 51 | 78 |
| 1986 | SF........ | 0 | 0 | 1 | 7.62 | 13.0 | 16 | 13 | 9 |
| 1987 | Pit....... | 0 | 2 | 13 | 1.45 | 31.0 | 28 | 8 | 27 |
| 1987 | SF........ | 1 | 0 | 0 | 4.50 | 56.0 | 53 | 32 | 63 |
| 1988 | Pit....... | 6 | 6 | 34 | 3.49 | 77.1 | 68 | 22 | 76 |
| 1989 | Pit....... | 0 | 0 | 0 | 0.00 | 0.2 | 1 | 1 | 1 |
| | | 35 | 48 | 50 | 4.17 | 748.2 | 732 | 310 | 530 |

# Mark Grant

**Birth Date: 10/24/63**
**Throws: Right**
**1989 Club:**
**San Diego Padres**
**Contest Code #: 367**

**Rating: 2**

In my evolution as a baseball appraiser I've learned how crucial mental toughness is for success. A case in point is Mark Grant.

Grant, selected by the Giants in the first round of the 1981 draft—the player chosen after the Mets selected Ron Darling—has always had great stuff. At Class A in 1982 he led all of minor-league baseball with 243 strikeouts, including 19 in one game, and at Triple A in 1986 he led the Pacific Coast League in victories (14), complete games (10), and shutouts (3).

I first observed Grant, a jovial person, while traveling for 10 days with the Giants on assignment for *Sport* magazine. Grant was struggling as a starter, his teammates told me, because he was too good-natured and not intense enough. Nonetheless, I picked him up for my fantasy team, believing he'd mature soon enough. I was willing to wait, even as Grant's outings grew shorter and shorter following his trade to the Padres. I took him again in 1988 and had to endure his 2–8, 3.69 ERA. Last year I decided I wanted no part of him, funny guy or no.

However, last year Padres manager Jack McKeon put Grant in middle relief. Grant settled down and became one of the division's most dependable setup men. He reversed his 1988 won-lost record, picked up 2 saves, and finished 19 games.

| Year | Team | W | L | SV | ERA | IP | H | BB | K |
|------|------|---|---|-----|------|-------|------|-----|-----|
| 1984 | SF...... | 1 | 4 | 1 | 6.37 | 53.2 | 56 | 19 | 32 |
| 1986 | SF...... | 0 | 1 | 0 | 3.60 | 10.0 | 6 | 5 | 5 |
| 1987 | SD...... | 6 | 7 | 0 | 4.66 | 102.1 | 104 | 52 | 58 |
| 1987 | SF...... | 1 | 2 | 1 | 3.54 | 61.0 | 66 | 21 | 32 |
| 1988 | SD...... | 2 | 8 | 0 | 3.69 | 97.2 | 97 | 36 | 61 |
| 1989 | SD...... | 8 | 2 | 2 | 3.33 | 116.1 | 105 | 32 | 69 |
| | | 18 | 24 | 4 | 4.12 | 441.0 | 434 | 165 | 257 |

# Kevin Gross

**Birth Date: 6/8/61**
**Throws: Right**
**1989 Club:**
**Montreal Expos**
**Contest Code #: 368**

**Rating: 1**

You're probably thinking that Kevin Gross is being underrated. After all, he's won in double figures for four of his seven seasons. He's pitched more than 200 innings in 5 consecutive seasons. Scouts say Gross has one of the league's best curveballs. I still wouldn't pick Gross.

He has lost in double figures for five straight seasons. Over this period he's issued an average of 88 walks. In three of the last four seasons he's either led or tied for the league lead in hit batsmen. In the last two seasons he's served up a total of 38 gopher balls. And what about that great curveball? It's Gross' only effective pitch, and he throws it so often that he lives and dies by it. In 1987 Gross was suspended for 10 days by the league president for adding a new pitch—a sandpaper ball.

| Year | Team | W | L | SV | ERA | IP | H | BB | K |
|------|------|---|---|-----|------|-------|------|-----|-----|
| 1983 | Phi ...... | 4 | 6 | 0 | 3.56 | 96.0 | 100 | 35 | 66 |
| 1984 | Phi ...... | 8 | 5 | 1 | 4.12 | 129.0 | 140 | 44 | 84 |
| 1985 | Phi ...... | 15 | 13 | 0 | 3.41 | 205.2 | 194 | 81 | 151 |
| 1986 | Phi ...... | 12 | 12 | 0 | 4.02 | 241.2 | 240 | 94 | 154 |
| 1987 | Phi ...... | 9 | 16 | 0 | 4.35 | 200.2 | 205 | 87 | 110 |
| 1988 | Phi ...... | 12 | 14 | 0 | 3.69 | 231.2 | 209 | 89 | 162 |
| 1989 | Mon ..... | 11 | 12 | 0 | 4.38 | 201.1 | 188 | 88 | 158 |
| | | 71 | 78 | 1 | 3.95 | 1306.0 | 1276 | 518 | 885 |

# Atlee Hammaker

**Birth Date: 1/24/58**
**Throws: Left**
**1989 Club:**
**San Francisco Giants**
**Contest Code #: 369**

**Rating: 1**

Atlee Hammaker has been on my fantasy teams in the past. When healthy, he'll show flashes of the form he displayed in 1983—a year in which he led the league in ERA (2.25) and issued the fewest walks per game (1.67 per nine innings)—but also get pounded every third or fourth outing. Because he is of his proneness to injury—he's been disabled 8 times in 11 pro seasons—he's bounced from the starting rotation to the bullpen and back.

Last year, I ran out of patience with Hammaker. I know he's not hurting himself intentionally, but his hurts hurt my team as much as his.

No doubt he'll be back in camp this spring vying for a spot in the rotation. If he escapes injury, he'll probably be a .500 pitcher for the fourth year in a row.

| Year | Team | W | L | SV | ERA | IP | H | BB | K |
|------|------|---|---|-----|------|-------|------|-----|-----|
| 1981 | KC....... | 1 | 3 | 0 | 5.54 | 39.0 | 44 | 12 | 11 |
| 1982 | SF....... | 12 | 8 | 0 | 4.11 | 175.0 | 189 | 28 | 102 |
| 1983 | SF....... | 10 | 9 | 0 | 2.25 | 172.1 | 147 | 32 | 127 |
| 1984 | SF....... | 2 | 0 | 0 | 2.18 | 33.0 | 32 | 9 | 24 |
| 1985 | SF....... | 5 | 12 | 0 | 3.74 | 170.2 | 161 | 47 | 100 |
| 1987 | SF....... | 10 | 10 | 0 | 3.58 | 168.1 | 159 | 57 | 107 |
| 1988 | SF....... | 9 | 9 | 5 | 3.73 | 144.2 | 136 | 41 | 65 |
| 1989 | SF....... | 6 | 6 | 0 | 3.76 | 76.2 | 78 | 23 | 30 |
| | | 55 | 57 | 5 | 3.54 | 979.2 | 946 | 249 | 566 |

# Greg W. Harris

Birth Date: 12/1/63
Throws: Right
1989 Club:
San Diego Padres
Contest Code #: 370

Rating: 3

Last year there were two pitchers in the National League named Greg Harris: right-hander Gregory Allen Harris, a well-traveled veteran reliever who spent most of last season with the Philllies; and right-hander Gregory Wade Harris, a top prospect destined to spend many productive years with the Padres.

Harris, selected in the tenth round of the June 1985 draft, has twice been named the Padres' minor-league pitcher of the year. From 1986 to 1988 he averaged 6 strikeouts per game and 11 victories per season. In a September 1988 call-up, Harris pitched in 3 games—2 as a starter—and completed 1, allowing 3 earned runs in 18 innings.

Last season, in 48 relief appearances and 8 starts, Harris notched 8 victories and 6 saves, was second on the Padres' staff in ERA, and third in strikeouts. This year Harris could be ready to join the Padres' rotation full-time.

| Year | Team | W | L | SV | ERA | IP | H | BB | K |
|------|------|---|---|----|-----|----|----|----|----|
| 1988 | SD....... | 2 | 0 | 0 | 1.50 | 18.0 | 13 | 3 | 15 |
| 1989 | SD....... | 8 | 9 | 6 | 2.60 | 135.0 | 106 | 52 | 106 |
| | | 10 | 9 | 6 | 2.47 | 153.0 | 119 | 55 | 121 |

# Neil Heaton

Birth Date: 3/3/60
Throws: Left
1989 Club:
Pittsburgh Pirates
Contest Code #: 371

Rating: 1

What a goofy franchise the Pirates are. They fired senior vice-president and general manager Syd Thrift following the 1988 season in part because of his acquisition of productive, well-paid veterans Dave LaPoint, Ken Oberkfell, Glenn Wilson, and Gary Redus to fortify the young Bucs' bench, then turned around and acquired such unproductive, well-paid veterans as Neil Heaton.

Heaton, who even in winning seasons with the Expos and Cleveland Indians allowed close to five runs a game, arrived in Pittsburgh after the start of the season. His annual salary of $650,000 made him the fifth-highest-paid player on the Pirates' payroll. In fairly short order Heaton pitched his way out of the Pittsburgh starting rotation. His 1989 numbers could have been worse, but he was relegated to a mop-up relief role, a safer environment for a pitcher who in his 8-year career has allowed an average of 13 base runners per 9 innings.

| Year | Team | W | L | SV | ERA | IP | H | BB | K |
|------|------|---|---|----|-----|----|----|----|----|
| 1982 | Cle ...... | 0 | 2 | 0 | 5.23 | 31.0 | 32 | 16 | 14 |
| 1983 | Cle ...... | 11 | 7 | 7 | 4.16 | 149.1 | 157 | 44 | 75 |
| 1984 | Cle ...... | 12 | 15 | 0 | 5.21 | 198.2 | 231 | 75 | 75 |
| 1985 | Cle ...... | 9 | 17 | 0 | 4.90 | 207.2 | 244 | 80 | 82 |
| 1986 | Cle ...... | 3 | 6 | 0 | 4.24 | 74.1 | 73 | 34 | 24 |
| 1986 | Min ...... | 4 | 9 | 1 | 3.98 | 124.1 | 128 | 47 | 66 |
| 1987 | Mon ..... | 13 | 10 | 0 | 4.52 | 193.1 | 207 | 37 | 105 |
| 1988 | Mon ..... | 3 | 10 | 2 | 4.99 | 97.1 | 98 | 43 | 43 |
| 1989 | Pit....... | 6 | 7 | 0 | 3.05 | 147.1 | 127 | 55 | 67 |
| | | 61 | 83 | 10 | 4.46 | 1223.1 | 1297 | 431 | 551 |

# Orel Hershiser

**Birth Date:** 9/16/58
**Throws:** Right
**1989 Club:**
**Los Angeles Dodgers**
**Contest Code #: 372**

**Rating: 5**

**W**hy is Orel Hershiser worth $3 million a season? Because he gives the Dodgers good innings by the truckload. He's led the National League in innings pitched for the last three seasons, averaging 263 innings during the regular season, and been among the ERA leaders each year.

In 1988 Hershiser had one of the greatest pitching seasons of all time. During the regular campaign he won 23 games, hurled a record-setting 59 consecutive scoreless innings, and was named the Cy Young Award winner. In post-season, he set a National League Championship Series record by pitching 24⅔ innings and was named World Series MVP by virtue of his 2 victories and 1.09 ERA. Adding his regular season, All-Star game and post-season statistics, Hershiser won 26 games and lost 8, gave up 223 hits, 86 walks, 72 earned runs (a 2.08 ERA), and struck out 210 in 310⅔ innings.

The only reason Hershiser went 15–15 last year was because the Dodgers' injury-plagued offense, which ranked tenth in the league, didn't support him. With any improvement in the Dodgers' offense, Hershiser will return to the 20-win club this season.

| Year | Team | W | L | SV | ERA | IP | H | BB | K |
|------|------|---|---|----|----|----|---|----|---|
| 1983 | LA....... | 0 | 0 | 1 | 3.37 | 8.0 | 7 | 6 | 5 |
| 1984 | LA....... | 11 | 8 | 2 | 2.66 | 189.2 | 160 | 50 | 150 |
| 1985 | LA....... | 19 | 3 | 0 | 2.03 | 239.2 | 179 | 68 | 157 |
| 1986 | LA....... | 14 | 14 | 0 | 3.85 | 231.1 | 213 | 86 | 153 |
| 1987 | LA....... | 16 | 16 | 1 | 3.06 | 264.2 | 247 | 74 | 190 |
| 1988 | LA....... | 23 | 8 | 1 | 2.26 | 267.0 | 208 | 73 | 178 |
| 1989 | LA....... | 15 | 15 | 0 | 2.31 | 256.2 | 226 | 77 | 178 |
| | | 98 | 64 | 5 | 2.69 | 1457.0 | 1240 | 434 | 1011 |

# Ken Hill

**Birth Date:** 12/14/65
**Throws:** Right
**1989 Club:**
**St. Louis Cardinals**
**Contest Code #: 373**

**Rating: 2**

**K**en Hill is a pitcher scouts describe as a "short-armer." As he starts his coil he brings his arm straight back, and as he uncoils, he slings it forward. Short-armers like Hill and veteran right-hander Walt Terrell need pinpoint control to be effective.

Hill, called up by the Cardinals after injuries shelved starters Danny Cox, Greg Mathews, and Joe Magrane, showed good control early on but was less effective his second time around the league. By season's end Hill had given up 99 walks and 186 hits in 196⅔ innings, an average of 1.5 base runners per inning.

Hill probably could have used a full season in Triple A last year. If he does begin the 1990 season in the minors, he'll benefit from the fine pitching instruction available in the Cardinals' system.

| Year | Team | W | L | SV | ERA | IP | H | BB | K |
|------|------|---|---|----|----|----|---|----|---|
| 1988 | StL ...... | 0 | 1 | 0 | 5.14 | 14.0 | 16 | 6 | 6 |
| 1989 | StL ...... | 7 | 15 | 0 | 3.80 | 196.2 | 186 | 99 | 112 |
| | | 7 | 16 | 0 | 3.89 | 210.2 | 202 | 105 | 118 |

# Ricky Horton

**Birth Date:** 7/30/59
**Throws:** Left
**1989 Clubs:**
**Los Angeles Dodgers &**
**St. Louis Cardinals**
**Contest Code #:** 374

### Rating: 1

Ricky Horton's style makes him one of the league's toughest left-handers to read. He hides the ball well during his windup and delays for a split-second before delivering the ball. And he has one of the league's best pickoff moves; his right leg hangs in the air long enough to make the runner at first commit himself.

Recently, however, Horton's problems have come once the ball's on its way to the plate. In 1988, Horton, a middle reliever and setup man, gave up 131 hits in 118⅓ innings, and last season allowed 85 in 72⅓ innings. The Dodgers released him during the 1989 season, but the Cardinals, desperate for help, claimed him for a second tour of duty in St. Louis and put him into the rotation. Should Horton remain with the Cards this year, he'll likely return to middle relief, a role he filled well in 1986 and 1987.

| Year | Team | W | L | SV | ERA | IP | H | BB | K |
|------|------|---|---|----|-----|-----|---|----|---|
| 1984 | StL . . . . . . | 9 | 4 | 1 | 3.44 | 125.2 | 140 | 39 | 76 |
| 1985 | StL . . . . . . | 3 | 2 | 1 | 2.91 | 89.2 | 84 | 34 | 59 |
| 1986 | StL . . . . . . | 4 | 3 | 3 | 2.24 | 100.1 | 77 | 26 | 49 |
| 1987 | StL . . . . . . | 8 | 3 | 7 | 3.82 | 125.0 | 127 | 42 | 55 |
| 1988 | ChA. . . . . . | 6 | 10 | 2 | 4.86 | 109.1 | 120 | 36 | 28 |
| 1988 | LA. . . . . . . | 1 | 1 | 0 | 5.00 | 9.0 | 11 | 2 | 8 |
| 1989 | LA. . . . . . . | 0 | 0 | 0 | 5.06 | 26.2 | 35 | 11 | 12 |
| 1989 | StL . . . . . . | 0 | 3 | 0 | 4.73 | 45.2 | 50 | 10 | 14 |
| | | 31 | 26 | 14 | 3.68 | 631.1 | 644 | 200 | 301 |

# Jay Howell

**Birth Date:** 11/26/55
**Throws:** Right
**1989 Club:**
**Los Angeles Dodgers**
**Contest Code #:** 375

### Rating: 5

The Dodgers have made some awful trades trying to bolster their bullpen over the past six years. (Do the names Carlos Diaz, Ed Vande Berg, and Matt Young ring a bell?) But at the 1987 winter meetings rookie general manager Fred Claire made a three-way deal with the Mets and A's that brought Dodgers closer Jay Howell from Oakland. Howell, who'd previously been written off by the Reds, Cubs, and Yankees, and spent a good deal of time on the disabled list in 1986 and 1987, settled in, healed up, and put a stop to L.A.'s leaky pen.

In 1988 the Dodgers used Howell, a power pitcher who throws an overhand fastball, big-breaking curve, and hard slider, as part of a bullpen-by-committee since he'd undergone shoulder surgery the season before. Last year Howell took a more dominant role and figured in 33 of the Dodgers' 77 victories.

Howell, who led the Dodgers in ERA, deserves credit for overcoming a dark incident during the 1988 playoffs in which he was suspended for three games by then-league president A. Bartlett Giamatti after being caught with pine tar in his glove.

| Year | Team | W | L | SV | ERA | IP | H | BB | K |
|------|------|---|---|----|-----|-----|---|----|---|
| 1980 | Cin . . . . . . | 0 | 0 | 0 | 15.00 | 3.0 | 8 | 0 | 1 |
| 1981 | ChN. . . . . . | 2 | 0 | 0 | 4.91 | 22.0 | 23 | 10 | 10 |
| 1982 | NYA. . . . . . | 2 | 3 | 0 | 7.71 | 28.0 | 42 | 13 | 21 |
| 1983 | NYA. . . . . . | 1 | 5 | 0 | 5.38 | 82.0 | 89 | 35 | 61 |
| 1984 | NYA. . . . . . | 9 | 4 | 7 | 2.69 | 103.2 | 86 | 34 | 109 |
| 1985 | Oak . . . . . . | 9 | 8 | 29 | 2.85 | 98.0 | 98 | 31 | 68 |
| 1986 | Oak . . . . . . | 3 | 6 | 16 | 3.38 | 53.1 | 53 | 23 | 42 |
| 1987 | Oak . . . . . . | 3 | 4 | 16 | 5.89 | 44.1 | 48 | 21 | 35 |
| 1988 | LA. . . . . . . | 5 | 3 | 21 | 2.08 | 65.0 | 44 | 21 | 70 |
| 1989 | LA. . . . . . . | 5 | 3 | 28 | 1.58 | 79.2 | 60 | 22 | 55 |
| | | 39 | 36 | 117 | 3.58 | 579.0 | 551 | 210 | 472 |

# Ken Howell

**Birth Date:** 11/28/60
**Throws:** Right
**1989 Club:**
**Philadelphia Phillies**
**Contest Code #:** 376

**Rating: 3**

**B**eing the staff ace of the National League's second-worst team is not exactly something one would list at the top of a resume, but, all things considered, Ken Howell, the Phillies' number-one starter, had a pretty good season.

Howell may not be in the class of former Dodger teammate Orel Hershiser, but he had the same average of hits and walks to innings pitched as Hershiser (1.18); the same winning percentage (.500); and earned 18 percent of the Phillies' victories, a shade under Hershiser's percentage.

Though Howell's won-lost record was 7–5 at the All-Star break and 5–7 after, he actually pitched better in the second half. His ERA was 3.90 (45 earned runs in 104 innings) on July 11, but 2.97 (33 earned runs in 100 innings) the rest of the way.

| Year | Team | W | L | SV | ERA | IP | H | BB | K |
|------|------|---|---|----|-----|----|----|----|----|
| 1984 | LA...... | 5 | 5 | 6 | 3.33 | 51.1 | 51 | 9 | 54 |
| 1985 | LA...... | 4 | 7 | 12 | 3.77 | 86.0 | 66 | 35 | 85 |
| 1986 | LA...... | 6 | 12 | 12 | 3.87 | 97.2 | 86 | 63 | 104 |
| 1987 | LA...... | 3 | 4 | 1 | 4.91 | 55.0 | 54 | 29 | 60 |
| 1988 | LA...... | 0 | 1 | 0 | 6.40 | 12.2 | 16 | 4 | 12 |
| 1989 | Phi ...... | 12 | 12 | 0 | 3.44 | 204.0 | 155 | 86 | 164 |
| | | 30 | 41 | 31 | 3.80 | 506.2 | 428 | 226 | 479 |

# Bruce Hurst

**Birth Date:** 3/24/58
**Throws:** Left
**1989 Club:**
**San Diego Padres**
**Contest Code #:** 377

**Rating: 5**

**N**ational League fantasy-team owners bid up a storm for Bruce Hurst in their 1989 drafts, and as the season ensued it became clear that Hurst was worth his fantasy salary.

Working 244⅔ innings, Hurst won 15 games with a career-low ERA of 2.69, fifth-best in the league, and tied Tim Belcher for most complete games (10). Hurst, a control pitcher who mixes his forkball, fastball, curve, and change-up, allowed an average of 10 base runners per 9 innings, 2 below his career average. Over the second half of the season, Hurst helped the Padres make a run at the top by winning 8 games and posting an ERA of 2.38.

The Padres' late-season momentum should carry over into the 1990 season now that all the new Padres—Jack Clark, Mike Pagliarulo, Andy Benes, Greg Harris, and Hurst—have meshed. This puts 20 victories within Hurst's grasp.

| Year | Team | W | L | SV | ERA | IP | H | BB | K |
|------|------|---|---|----|-----|----|----|----|----|
| 1980 | Bos...... | 2 | 2 | 0 | 9.00 | 31.0 | 39 | 16 | 16 |
| 1981 | Bos...... | 2 | 0 | 0 | 4.30 | 23.0 | 23 | 12 | 11 |
| 1982 | Bos...... | 3 | 7 | 0 | 5.77 | 117.0 | 161 | 40 | 53 |
| 1983 | Bos...... | 12 | 12 | 0 | 4.09 | 211.1 | 241 | 62 | 115 |
| 1984 | Bos...... | 12 | 12 | 0 | 3.92 | 218.0 | 232 | 88 | 136 |
| 1985 | Bos...... | 11 | 13 | 0 | 4.51 | 229.1 | 243 | 70 | 189 |
| 1986 | Bos...... | 13 | 8 | 0 | 2.99 | 174.1 | 169 | 50 | 167 |
| 1987 | Bos...... | 15 | 13 | 0 | 4.41 | 238.2 | 239 | 76 | 190 |
| 1988 | Bos...... | 18 | 6 | 0 | 3.66 | 216.2 | 222 | 65 | 166 |
| 1989 | SD....... | 15 | 11 | 0 | 2.69 | 244.2 | 214 | 66 | 179 |
| | | 103 | 84 | 0 | 4.01 | 1704.0 | 1783 | 545 | 1222 |

# Jeff Innis

**Birth Date: 7/5/62**
**Throws: Right**
**1989 Club:**
**New York Mets**
**Contest Code #: 378**

## Rating: 2

**J**eff Innis was a good closer in his minor-league career. In 1983 the submariner, an All Star in the Class-A New York-Penn League, was third in saves (8) and games finished (25), fourth in games and fifth in victories (8). Two seasons later Innis earned 14 saves and was second in the Carolina League in appearances (53) and games finished (39). In 1986, Innis, pitching for Double-A Jackson, notched a league-leading 25 saves and was again named an All-Star.

However, in parts of three seasons on the major-league level, Innis has been overlooked by manager Davey Johnson in favor of left-hander Randy Myers and righty Roger McDowell. And when McDowell was traded to the Phillies, thirty-four-year-old Don Aase stepped ahead of Innis.

So during the 1989 off season Innis learned to throw a knuckleball while attending the Mets' Instructional League. Since teams aren't keen on knuckleball closers, Innis may have a hidden value to the Mets or another team as a starting pitcher.

| Year | Team | W | L | SV | ERA | IP | H | BB | K |
|------|------|---|---|----|----|----|---|----|---|
| 1987 | NYN ..... | 0 | 1 | 0 | 3.16 | 25.2 | 29 | 4 | 28 |
| 1988 | NYN ..... | 1 | 1 | 0 | 1.89 | 19.0 | 19 | 2 | 14 |
| 1989 | NYN ..... | 0 | 1 | 0 | 3.18 | 39.2 | 38 | 8 | 16 |
| | | 1 | 3 | 0 | 2.88 | 84.1 | 86 | 14 | 58 |

# Danny Jackson

**Birth Date: 1/5/62**
**Throws: Left**
**1989 Club:**
**Cincinnati Reds**
**Contest Code #: 379**

## Rating: 3

**I**f Danny Jackson were an automobile, an insurance appraiser might have written him off as a total loss last season. Jackson was a physical mess—one of his toes calcified, and the muscles in his left rotator cuff frayed.

Jackson had known hard luck in Kansas City, where he pitched superbly but got little run support. The clouds parted in 1988, when Jackson won a major-league-leading 23 games, including 6 shutouts and 15 complete games, and walked only 71 batters in 260⅔ innings while striking out 161. But everything went wrong last year. Jackson allowed 122 hits and 72 earned runs in 115⅔ innings.

During the off season, the Reds' front office was calling around for pitching help as insurance should Jackson remain ineffective.

| Year | Team | W | L | SV | ERA | IP | H | BB | K |
|------|------|---|---|----|----|----|---|----|---|
| 1983 | KC....... | 1 | 1 | 0 | 5.21 | 19.0 | 26 | 6 | 9 |
| 1984 | KC....... | 2 | 6 | 0 | 4.26 | 76.0 | 84 | 35 | 40 |
| 1985 | KC....... | 14 | 12 | 0 | 3.42 | 208.0 | 209 | 76 | 114 |
| 1986 | KC....... | 11 | 12 | 1 | 3.20 | 185.2 | 177 | 79 | 115 |
| 1987 | KC....... | 9 | 18 | 0 | 4.02 | 224.0 | 219 | 109 | 152 |
| 1988 | Cin ...... | 23 | 8 | 0 | 2.73 | 260.2 | 206 | 71 | 161 |
| 1989 | Cin ...... | 6 | 11 | 0 | 5.60 | 115.2 | 122 | 57 | 70 |
| | | 66 | 68 | 1 | 3.66 | 1089.0 | 1043 | 433 | 661 |

# Bob Kipper

Birth Date: 7/8/64
Throws: Left
1989 Club:
Pittsburgh Pirates
Contest Code #: 380

Rating: 1

**B**ob Kipper was a capable middle-inning reliever in his first full season with the Pirates. Called on to face one or two left-handed hitters per game, Kipper posted the staff's fifth-best ERA. And when the Pirates' pen was in disarray, Kipper chipped in with four saves. All told, he finished 15 games in 52 appearances.

Kipper, chosen by the California Angels in the first round of the June 1982 draft, arrived in Pittsburgh as part of a six-player swap with the Angels. If the Pirates can get their act together in 1990, Kipper could find himself in an ideal middle-reliever situation—lots of victories facing few batters.

| Year | Team | W | L | SV | ERA | IP | H | BB | K |
|------|------|---|---|----|----|----|---|----|---|
| 1985 | Cal ...... | 0 | 1 | 0 | 21.62 | 3.1 | 7 | 3 | 0 |
| 1985 | Pit ....... | 1 | 2 | 0 | 5.11 | 24.2 | 21 | 7 | 13 |
| 1986 | Pit ....... | 6 | 8 | 0 | 4.03 | 114.0 | 123 | 34 | 81 |
| 1987 | Pit ....... | 5 | 9 | 0 | 5.94 | 110.2 | 117 | 52 | 83 |
| 1988 | Pit ....... | 2 | 6 | 0 | 3.74 | 65.0 | 54 | 26 | 39 |
| 1989 | Pit ....... | 3 | 4 | 4 | 2.93 | 83.0 | 55 | 33 | 58 |
| | | 17 | 30 | 4 | 4.49 | 400.2 | 377 | 155 | 274 |

# Bob Knepper

Birth Date: 5/25/54
Throws: Left
1989 Clubs:
Houston Astros &
San Francisco Giants
Contest Code #: 381

Rating: 1

**B**ob Knepper exhausted the patience of the Astros' management last season through ineffective pitching and frequent grumbling. If Knepper had pitched the way he did in 1988, perhaps things could have been smoothed over. But by July 25 the thirty-five-year-old junkballer had served up 43 hits and 15 walks in 27 ⅓ innings, with a frightening 9.55 ERA. The Astros released him, even though it cost them $1 million to terminate his contract.

Weeks later the Giants, in dire need of starters because of injuries to Rick Reuschel, Atlee Hammaker, Mike Krukow, Kelly Downs, and Scott Garrelts, reached out for Knepper. Apparently, Knepper's torch was still blazing. Over the rest of the season Knepper went 6–10 with an ERA of 4.25.

| Year | Team | W | L | SV | ERA | IP | H | BB | K |
|------|------|---|---|----|----|----|---|----|---|
| 1976 | SF ....... | 1 | 2 | 0 | 3.24 | 25.0 | 26 | 7 | 11 |
| 1977 | SF ....... | 11 | 9 | 0 | 3.36 | 166.0 | 151 | 72 | 100 |
| 1978 | SF ....... | 17 | 11 | 0 | 2.63 | 260.0 | 218 | 85 | 147 |
| 1979 | SF ....... | 9 | 12 | 0 | 4.65 | 207.0 | 241 | 77 | 123 |
| 1980 | SF ....... | 9 | 16 | 0 | 4.10 | 215.0 | 242 | 61 | 103 |
| 1981 | Hou ...... | 9 | 5 | 0 | 2.18 | 157.0 | 128 | 38 | 75 |
| 1982 | Hou ...... | 5 | 15 | 1 | 4.45 | 180.0 | 193 | 60 | 108 |
| 1983 | Hou ...... | 6 | 13 | 0 | 3.19 | 203.0 | 202 | 71 | 125 |
| 1984 | Hou ...... | 15 | 10 | 0 | 3.20 | 233.2 | 223 | 55 | 140 |
| 1985 | Hou ...... | 15 | 13 | 0 | 3.55 | 241.0 | 253 | 54 | 131 |
| 1986 | Hou ...... | 17 | 12 | 0 | 3.14 | 258.0 | 232 | 62 | 143 |
| 1987 | Hou ...... | 8 | 17 | 0 | 5.27 | 177.2 | 226 | 54 | 76 |
| 1988 | Hou ...... | 14 | 5 | 0 | 3.14 | 175.0 | 156 | 67 | 103 |
| 1989 | Hou ...... | 4 | 10 | 0 | 5.89 | 113.0 | 135 | 60 | 45 |
| 1989 | SF ....... | 3 | 2 | 0 | 3.46 | 52.0 | 55 | 15 | 19 |
| | | 143 | 152 | 1 | 3.64 | 2663.1 | 2681 | 838 | 1449 |

# Randy Kramer

**Birth Date: 9/20/60**
**Throws: Right**
**1989 Club:**
**Pittsburgh Pirates**
**Contest Code #: 382**

**Rating: 2**

**H**ere's a wacky scenario: After one of your starters pitches a nine-inning, one-hit shutout, you bring him in from the bullpen *two days later* to pitch two innings of relief. That's just what Pirates manager Jim Leyland did with Randy Kramer last summer. Luckily, Kramer survived without injury.

From the moment Kramer was summoned from the minors last year, Leyland couldn't decide how to use him. Kramer started 15 games and relieved in 20 more. One day he was in the rotation, the next day he was the closer. Leyland should have let Kramer settle in as a starter.

The Pirates had acquired Kramer, then a six-year minor player eligible for free agency, from the Texas Rangers in 1986 and schooled him well in the art of pitching. In 1988 Kramer led the American Association in innings pitched (198⅓), was third in strikeouts (120), tied for third in games started (28), and was ninth in ERA (3.13).

National League scouts say Kramer has the makings of a dependable major-league starter. I wonder if Leyland is aware of this.

| Year | Team | W | L | SV | ERA | IP | H | BB | K |
|------|------|---|---|----|----|----|----|----|----|
| 1988 | Pit....... | 1 | 2 | 0 | 5.40 | 10.0 | 12 | 1 | 7 |
| 1989 | Pit....... | 5 | 9 | 2 | 3.96 | 111.1 | 90 | 61 | 52 |
| | | 6 | 11 | 2 | 4.08 | 121.1 | 102 | 62 | 59 |

# Mike LaCoss

**Birth Date: 5/30/56**
**Throws: Right**
**1989 Club:**
**San Francisco Giants**
**Contest Code #: 383**

**Rating: 2**

**F**or 12 major-league seasons Mike LaCoss has tantalized many a general manager by pitching well over stretches but never over a full season.

LaCoss' first streak was in 1979, his second big-league season. He reeled off eight consecutive victories and was named to the National League All-Star team, then won only six games the rest of the season. After he won 10 games in 1980 and four in 1981, the Reds sold him to the Astros. LaCoss, used in relief, pitched so nicely late in 1982 that the Astros put him into their rotation in 1983. Fifteen starts later, LaCoss was back in the bullpen. A swingman in 1984, LaCoss signed as a free agent with the Kansas City Royals following the season. Six months into the season, the Royals sent him outright to Triple A.

LaCoss then took his act to San Francisco. In 1986 he was 9–3, with a 2.76 ERA in 22 games before the All-Star break, but 1–10, with a 4.91 ERA, the rest of the way. In 1987 he led the Giants in victories (13) but allowed 3.6 runs and 13 base runners per 9 innings. In 1988 he started out 1–4, won 6 of 9 decisions between May 15 and July 8, then underwent season-ending surgery to remove bone chips in his elbow. Last season LaCoss shared closing duties with Craig Lefferts until Steve Bedrosian arrived. Early on he had a 50-inning stretch in which he gave up 50 hits and 27 walks, an average of 1.54

base runners per inning. Over his last 83⅔ innings, however, LaCoss lowered that average to 1.34 while notching 6 victories.

Don't let LaCoss break *your* heart.

| Year | Team | W | L | SV | ERA | IP | H | BB | K |
|------|------|---|---|----|----|----|----|----|----|
| 1978 | Cin ...... | 4 | 8 | 0 | 4.50 | 96.0 | 104 | 46 | 31 |
| 1979 | Cin ...... | 14 | 8 | 0 | 3.50 | 206.0 | 202 | 79 | 73 |
| 1980 | Cin ...... | 10 | 12 | 0 | 4.63 | 169.0 | 207 | 68 | 59 |
| 1981 | Cin ...... | 4 | 7 | 1 | 6.12 | 78.0 | 102 | 30 | 22 |
| 1982 | Hou...... | 6 | 6 | 0 | 2.90 | 115.0 | 107 | 54 | 51 |
| 1983 | Hou...... | 5 | 7 | 1 | 4.43 | 138.0 | 142 | 56 | 53 |
| 1984 | Hou...... | 7 | 5 | 3 | 4.02 | 132.0 | 132 | 55 | 86 |
| 1985 | KC....... | 1 | 1 | 1 | 5.09 | 40.2 | 49 | 29 | 26 |
| 1986 | SF....... | 10 | 13 | 0 | 3.57 | 204.1 | 179 | 70 | 86 |
| 1987 | SF....... | 13 | 10 | 0 | 3.68 | 171.0 | 184 | 63 | 79 |
| 1988 | SF....... | 7 | 7 | 0 | 3.62 | 114.1 | 99 | 47 | 70 |
| 1989 | SF....... | 10 | 10 | 6 | 3.17 | 150.1 | 143 | 65 | 78 |
| | | 91 | 94 | 12 | 3.93 | 1614.2 | 1650 | 662 | 714 |

# Les Lancaster

**Birth Date: 4/21/62**
**Throws: Right**
**1989 Club:**
**Chicago Cubs**
**Contest Code #: 384**

**Rating: 3**

If I were Les Lancaster, I'd seriously consider giving part of my 1989 playoff share to Calvin Schiraldi. If Schiraldi had not suffered a hamstring pull, Lancaster would not have been promoted from Triple A.

Lancaster, who appeared in 44 games for the Cubbies in 1988, was so disappointed at not breaking camp with the 1989 Cubs that he affixed pictures of manager Don Zimmer and general manager Jim Frey to a dart board hung above his minor-league locker. When word of the dart board got back to Chicago, Frey shopped Lancaster around. But when right-hander Schiraldi went down, leaving a gaping hole in the Cubs' pen, Zimmer and Frey had little choice but to summon Lancaster from Iowa. Alternating as a setup man for and closer with left-hander Mitch Williams, Lancaster pitched 30 consecutive scoreless innings. By season's end he earned eight saves and led the Cubs staff in ERA.

A postscript to the dart-board story: Frey never forgave Iowa manager Pete Mackanin for allowing Lancaster to keep the dart board above his locker. Mackanin, one of the managers in last July's Triple-A All-Star Game, was fired at the end of the season.

| Year | Team | W | L | SV | ERA | IP | H | BB | K |
|------|------|---|---|----|----|----|----|----|----|
| 1987 | ChN...... | 8 | 3 | 0 | 4.90 | 132.1 | 138 | 51 | 78 |
| 1988 | ChN...... | 4 | 6 | 5 | 3.78 | 85.2 | 89 | 34 | 36 |
| 1989 | ChN...... | 4 | 2 | 8 | 1.36 | 72.2 | 60 | 15 | 56 |
| | | 16 | 11 | 13 | 3.68 | 290.2 | 287 | 100 | 170 |

# Bill Landrum

**Birth Date: 8/17/58**
**Throws: Right**
**1989 Club:**
**Pittsburgh Pirates**
**Contest Code #: 385**

## Rating: 2

I t took Bill Landrum 10 years to outdo his father. In 1988, Landrum, playing for his tenth pro team in nine years, pitched in his third major-league season, one more than his father, Joe, who pitched for the Brooklyn Dodgers in 1950 and 1952.

But after last season, it would appear that Landrum's wayfaring days have come to a halt. Called up from the Pirates' Triple A team in Buffalo after five relievers couldn't fill in for injured closer Jim Gott, Landrum shocked the National League by saving 26 games—24 more than he'd earned in his entire career. Landrum, a short-armer, had exceptional control, hitting the outside corners of the plate over and again.

Only time will tell if Landrum can continue to pitch as never before. If Gott returns to form, Landrum will most likely be used as a right-handed setup man, so he'll see fewer save opportunities. But judging by manager Jim Leyland's faith in the "hot-hand" theory, Landrum may surprise us again in 1990.

| Year | Team | W | L | SV | ERA | IP | H | BB | K |
|------|------|---|---|----|----|-----|----|----|----|
| 1986 | Cin ...... | 0 | 0 | 0 | 6.75 | 13.1 | 23 | 4 | 14 |
| 1987 | Cin ...... | 3 | 2 | 2 | 4.71 | 65.0 | 68 | 34 | 42 |
| 1988 | ChN...... | 1 | 0 | 0 | 5.84 | 12.1 | 19 | 3 | 6 |
| 1989 | Pit....... | 2 | 3 | 26 | 1.67 | 81.0 | 60 | 28 | 51 |
| | | 6 | 5 | 28 | 3.51 | 171.2 | 170 | 69 | 113 |

# Tim Leary

**Birth Date: 12/23/58**
**Throws: Right**
**1989 Club:**
**Los Angeles Dodgers &**
**Cincinnati Reds**
**Contest Code #: 387**

## Rating: 3

W e sometimes forget how terrible the Mets were during the early 1980s, but Tim Leary never will. In 1980, Leary, billed as the next Tom Seaver, had an exceptional year at Double A Jackson, leading the Texas League in victories (15) and shutouts (6). The following spring, manager Joe Torre convinced the Mets' brass to let Leary break camp with the big club. Leary's first start, against the Cubs, lasted just two innings; he strained a muscle in his right elbow and did not pitch again until August. Then Leary damaged nerves in his throwing shoulder, an injury that took doctors a year to diagnose, and didn't pitch again until 1983.

With the damage done, the Mets shipped Leary to the Brewers in 1985 as part of a six-player, four-team deal. Two years later Leary was traded to the Dodgers. Following a poor 1987 season, Leary learned to throw a split-fingered fastball during winter ball. His career was reborn.

Leary pitched reasonably well in the first half of last season, winning 6 games with an ERA of 3.18. In July the Dodgers, stuffed to the gills with starters and starved for power hitters, traded Leary to the Reds for outfielder Kal Daniels. Pitching for a team in turmoil, Leary managed only two more wins. And he missed two turns late in the season because of sprained ligaments in his pitching hand, which hampered his ability to throw his splitter.

In recent seasons Leary has pitched to the level of his teams. Since I project the 1990 Reds as a threat to wrest the Braves' claim on last place, I foresee Leary winning no more than 10 games.

| Year | Team | W | L | SV | ERA | IP | H | BB | K |
|---|---|---|---|---|---|---|---|---|---|
| 1981 | NYN ..... | 0 | 0 | 0 | 0.00 | 2.0 | 0 | 1 | 3 |
| 1983 | NYN ..... | 1 | 1 | 0 | 3.38 | 10.2 | 15 | 4 | 9 |
| 1984 | NYN ..... | 3 | 3 | 0 | 4.03 | 53.2 | 61 | 18 | 29 |
| 1985 | Mil ...... | 1 | 4 | 0 | 4.05 | 33.1 | 40 | 8 | 29 |
| 1986 | Mil ...... | 12 | 12 | 0 | 4.21 | 188.1 | 216 | 53 | 110 |
| 1987 | LA........ | 3 | 11 | 1 | 4.76 | 107.2 | 121 | 36 | 61 |
| 1988 | LA........ | 17 | 11 | 0 | 2.91 | 228.2 | 201 | 56 | 180 |
| 1989 | LA........ | 6 | 7 | 0 | 3.38 | 117.1 | 107 | 37 | 59 |
| 1989 | Cin ...... | 2 | 7 | 0 | 3.71 | 89.2 | 98 | 31 | 64 |
| | | 45 | 56 | 1 | 3.71 | 831.1 | 859 | 244 | 544 |

# Craig Lefferts

**Birth Date: 9/29/57**
**Throws: Left**
**1989 Club:**
**San Francisco Giants**
**Contest Code #: 388**

**Rating: 3**

When Roger Craig signaled to the bullpen for Craig Lefferts, the thirty-two-year-old screwballer would always sprint to the mound so rapidly that one would think his pants were on fire.

One has to like Lefferts' style, and, looking over his stats, one has got to like him as a pitcher. His unorthodox motion is tough to read, and his screwball is tough to hit. His save totals have increased each year, and, except for 1987, when he was traded during the season, he's been a consistently effective setup man. Last season Lefferts took charge of the late innings until the Steve Bedrosian trade, then picked up the slack when Bedrosian faltered in July. Lefferts, a free agent, signed during the off-season with the San Diego Padres for three years at $5.35 million, nearly three times what he was earning as a Giant.

| Year | Team | W | L | SV | ERA | IP | H | BB | K |
|---|---|---|---|---|---|---|---|---|---|
| 1983 | ChN...... | 3 | 4 | 1 | 3.13 | 89.0 | 80 | 29 | 60 |
| 1984 | SD....... | 3 | 4 | 10 | 2.13 | 105.2 | 88 | 24 | 56 |
| 1985 | SD....... | 7 | 6 | 2 | 3.35 | 83.1 | 75 | 30 | 48 |
| 1986 | SD....... | 9 | 8 | 4 | 3.09 | 107.2 | 98 | 44 | 72 |
| 1987 | SF....... | 3 | 3 | 4 | 3.23 | 47.1 | 36 | 18 | 18 |
| 1987 | SD....... | 2 | 2 | 2 | 4.38 | 51.1 | 56 | 15 | 39 |
| 1988 | SF....... | 3 | 8 | 11 | 2.92 | 92.1 | 74 | 23 | 58 |
| 1989 | SF....... | 2 | 4 | 20 | 2.69 | 107.0 | 93 | 22 | 71 |
| | | 32 | 39 | 54 | 3.00 | 683.2 | 600 | 205 | 422 |

# Derek Lilliquist

**Birth Date: 2/20/66**
**Throws: Left**
**1989 Club:**
**Atlanta Braves**
**Contest Code #: 389**

**Rating: 2**

In a 1988 episode of the television program "Married ...with Children", beleaguered shoe salesman Al Bundy tells the matronly librarian of the elementary school he'd attended why he believes he's had a successful life: "I can put a gun to my mouth and not pull the trigger." Despite a fifth-place finish in my fantasy league last season, the silver lining was that I survived a year of Derek Lilliquist.

The portly Lilliquist, highly touted since his days at the University of Georgia, was two pitchers in one: There was Derek the Controller, who issued a mere 34 walks in 165⅔ innings: and there was Derek the Destroyer, who was shelled for 202 hits in 165⅔ innings.

Watching Lilliquist develop a mid-season allergy for the sixth inning was as joyous as ripping adhesive tape off a thigh wound. The Lilliquist line in five starts from

June 21 to July 15: 5 IP, 2 ER, 10 H, 0 BB; 4 IP, 4 ER, 7 H, 1 BB; 6⅓ IP, 1 ER, 5 H, 2 BB; 5 IP, 3 ER, 8 H, 2 BB; 3 IP, 4 ER, 7 H, 2 BB.

When Lilliquist told reporters in August that he was thinking of abandoning his side-arm style and returning to the three-quarter delivery he used in college, I was already too numb to cry.

| Year | Team | W | L | SV | ERA | IP | H | BB | K |
|------|------|---|---|----|-----|-----|-----|----|----|
| 1989 | Atl....... | 8 | 10 | 0 | 3.97 | 165.2 | 202 | 34 | 79 |
| | | 8 | 10 | 0 | 3.97 | 165.2 | 202 | 34 | 79 |

# Greg Maddux

Birth Date: 4/14/66
Throws: Right
1989 Club:
Chicago Cubs
Contest Code #: 390

Rating: 5

Greg Maddux has made great strides in becoming one of the league's top starting pitchers. Just two seasons ago, Maddux, rushed into the Cubs' rotation at age twenty-one, won 6 games and lost 14, with an ERA of 5.61. In 1988 Maddux was a sizzling 15–3 with a 2.14 ERA at the All-Star break, but only 3–5 (plus 7 no-decisions) with an ERA of 4.92 after the break. But last year Maddux pitched well in the first half—8–7 with a 2.93 ERA—and in the second half, when manager Don Zimmer relied on a three-man rotation, Maddux went 11–5 with a 2.95 ERA.

Maddux has an above-average fastball that rides in and out in the hitting zone, a good curve and a superior change-up. He gets a lot of ground-ball outs, a plus at homer-friendly Wrigley Field. He is also a fine athlete who hits well (his 19 hits in 1988 led all pitchers) and is frequently used as a pinch-runner.

With two strong seasons under his belt, the twenty-four-year-old Maddux is ready to join the 20-win club for many seasons to come.

| Year | Team | W | L | SV | ERA | IP | H | BB | K |
|------|------|---|---|----|-----|-----|-----|----|----|
| 1986 | ChN...... | 2 | 4 | 0 | 5.52 | 31.0 | 44 | 11 | 20 |
| 1987 | ChN...... | 6 | 14 | 0 | 5.61 | 155.2 | 181 | 74 | 101 |
| 1988 | ChN...... | 18 | 8 | 0 | 3.18 | 249.0 | 230 | 81 | 140 |
| 1989 | ChN...... | 19 | 12 | 0 | 2.95 | 238.1 | 222 | 82 | 135 |
| | | 45 | 38 | 0 | 3.77 | 674.0 | 677 | 248 | 396 |

# Joe Magrane

Birth Date: 7/2/64
Throws: Left
1989 Club:
St. Louis Cardinals
Contest Code #: 391

Rating: 5

Joking Joe Magrane has some flaky statistics. In 1987 he won nine games but led the National League in hit batsmen. In 1988 he led the league in ERAs but won only five games, the lowest victory total for an ERA winner in baseball history. In 1989 his ERA rose to 2.91 but he tied for third in the league in victories (18) and complete games (9).

Unfortunately, the one constant is that the 6'5", 225-pound Magrane has spent time on the disabled list in each of his three major-league seasons, which helps account for his relatively low victory totals in 1987 and 1988 and his failure to win 20 games last year. Actually, Magrane could have exceeded 20 victories in 1989 but was winless over the last four weeks of the season.

The Cards' top draft pick in 1985, Magrane has the tools for stardom: He throws a good fastball, curve, slider, and change-up; he hides the ball well in his delivery; and he allows few home runs (11 in his last 400 innings). If he can keep off the disabled list, he should be listed among the pitching leaders in 1990.

| Year | Team | W | L | SV | ERA | IP | H | BB | K |
|---|---|---|---|---|---|---|---|---|---|
| 1987 | StL ...... | 9 | 7 | 0 | 3.54 | 170.1 | 157 | 60 | 101 |
| 1988 | StL ...... | 5 | 9 | 0 | 2.18 | 165.1 | 133 | 51 | 100 |
| 1989 | StL ...... | 18 | 9 | 0 | 2.91 | 234.2 | 219 | 72 | 127 |
| | | 32 | 25 | 0 | 2.89 | 570.1 | 509 | 183 | 328 |

# Rick Mahler

**Birth Date: 8/5/53**
**Throws: Right**
**1989 Club:**
**Cincinnati Reds**
**Contest Code #: 392**

**Rating: 1**

The common answer National League managers give when asked to assess Rick Mahler is, "He gives you plenty of innings." The common answer fantasy-league owners give when asked to assess Mahler is, "He gives you plenty of bad innings." In fantasy leagues that use the category known as "ratio"—hits plus walks divided by innings pitched—Mahler has been known as "The Ratio Killer."

Mahler, a junkball pitcher, has earned quite a few dubious achievements. From 1984, in 1,393 innings he has allowed 1,497 hits, topping the league three times, and 769 earned runs, twice a league leader. He's also lost in double digits for six consecutive seasons, including a league-high 18 in 1986.

| Year | Team | W | L | SV | ERA | IP | H | BB | K |
|---|---|---|---|---|---|---|---|---|---|
| 1979 | Atl ...... | 0 | 0 | 0 | 6.14 | 22.0 | 28 | 11 | 12 |
| 1980 | Atl ...... | 0 | 0 | 0 | 2.25 | 4.0 | 2 | 0 | 1 |
| 1981 | Atl ...... | 8 | 6 | 2 | 2.81 | 112.0 | 109 | 43 | 54 |
| 1982 | Atl ...... | 9 | 10 | 0 | 4.21 | 205.1 | 213 | 62 | 105 |
| 1983 | Atl ...... | 0 | 0 | 0 | 5.02 | 14.1 | 16 | 9 | 7 |
| 1984 | Atl ...... | 13 | 10 | 0 | 3.12 | 222.0 | 209 | 62 | 106 |
| 1985 | Atl ...... | 17 | 15 | 0 | 3.48 | 266.2 | 272 | 79 | 107 |
| 1986 | Atl ...... | 14 | 18 | 0 | 4.89 | 237.2 | 283 | 95 | 137 |
| 1987 | Atl ...... | 8 | 13 | 0 | 4.98 | 197.0 | 212 | 85 | 95 |
| 1988 | Atl ...... | 9 | 16 | 0 | 3.69 | 249.0 | 279 | 42 | 131 |
| 1989 | Cin ...... | 9 | 13 | 0 | 3.83 | 220.2 | 242 | 51 | 102 |
| | | 87 | 101 | 2 | 3.95 | 1750.2 | 1865 | 539 | 857 |

# Dennis Martinez

**Birth Date: 5/14/55**
**Throws: Right**
**1989 Club:**
**Montreal Expos**
**Contest Code #: 393**

**Rating: 4**

Dennis Martinez, the first Nicaraguan-born player in the major leagues, has made a commendable comeback from shoulder problems and alcohol abuse.

At the start of his major-league career, Martinez was a double-digit winner for the Orioles, averaging 13.5 victories from 1977 through 1982. When his physical and emotional problems robbed him of his effectiveness, Martinez bounced from the Orioles to the Expos to the Miami Marlins, an independent Class-A team. Then in 1986, after he overcame his problems, the Expos re-signed him and soon after he returned to his winning ways.

Martinez is an intelligent pitcher who uses two-seam and four-seam fastballs to set up his curve, considered

among the league's finest. As with most control pitchers, Martinez gives up a lot of home runs—23 last season—but issues few walks—55 in 1988 and 49 last season. In 1989 Martinez led the Expos' staff in victories (16), games started (33), complete games (5) and innings pitched (232).

| Year | Team | W | L | SV | ERA | IP | H | BB | K |
|---|---|---|---|---|---|---|---|---|---|
| 1976 | Bal ...... | 1 | 2 | 0 | 2.57 | 28.0 | 23 | 8 | 18 |
| 1977 | Bal ...... | 14 | 7 | 4 | 4.10 | 167.0 | 157 | 64 | 107 |
| 1978 | Bal ...... | 16 | 11 | 0 | 3.52 | 276.0 | 257 | 93 | 142 |
| 1979 | Bal ...... | 15 | 16 | 0 | 3.67 | 292.0 | 279 | 78 | 132 |
| 1980 | Bal ...... | 6 | 4 | 1 | 3.96 | 100.0 | 103 | 44 | 42 |
| 1981 | Bal ...... | 14 | 5 | 0 | 3.32 | 179.0 | 173 | 62 | 88 |
| 1982 | Bal ...... | 16 | 12 | 0 | 4.21 | 252.0 | 262 | 87 | 111 |
| 1983 | Bal ...... | 7 | 16 | 0 | 5.53 | 153.0 | 209 | 45 | 71 |
| 1984 | Bal ...... | 6 | 9 | 0 | 5.02 | 141.2 | 145 | 37 | 72 |
| 1985 | Bal ...... | 13 | 11 | 0 | 5.15 | 180.0 | 203 | 63 | 68 |
| 1986 | Bal ...... | 0 | 0 | 0 | 6.76 | 6.2 | 11 | 2 | 2 |
| 1986 | Mon ..... | 3 | 6 | 0 | 4.59 | 98.0 | 103 | 28 | 63 |
| 1987 | Mon ..... | 11 | 4 | 0 | 3.30 | 144.2 | 133 | 40 | 84 |
| 1988 | Mon ..... | 15 | 13 | 0 | 2.72 | 235.1 | 215 | 55 | 120 |
| 1989 | Mon ..... | 16 | 7 | 0 | 3.18 | 232.0 | 227 | 49 | 142 |
| | | 153 | 123 | 5 | 3.90 | 2485.1 | 2500 | 755 | 1262 |

# Ramon Martinez

**Birth Date: 3/22/68**
**Throws: Right**
**1989 Club:**
**Los Angeles Dodgers**
**Contest Code #: 394**

**Rating: 3**

Amid great fanfare, Ramon Martinez has shown flashes of brilliance over the past two seasons. His fastball has always been above average, but no starter can survive with one pitch. As soon as he improves his curveball and masters an off-speed pitch, Martinez will fulfill his vast potential.

Martinez first caught the attention of the baseball community in 1987 while pitching in the Florida State League. In 170⅓ innings, Martinez went 16–5 with 148 strikeouts and an ERA of 2.17. Martinez started the 1988 season at Double-A San Antonio. After going 8–4 with a 2.46 ERA, he was promoted to Triple A, where he won five of seven decisions. That September, the Dodgers brought him up to get a taste of the major leagues.

Martinez went back to Triple A at the start of 1989 to work on his curveball. He was called up in June for an emergency start, pitched a complete-game shutout, and, to his dismay, was sent back to Albuquerque. But in August, after going 10–2 at Triple A, he rejoined the Dodgers' rotation for the rest of the season.

| Year | Team | W | L | SV | ERA | IP | H | BB | K |
|---|---|---|---|---|---|---|---|---|---|
| 1988 | LA....... | 1 | 3 | 0 | 3.79 | 35.2 | 27 | 22 | 23 |
| 1989 | LA....... | 6 | 4 | 0 | 3.19 | 98.2 | 79 | 41 | 89 |
| | | 7 | 7 | 0 | 3.35 | 134.1 | 106 | 63 | 112 |

# Randy McCament

**Birth Date: 7/29/62**
**Throws: Right**
**1989 Club:**
**San Francisco Giants**
**Contest Code #: 395**

**Rating: 1**

Randy McCament made his major-league debut last season after injuries KO'ed most of the Giants' staff. His numbers are an improvement over his minor-league totals.

In 1988 McCament split time at Double-A Shreveport and Triple-A Phoenix. At Shreveport McCament was 3–4 with an ERA of 5.36. In 24 games he pitched 42 innings of relief, allowing 56 hits and 14 walks, striking out 15 and saving two games. In 19 games at the Pacific Coast League, McCament was 0–1 with a 7.56 ERA, giving up 40 hits and 16 walks, striking out 7 and earning 1 save in 25 innings. Last season McCament was a middle-inning mop-up man, finishing 10 of 25 games.

| Year | Team | W | L | SV | ERA | IP | H | BB | K |
|------|------|---|---|----|----|----|---|----|---|
| 1989 | SF....... | 1 | 1 | 0 | 3.93 | 36.2 | 32 | 23 | 12 |
| | | 1 | 1 | 0 | 3.93 | 36.2 | 32 | 23 | 12 |

# Roger McDowell

**Birth Date: 12/21/60**
**Throws: Right**
**1989 Clubs:**
**New York Mets &**
**Philadelphia Phillies**
**Contest Code #: 396**

**Rating: 4**

Roger McDowell, baseball's best practical joker, pulled a fast one on the Mets last season. Though McDowell had been a mainstay of their bullpen since 1985, the Mets thought he'd lost his effectiveness and traded him to the Phillies. But McDowell had the last laugh. While the Mets could not find a right-hander to fill the void in the bullpen, McDowell wound up with 23 saves, two short of his career high, and a career-low 1.96 ERA.

McDowell's emergence as a top reliever can be traced back to the elbow surgery he underwent in 1984 to remove bone chips. Up to that time McDowell had been a starting pitcher. But two things happened after the surgery: The Mets converted him to relief to minimize his innings; and his pitches developed a natural sinking movement.

McDowell made the Mets' major-league team in 1985 as a middle reliever, and a year later he became the Mets' main man in the pen. He slumped at the end of 1988 and the start of 1989 because he lost control of his sinker. Last year's trade may have given jolly Roger the resolve he needed to reclaim his closing role.

| Year | Team | W | L | SV | ERA | IP | H | BB | K |
|------|------|---|---|----|----|----|---|----|---|
| 1985 | NYN ..... | 6 | 5 | 17 | 2.83 | 127.1 | 108 | 37 | 70 |
| 1986 | NYN ..... | 14 | 9 | 22 | 3.02 | 128.0 | 107 | 42 | 65 |
| 1987 | NYN ..... | 7 | 5 | 25 | 4.16 | 88.2 | 95 | 28 | 32 |
| 1988 | NYN ..... | 5 | 5 | 16 | 2.63 | 89.0 | 80 | 31 | 46 |
| 1989 | NYN ..... | 1 | 5 | 4 | 3.31 | 35.1 | 34 | 16 | 15 |
| 1989 | Phi ...... | 3 | 3 | 19 | 1.11 | 56.2 | 45 | 22 | 32 |
| | | 36 | 32 | 103 | 2.91 | 525.0 | 469 | 176 | 260 |

# Larry McWilliams

Birth Date: 2/10/54
Throws: Left
1989 Club:
Philadelphia Phillies
Contest Code #: 397

Rating: 1

Here's a lesson in baseball economics for all you aspiring general managers. In 1983 starting pitcher Larry McWilliams had a fine season for the Pirates. A year later, though his wins shrank and losses grew, he allowed fewer runs. So the Pirates signed him to a multimillion-dollar, long-term contract. Since 1985, McWilliams has won a total of 20 games for five different clubs. And even though the Pirates released McWilliams in May 1987, under the terms of their contract they were still obligated to pay his 1989 salary of $1,050,000.

McWilliams, who was plagued by arm trouble for a few years, has been a ghost of his old self. He's good only in spurts. Last September the Phillies traded him to the Royals, who used him as a spot starter.

| Year | Team | W | L | SV | ERA | IP | H | BB | K |
|------|------|---|---|----|----|----|---|----|---|
| 1978 | Atl....... | 9 | 3 | 0 | 2.82 | 99.0 | 84 | 35 | 42 |
| 1979 | Atl....... | 3 | 2 | 0 | 5.59 | 66.0 | 69 | 22 | 32 |
| 1980 | Atl....... | 9 | 14 | 0 | 4.94 | 164.0 | 188 | 39 | 77 |
| 1981 | Atl....... | 2 | 1 | 0 | 3.08 | 38.0 | 31 | 8 | 23 |
| 1982 | Pit....... | 6 | 5 | 1 | 3.11 | 121.2 | 106 | 24 | 94 |
| 1982 | Atl....... | 2 | 3 | 0 | 6.21 | 37.2 | 52 | 20 | 24 |
| 1983 | Pit....... | 15 | 8 | 0 | 3.25 | 238.0 | 205 | 87 | 199 |
| 1984 | Pit....... | 12 | 11 | 1 | 2.93 | 227.1 | 226 | 78 | 149 |
| 1985 | Pit....... | 7 | 9 | 0 | 4.70 | 126.1 | 139 | 62 | 52 |
| 1986 | Pit....... | 3 | 11 | 0 | 5.15 | 122.1 | 129 | 49 | 80 |
| 1987 | Atl....... | 0 | 1 | 0 | 5.76 | 20.1 | 25 | 7 | 13 |
| 1988 | StL ...... | 6 | 9 | 1 | 3.90 | 136.0 | 130 | 45 | 70 |
| 1989 | KC....... | 2 | 2 | 0 | 4.13 | 32.2 | 31 | 8 | 24 |
| 1989 | Phi ...... | 2 | 11 | 0 | 4.10 | 120.2 | 123 | 49 | 54 |
| | | 78 | 90 | 3 | 3.95 | 1550.0 | 1538 | 533 | 933 |

# John Mitchell

Birth Date: 8/11/65
Throws: Right
1989 Club:
New York Mets
Contest Code #: 398

Rating: 1

John Mitchell, who came to the Mets not from the Nixon White House but from the Red Sox as part of the Bob Ojeda trade, has yet to pan out as a major leaguer.

Mitchell, a short-armer with a below-average fastball, has suffered from poor control in most of his 27 big-league appearances. In 1987, when the Mets lost half their starting staff to injuries, Mitchell got the call and gave up 124 hits and 36 walks in 111⅔ innings. Though he's fared better at Triple A, Mitchell has pitched in only three games for the Mets since 1987.

Considering the depth in the Mets' starting staff, Mitchell has virtually no chance of starting for the Mets in 1990. If he moves to another team, he still must show some control if he hopes to stick around.

| Year | Team | W | L | SV | ERA | IP | H | BB | K |
|------|------|---|---|----|----|----|---|----|---|
| 1986 | NYN ..... | 0 | 1 | 0 | 3.60 | 10.0 | 10 | 4 | 2 |
| 1987 | NYN ..... | 3 | 6 | 0 | 4.11 | 111.2 | 124 | 36 | 57 |
| 1988 | NYN ..... | 0 | 0 | 0 | 0.00 | 1.0 | 2 | 1 | 1 |
| 1989 | NYN ..... | 0 | 1 | 0 | 6.00 | 3.0 | 3 | 4 | 4 |
| | | 3 | 8 | 0 | 4.08 | 125.2 | 139 | 45 | 64 |

# Mike Morgan

**Birth Date:** 10/8/59
**Throws:** Right
**1989 Club:**
**Los Angeles Dodgers**
**Contest Code #: 399**

**Rating: 2**

We writers learn in journalism school that the sensational stories make page one, but the follow-ups and retractions are on page 27. When Mike Morgan was among the National League leaders in ERA (1.55) and fewest percentage of base runners (0.92) for the first three months of the 1989 season, scores of publications lauded the Dodgers' foresight in obtaining him from the Orioles. But little was written after Morgan went into a tailspin and was pulled from the Dodgers' rotation. The point with Morgan was that he simply found his level after that sensational start.

Morgan was a victim of former A's owner Charlie Finley's dire need for fresh, inexpensive players. After taking Morgan in the first round of the June 1978 draft, Finley brought him, then age eighteen, to the big leagues. Three games later, Morgan was demoted to Triple A. He returned in 1979 and went 2–10 in 13 games. A year later he was traded to the Yankees' organization. Two years later he was sent to the Blue Jays. In December 1984 he was claimed by the Mariners. In 1987 he was traded to the Orioles. All told, Morgan's been to 12 cities in 12 years.

| Year | Team | W | L | SV | ERA | IP | H | BB | K |
|------|------|---|---|----|----|----|----|----|----|
| 1978 | Oak...... | 0 | 3 | 0 | 7.50 | 12.0 | 19 | 8 | 0 |
| 1979 | Oak...... | 2 | 10 | 0 | 5.96 | 77.0 | 102 | 50 | 17 |
| 1982 | NYA...... | 7 | 11 | 0 | 4.37 | 150.1 | 167 | 67 | 71 |
| 1983 | Tor...... | 0 | 3 | 0 | 5.16 | 45.1 | 48 | 21 | 22 |
| 1985 | Sea..... | 1 | 1 | 0 | 12.00 | 6.0 | 11 | 5 | 2 |
| 1986 | Sea..... | 11 | 17 | 1 | 4.53 | 216.1 | 243 | 86 | 116 |
| 1987 | Sea..... | 12 | 17 | 0 | 4.65 | 207.0 | 245 | 53 | 85 |
| 1988 | Bal ...... | 1 | 6 | 1 | 5.43 | 71.1 | 70 | 23 | 29 |
| 1989 | LA....... | 8 | 11 | 0 | 2.54 | 152.2 | 130 | 33 | 72 |
| | | 42 | 79 | 2 | 4.51 | 938.0 | 1035 | 346 | 414 |

# Terry Mulholland

**Birth Date:** 3/9/63
**Throws:** Left
**1989 Clubs:**
**San Francisco Giants &**
**Philadelphia Phillies**
**Contest Code #: 400**

**Rating: 2**

Terry Mulholland will always be remembered for an inventive fielding play during a 1986 game against the Mets. Mulholland, then pitching for the Giants, fielded a ground ball hit back to the mound but couldn't get it out of his glove. So Mulholland quickly slid his glove off his right hand and tossed the glove-enclosed ball to first base for the out.

Mulholland has had little to laugh about since then. In 1987 he went 7–12 at Triple-A Phoenix, led the Pacific Coast League in runs allowed (124), and all of Triple A in earned runs (97). He turned things around in 1988, earning a return to the Giants after going 7–3 at Phoenix. But in August, arm problems shelved him for the rest of the season. Last year he was traded from the National League's eventual pennant winner to the Phillies, doormats of the National League East.

Mulholland has a rough time in his new surroundings. Over his last 65 innings he gave up 86 hits, 18 walks, and 39 earned runs. But the Phillies believe that Mulholland, who three seasons ago was among the Giants' best pitching prospects, possesses the moving fastball and sharp-breaking curve that can make him a good third starter.

| Year | Team | W | L | SV | ERA | IP | H | BB | K |
|------|------|---|---|----|----|-----|---|----|---|
| 1986 | SF....... | 1 | 7 | 0 | 4.94 | 54.2 | 51 | 35 | 27 |
| 1988 | SF....... | 2 | 1 | 0 | 3.72 | 46.0 | 50 | 7 | 18 |
| 1989 | SF....... | 0 | 0 | 0 | 4.09 | 11.0 | 15 | 4 | 6 |
| 1989 | Phi ...... | 4 | 7 | 0 | 5.00 | 104.1 | 122 | 32 | 60 |
| | | 7 | 15 | 0 | 4.67 | 216.0 | 238 | 78 | 111 |

# Dan Murphy

**Birth Date: 9/18/64**
**Throws: Right**
**1989 Club:**
**San Diego Padres**
**Contest Code #: 401**

**Rating: 1**

Swingman Dan Murphy got clocked during a late-season call-up to the Padres. Appearing in seven games—four as a starter—Murphy gave up six hits, four walks, four earned runs, and gave up one home run. Unfortunately, Murphy's big-league stats were consistent with his 1989 Triple-A outings.

Pitching for the Las Vegas Stars, Murphy allowed an average of 4.2 runs per game and 1.6 base runners per inning. On the plus side, he did pitch three complete games and earn two saves.

In 1988 Murphy was strafed for 25 hits and 18 earned runs in 26 innings for the Brewers' Class-A team in Stockton.

| Year | Team | W | L | SV | ERA | IP | H | BB | K |
|------|------|---|---|----|----|-----|---|----|---|
| 1989 | SD....... | 0 | 0 | 0 | 5.69 | 6.1 | 6 | 4 | 1 |
| | | 0 | 0 | 0 | 5.69 | 6.1 | 6 | 4 | 1 |

# Jeff Musselman

**Birth Date: 6/21/63**
**Throws: Left**
**1989 Club:**
**Toronto Blue Jays**
**& New York Mets**
**Contest Code #: 402**

**Rating: 1**

Jeff Musselman had run out of chances with the Blue Jays last season. Once a promising prospect, Musselman, who'd earned his bachelor of arts degree in economics from Harvard University, became a liability after a battle with substance abuse.

He was traded last July to the Mets, who hoped he could fill their need for a left-handed, middle-inning reliever. The results were mixed. Though his end-of-season ERA was a reasonable 3.08, he had a rough stretch of 19 innings in which he permitted 23 hits, 13 walks, and 9 earned runs. Overall, he allowed an average of 1.56 base runners, far too many for a reliever called in primarily to keep the score within the Mets' reach.

| Year | Team | W | L | SV | ERA | IP | H | BB | K |
|------|------|---|---|----|----|-----|---|----|---|
| 1986 | Tor....... | 0 | 0 | 0 | 10.13 | 5.1 | 8 | 5 | 4 |
| 1987 | Tor....... | 12 | 5 | 3 | 4.15 | 89.0 | 75 | 54 | 54 |
| 1988 | Tor....... | 8 | 5 | 0 | 3.18 | 85.0 | 80 | 30 | 39 |
| 1989 | Tor....... | 0 | 1 | 0 | 10.64 | 11.0 | 19 | 9 | 3 |
| 1989 | NYN ..... | 3 | 2 | 0 | 3.08 | 26.1 | 27 | 14 | 11 |
| | | 23 | 13 | 3 | 4.11 | 216.2 | 209 | 112 | 111 |

# Randy Myers

**Birth Date:** 9/19/62
**Throws:** Left
**1989 Club:**
**New York Mets**
**Contest Code #:** 403

**Rating: 5**

**I**'m an advocate of individualized, properly supervised-conditioning programs for baseball players. What drives me wild is when players design their own programs that bulk muscles. Pitchers, especially, don't need bulging biceps and pectorals; they need lower body strength to generate force from their legs and midsections, and upper body flexibility to prevent shoulder and arm injuries.

Will someone please tell this to Randy "Rambo" Myers? After most Mets games, Myers could be found pumping iron. Despite his pumped-up macho look, he wore out as last season wore down. In the first half of the season Myers won 6 games and saved 12, allowed only 8 earned runs (1.45), 35 hits, and 21 walks (an average of 1.12 base runners) in 49⅔ innings. In the second half Myers won 1 game and saved 12, gave up 14 earned runs (3.64), 27 hits, and 19 walks (1.32) in 34⅔ innings.

You may think I'm quibbling, since Myers' blazing fastball earns him a place with the league's best left-handed closers. I simply think he can be the league's best closer—lefty or righty—with a more balanced conditioning program. Listen, Randy: Stop trying to sculpt yourself a torso like Stallone's. Your role model should be Nolan Ryan, who builds his legs and midsection while toning his arms. In a surprise move during baseball's Winter Meetings, Myers was traded straight-up for the Reds' John Franco. "I'm in a state of shock," Myers was reported to have said. Many think he'll come out firing.

| Year | Team | W | L | SV | ERA | IP | H | BB | K |
|------|------|---|---|----|----|----|----|----|----|
| 1985 | NYN ..... | 0 | 0 | 0 | 0.00 | 2.0 | 0 | 1 | 2 |
| 1986 | NYN ..... | 0 | 0 | 0 | 4.22 | 10.2 | 11 | 9 | 13 |
| 1987 | NYN ..... | 3 | 6 | 6 | 3.96 | 75.0 | 61 | 30 | 92 |
| 1988 | NYN ..... | 7 | 3 | 26 | 1.72 | 68.0 | 45 | 17 | 69 |
| 1989 | NYN ..... | 7 | 4 | 24 | 2.35 | 84.1 | 62 | 40 | 88 |
| | | 17 | 13 | 56 | 2.74 | 240.0 | 179 | 97 | 264 |

# Bob Ojeda

**Birth Date:** 12/17/57
**Throws:** Left
**1989 Club:**
**New York Mets**
**Contest Code #:** 404

**Rating: 3**

**U**ntil the arrival of Frank Viola, offspeed specialist Bob Ojeda was the perfect number-three starter for the Mets. With Dwight Gooden and Ron Darling preceding him, and David Cone and Sid Fernandez behind, Ojeda gave the staff a different look. Once opposing batters had adjusted to the speed of Gooden and Darling, along came Ojeda and his "dead fish" change-up to throw off their timing. After swinging at Ojeda's junk, batters found that Cone and Fernandez looked even faster.

But Viola's presence will change Ojeda's previous good fortune. As he's gotten older, Viola's pitch selection has become more like Ojeda's. Therefore, batters won't have as great an adjustment.

Ojeda is a good pitcher who's benefited greatly from his place in a hard-throwing rotation on a consistent division contender. Take away those advantages and you're left with a crafty pitcher who will win 10 to 12 games a season.

| Year | Team | W | L | SV | ERA | IP | H | BB | K |
|------|------|---|---|----|----|----|----|----|----|
| 1980 | Bos...... | 1 | 1 | 0 | 6.92 | 26.0 | 39 | 14 | 12 |
| 1981 | Bos...... | 6 | 2 | 0 | 3.14 | 66.0 | 50 | 25 | 28 |
| 1982 | Bos...... | 4 | 6 | 0 | 5.63 | 78.1 | 95 | 29 | 52 |
| 1983 | Bos...... | 12 | 7 | 0 | 4.04 | 173.2 | 173 | 73 | 94 |
| 1984 | Bos...... | 12 | 12 | 0 | 3.99 | 216.2 | 211 | 96 | 137 |
| 1985 | Bos...... | 9 | 11 | 1 | 4.00 | 157.2 | 166 | 48 | 102 |
| 1986 | NYN..... | 18 | 5 | 0 | 2.57 | 217.1 | 185 | 52 | 148 |
| 1987 | NYN..... | 3 | 5 | 0 | 3.89 | 46.1 | 45 | 10 | 21 |
| 1988 | NYN..... | 10 | 13 | 0 | 2.88 | 190.1 | 158 | 33 | 133 |
| 1989 | NYN..... | 13 | 11 | 0 | 3.47 | 192.0 | 179 | 78 | 95 |
|  |  | 88 | 73 | 1 | 3.65 | 1364.1 | 1301 | 458 | 822 |

# Randy O'Neal

**Birth Date:** 8/30/60
**Throws:** Left
**1989 Club:**
**Philadelphia Phillies**
**Contest Code #:** 405

**Rating: 1**

Randy O'Neal was so coveted a prospect from 1979 to 1981 that he could virtually pick his ball club. O'Neal refused to sign with the Expos, who selected him in the January 1979 draft. He turned down the Minnesota Twins, who selected him in the secondary phase of the June 1979 draft. He snubbed the Brewers, who drafted him in January 1980. And he said no to the Reds, who took him in the secondary phase of the June 1980 draft. A year later he finally signed with the Tigers, who drafted him in June 1981.

Then the tables turned on O'Neal. After parts of three major-league seasons with the Tigers, he was traded to the Braves in January 1987 with pitcher Chuck Cary for outfielders Terry Harper and Freddie Tiburco. Six months later the Braves sent him to the Cardinals for Joe Boever. Four months later he signed as a free agent with the Phillies. And through all his travels he has yet to pitch a full season in the majors.

| Year | Team | W | L | SV | ERA | IP | H | BB | K |
|------|------|---|---|----|----|----|----|----|----|
| 1984 | Det...... | 2 | 1 | 0 | 3.38 | 18.2 | 16 | 6 | 12 |
| 1985 | Det...... | 5 | 5 | 1 | 3.24 | 94.1 | 82 | 36 | 52 |
| 1986 | Det...... | 3 | 7 | 2 | 4.33 | 122.2 | 121 | 44 | 68 |
| 1987 | StL...... | 0 | 0 | 0 | 1.80 | 5.0 | 2 | 2 | 4 |
| 1987 | Atl...... | 4 | 2 | 0 | 5.61 | 61.0 | 79 | 24 | 33 |
| 1988 | StL...... | 2 | 3 | 0 | 4.58 | 53.0 | 57 | 10 | 20 |
| 1989 | Phi...... | 0 | 1 | 0 | 6.23 | 39.0 | 46 | 9 | 29 |
|  |  | 16 | 19 | 3 | 4.41 | 393.2 | 403 | 131 | 218 |

# Jeff Parrett

**Birth Date:** 8/26/61
**Throws:** Right
**1989 Club:**
**Philadelphia Phillies**
**Contest Code #:** 406

**Rating: 3**

If you get a cut on your finger, usually it's no big deal. Some antiseptic, a Band-Aid, maybe a stitch or two and you're back in action. But if you're a pitcher, a laceration of a finger on your pitching hand can wreak havoc.

In 1988, Jeff Parrett, groomed in the Expos' minor-league system as a closer, had taken charge of Montreal's pen, winning 10 games and saving 6 by mid-July. Then he lacerated a finger during batting practice. He returned a month later and pitched just 26 ⅓ innings the rest of the season.

During the 1988 off season the Expos traded Parrett to the Phillies for starter Kevin Gross. Initially, the move seemed like a career setback for Parrett because of the presence of Steve Bedrosian. When the Phillies dealt Bedrock to the Giants, Parrett thought the closing job was his. But a day later the Phillies picked up Roger McDowell and kept Parrett in a setup role.

Nonetheless, Parrett, a fastball, slider, change-up pitcher, is an excellent insurance policy in the event that McDowell slumps. Parrett gives up few earned runs, picks up a lot of victories, and chips in a few saves.

| Year | Team | W | L | SV | ERA | IP | H | BB | K |
|------|------|---|---|----|-----|-----|-----|-----|-----|
| 1986 | Mon ..... | 0 | 1 | 0 | 4.87 | 20.1 | 19 | 13 | 21 |
| 1987 | Mon ..... | 7 | 6 | 6 | 4.21 | 62.0 | 53 | 30 | 56 |
| 1988 | Mon ..... | 12 | 4 | 6 | 2.65 | 91.2 | 66 | 45 | 62 |
| 1989 | Phi ...... | 12 | 6 | 6 | 2.98 | 105.2 | 90 | 44 | 98 |
| | | 31 | 17 | 18 | 3.28 | 279.2 | 228 | 132 | 237 |

# Alejandro Pena

**Birth Date: 6/25/59**
**Throws: Right**
**1989 Club:**
**Los Angeles Dodgers**
**Contest Code #: 407**

**Rating: 3**

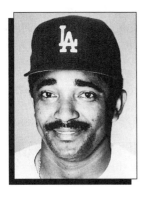

**O**nce a gifted starting pitcher with a 95-mile-an-hour fastball, Alejandro Pena has come back from three years of shoulder ailments to become a dependable setup man and occasional closer.

In fact, because of Pena and teammate Jay Howell's histories of arm problems, Pena gets a little more work than Howell, the Dodgers' titular closer. Over the past two seasons Pena has appeared in 113 games to Howell's 106, and has hurled 170⅓ innings to Howell's 144⅔. They have the same number of victories over that period (10) and similar earned run averages. The difference is saves. Pena had 12 in 1988 because he filled in as the closer when Howell was injured, but last season, with Howell healthy, Pena notched only 5.

We can't be sure that Pena, because of past injuries, can take on regular closing duties, but in his current role he's a valuable pitcher to have. Apparently, the Mets agree; Pena came to the Mets during the off-season along with Mike Marshall in exchange for centerfielder Juan Samuel.

| Year | Team | W | L | SV | ERA | IP | H | BB | K |
|------|------|---|---|----|-----|-----|-----|-----|-----|
| 1981 | LA ....... | 1 | 1 | 2 | 2.88 | 25.0 | 18 | 11 | 14 |
| 1982 | LA ....... | 0 | 2 | 0 | 4.80 | 35.2 | 37 | 21 | 20 |
| 1983 | LA ....... | 12 | 9 | 1 | 2.75 | 177.0 | 152 | 51 | 120 |
| 1984 | LA ....... | 12 | 6 | 0 | 2.48 | 199.1 | 186 | 46 | 135 |
| 1985 | LA ....... | 0 | 1 | 0 | 8.31 | 4.1 | 7 | 3 | 2 |
| 1986 | LA ....... | 1 | 2 | 1 | 4.89 | 70.0 | 74 | 30 | 46 |
| 1987 | LA ....... | 2 | 7 | 11 | 3.50 | 87.1 | 82 | 37 | 76 |
| 1988 | LA ....... | 6 | 7 | 12 | 1.91 | 94.1 | 75 | 27 | 83 |
| 1989 | LA ....... | 4 | 3 | 5 | 2.13 | 76.0 | 62 | 18 | 75 |
| | | 38 | 38 | 32 | 2.93 | 769.0 | 693 | 244 | 571 |

# Mark Portugal

**Birth Date: 10/30/62**
**Throws: Right**
**1989 Club:**
**Houston Astros**
**Contest Code #: 409**

**Rating: 3**

**L**ast season Mark Portugal was one of those "Where did he come from?" stories. After toiling eight years in the Twins system, including one full season and parts of three others with the big club, Portugal was traded to the Astros in December 1988. He opened the season at Triple A, but became one of the Astros' most important pitchers after his mid-season call-up.

Portugal had been plagued by control problems through most of his career. Following a 6–10 season for the Twins in 1986, Portugal hit rock bottom at Triple A in 1987. In 102 innings for Portland of the Pacific Coast

League, Portugal went 1–10, gave up 108 hits, 50 walks, and 68 earned runs. He issued far fewer walks per inning at Triple A in 1988, and last year with the Astros he walked only 37 batters in 108 innings. In 20 games—15 as a starter—Portugal won 7, including a complete-game shutout. In 108 innings, he permitted 91 hits and struck out 86.

Sometimes it takes a pitcher years to find himself. Mike Bielecki didn't become a good major league starter until he was twenty-nine. I'm not saying Portugal is the next Bielecki, but he bears watching.

| Year | Team | W | L | SV | ERA | IP | H | BB | K |
|------|------|---|---|----|----|----|----|----|----|
| 1985 | Min...... | 1 | 3 | 0 | 5.55 | 24.1 | 24 | 14 | 12 |
| 1986 | Min...... | 6 | 10 | 1 | 4.31 | 112.2 | 112 | 50 | 67 |
| 1987 | Min...... | 1 | 3 | 0 | 7.77 | 44.0 | 58 | 24 | 28 |
| 1988 | Min...... | 3 | 3 | 3 | 4.53 | 57.2 | 60 | 17 | 31 |
| 1989 | Hou...... | 7 | 1 | 0 | 2.75 | 108.0 | 91 | 37 | 86 |
| | | 18 | 20 | 4 | 4.39 | 346.2 | 345 | 142 | 224 |

# Ted Power

**Birth Date: 1/31/55**
**Throws: Right**
**1989 Club:**
**St. Louis Cardinals**
**Contest Code #: 410**

**Rating: 1**

Twice in his nine-year career, Ted Power has made his teams' general managers look like geniuses. In October 1982 the Reds acquired Power from the Dodgers, and within two seasons Power became the tower of the Reds' bullpen. In 1984 he led the National League with 78 appearances, and in 1985 he earned 27 saves, tied with Dave Smith for third-best in the league. When John Franco took over as the Reds' closer in 1986, Power joined the starting rotation and won 10 games.

But Power's success was short-lived. In 1987 he gave up 213 hits and 71 walks in 204 innings, an average of 1.4 base runners per inning. The Reds sent him to the Royals, and in August 1988 the Royals passed him along to the Tigers.

Last year the Cardinals, in dire need of starting pitchers, plucked Power from the minors and he emerged as a steady performer. Over one stretch Power and fellow castoff Ricky Horton were manager Whitey Herzog's most dependable starters.

Now that the Cardinals' injury crises have passed, Power, who still gives up a lot of hits, may struggle to make the 1990 staff.

| Year | Team | W | L | SV | ERA | IP | H | BB | K |
|------|------|---|---|----|----|----|----|----|----|
| 1981 | LA........ | 1 | 3 | 0 | 3.21 | 14.0 | 16 | 7 | 7 |
| 1982 | LA........ | 1 | 1 | 0 | 6.68 | 33.2 | 38 | 23 | 15 |
| 1983 | Cin ...... | 5 | 6 | 2 | 4.54 | 111.0 | 120 | 49 | 57 |
| 1984 | Cin ...... | 9 | 7 | 11 | 2.82 | 108.2 | 93 | 46 | 81 |
| 1985 | Cin ...... | 8 | 6 | 27 | 2.70 | 80.0 | 65 | 45 | 42 |
| 1986 | Cin ...... | 10 | 6 | 1 | 3.70 | 129.0 | 115 | 52 | 95 |
| 1987 | Cin ...... | 10 | 13 | 0 | 4.50 | 204.0 | 213 | 71 | 133 |
| 1988 | KC........ | 5 | 6 | 0 | 5.94 | 80.1 | 98 | 30 | 44 |
| 1988 | Det ...... | 1 | 1 | 0 | 5.79 | 18.2 | 23 | 8 | 13 |
| 1989 | StL ...... | 7 | 7 | 0 | 3.71 | 97.0 | 96 | 21 | 43 |
| | | 57 | 56 | 41 | 4.15 | 876.1 | 877 | 352 | 530 |

# Dan Quisenberry

**Birth Date:** 2/7/53
**Throws:** Right
**1989 Club:**
**St. Louis Cardinals**
**Contest Code #:** 411

**Rating: 2**

**D**an Quisenberry is truly fortunate that the Cardinals were willing to let him work through his problems in 1988. Quisenberry, the best reliever in the American League during the mid-1980s, appeared to have reached the end of the line by 1987. His ineffectiveness and lucrative, long-term contract wiped out his trade value, so the Royals released him on Independence Day in 1988. Ten days later, the Cards added him to their roster as a middle reliever, and through the rest of that season Quiz was pounded for 54 hits and 26 earned runs in 38 innings.

In 1989 Quisenberry repaid the Cards' patience. Used as a middle man, setup man, and, when Todd Worrell got hurt, a co-closer, Quiz gave up only 2 home runs in 78⅓ innings, earning 3 victories and 6 saves in 63 appearances.

Now in his baseball golden years, Quisenberry, who has a great sense of humor, is a good man to have in a committee-style bullpen.

| Year | Team | W | L | SV | ERA | IP | H | BB | K |
|------|------|---|---|----|-----|----|---|----|---|
| 1979 | KC....... | 3 | 2 | 5 | 3.15 | 40.0 | 42 | 7 | 13 |
| 1980 | KC....... | 12 | 7 | 33 | 3.09 | 128.0 | 129 | 27 | 37 |
| 1981 | KC....... | 1 | 4 | 18 | 1.74 | 62.0 | 59 | 15 | 20 |
| 1982 | KC....... | 9 | 7 | 35 | 2.57 | 136.2 | 126 | 12 | 46 |
| 1983 | KC....... | 5 | 3 | 45 | 1.94 | 139.0 | 118 | 11 | 48 |
| 1984 | KC....... | 6 | 3 | 44 | 2.64 | 129.1 | 121 | 12 | 41 |
| 1985 | KC....... | 8 | 9 | 37 | 2.37 | 129.0 | 142 | 16 | 54 |
| 1986 | KC....... | 3 | 7 | 12 | 2.77 | 81.1 | 92 | 24 | 36 |
| 1987 | KC....... | 4 | 1 | 8 | 2.76 | 49.0 | 58 | 10 | 17 |
| 1988 | KC....... | 0 | 1 | 1 | 3.55 | 25.1 | 32 | 5 | 9 |
| 1988 | StL ...... | 2 | 0 | 0 | 6.16 | 38.0 | 54 | 6 | 19 |
| 1989 | StL ...... | 3 | 1 | 6 | 2.64 | 78.1 | 78 | 14 | 37 |
| | | 56 | 45 | 244 | 2.69 | 1036.0 | 1051 | 159 | 377 |

# Dennis Rasmussen

**Birth Date:** 4/18/59
**Throws:** Left
**1989 Club:**
**San Diego Padres**
**Contest Code #:** 412

**Rating: 1**

**I**'m a believer in the tenets Pirates pitching coach Ray Miller teaches his staff: "Work fast, change speeds, throw strikes." By working quickly, you keep your fielders alert and give opposing batters less time to adjust to your pitches. Changing speeds keeps the hitters off balance. Throwing strikes ensures success. Too bad Miller can't work with Dennis Rasmussen of the Padres.

Rasmussen is one of the National League's slowest workers. He takes between 30 seconds to a minute between pitches. All his pitches—below-average fastball; slow curveball and changeup—are within the same range of speeds. So when he throws strikes, the hitters, who've had time to prepare and adjust to basically the same pitches, salivate like Pavlov's dog.

Rasmussen has taxed the patience of four organizations: the Angels, who drafted him; the Yankees, who traded for him; the Padres, who've twice traded for him; and the Reds, who shipped him out after a season and change. Rasmussen routinely follows a good season with a poor one. Judging by his record, one may think Rasmussen is ready to rebound in 1990. I wouldn't, having seen Rasmussen give up 190 hits in 183⅔ innings last year.

| Year | Team | W | L | SV | ERA | IP | H | BB | K |
|------|------|---|---|----|----|----|----|----|---|
| 1983 | SD....... | 0 | 0 | 0 | 1.98 | 13.2 | 10 | 8 | 13 |
| 1984 | NYA...... | 9 | 6 | 0 | 4.57 | 147.2 | 127 | 60 | 110 |
| 1985 | NYA...... | 3 | 5 | 0 | 3.98 | 101.2 | 97 | 42 | 63 |
| 1986 | NYA...... | 18 | 6 | 0 | 3.88 | 202.0 | 160 | 74 | 131 |
| 1987 | NYA...... | 9 | 7 | 0 | 4.75 | 146.0 | 145 | 55 | 89 |
| 1987 | Cin ...... | 4 | 1 | 0 | 3.97 | 45.1 | 39 | 12 | 39 |
| 1988 | Cin ...... | 2 | 6 | 0 | 5.75 | 56.1 | 68 | 22 | 27 |
| 1988 | SD....... | 14 | 4 | 0 | 2.55 | 148.1 | 131 | 36 | 85 |
| 1989 | SD....... | 10 | 10 | 0 | 4.26 | 183.2 | 190 | 72 | 87 |
| | | 69 | 45 | 0 | 4.07 | 1044.2 | 967 | 381 | 644 |

# Rick Reed

**Birth Date: 8/16/64**
**Throws: Right**
**1989 Club:**
**Pittsburgh Pirates**
**Contest Code #: 413**

**Rating: 2**

Rick Reed, chosen by the Pirates in the twenty-sixth round of the June 1986 draft, had developed nicely in their organization. In 1987, Reed went 8–4 with a 2.50 ERA in the Class-A South Atlantic League. In 1988, he was 6–2 with a 2.74 ERA in Double A; 5–2, 1.64 at Triple A; and 1–0, 1.13, in two starts on the major-league level. But when the Pirates changed general managers following the 1988 season and got off to a horrible start in 1989, the players were used and yanked depending on their last performances. Sadly, Reed had to deal with that as well.

Reed was treated like a yo-yo, splitting time between Pittsburgh and Triple-A Buffalo. With the big club, he jockeyed between the rotation and bullpen, starting seven games and relieving in eight. Reed, a control pitcher, wasn't given the chance to settle in and weather rough outings.

Reed can be a good starter on many teams. Hopefully, scouts from other teams will not judge Reed solely on his 1989 stats.

| Year | Team | W | L | SV | ERA | IP | H | BB | K |
|------|------|---|---|----|----|----|----|----|---|
| 1988 | Pit....... | 1 | 0 | 0 | 3.00 | 12.0 | 10 | 2 | 6 |
| 1989 | Pit....... | 1 | 4 | 0 | 5.60 | 54.2 | 62 | 11 | 34 |
| | | 2 | 4 | 0 | 5.13 | 66.2 | 72 | 13 | 40 |

# Rick Reuschel

**Birth Date: 5/16/49**
**Throws: Right**
**1989 Club:**
**San Francisco Giants**
**Contest Code #: 414**

**Rating: 5**

Rick Reuschel, fondly referred to by his teammates as "Big Daddy," remains among the National League's best right-handed starters even at his advanced age. His sinking fastball induces a steady stream of ground-ball outs, and his low ratio of walks to innings pitched (.17 in 1988, .26 in 1989) keeps him in every ball game. The old man knows how to pitch, but he'd do well to work on his physical conditioning.

Reuschel is from the old school, which believes less off-the-field exertion means more on-field success. The only time Reuschel dedicated himself to a conditioning program was between 1982 and 1983, when he had to rehabilitate his surgically repaired rotator cuff. Last season Reuschel was 12–3 with a 2.12 ERA at the All-Star break, but he suffered a groin pull that dogged him through the second half of the season and into the post-season.

Last year the Giants hired Mackie Shilstone, a nationally recognized expert in conditioning and nutrition, as a team consultant. It would be wise for Reuschel to begin a conditioning program under Shilstone's supervision to ensure his continued success.

| Year | Team | W | L | SV | ERA | IP | H | BB | K |
|------|------|---|---|----|----|----|---|----|---|
| 1972 | ChN..... | 10 | 8 | 0 | 2.93 | 129.0 | 127 | 29 | 87 |
| 1973 | ChN..... | 14 | 15 | 0 | 3.00 | 237.0 | 244 | 62 | 168 |
| 1974 | ChN..... | 13 | 12 | 0 | 4.29 | 241.0 | 262 | 83 | 160 |
| 1975 | ChN..... | 11 | 17 | 1 | 3.73 | 234.0 | 244 | 67 | 155 |
| 1976 | ChN..... | 14 | 12 | 1 | 3.46 | 260.0 | 260 | 64 | 146 |
| 1977 | ChN..... | 20 | 10 | 1 | 2.79 | 252.0 | 233 | 74 | 166 |
| 1978 | ChN..... | 14 | 15 | 0 | 3.41 | 243.0 | 235 | 54 | 115 |
| 1979 | ChN..... | 18 | 12 | 0 | 3.62 | 239.0 | 251 | 75 | 125 |
| 1980 | ChN..... | 11 | 13 | 0 | 3.40 | 257.0 | 281 | 76 | 140 |
| 1981 | NYA..... | 4 | 4 | 0 | 2.66 | 71.0 | 75 | 10 | 22 |
| 1981 | ChN..... | 4 | 7 | 0 | 3.45 | 86.0 | 87 | 23 | 53 |
| 1983 | ChN..... | 1 | 1 | 0 | 3.92 | 20.2 | 18 | 10 | 9 |
| 1984 | ChN..... | 5 | 5 | 0 | 5.17 | 92.1 | 123 | 23 | 43 |
| 1985 | Pit...... | 14 | 8 | 1 | 2.27 | 194.0 | 153 | 52 | 138 |
| 1986 | Pit...... | 9 | 16 | 0 | 3.96 | 215.2 | 232 | 57 | 125 |
| 1987 | SF....... | 5 | 3 | 0 | 4.32 | 50.0 | 44 | 7 | 27 |
| 1987 | Pit...... | 8 | 6 | 0 | 2.75 | 177.0 | 163 | 35 | 80 |
| 1988 | SF....... | 19 | 11 | 0 | 3.12 | 245.0 | 242 | 42 | 92 |
| 1989 | SF....... | 17 | 8 | 0 | 2.94 | 208.1 | 195 | 54 | 111 |
| | | 211 | 183 | 4 | 3.36 | 3452.0 | 3469 | 897 | 1962 |

# Rick Rhoden

**Birth Date: 5/16/53**
**Throws: Right**
**1989 Club:**
**Houston Astros**
**Contest Code #: 415**

**Rating: 2**

The Astros had hoped Rick Rhoden would help fill Nolan Ryan's spot in the rotation last year. However, Rhoden spent much of the season on the disabled list with a pulled rib-cage muscle. It was the second straight season Rhoden has had to be disabled, a bad omen for a thirty-six-year-old pitcher whose best seasons are behind him.

At his best, Rhoden was capable of winning 15 games and throwing 200 innings a season. Rhoden reached his zenith in 1987, winning 16 games in his role as the Yankees' number-one starter. In 1988, battling a back injury, he gave up 206 hits and 94 earned runs in 197 innings.

Rhoden, who throws a fastball, curve, slider, and change-up, has long been accused of tampering with the baseball. Whether it's true, this season he'll have to pull every trick in the book to be an effective pitcher.

| Year | Team | W | L | SV | ERA | IP | H | BB | K |
|------|------|---|---|----|----|----|---|----|---|
| 1974 | LA....... | 1 | 0 | 0 | 2.00 | 9.0 | 5 | 4 | 7 |
| 1975 | LA....... | 3 | 3 | 0 | 3.09 | 99.0 | 94 | 32 | 40 |
| 1976 | LA....... | 12 | 3 | 0 | 2.98 | 181.0 | 165 | 53 | 77 |
| 1977 | LA....... | 16 | 10 | 0 | 3.75 | 216.0 | 223 | 63 | 122 |
| 1978 | LA....... | 10 | 8 | 0 | 3.65 | 165.0 | 160 | 51 | 79 |
| 1979 | Pit...... | 0 | 1 | 0 | 7.20 | 5.0 | 5 | 2 | 2 |
| 1980 | Pit...... | 7 | 5 | 0 | 3.83 | 127.0 | 133 | 40 | 70 |
| 1981 | Pit...... | 9 | 4 | 0 | 3.90 | 136.0 | 147 | 53 | 76 |
| 1982 | Pit...... | 11 | 14 | 0 | 4.14 | 230.1 | 239 | 70 | 128 |
| 1983 | Pit...... | 13 | 13 | 1 | 3.09 | 244.1 | 256 | 68 | 153 |
| 1984 | Pit...... | 14 | 9 | 0 | 2.72 | 238.1 | 216 | 62 | 136 |
| 1985 | Pit...... | 10 | 15 | 0 | 4.47 | 213.1 | 254 | 69 | 128 |
| 1986 | Pit...... | 15 | 12 | 0 | 2.84 | 253.2 | 211 | 76 | 159 |
| 1987 | NYA..... | 16 | 10 | 0 | 3.86 | 181.2 | 184 | 61 | 107 |
| 1988 | NYA..... | 12 | 12 | 0 | 4.29 | 197.0 | 206 | 56 | 94 |
| 1989 | Hou..... | 2 | 6 | 0 | 4.28 | 96.2 | 108 | 41 | 41 |
| | | 151 | 125 | 1 | 3.60 | 2593.1 | 2606 | 801 | 1419 |

# Jose Rijo

Birth Date: 5/13/65
Throws: Right
1989 Club:
Cincinnati Reds
Contest Code #: 416

Rating: 4

**T**he beauty of George Steinbrenner is that he'll discard a good young prospect like Jose Rijo well before his time, but sign a rehab veteran like Pascual Perez.

That may seem like ancient history to Rijo, but this season he may get a history lesson. Bob Quinn, the Reds' new general manager, was schooled in the art of contract negotiations by former Indians honchos Gabe Paul and Phil Seghi, and tutored in the art of the misdeal by Steinbrenner. Quinn knows that Rijo, plagued by back spasms last season, is in the final year of his contract. With five other Reds in their option years, someone may go—someone like Rijo. Perhaps a cooler head—like Reds manager Lou Piniella, who was Rijo's teammate on the Yankees in 1984—may understand that pitchers like Rijo are hard to come by.

| Year | Team | W | L | SV | ERA | IP | H | BB | K |
|------|------|---|---|----|----|----|----|----|----|
| 1984 | NYA...... | 2 | 8 | 2 | 4.76 | 62.1 | 74 | 33 | 47 |
| 1985 | Oak...... | 6 | 4 | 0 | 3.53 | 63.2 | 57 | 28 | 65 |
| 1986 | Oak...... | 9 | 11 | 1 | 4.65 | 193.2 | 172 | 108 | 176 |
| 1987 | Oak...... | 2 | 7 | 0 | 5.90 | 82.1 | 106 | 41 | 67 |
| 1988 | Cin ...... | 13 | 8 | 0 | 2.39 | 162.0 | 120 | 63 | 160 |
| 1989 | Cin ...... | 7 | 6 | 0 | 2.84 | 111.0 | 101 | 48 | 86 |
| | | 39 | 44 | 3 | 3.87 | 675.0 | 630 | 321 | 601 |

# Don Robinson

Birth Date: 6/8/57
Throws: Right
1989 Club:
San Francisco Giants
Contest Code #: 417

Rating: 3

**D**on Robinson, a good, naturally gifted athlete, has never let baseball stop him from having a good time after hours. Over the course of his career he'd been through three operations on his right shoulder, one on his right elbow, and another on his right knee and never missed a last call. But at some point in every person's life his body becomes less resilient to a dusk-to-dawn lifestyle.

Robinson was merrily rolling along last season until suffering a knee injury during the second half. The knee was slow to heal in part because Robinson had gained 25 pounds, which put more stress on the knee joint. Insiders tell me Giants' team officials suggested—then demanded—Robinson shed his excess baggage, to no avail. During the post-season Robinson strapped on a corsetlike knee brace and tried to pitch on one leg.

The loss of Robinson in the Giants' post-season rotation was keenly felt, so it behooves him to arrive at spring training in shape and ready to pitch.

| Year | Team | W | L | SV | ERA | IP | H | BB | K |
|------|------|---|---|----|----|----|----|----|----|
| 1978 | Pit....... | 14 | 6 | 1 | 3.47 | 228.0 | 203 | 57 | 135 |
| 1979 | Pit....... | 8 | 8 | 0 | 3.86 | 161.0 | 171 | 52 | 96 |
| 1980 | Pit....... | 7 | 10 | 1 | 3.99 | 160.0 | 157 | 45 | 103 |
| 1981 | Pit....... | 0 | 3 | 2 | 5.92 | 38.0 | 47 | 23 | 17 |
| 1982 | Pit....... | 15 | 13 | 0 | 4.28 | 227.0 | 213 | 103 | 165 |
| 1983 | Pit....... | 2 | 2 | 0 | 4.46 | 36.1 | 43 | 21 | 28 |
| 1984 | Pit....... | 5 | 6 | 10 | 3.02 | 122.0 | 99 | 49 | 110 |
| 1985 | Pit....... | 5 | 11 | 3 | 3.87 | 95.1 | 95 | 42 | 65 |
| 1986 | Pit....... | 3 | 4 | 14 | 3.38 | 69.1 | 61 | 27 | 53 |
| 1987 | SF ....... | 5 | 1 | 7 | 2.74 | 42.2 | 39 | 18 | 26 |
| 1987 | Pit....... | 6 | 6 | 12 | 3.86 | 65.1 | 66 | 22 | 53 |
| 1988 | SF ....... | 10 | 5 | 6 | 2.45 | 176.2 | 152 | 49 | 122 |
| 1989 | SF ....... | 12 | 11 | 0 | 3.43 | 197.0 | 184 | 37 | 96 |
| | | 92 | 86 | 56 | 3.62 | 1618.2 | 1530 | 545 | 1069 |

# Ron Robinson

**Birth Date:** 3/24/62
**Throws:** Right
**1989 Club:**
**Cincinnati Reds**
**Contest Code #:** 419

## Rating: 1

On May 2, 1988, Ron Robinson was on the threshold of greatness, one strike away from a perfect game against the Expos. A two-out single by Wallace Johnson prevented Robinson's entry into the record books. Then a bone spur in his right elbow took two strikes from Robinson's career.

Robinson underwent corrective surgery in September 1988, but the pain returned last season, restricting him to 15 games. In all, he's pitched only 89⅔ innings since the 1988 All-Star break. The elbow problem is particularly significant for Robinson because his best pitch is his curveball, which in itself puts stress on the elbow.

If his elbow heals fully, Robinson may be better off returning to the bullpen as a middle reliever.

| Year | Team | W | L | SV | ERA | IP | H | BB | K |
|------|------|---|---|----|-----|-----|-----|-----|-----|
| 1984 | Cin ...... | 1 | 2 | 0 | 2.72 | 39.2 | 35 | 13 | 24 |
| 1985 | Cin ...... | 7 | 7 | 1 | 3.99 | 108.1 | 107 | 32 | 76 |
| 1986 | Cin ...... | 10 | 3 | 14 | 3.24 | 116.2 | 110 | 43 | 117 |
| 1987 | Cin ...... | 7 | 5 | 4 | 3.68 | 154.0 | 148 | 43 | 99 |
| 1988 | Cin ...... | 3 | 7 | 0 | 4.12 | 78.2 | 88 | 26 | 38 |
| 1989 | Cin ...... | 5 | 3 | 0 | 3.35 | 83.1 | 80 | 28 | 36 |
| | | 33 | 27 | 19 | 3.60 | 580.2 | 568 | 185 | 390 |

# Mike Roesler

**Birth Date:** 9/12/63
**Throws:** Right
**1989 Club:**
**Cincinnati Reds**
**Contest Code #:** 420

## Rating: 2

Mike Roesler (pronounced *Ress-ler*) was selected by the Reds in the seventeenth round of the June 1985 draft. Over the rest of that season the 6'5", 195-pound right-hander won eight of ten decisions as a starter in the Rookie League. The following season at Class A, Roesler was pounded as a starter, so the Reds converted him to short relief.

In 1987, Roesler, splitting time between the A and Double-A levels, earned 11 victories and 22 saves as a closer. The next season he won 4 and saved 10 in Double A and Triple A. During the 1989 season, Roesler was promoted to the bigs and used in middle relief.

Roesler, who played college baseball for Ball State University, has good athletic abilities; in high school he played baseball, basketball, and tennis. He should break camp in 1990 as a member of the Reds' middle-relief corps.

| Year | Team | W | L | SV | ERA | IP | H | BB | K |
|------|------|---|---|----|-----|-----|-----|-----|-----|
| 1989 | Cin ...... | 0 | 1 | 0 | 3.96 | 25.0 | 22 | 9 | 14 |
| | | 0 | 1 | 0 | 3.96 | 25.0 | 22 | 9 | 14 |

# Bruce Ruffin

Birth Date: 10/4/63
Throws: Left
1989 Club:
Philadelphia Phillies
Contest Code #: 421

## Rating: 1

The Phillies have had their hands full with former University of Texas star Bruce Wayne Ruffin since his 9–4 rookie season. As a starter in 1987 he went 11–14 with a 4.35 ERA and coughed up 236 hits and 73 walks in 204 ⅔ innings. As a reliever in 1988, Ruffin was 6–10 with a 4.43 ERA, allowing 151 hits and (hold on to your hat) 80 walks in 144 ⅓ innings.

Last year Bruce Ruffin was back in the Phillies' rotation and as wild as *Bull Durham's* Nuke Laloosh. In his first 9 games he was 2–3, allowing 59 hits and 24 walks (an average of 2 base runners per inning) and 27 earned runs (5.98 per 9 innings) in 40 ⅔ innings. After a pit stop in the minors, Ruffin went 4–7 the rest of the way, giving up 93 hits and 38 walks (1.5 base runners), and 35 earned runs (3.70) over 85 innings. Guess you could say ol' Nuke settled down.

If the Phils are hurting for starting pitchers this season, as they were at the start of 1989, Ruffin will get another shot in the rotation.

| Year | Team | W | L | SV | ERA | IP | H | BB | K |
|---|---|---|---|---|---|---|---|---|---|
| 1986 | Phi ...... | 9 | 4 | 0 | 2.46 | 146.1 | 138 | 44 | 70 |
| 1987 | Phi ...... | 11 | 14 | 0 | 4.35 | 204.2 | 236 | 73 | 93 |
| 1988 | Phi ...... | 6 | 10 | 3 | 4.43 | 144.1 | 151 | 80 | 82 |
| 1989 | Phi ...... | 6 | 10 | 0 | 4.44 | 125.2 | 152 | 62 | 70 |
| | | 32 | 38 | 3 | 3.94 | 621.0 | 677 | 259 | 315 |

# Scott Sanderson

Birth Date: 7/22/56
Throws: Right
1989 Club:
Chicago Cubs
Contest Code #: 422

## Rating: 1

Since joining the Cubs in 1984, Scott Sanderson has had the body of a twig. He's been on the disabled list in 1984 (back spasms), 1985 (a partial tear of the medial collateral ligament in his right knee), 1987 (tenderness of the right shoulder), and 1988 (removal of a disc in his back).

When healthy, Sanderson has been quite hittable. In 737 ⅓ innings since 1984 he's given up 312 earned runs (3.8 per 9 innings). Last season Sanderson became a forgotten man on the Cubs' staff when manager Don Zimmer excluded him from the three-man rotation he used the last two months of 1989. Sanderson, who'd hurled 92 ⅓ innings before the All-Star break, pitched only 54 innings over the second half.

Sanderson needs pinpoint control in the lower half of the strike zone to be effective. Whenever his pitches are waist-level or higher, hitters bang them out to Waverly Avenue.

| Year | Team | W | L | SV | ERA | IP | H | BB | K |
|---|---|---|---|---|---|---|---|---|---|
| 1978 | Mon ..... | 4 | 2 | 0 | 2.51 | 61.0 | 52 | 21 | 50 |
| 1979 | Mon ..... | 9 | 8 | 1 | 3.43 | 168.0 | 148 | 54 | 138 |
| 1980 | Mon ..... | 16 | 11 | 0 | 3.11 | 211.0 | 206 | 56 | 125 |
| 1981 | Mon ..... | 9 | 7 | 0 | 2.96 | 137.0 | 122 | 31 | 77 |
| 1982 | Mon ..... | 12 | 12 | 0 | 3.46 | 224.0 | 212 | 58 | 158 |
| 1983 | Mon ..... | 6 | 7 | 1 | 4.65 | 81.1 | 98 | 20 | 55 |
| 1984 | ChN...... | 8 | 5 | 0 | 3.14 | 140.2 | 140 | 24 | 76 |
| 1985 | ChN...... | 5 | 6 | 0 | 3.12 | 121.0 | 100 | 27 | 80 |
| 1986 | ChN...... | 9 | 11 | 1 | 4.19 | 169.2 | 165 | 37 | 124 |
| 1987 | ChN...... | 8 | 9 | 2 | 4.29 | 144.2 | 156 | 50 | 106 |
| 1988 | ChN...... | 1 | 2 | 0 | 5.28 | 15.1 | 13 | 3 | 6 |
| 1989 | ChN...... | 11 | 9 | 0 | 3.94 | 146.1 | 155 | 31 | 86 |
| | | 98 | 89 | 5 | 3.55 | 1620.0 | 1567 | 412 | 1081 |

# Calvin Schiraldi

**Birth Date:** 6/16/62
**Throws:** Right
**1989 Clubs:**
**Chicago Cubs &**
**San Diego Padres**
**Contest Code #:** 423

**Rating:** 2

All through the 1989 National League Championship Series NBC's Tom Seaver clucked the praises of Cubs' general manager "Jimmy" Frey for boldly acquiring Mitch Williams to fill the gaping hole in the Cubs' pen. To refresh Seaver's memory, it was Jim Frey who created the gaping hole in the Cubs' 1988 pen by trading Lee Smith to the Red Sox for reliever Calvin Schiraldi and swingman Al Nipper.

Schiraldi, a standout at the University of Texas, has long possessed the ability to be a successful pitcher. After being traded by the Mets to the Red Sox, in 1986 Schiraldi became Boston's closer. But scouts say he has never recovered from his horrendous performances in the 1986 World Series, during which he lost two of three games he appeared in, allowing seven hits, three walks and six earned runs in four innings of work. The Cubs were forced to shift him into their rotation, where he also was ineffective, and last season into middle relief. Just before the August 31 deadline, Frey traded Schiraldi to the Padres.

Under the tutelage of Padres manager Jack McKeon and pitching coach Pat Dobson, Schiraldi is now in an environment where he may regain his skills.

| Year | Team | W | L | SV | ERA | IP | H | BB | K |
|------|------|---|---|----|-----|----|----|----|----|
| 1984 | NYN ..... | 0 | 2 | 0 | 5.71 | 17.1 | 20 | 10 | 16 |
| 1985 | NYN ..... | 2 | 1 | 0 | 8.89 | 26.1 | 43 | 11 | 21 |
| 1986 | Bos ...... | 4 | 2 | 9 | 1.41 | 51.0 | 36 | 15 | 55 |
| 1987 | Bos ...... | 8 | 5 | 6 | 4.41 | 83.2 | 75 | 40 | 93 |
| 1988 | ChN...... | 9 | 13 | 1 | 4.38 | 166.1 | 166 | 63 | 140 |
| 1989 | ChN...... | 3 | 6 | 4 | 3.78 | 78.2 | 60 | 50 | 54 |
| 1989 | SD....... | 3 | 1 | 0 | 2.53 | 21.1 | 12 | 13 | 17 |
| | | 29 | 30 | 20 | 4.17 | 444.2 | 412 | 202 | 396 |

# Don Schulze

**Birth Date:** 9/27/62
**Throws:** Right
**1989 Club:**
**San Diego Padres**
**Contest Code #:** 424

**Rating:** 1

If this book were titled *Triple A Baseball Contest*, Don Schulze would be your number-one starter. Schulze has won in double figures three times at the Triple A level. In 1987, Schulze had a glittering 11–1 record with the Mets' Tidewater club, and in 1988 he posted a 3.11 ERA over 185⅓ for the Tigers' team in Toledo.

Unfortunately, Schulze, now with the Padres, doesn't have enough of the equipment necessary to win on the major-league level. When he's on his game, Schulze has good control, but his below-average fastball isn't that much faster than his offspeed pitches.

Perhaps Schulze's greatest claim to fame is that he once sued Ted Gianounis, better known as "The San Diego Chicken," claiming the well-known mascot inflicted a shoulder injury on him while wrestling with him between innings of a minor-league game. Schulze lost the suit.

| Year | Team | W | L | SV | ERA | IP | H | BB | K |
|------|------|---|---|----|-----|----|----|----|----|
| 1983 | ChN...... | 0 | 1 | 0 | 7.07 | 14.0 | 19 | 7 | 8 |
| 1984 | Cle ...... | 3 | 6 | 0 | 4.83 | 85.2 | 105 | 27 | 39 |
| 1984 | ChN...... | 0 | 0 | 0 | 12.00 | 3.0 | 8 | 1 | 2 |
| 1985 | Cle ...... | 4 | 10 | 0 | 6.01 | 94.1 | 128 | 19 | 37 |
| 1986 | Cle ...... | 4 | 4 | 0 | 5.00 | 84.2 | 88 | 34 | 33 |
| 1987 | NYN ..... | 1 | 2 | 0 | 6.23 | 21.2 | 24 | 6 | 5 |

| Year | Team | W | L | SV | ERA | IP | H | BB | K |
|------|------|---|---|----|----|----|---|----|---|
| 1989 | NYA...... | 1 | 1 | 0 | 4.09 | 11.0 | 12 | 5 | 5 |
| 1989 | SD....... | 2 | 1 | 0 | 5.55 | 24.1 | 38 | 6 | 15 |
|  |  | 15 | 25 | 0 | 5.47 | 338.2 | 422 | 105 | 144 |

# Mike Scott

**Birth Date: 4/26/55**
**Throws: Right**
**1989 Club:**
**Houston Astros**
**Contest Code #: 425**

**Rating: 5**

Since 1985 Mike Scott has been accused of defacing the baseball to make his split-fingered fastball drop like an anvil when it reaches the hitting zone. Call him a scuffer; I call him a craftsman.

Check out his victory totals over the past five seasons since 1985: 18, 18, 16, 14, and a league-leading 20. Check out his earned run averages: 3.29, a league-leading 2.22, 3.23, 2.92, and 3.10. Last season he allowed an average of only 1.06 base runners (180 hits and 62 walks) over 229 innings. And talk about innings: Scott has hurled 218 or better per season since 1985, including a league-best 275⅓ in 1986. Strikeouts? He's averaged 208 a season the past five years.

Call Scott whatever you will, but five years after his career has ended you may be calling him a Hall of Famer.

| Year | Team | W | L | SV | ERA | IP | H | BB | K |
|------|------|---|---|----|----|----|---|----|---|
| 1979 | NYN ..... | 1 | 3 | 0 | 5.37 | 52.0 | 59 | 20 | 21 |
| 1980 | NYN ..... | 1 | 1 | 0 | 4.34 | 29.0 | 40 | 8 | 13 |
| 1981 | NYN ..... | 5 | 10 | 0 | 3.90 | 136.0 | 130 | 34 | 54 |
| 1982 | NYN ..... | 7 | 13 | 3 | 5.14 | 147.0 | 185 | 60 | 63 |
| 1983 | Hou...... | 10 | 6 | 0 | 3.72 | 145.0 | 143 | 46 | 73 |
| 1984 | Hou...... | 5 | 11 | 0 | 4.68 | 154.0 | 179 | 43 | 83 |
| 1985 | Hou...... | 18 | 8 | 0 | 3.29 | 221.2 | 194 | 80 | 137 |
| 1986 | Hou...... | 18 | 10 | 0 | 2.22 | 275.1 | 182 | 72 | 306 |
| 1987 | Hou...... | 16 | 13 | 0 | 3.23 | 247.2 | 199 | 79 | 233 |
| 1988 | Hou...... | 14 | 8 | 0 | 2.92 | 218.2 | 162 | 53 | 190 |
| 1989 | Hou...... | 20 | 10 | 0 | 3.10 | 229.0 | 180 | 62 | 172 |
|  |  | 115 | 93 | 3 | 3.47 | 1855.1 | 1653 | 557 | 1345 |

# Scott Scudder

**Birth Date: 2/14/68**
**Throws: Right**
**1989 Club:**
**Cincinnati Reds**
**Contest Code #: 426**

**Rating: 4**

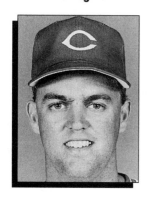

I'd always been leery of the way former Reds manager Pete Rose handled young pitchers promoted from the Reds' system. When they pitched well he'd used them, but after one bad outing he'd relegate them to long relief. I recall how in 1988 he never showed confidence in right-hander Jack Armstrong, and in 1989 he never seemed comfortable with Scott Scudder.

Scudder is one of the best right-handed pitching prospects in baseball. The Reds' first pick in the June 1986 draft, Scudder was voted by league managers as the third-best pitching prospect in the Pioneer League in 1986 even though he'd won only one game. In 1987 Scudder pitched a no-hitter for Class-A Cedar Rapids and was cited by Midwest League managers as the league's second-best pitching prospect. The following year Scudder went 7–3 with a 2.02 ERA for Cedar Rapids, and 7–0 with a 2.96 ERA for Double-A Chattanooga, as both teams won league championships.

Last year Scudder was promoted from Triple A and appeared in 23 games with the Reds, 17 as a starter. The new manager of the Reds should put Scudder in the 1990 rotation right away and keep him there.

| Year | Team | W | L | SV | ERA | IP | H | BB | K |
|------|------|---|---|----|----|----|---|----|----|
| 1989 | Cin ...... | 4 | 9 | 0 | 4.49 | 100.1 | 91 | 61 | 66 |
| | | 4 | 9 | 0 | 4.49 | 100.1 | 91 | 61 | 66 |

# Ray Searage

**Birth Date: 5/1/55**
**Throws: Left**
**1989 Club:**
**Los Angeles Dodgers**
**Contest Code #: 427**

**Rating: 1**

Ray Searage is the poster boy for those who say there's a shortage of left-handed relievers in baseball. Originally drafted in the twenty-second round of the June draft 16 years ago, Searage is still hanging in despite having played just six major-league seasons.

Searage has since served time in six organizations—the Mets, Cleveland Indians, Padres, Brewers, White Sox, and Dodgers. He's been traded four times, three times for other players—catcher Jody Davis in 1979; utility infielder Tom Veryzer in 1982; pitcher Al Jones and outfielder Tom Hartley in 1986—and once for himself. On December 15, 1982, the Indians traded Searage to the Padres for a player to be named later; on March 28, 1983, the Padres returned Searage to the Indians to complete the trade.

Last year the Dodgers called him up from Triple A and used him to pitch one batter or one inning at a time. That means that his ERA can catch fire in one bad outing.

| Year | Team | W | L | SV | ERA | IP | H | BB | K |
|------|------|---|---|----|----|----|---|----|----|
| 1981 | NYN ..... | 1 | 0 | 1 | 3.65 | 37.0 | 34 | 17 | 16 |
| 1984 | Mil ...... | 2 | 1 | 6 | 0.70 | 38.1 | 20 | 16 | 29 |
| 1985 | Mil ...... | 1 | 4 | 1 | 5.92 | 38.0 | 54 | 24 | 36 |
| 1986 | Mil ...... | 0 | 1 | 1 | 6.95 | 22.0 | 29 | 9 | 10 |
| 1986 | ChA..... | 1 | 0 | 0 | 0.62 | 29.0 | 15 | 19 | 26 |
| 1987 | ChA..... | 2 | 3 | 2 | 4.20 | 55.2 | 56 | 24 | 33 |
| 1989 | LA ....... | 3 | 4 | 0 | 3.53 | 35.2 | 29 | 18 | 24 |
| | | 10 | 13 | 11 | 3.59 | 255.2 | 237 | 127 | 174 |

# Eric Show

**Birth Date: 5/19/56**
**Throws: Right**
**1989 Club:**
**San Diego Padres**
**Contest Code #: 428**

**Rating: 2**

Eric Show has always been right smack in the middle of many Padres clubhouse controversies. Where do we begin? With his ongoing feud with catcher Benito Santiago? With his 1987 beaning of Andre Dawson? Or with his acting career, on which teammates felt he was focusing too much attention last year?

Show was once a promising pitcher, but he's never been the same since his post season pastings by the Cubs and Tigers in 1984. During the 1984 National League Championship Series, he gave up a record-tying eight earned runs (in only 5 ⅓ innings), and in the Fall Classic he went 2 ⅔ innings, giving up four hits and three earned runs for an ERA of 10.13.

Since then, he's been an average pitcher. He tends to pitch in streaks, and you don't want to have him on your team when he's in the midst of a bad one.

| Year | Team | W | L | SV | ERA | IP | H | BB | K |
|------|------|---|---|----|----|----|---|----|----|
| 1981 | SD....... | 1 | 3 | 3 | 3.13 | 23.0 | 17 | 9 | 22 |
| 1982 | SD....... | 10 | 6 | 3 | 2.64 | 150.0 | 117 | 48 | 88 |
| 1983 | SD....... | 15 | 12 | 0 | 4.17 | 200.2 | 201 | 74 | 120 |
| 1984 | SD....... | 15 | 9 | 0 | 3.40 | 206.2 | 175 | 88 | 104 |
| 1985 | SD....... | 12 | 11 | 0 | 3.09 | 233.0 | 212 | 87 | 141 |
| 1986 | SD....... | 9 | 5 | 0 | 2.97 | 136.1 | 109 | 69 | 94 |

| Year | Team | W | L | SV | ERA | IP | H | BB | K |
|---|---|---|---|---|---|---|---|---|---|
| 1987 | SD....... | 8 | 16 | 0 | 3.84 | 206.1 | 188 | 85 | 117 |
| 1988 | SD....... | 16 | 11 | 0 | 3.26 | 234.2 | 201 | 53 | 144 |
| 1989 | SD....... | 8 | 6 | 0 | 4.23 | 106.1 | 113 | 39 | 66 |
| | | 94 | 79 | 6 | 3.43 | 1497.0 | 1333 | 552 | 896 |

# John Smiley

**Birth Date:** 3/17/65
**Throws:** Left
**1989 Club:**
**Pittsburgh Pirates**
**Contest Code #: 429**

**Rating: 5**

John Smiley is my kind of pitcher. He has the aptitude and athletic abilities of a steady 20-game winner. In September 1986 former Pirates general manager Syd Thrift promoted Smiley from Class A to the big leagues, and after getting his feet wet as a reliever in 1987 Smiley has become the league's best young left-hander.

He uses his fastball, slider, change-up, and curve to perfection, routinely breaking hitters' bats. His control is outstanding, as evidenced by his 46 walks in 205 innings in 1988, and 49 in 205⅓ last year.

With better offensive support—the Pirates' eighth-ranked offense batted .241 and averaged 3.9 runs per game—Smiley will win 20 games in 1990. If the Pirates don't score many runs, Smiley will still come close to 20 wins.

| Year | Team | W | L | SV | ERA | IP | H | BB | K |
|---|---|---|---|---|---|---|---|---|---|
| 1986 | Pit....... | 1 | 0 | 0 | 3.86 | 11.2 | 4 | 4 | 9 |
| 1987 | Pit....... | 5 | 5 | 4 | 5.76 | 75.0 | 69 | 50 | 58 |
| 1988 | Pit....... | 13 | 11 | 0 | 3.25 | 205.0 | 185 | 46 | 129 |
| 1989 | Pit....... | 12 | 8 | 0 | 2.81 | 205.1 | 174 | 49 | 123 |
| | | 31 | 24 | 4 | 3.46 | 497.0 | 432 | 149 | 319 |

# Bryn Smith

**Birth Date:** 8/11/55
**Throws:** Right
**1989 Club:**
**Montreal Expos**
**Contest Code #: 430**

**Rating: 3**

Though Bryn Smith's winningest season was five years ago, he's still an effective pitcher. In his last 413⅔ innings, from 1988 through 1989, Smith has averaged 11 victories and 11 losses, 1.07 base runners per inning, and 2.92 runs per 9 innings. These numbers were good enough for the St. Louis Cardinals, who signed Smith during the off-season.

Smith's fastball is below average, so he controls the strike zone with four pitches—fastball, curves, palm balls, and slider—thrown at different speeds. Smith's value on a fantasy team grows as the season moves along because he gives you enough good innings to help lower your team ERA.

| Year | Team | W | L | SV | ERA | IP | H | BB | K |
|---|---|---|---|---|---|---|---|---|---|
| 1981 | Mon ..... | 1 | 0 | 0 | 2.77 | 13.0 | 14 | 3 | 9 |
| 1982 | Mon ..... | 2 | 4 | 3 | 4.20 | 79.1 | 81 | 23 | 50 |
| 1983 | Mon ..... | 6 | 11 | 3 | 2.49 | 155.1 | 142 | 43 | 101 |
| 1984 | Mon ..... | 12 | 13 | 0 | 3.32 | 179.0 | 178 | 51 | 101 |
| 1985 | Mon ..... | 18 | 5 | 0 | 2.91 | 222.1 | 193 | 41 | 127 |
| 1986 | Mon ..... | 10 | 8 | 0 | 3.94 | 187.1 | 182 | 63 | 105 |
| 1987 | Mon ..... | 10 | 9 | 0 | 4.37 | 150.1 | 164 | 31 | 94 |
| 1988 | Mon ..... | 12 | 10 | 0 | 3.00 | 198.0 | 179 | 32 | 122 |
| 1989 | Mon ..... | 10 | 11 | 0 | 2.84 | 215.2 | 177 | 54 | 129 |
| | | 81 | 71 | 6 | 3.28 | 1400.1 | 1310 | 341 | 838 |

# Dave Smith

Birth Date: 1/21/55
Throws: Right
1989 Club:
Houston Astros
Contest Code #: 431

Rating: 5

**D**ave Smith gets a high rating because he has consistently ranked among the National League's save leaders the past five seasons. But if you're considering Smith for your staff, bear in mind that:

Over the past four seasons, injuries have limited him to an average of 52 appearances a year, 10 to 20 games below the appearances made by most closers. Over the past two seasons, he's allowed an average of 1.27 base runners per inning and 2.65 earned runs per 9 innings—good numbers, but well below his 1987 averages.

The point is, Smith may still be a fine closer, but he's not the pitcher he once was.

| Year | Team | W | L | SV | ERA | IP | H | BB | K |
|------|------|---|---|----|----|----|---|----|---|
| 1980 | Hou...... | 7 | 5 | 10 | 1.92 | 103.0 | 90 | 32 | 85 |
| 1981 | Hou...... | 5 | 3 | 8 | 2.76 | 75.0 | 54 | 23 | 52 |
| 1982 | Hou...... | 5 | 4 | 11 | 3.84 | 63.1 | 69 | 31 | 28 |
| 1983 | Hou...... | 3 | 1 | 6 | 3.10 | 72.2 | 72 | 36 | 41 |
| 1984 | Hou...... | 5 | 4 | 5 | 2.21 | 77.1 | 60 | 20 | 45 |
| 1985 | Hou...... | 9 | 5 | 27 | 2.27 | 79.1 | 69 | 17 | 40 |
| 1986 | Hou...... | 4 | 7 | 33 | 2.73 | 56.0 | 39 | 22 | 46 |
| 1987 | Hou...... | 2 | 3 | 24 | 1.65 | 60.0 | 39 | 21 | 73 |
| 1988 | Hou...... | 4 | 5 | 27 | 2.67 | 57.1 | 60 | 19 | 38 |
| 1989 | Hou...... | 3 | 4 | 25 | 2.64 | 58.0 | 49 | 19 | 31 |
| | | 47 | 41 | 176 | 2.54 | 702.0 | 601 | 240 | 479 |

# Mike Smith

Birth Date: 10/31/63
Throws: Right
1989 Club:
Pittsburgh Pirates
Contest Code #: 432

Rating: 1

**T**here are two pitchers in pro baseball named Michael Anthony Smith. The Smith born in Jackson, Mississippi, on February 23, 1961, has sojourned through many organizations, from the Reds to the Expos, back to the Reds and back to the Expos, and on to the Orioles. The Smith born in San Antonio, Texas, on October 31, 1963, has wandered through four organizations, from the Padres to the Reds to the Orioles and now to the Pirates.

"Texas Mike" has had a wild minor league career. In 1986 he tied for the Midwest League lead in wild pitches (19). In 1987 he led the Eastern League in walks issued (117, in 171⅓ innings). In 1988 he led the Southern League in hit batsmen (10) and walks issued (98, in 194⅓ innings).

In 1989, Texas Mike was called up by the Pirates. In 28 innings of relief he allowed 28 hits, 10 walks and 10 earned runs. Some relief.

| Year | Team | W | L | SV | ERA | IP | H | BB | K |
|------|------|---|---|----|----|----|---|----|---|
| 1984 | Cin ...... | 1 | 0 | 0 | 5.23 | 10.1 | 12 | 5 | 7 |
| 1985 | Cin ...... | 0 | 0 | 0 | 5.41 | 3.1 | 2 | 1 | 2 |
| 1986 | Cin ...... | 0 | 0 | 0 | 13.51 | 3.1 | 7 | 1 | 1 |
| 1988 | Mon ..... | 0 | 0 | 1 | 3.12 | 8.2 | 6 | 5 | 4 |
| 1989 | Pit....... | 0 | 1 | 0 | 3.75 | 24.0 | 28 | 10 | 12 |
| | | 1 | 1 | 1 | 4.71 | 49.2 | 55 | 22 | 26 |

# Peter Smith

**Birth Date:** 2/27/66
**Throws:** Right
**1989 Club:**
**Atlanta Braves**
**Contest Code #:** 433

**Rating: 2**

If players could sue their teams for rushing them to the big leagues and throwing them to the wolves, Peter Smith would win a huge award for damages.

The Braves acquired the well-touted Smith from the Phillies organization in December 1985 along with catcher Ozzie Virgil for Steve Bedrosian and outfielder Milt Thompson. Smith, who in 1985 was 12–10 with a 3.29 ERA for the Phillies' Clearwater (Florida State League) club, slid to 1–8 with a 5.85 ERA for the Braves' Greenville (Southern League) club in 1986. The following year, after going 9–9 with a 3.35 ERA, Smith, then age twenty-one, was called up by the Braves late in the season.

In 1988 the Braves should have kept Smith in Triple A so that he could have experienced some success to build his confidence. But, no; the Braves, starved for starters, put Smith in their regular rotation. He survived a horrible first half and managed to win four of six decisions with a 2.27 ERA in the second half. Last year Smith was ineffective all season long. Now twenty-four, Smith is saddled with a 13–31 record.

| Year | Team | W | L | SV | ERA | IP | H | BB | K |
|------|------|---|---|----|----|----|----|----|----|
| 1987 | Atl....... | 1 | 2 | 0 | 4.83 | 31.2 | 39 | 14 | 11 |
| 1988 | Atl....... | 7 | 15 | 0 | 3.69 | 195.1 | 183 | 88 | 124 |
| 1989 | Atl....... | 5 | 14 | 0 | 4.75 | 142.0 | 144 | 57 | 115 |
| | | 13 | 31 | 0 | 4.20 | 369.0 | 366 | 159 | 250 |

# Zane Smith

**Birth Date:** 12/28/60
**Throws:** Left
**1989 Clubs:**
**Atlanta Braves &**
**Montreal Expos**
**Contest Code #:** 434

**Rating: 1**

When he was healthy, Zane Smith could have used an offspeed pitch to go with his fastball and slider. But years of elbow problems have slowed his fastball and slider to the point where they are now in the offspeed category.

Smith is nowhere close to the pitcher he was in 1987. Last year the Braves wrung out whatever he had left as a starter, then traded him to the Expos. Smith finished the season in middle relief. If Smith can develop an assortment of offspeed pitches that don't tax his elbow, he may have a few productive years left.

| Year | Team | W | L | SV | ERA | IP | H | BB | K |
|------|------|---|---|----|----|----|----|----|----|
| 1984 | Atl....... | 1 | 0 | 0 | 2.25 | 20.0 | 16 | 13 | 16 |
| 1985 | Atl....... | 9 | 10 | 0 | 3.80 | 147.0 | 135 | 80 | 85 |
| 1986 | Atl....... | 8 | 16 | 1 | 4.05 | 204.2 | 209 | 105 | 139 |
| 1987 | Atl....... | 15 | 10 | 0 | 4.09 | 242.0 | 245 | 91 | 130 |
| 1988 | Atl....... | 5 | 10 | 0 | 4.30 | 140.1 | 159 | 44 | 59 |
| 1989 | Atl....... | 1 | 12 | 0 | 4.45 | 99.0 | 102 | 33 | 58 |
| 1989 | Mon ..... | 0 | 1 | 2 | 1.50 | 48.0 | 39 | 19 | 35 |
| | | 39 | 59 | 3 | 3.93 | 901.0 | 905 | 385 | 522 |

# John Smoltz

**Birth Date:** 5/15/67
**Throws:** Right
**1989 Club:**
Atlanta Braves
**Contest Code #:** 435

**Rating: 4**

On most other teams, John Smoltz would have won 20 games last season. By July 11, Smoltz, named to the National League All-Star team, was 11–6 with a 2.11 ERA. In 132⅔ innings he allowed 98 hits and struck out 104. But pitching for the Braves, who had the National League's worst offense, Smoltz won just one more game the rest of the way.

Smoltz has a great arm and a fine aptitude for pitching. Scouts expect him to become a consistent winner, even if he doesn't get better offensive support. Dubbed "Holy Smoltz" during his days in the Tigers organization, Smoltz should terrorize batters this season.

| Year | Team | W | L | SV | ERA | IP | H | BB | K |
|------|------|---|---|----|----|----|----|----|----|
| 1988 | Atl……. | 2 | 7 | 0 | 5.48 | 64.0 | 74 | 33 | 37 |
| 1989 | Atl……. | 12 | 11 | 0 | 2.94 | 208.0 | 160 | 72 | 168 |
| | | 14 | 18 | 0 | 3.54 | 272.0 | 234 | 105 | 205 |

# Mike Stanton

**Birth Date:** 6/2/67
**Throws:** Left
**1989 Club:**
Atlanta Braves
**Contest Code #:** 436

**Rating: 3**

The Braves were so thrilled to acquire young Mike Stanton last August that they simply couldn't wait to make him their closer. Within days of his arrival, Stanton replaced Joe Boever as their bullpen's top banana. Stanton finished 10 games, saving 7, and struck out 27 batters in 24 innings.

Looking at the Braves' long-term picture, the hard-throwing Stanton should be used a a co-closer and setup man this season. He should not be expected to take on all the closing responsibilities so early in his career. Trouble is, the Braves' management has reached the point where their jobs are on the line. It's always the young and innocent who suffer most.

| Year | Team | W | L | SV | ERA | IP | H | BB | K |
|------|------|---|---|----|----|----|----|----|----|
| 1989 | Atl……. | 0 | 1 | 7 | 1.50 | 24.0 | 17 | 8 | 27 |
| | | 0 | 1 | 7 | 1.50 | 24.0 | 17 | 8 | 27 |

# Rick Sutcliffe

**Birth Date:** 6/21/56
**Throws:** Right
**1989 Club:**
Chicago Cubs
**Contest Code #:** 437

**Rating: 3**

In his 13-year career, Rick Sutcliffe has established himself as a double-figure winner who gives up lots of earned runs, hits, and walks, gets hurt often, and will have horrible seasons when you least expect them.

After earning National League Rookie of the Year honors in 1979, Sutcliffe feuded with manager Tom Lasorda and was dealt to Cleveland in December 1981. Sutcliffe returned to his first-year form in 1982, but slid in 1983. Right before the June 1984 trading deadline, Sutcliffe was traded to the Cubs. Over his next 20 starts, Sutcliffe was the best pitcher in baseball.

But that was six years ago. Since then Sutcliffe has averaged 12 victories, 11 losses, a 3.82 ERA, and almost 1 appearance on the disabled list per season.

| Year | Team | W | L | SV | ERA | IP | H | BB | K |
|------|------|---|---|----|----|----|----|----|----|
| 1976 | LA……. | 0 | 0 | 0 | 0.00 | 5.0 | 2 | 1 | 3 |
| 1978 | LA……. | 0 | 0 | 0 | 0.00 | 2.0 | 2 | 1 | 0 |
| 1979 | LA……. | 17 | 10 | 0 | 3.46 | 242.0 | 217 | 97 | 117 |
| 1980 | LA……. | 3 | 9 | 5 | 5.56 | 110.0 | 122 | 55 | 59 |

| 1981 | LA....... | 2 | 2 | 0 | 4.02 | 47.0 | 41 | 20 | 16 |
| 1982 | Cle ...... | 14 | 8 | 1 | 2.96 | 216.0 | 174 | 98 | 142 |
| 1983 | Cle ...... | 17 | 11 | 0 | 4.29 | 243.1 | 251 | 102 | 160 |
| 1984 | Cle ...... | 4 | 5 | 0 | 5.15 | 94.1 | 111 | 46 | 58 |
| 1984 | ChN..... | 16 | 1 | 0 | 2.69 | 150.1 | 123 | 39 | 155 |
| 1985 | ChN..... | 8 | 8 | 0 | 3.18 | 130.0 | 119 | 44 | 102 |
| 1986 | ChN..... | 5 | 14 | 0 | 4.64 | 176.2 | 166 | 96 | 122 |
| 1987 | ChN..... | 18 | 10 | 0 | 3.68 | 237.1 | 223 | 106 | 174 |
| 1988 | ChN..... | 13 | 14 | 0 | 3.86 | 226.0 | 232 | 70 | 144 |
| 1989 | ChN..... | 16 | 11 | 0 | 3.66 | 229.0 | 202 | 69 | 153 |
| | | 133 | 103 | 6 | 3.81 | 2109.0 | 1985 | 844 | 1405 |

# Rick Thompson

Birth Date: 11/1/58
Throws: Right
1989 Club:
Montreal Expos
Contest Code #: 438

**Rating: 2**

Reliever Rich Thompson gave a big lift to the Expos' wounded middle-inning corps last season. In 19 games (including one start) he finished 9, allowing only 8 earned runs and 11 walks in 33 innings.

In 1988, Thompson pitched for the Royals' Triple-A club in Omaha. As a spot starter and middle reliever, Thompson won six games, completed four, and saved two. He issued just 15 walks and 31 earned runs in 96 innings.

Judging from the way Expos manager Buck Rodgers uses all his relief pitchers in clearly defined roles, Thompson should see plenty of middle-inning action in 1990.

| Year | Team | W | L | SV | ERA | IP | H | BB | K |
|---|---|---|---|---|---|---|---|---|---|
| 1985 | Cle ...... | 3 | 8 | 5 | 6.30 | 80.0 | 95 | 48 | 30 |
| 1989 | Mon ..... | 0 | 2 | 0 | 2.18 | 33.0 | 27 | 11 | 15 |
| | | 3 | 10 | 5 | 5.10 | 113.0 | 122 | 59 | 45 |

# Sergio Valdez

Birth Date: 9/7/65
Throws: Right
1989 Club:
Atlanta Braves
Contest Code #: 439

**Rating: 1**

Hard-throwing Sergio Valdez was pounded last year in his second go-round on the major-league level. His first call-up came in 1986, when the Expos' pitching staff was decimated by injuries. Valdez vaulted from Class A to a start against the Mets, that season's eventual World Series winner. Sergio didn't make it through the first inning.

The following season Valdez won 10 games at Triple-A Indianapolis and tied for the American Association lead in shutouts. In 1988 he won half as many games and last season was sent to the Braves.

Watching Valdez last season reminded me of my 1986 impressionof him: good arm, inconsistent motion, needs to learn the strike zone.

| Year | Team | W | L | SV | ERA | IP | H | BB | K |
|---|---|---|---|---|---|---|---|---|---|
| 1986 | Mon ..... | 0 | 4 | 0 | 6.84 | 25.0 | 39 | 11 | 20 |
| 1989 | Atl....... | 1 | 2 | 0 | 6.06 | 32.2 | 31 | 17 | 26 |
| | | 1 | 6 | 0 | 6.40 | 57.2 | 70 | 28 | 46 |

# Fernando Valenzuela

**Birth Date: 11/1/60**
**Throws: Left**
**1989 Club:**
**Los Angeles Dodgers**
**Contest Code #: 440**

**Rating: 3**

Fernando, welcome back from your two-year hide-away. You may not look like the Fernando of old—and, may I say, those glasses make you look quite old—but for a pitcher everyone gave up for dead, you look mahvelous, absolutely mahvelous.

Valenzuela, who once looked like the next Sandy Koufax, now looks more and more like Frank Tanana. Valenzuela has become a master of throwing junk at different speeds to different locations.

Actually, Valenzuela blends in well with the hard throwers in the Dodgers' rotation. As a number-three or -four pitcher, Valenzuela can mess up the timing of opposing batters who've grown accustomed to the heat from Orel Hershiser, Tim Belcher, and Ramon Martinez. And though Valenzuela is no longer a staff ace, he still knows how to pitch.

| Year | Team | W | L | SV | ERA | IP | H | BB | K |
|------|------|---|---|----|----|----|----|----|----|
| 1980 | LA....... | 2 | 0 | 1 | 0.00 | 18.0 | 8 | 5 | 16 |
| 1981 | LA....... | 13 | 7 | 0 | 2.48 | 192.0 | 140 | 61 | 180 |
| 1982 | LA....... | 19 | 13 | 0 | 2.87 | 285.0 | 247 | 83 | 199 |
| 1983 | LA....... | 15 | 10 | 0 | 3.75 | 257.0 | 245 | 99 | 189 |
| 1984 | LA....... | 12 | 17 | 0 | 3.03 | 261.0 | 218 | 106 | 240 |
| 1985 | LA....... | 17 | 10 | 0 | 2.45 | 272.1 | 211 | 101 | 208 |
| 1986 | LA....... | 21 | 11 | 0 | 3.14 | 269.1 | 226 | 85 | 242 |
| 1987 | LA....... | 14 | 14 | 0 | 3.98 | 251.0 | 254 | 124 | 190 |
| 1988 | LA....... | 5 | 8 | 1 | 4.24 | 142.1 | 142 | 76 | 64 |
| 1989 | LA....... | 10 | 13 | 0 | 3.43 | 196.2 | 185 | 98 | 116 |
| | | 128 | 103 | 2 | 3.19 | 2144.2 | 1876 | 838 | 1644 |

# Frank Viola

**Birth Date: 4/19/60**
**Throws: Left**
**1989 Club:**
**Minnesota Twins**
**& New York Mets**
**Contest Code #: 441**

**Rating: 4**

Frank Viola, in the final year of his contract, made a lot of enemies in Minnesota after signing a new pact in line with Orel Hershiser's. After a slow start, Twins fans called Viola "greedy." And after trading Viola to the Mets last July, the executive vice-president of the Twins delivered a nasty parting shot by contending that Viola, the 1988 American League Cy Young Award winner, had lost four to five miles an hour off his fastball.

How quickly they dismissed Viola's past achievements: 200-plus innings for 7 straight seasons; 112 victories over 8 seasons; an ERA under 3.00 in both 1987 and 1988, despite pitching in the Hubert Humphrey "Homer Dome," and an outstanding ratio of walks to innings pitched.

But MacPhail's allegation about Viola's velocity should not be dismissed out of hand. Viola pitched well in his first few Mets starts, but the league caught up with him pretty quickly. If Viola has in fact lost something off his fastball (others who timed him last season agree with MacPhail), Viola's change-up—his best pitch—won't be as effective because it won't be that much slower than his fastball.

| Year | Team | W | L | SV | ERA | IP | H | BB | K |
|------|------|---|---|----|----|----|----|----|----|
| 1982 | Min...... | 4 | 10 | 0 | 5.21 | 126.0 | 152 | 38 | 84 |
| 1983 | Min...... | 7 | 15 | 0 | 5.49 | 210.0 | 242 | 92 | 127 |
| 1984 | Min...... | 18 | 12 | 0 | 3.21 | 257.2 | 225 | 73 | 149 |
| 1985 | Min...... | 18 | 14 | 0 | 4.09 | 250.2 | 262 | 68 | 135 |
| 1986 | Min...... | 16 | 13 | 0 | 4.51 | 245.2 | 257 | 83 | 191 |
| 1987 | Min...... | 17 | 10 | 0 | 2.90 | 251.2 | 230 | 66 | 197 |

| 1988 | Min...... | 24 | 7 | 0 | 2.64 | 255.1 | 236 | 54 | 193 |
| 1989 | Min...... | 8 | 12 | 0 | 3.79 | 175.2 | 171 | 47 | 138 |
| 1989 | NYN ..... | 5 | 5 | 0 | 3.38 | 85.1 | 75 | 27 | 73 |
| | | 117 | 98 | 0 | 3.84 | 1858.0 | 1850 | 548 | 1287 |

# Bob Walk

**Birth Date: 11/26/56**
**Throws: Right**
**1989 Club:**
**Pittsburgh Pirates**
**Contest Code #: 442**

**Rating: 2**

For many years Bob Walk has been his own worst enemy. He's prone to losing his temper when things go wrong, then loses control of the strike zone.

Baseball observers thought Walk had finally matured in 1988, but last season he returned to his erratic ways: 208 hits and 65 walks (an average of 1.4 base runners per inning), and 96 earned runs in 196 innings.

Walk, who has an above-average fastball, slider, and change-up, and a fair curve, rarely pitches a complete game (three in the past three seasons). Therefore, he needs a deep bullpen behind him. If the Pirates can't plug the leaks in their pen this season, Walk is doomed to an encore of 1989.

| Year | Team | W | L | SV | ERA | IP | H | BB | K |
|------|------|---|---|----|----|----|----|----|----|
| 1980 | Phi ..... | 11 | 7 | 0 | 4.56 | 152.0 | 163 | 71 | 94 |
| 1981 | Atl....... | 1 | 4 | 0 | 4.60 | 43.0 | 41 | 23 | 16 |
| 1982 | Atl....... | 11 | 9 | 0 | 4.87 | 164.1 | 179 | 59 | 84 |
| 1983 | Atl....... | 0 | 0 | 0 | 7.38 | 3.2 | 7 | 2 | 4 |
| 1984 | Pit....... | 1 | 1 | 0 | 2.61 | 10.1 | 8 | 4 | 10 |
| 1985 | Pit....... | 2 | 3 | 0 | 3.68 | 58.2 | 60 | 18 | 40 |
| 1986 | Pit....... | 7 | 8 | 2 | 3.75 | 141.2 | 129 | 64 | 78 |
| 1987 | Pit....... | 8 | 2 | 0 | 3.31 | 117.0 | 107 | 51 | 78 |
| 1988 | Pit....... | 12 | 10 | 0 | 2.71 | 212.2 | 183 | 65 | 81 |
| 1989 | Pit....... | 13 | 10 | 0 | 4.41 | 196.0 | 208 | 65 | 83 |
| | | 66 | 54 | 2 | 3.93 | 1099.1 | 1085 | 422 | 568 |

# John Wetteland

**Birth Date: 8/21/66**
**Throws: Right**
**1989 Club:**
**Los Angeles Dodgers**
**Contest Code #: 443**

**Rating: 3**

When John Wetteland was summoned by the Dodgers last season, fans who'd never heard of him didn't know whether he was a pitcher or a theme park. Wetteland was wild in the minors—in 1987 he led the Florida State League in home runs allowed and wild pitches, and in 1988 he led the Texas League in wild pitches. But last year he convinced National League scouts that he has the makings of an above-average major-league starter.

Wetteland had originally been selected by the Mets in the June 1984 draft but chose not to sign with them. He was chosen by—and signed with—the Dodgers in the January 1985 draft. The Tigers claimed Wetteland in the December 1987 draft after the Dodgers left him off their 40-man roster. According to the rules of the winter draft, the Tigers would have had to keep Wetteland on their major-league roster the entire season in order to retain his future rights. When the Detroit decision-makers felt Wetteland wouldn't make their staff, they sent him back to L.A.

Wetteland is a strikeout pitcher. In 1988 he was second in the Texas League in K's (140) and last season fanned 96 in 102⅔ innings. More encouraging was his average of 1.12 base runners per inning in 31 games—12 starts—with the Dodgers.

| Year | Team | W | L | SV | ERA | IP | H | BB | K |
|------|------|---|---|----|-----|----|---|----|----|
| 1989 | LA....... | 5 | 8 | 1 | 3.77 | 102.2 | 81 | 34 | 96 |
| | | 5 | 8 | 1 | 3.77 | 102.2 | 81 | 34 | 96 |

# Ed Whitson

**Birth Date: 5/19/55**
**Throws: Right**
**1989 Club:**
**San Diego Padres**
**Contest Code #: 444**

**Rating: 3**

**W**hich San Diego pitcher led all Padres starters in victories and ERA in 1989? Not high-priced Bruce Hurst, but steady Eddie Whitson.

It took Whitson years to get over his nightmarish season and a half with the Yankees, years in which he was tormented not only by the owner but by unruly fans who vandalized his property and threatened his safety. It wasn't until the second half of the 1988 season that Whitson settled down and regained the form of his early days with the Padres. From the 1988 All-Star break to the end of that season, Whitson posted a 2.74 ERA; in one stretch he allowed only 10 earned runs over 45⅔ innings. Last season Whitson won a career-high 16 games with a career-best 2.66 ERA.

The key to Whitson's success is that he changes speeds—mixing his palm ball with his fastball and slider—and consistently hits the corners of the strike zone.

| Year | Team | W | L | SV | ERA | IP | H | BB | K |
|------|------|---|---|----|-----|----|---|----|----|
| 1977 | Pit....... | 1 | 0 | 0 | 3.37 | 16.0 | 11 | 9 | 10 |
| 1978 | Pit....... | 5 | 6 | 4 | 3.28 | 74.0 | 66 | 37 | 64 |
| 1979 | Pit....... | 2 | 3 | 1 | 4.34 | 58.0 | 53 | 36 | 31 |
| 1979 | SF....... | 5 | 8 | 0 | 3.96 | 100.0 | 98 | 39 | 62 |
| 1980 | SF....... | 11 | 13 | 0 | 3.10 | 212.0 | 222 | 56 | 90 |
| 1981 | SF ....... | 6 | 9 | 0 | 4.02 | 123.0 | 130 | 47 | 65 |
| 1982 | Cle ....... | 4 | 2 | 2 | 3.26 | 107.2 | 91 | 58 | 61 |
| 1983 | SD....... | 5 | 7 | 1 | 4.30 | 144.1 | 143 | 50 | 81 |
| 1984 | SD....... | 14 | 8 | 0 | 3.24 | 189.0 | 181 | 42 | 103 |
| 1985 | NYA...... | 10 | 8 | 0 | 4.88 | 158.2 | 201 | 43 | 89 |
| 1986 | NYA...... | 5 | 2 | 0 | 7.54 | 37.0 | 54 | 23 | 27 |
| 1986 | SD....... | 1 | 7 | 0 | 5.59 | 75.2 | 85 | 37 | 46 |
| 1987 | SD....... | 10 | 13 | 0 | 4.73 | 205.2 | 197 | 64 | 135 |
| 1988 | SD....... | 13 | 11 | 0 | 3.77 | 205.1 | 202 | 45 | 118 |
| 1989 | SD....... | 16 | 11 | 0 | 2.66 | 227.0 | 198 | 48 | 117 |
| | | 108 | 108 | 8 | 3.88 | 1933.1 | 1932 | 634 | 1099 |

# Dean Wilkins

**Birth Date: 8/24/66**
**Throws: Right**
**1989 Club:**
**Chicago Cubs**
**Contest Code #: 445**

**Rating: 2**

**D**urable Dean Wilkins, who in 1988 led all Double-A pitchers in appearances (59) while leading the Eastern League in saves (26) and games finished (49), visited the Cubs for 11 games last season. Though he allowed 13 hits, 9 walks, and 8 earned runs in 15⅔ innings, he did average close to a strikeout an inning.

Wilkins, a native of Chicago, was originally selected by the Yankees in the second round of the January 1986 draft. One and a half months later, the Yanks traded him with pitchers Bob Tewksbury and Rick Scheid for the Cubs' original "Wild Thing," left-hander Steve Trout.

If Wilkins breaks camp with the Cubs, expect him to be used in middle relief.

| Year | Team | W | L | SV | ERA | IP | H | BB | K |
|------|------|---|---|----|-----|----|---|----|----|
| 1989 | ChN...... | 1 | 0 | 0 | 4.60 | 15.2 | 13 | 9 | 14 |
| | | 1 | 0 | 0 | 4.60 | 15.2 | 13 | 9 | 14 |

# Mitch Williams

Birth Date: 11/17/64
Throws: Left
1989 Club:
Chicago Cubs
Contest Code #: 446

## Rating: 5

**M**ost baseball writers have a favorite Mitch Williams story. Mine goes back to August 15, 1987. The Rangers and Red Sox are tied, 6–6, in the eighth inning of a game at Fenway Park. The Sox have a runner on first with one out. Texas manager Bobby Valentine brings in Williams. The "Wild Thing" throws eight straight balls and walks the bases loaded.

Wade Boggs, the best hitter in the American League, steps to the plate. As Williams uncoils and delivers the ball home, he curses at Boggs, "Swing the bat, you {expletive}!" Boggs takes ball one. This continued through the next three pitches—windup, curse, ball—forcing home the winning run.

Scouts say that last year Williams chilled out. Did he mature, or was it that he had little reason to blow his cool last season? Will he come to training camp thinking of his success during the 1989 regular season, or his disappointment at being overlooked by manager Don Zimmer during the post-season? Take Williams, and you take a walk on the wild side.

| Year | Team | W | L | SV | ERA | IP | H | BB | K |
|------|------|---|---|----|----|----|----|----|----|
| 1986 | Tex ...... | 8 | 6 | 8 | 3.58 | 98.0 | 69 | 79 | 90 |
| 1987 | Tex ...... | 8 | 6 | 6 | 3.23 | 108.2 | 63 | 94 | 129 |
| 1988 | Tex ...... | 2 | 7 | 18 | 4.63 | 68.0 | 48 | 47 | 61 |
| 1989 | ChN...... | 4 | 4 | 36 | 2.65 | 81.2 | 71 | 52 | 67 |
| | | 22 | 23 | 68 | 3.46 | 356.1 | 251 | 272 | 347 |

# Steve Wilson

Birth Date: 12/13/64
Throws: Left
1989 Club:
Chicago Cubs
Contest Code #: 447

## Rating: 2

**S**teve Wilson could be a wild card on the Cubs' staff this season. As a middle reliever and spot starter last season, Wilson picked up 6 wins and 2 saves, striking out 65 batters in 85⅔ innings. It's possible that Wilson could again join the rotation when a fifth starter is needed, or serve as a left-handed setup man for Mitch Williams.

Wilson, a British Columbian originally selected by the Rangers on the fourth round of the June 1985 draft, had control problems early in his pro career (he led the Texas League with 103 walks in 1986), but went 9–5 with a 2.44 ERA at the Florida State League in 1987 and 15–7 with a 3.16 ERA with Triple-A Tulsa in 1988. He was traded to the Cubs following the 1988 season in the deal that included Mitch Williams.

In 1989, his first full season, Wilson pitched well until early August, going 5–0 with a 2.82 ERA, but his numbers swelled down the stretch. In his last 29⅓ innings he was rocked for 32 hits and 18 earned runs.

| Year | Team | W | L | SV | ERA | IP | H | BB | K |
|------|------|---|---|----|----|----|----|----|----|
| 1988 | Tex ...... | 0 | 0 | 0 | 5.87 | 7.2 | 7 | 4 | 1 |
| 1989 | ChN...... | 6 | 4 | 2 | 4.20 | 85.2 | 83 | 31 | 65 |
| | | 6 | 4 | 2 | 4.34 | 93.1 | 90 | 35 | 66 |

# Todd Worrell

Birth Date: 9/28/59
Throws: Right
1989 Club:
St. Louis Cardinals
Contest Code #: 448

Rating: 4

**U**nder normal circumstances I'd give Todd Worrell a rating of 5 without batting an eyelash. Worrell has been the league's most dominant closer since being called up late in the 1985 season. He shined in the 1985 World Series. In 1986 he led the league in saves (36) and was named Rookie of the Year. The flame-throwing right-hander earned 33 saves in 1987 and 32 in 1988. I've had Worrell on my fantasy team for most of his career and he never let me down.

But last September Worrell suffered a season-ending elbow injury. At first team doctors hoped rest would suffice. By November they had talked about ligament-replacement surgery, known in baseball circles as "the Tommy John operation."

Whatever the decision, figure Worrell will need time to heal and rehabilitate his arm. When Worrell returns to action, expect Whitey Herzog to ration his appearances carefully the remainder of the season. Therefore, even if Worrell makes a successful comeback, he will earn fewer saves, another reason why he falls short of a 5 rating this year.

| Year | Team | W | L | SV | ERA | IP | H | BB | K |
|------|------|---|---|----|----|----|----|----|----|
| 1985 | StL ...... | 3 | 0 | 5 | 2.91 | 21.2 | 17 | 7 | 17 |
| 1986 | StL ...... | 9 | 10 | 36 | 2.08 | 103.2 | 86 | 41 | 73 |
| 1987 | StL ...... | 8 | 6 | 33 | 2.66 | 94.2 | 86 | 34 | 92 |
| 1988 | StL ...... | 5 | 9 | 32 | 3.00 | 90.0 | 69 | 34 | 78 |
| 1989 | StL ...... | 3 | 5 | 20 | 2.96 | 51.2 | 42 | 26 | 41 |
| | | 28 | 30 | 126 | 2.64 | 361.2 | 300 | 142 | 301 |

# Charlie Leibrandt

Birth Date: 10/4/56
Throws: Left
1989 Club:
Kansas City Royals
Contest Code #: 450

Rating: 4

**T**hough Charlie Leibrandt remains a regular in the Kansas City rotation, it appears that some of his game has begun to slide backward. Nothing earth-shaking, mind you, but enough to get your attention. Leibrandt, who was 17-9 with a 2.69 ERA in his best season (1985), struggled to a 5-11 mark a year ago with a sky-high 5.14 ERA.

The major trouble is his fastball, which has fallen to way below average. As always, his straight change remains his best pitch, and his slider isn't bad. But Charlie has begun to struggle with his control (73 strikeouts, 54 walks in 161 innings last year), and that isn't a good sign.

Once Cincinnati Red property, Charlie jumped from Class A to the majors in under two seasons back in 1979, then spent all or part of the next four seasons with the Reds before being demoted to Indianapolis in 1983, from where he was dealt to the Kansas City organization. He arrived in Kaycee the following year and has remained on the Royals' starting staff ever since.

| Year | Team | W | L | SV | ERA | IP | H | BB | K |
|------|------|---|---|----|----|----|----|----|----|
| 1979 | Cin ...... | 0 | 0 | 0 | 0.00 | 4.0 | 2 | 2 | 1 |
| 1980 | Cin ...... | 10 | 9 | 0 | 4.24 | 174.0 | 200 | 54 | 62 |
| 1981 | Cin ...... | 1 | 1 | 0 | 3.60 | 30.0 | 28 | 15 | 9 |
| 1982 | Cin ...... | 5 | 7 | 2 | 5.10 | 107.2 | 130 | 48 | 34 |
| 1984 | KC....... | 11 | 7 | 0 | 3.63 | 143.2 | 158 | 38 | 53 |
| 1985 | KC....... | 17 | 9 | 0 | 2.69 | 237.2 | 223 | 68 | 108 |
| 1986 | KC....... | 14 | 11 | 0 | 4.09 | 231.1 | 238 | 63 | 108 |
| 1987 | KC....... | 16 | 11 | 0 | 3.41 | 240.1 | 235 | 74 | 151 |

| | | | | | | | | |
|---|---|---|---|---|---|---|---|---|
| 1988 | KC....... | 13 | 12 | 0 | 3.19 | 243.0 | 244 | 62 | 125 |
| 1989 | KC....... | 5 | 11 | 0 | 5.14 | 161.0 | 196 | 54 | 73 |
| | | 92 | 78 | 2 | 3.77 | 1572.2 | 1654 | 478 | 724 |

# Rick Luecken

**Birth Date: 11/15/60**
**Throws: Right**
**1989 Club:**
**Kansas City Royals**
**Contest Code #: 449**

**Rating: 2**

Rick Luecken made at least a few folks sit up and take notice when he finally made his major-league debut last year. A former Seattle Mariner farmhand, Luecken was dealt to the Kansas City Royals along with Danny Tartabull in 1986. A starter in the Seattle organization, Rick switched to the bullpen for the Royals and a combined 9-1 record in 1988 at AA Memphis and AAA Omaha finally won him at shot in Kaycee.

The big (6'6", 210 pounds) righthander pitched 23⅔ innings in 19 appearances, finishing 12 games, winning two of three decisions, and earning his first big-league save. Control remains a problem for the former Texas A&M star, who walked 13 (while striking out 16) last season.

| Year | Team | W | L | SV | ERA | IP | H | BB | K |
|---|---|---|---|---|---|---|---|---|---|
| 1989 | KC....... | 2 | 1 | 1 | 3.42 | 23.2 | 23 | 13 | 16 |
| | | 2 | 1 | 1 | 3.42 | 23.2 | 23 | 13 | 16 |

# OFFICIAL RULES

## NO PURCHASE NECESSARY TO ENTER

1. In the spaces provided on an official entry form, hand print your name, address, and the names and code numbers of the 24 players from the National League whom you have selected for your roster. Only those players profiled in this book may be selected. You must select 6 outfielders, 1 first baseman, 1 second baseman, 1 third baseman, 1 shortstop, 2 additional infielders, 2 catchers, and 10 pitchers. The positions assigned to the players in this book are the positions you must use in choosing your team. Each player profiled in this book has been assigned rating points. Your team's combined rating point total must not exceed 75. You must choose at least one player from at least 6 of the 12 National League teams.

2. Mail your completed entry to: Baseball Contest 1990: National League, P.O. Box 4863, Blair, NE 68009. All entries must be received by the day of the All-Star Game, July 10, 1990. Not responsible for lost, late or misdirected mail.

   Additional official entry forms and a complete listing of the National League players profiled in this book can be obtained by sending a self-addressed, stamped (state of WA residents need not affix return postage), #10 envelope by June 20, 1990 to: National League Baseball Entry Form, P.O. Box 4874, Blair, NE 68009. Limit one request per envelope.

3. One $10,000 prize will be awarded to the individual who has selected the roster with the highest combined actual statistics at the end of the 1990 regular season. Points will be based on actual player performance in 1990 and will be tabulated as follows:

   Batting Average = 1 point for each .001
   Number of Home Runs × 10
   Number of Runs Batted In × 3
   Number of Runs Scored × 3
   Earned Run Average = 1 point for each .01 below 6.00
   Number of Wins × 30
   Number of Losses × − 10
   Number of Saves × 10

   A batter must have at least 100 at bats to earn Batting Average points; a pitcher must pitch at least 20 innings to earn Earned Run Average points. In the event of a tie, the prize will be divided in equal shares among the winners.

Changes to an entrant's roster will not be permitted once mailed. If a chosen player is traded to the American League, sent to the minors, injured or retires during the season, the entrant will only earn points for the player's performance before he left the National League during the 1990 regular season.

4. Prizewinner selection will be under the supervision of the D. L. Blair Corporation, an independent judging organization whose decisions are final. Potential winners must respond to any required Affidavit of Eligibility/Prize Acceptance Form within 21 days of attempted delivery of same. Noncompliance within this time period will result in disqualification and an alternate will be selected. Winners will be notified by mail. Taxes on prize are the sole responsibility of the winner(s). No substitution or transfer of prize permitted. Chances of winning are determined by the total number of entries received.

5. Sweepstakes participation open to U.S. citizens residing in the U.S., except employees of Cloverdale Press Inc., Little, Brown & Co., their subsidiaries, affiliates, advertising and promotion agencies and their immediate family members. Offer is subject to all federal, state and local laws and regulations and is void in Puerto Rico and wherever prohibited by law. Winner's entry and acceptance of prize offered constitute permission to use name of winner(s), photograph, or other likeness for purposes of advertising and promotion on behalf of Cloverdale Press Inc. and/or Little, Brown & Co., without further compensation to the winner.

6. For the name of the winner(s), available after March 15, 1991, send a separate, self-addressed, stamped, #10 envelope to: Baseball Winner: National League, P. 0. Box 4888, Blair, NE 68009.

# BASEBALL CONTEST 1990: NATIONAL LEAGUE PLAYERS

# OFFICIAL ENTRY FORM

## NO PURCHASE NECESSARY TO ENTER

Please Print Clearly:

Name _____

Address _____

City _____ State _____ Zip _____

Clearly print the 3-digit codes (see player profiles for the correct codes) and names of the 24 players you have selected for your National League Roster. You must select 6 outfielders, 1 first baseman, 1 second baseman, 1 third baseman, 1 shortstop, 2 additional infielders, 2 catchers and 10 pitchers. (All players selected must be profiled in this book.) You have a total of 75 rating points to spend on your team, based on the ratings for each player in this book. Entries with more than 75 total rating points will be disqualified. You must choose one player from at least 6 of the 12 National League teams.

| Outfielders: | 3-Digit Code: | | Infielders: | 3-Digit Code: |
|---|---|---|---|---|
| 1. _____ | _____ | | 11. _____ | _____ |
| 2. _____ | _____ | | 12. _____ | _____ |
| 3. _____ | _____ | | **Catchers:** | |
| 4. _____ | _____ | | 13. _____ | _____ |
| 5. _____ | _____ | | 14. _____ | _____ |
| 6. _____ | _____ | | **Pitchers:** | |
| **First Baseman:** | | | 15. _____ | _____ |
| 7. _____ | _____ | | 16. _____ | _____ |
| **Second Baseman:** | | | 17. _____ | _____ |
| 8. _____ | _____ | | 18. _____ | _____ |
| | | | 19. _____ | _____ |
| **Third Baseman:** | | | 20. _____ | _____ |
| 9. _____ | _____ | | 21. _____ | _____ |
| | | | 22. _____ | _____ |
| **Shortstop:** | | | 23. _____ | _____ |
| 10. _____ | _____ | | 24. _____ | _____ |

# Mail your completed entry to:

Baseball Contest 1990:
National League Players
P.O. Box 4863
Blair, NE 68009

Entries must be received by the day of the All-Star Game, July 10, 1990. Entrants will receive 10 bonus points per day for each day their entry is received prior to the All-Star Game.

See Official Rules for complete details and to obtain an additional official entry form and complete listing of eligible players profiled in this book.

All federal, state and local laws and regulations apply. Offer void in Puerto Rico and wherever prohibited by law.